SONGS *of* OURSELVES

JOAN SHELLEY RUBIN

SONGS *of* OURSELVES

The Uses of Poetry in America

THE BELKNAP PRESS OF
HARVARD UNIVERSITY PRESS
Cambridge, Massachusetts
London, England
2007

ISBN-13: 978-0-674-02436-6
ISBN-10: 0-674-02436-2

Cataloging-in-Publication data is
available from the Library of Congress.

Designed by Gwen Nefsky Frankfeldt

For Tai, David, and Michael, with love

Acknowledgments

❧ READERS remake texts, but readers who share the professional commitments of the author also help to make texts in the first place. Foremost in that category are three people who read the entire manuscript: David D. Hall, who has influenced my thinking over many years; Stanley Engerman, the ideal intelligent reader; and Scott Casper, who wrote an insightful anonymous reader's report and subsequently identified himself to me. I am also indebted to my collaborators on *A History of the Book In America*, of which David Hall is general editor, and to its sponsor, the American Antiquarian Society, for giving me an invaluable sense of common purpose as I worked on this book. My colleagues in the University of Rochester History Department have been lively company as well.

For particular contributions—astute commentary, research leads, and various forms of support—I thank Norma Bagley, Daniel Borus, Rabbi Herbert Bronstein, Theodore Brown, John Cole, George Cotkin, David Brion Davis, Ellen Gruber Garvey, Lynn Gordon, Robert Gross, John Hench, Barbara Hochman, David Hollinger, John W. Hyland, Jr., Carl Kaestle, Meredith McGill, Brenda Meehan, David Nord, Lewis Perry, Morris Pierce, Janice Radway, Cynthia Rubin, Linda Rubin, Michael Schudson, Barbara Sicherman, Caroline Sloat, and Trysh Travis.

Robert Pinsky, Maggie Dietz, and Rosemary Ellis of the "Favorite Poem Project" generously made the project's database available to me. I greatly appreciate their encouragement and unstinting expenditure of time and effort on my behalf. My thanks also go to the ordinary readers who identified their favorite poems and who answered my "Author's Query" about schoolroom recitation; they enriched my study immeasurably. I have credited individual respondents in the endnotes, and have quoted from their comments with their permission. The late Rabbi Chaim Stern kindly granted me an interview in 1999. Staff members at the American Baptist Historical Society's Samuel Colgate Historical Library were especially gracious in arranging for me to use documents from their archives.

All material from the Henry Holt Archives, Manuscripts Division, Department of Rare Books and Special Collections, Princeton University Library is reprinted by permission of Henry Holt and Company, LLC, and the Princeton University Library. I have reprinted material from the Archives of Charles Scribner's Sons, Manuscripts Division, Department of Rare Books and Special Collections, Princeton University Library by permission of Scribner, an imprint of Simon & Schuster Adult Publishing Group, and the Princeton University Library. All material from the Macmillan Company Records, Manuscripts and Archives Division, The New York Public Library, Astor, Lenox and Tilden Foundations, is also reprinted by permission of Scribner, an imprint of Simon & Schuster Adult Publishing Group.

The following students eased many tasks by serving as research assistants: Daniel Apfel, Jessica Bell-Masterson, Corinne Carpenter, Laura Crane, Jason Gogniat, Sophia Lai, Justin Nordstrom, and Susan Thyne. My department's office staff, Rebecca Hurysz and Helen Hull, were unfailingly efficient, cheerful, and sympathetic. I am grateful to my editor at Harvard University Press, Joyce Seltzer, for bringing her wealth of experience and good judgment to bear on this project. Mary Ellen Geer, my copy editor at the Press and a poet herself, did a superb job of attending to language and style.

While I acknowledge in the Introduction my father's role in my decision to explore the uses of poetry, here I want to note the indelible influence of my mother, Pearl W. Rubin. In her passion for literary culture, her modernist sensibility, and her approach to life, she has powerfully and positively affected my own tastes and practices as a reader.

The John Simon Guggenheim Memorial Foundation awarded me a most welcome fellowship for research in 1997–1998. Earlier versions of some of the material in Chapter 7 appeared in "Listen, My Children: Modes and Functions of Poetry Reading in American Schools, 1880–1950," in Karen Halttunen and Lewis Perry, eds., *Moral Problems in American Life: New Perspectives on Cultural History* (Ithaca: Cornell University Press, 1998), and in "'They Flash Upon That Inward Eye': Poetry Recitation and American Readers," *Proceedings of the American Antiquarian Society,* vol. 160, part 1 (1997), 273–300, reprinted in Barbara Ryan and Amy M. Thomas, eds., *Reading Acts: U.S. Readers' Interactions with Literature, 1800–1950* (Knoxville: University of Tennessee Press, 2002). Portions of Chapters 7 and 9 appeared in "Modernism in Practice: Public Readings of the New Poetry," in Townsend Ludington, ed., *A Modern Mosaic: Art and Modernism in the United States* (Chapel Hill: University of North Carolina Press, 2000).

It is impossible to list all of the friends—singing companions, "Women's Weekenders," purveyors of laughter and wisdom—who saved me from scholarly isolation, but I hope they know how much they mean to me. Once more my greatest debt is to my husband, Tai C. Kwong, who has steadied me with perspective and plied me with Chinese food on innumerable occasions. To him I can only say, with Browning, that "the best is yet to be," although it has been awfully good up to now. My sons, David Rubin Kwong and Michael Rubin Kwong, are, as Longfellow wrote about children, "better than all the ballads / That were ever sung or said." I dedicate this book to Tai, David, and Michael with nothing more poetic than a simple declaration of love, but, in practice, the meaning of the words runs deep.

Contents

Illustrations

SONGS *of* OURSELVES

Introduction

ℒ My INTEREST in the subject of poetry reading initially derived from two sources—one personal, the other scholarly. The personal side concerns my father, a Rochester tax attorney, who, when he was in his seventies, rediscovered his high school poetry anthology in a local used bookstore. Entitled *Through Magic Casements,* the blue-and-gold-covered volume was the work of two Rochester English teachers who attained a national audience after Macmillan issued the book in 1927. Although not usually given to literary enthusiasms, my father was delighted with his find, and spent many hours reciting (to me and other captives) lines from such remembered favorites as Thomas Babington Macaulay's "Horatius" and James Russell Lowell's "The Vision of Sir Launfal." My father was not given to spending a great deal on telephone calls either, and after I heard him declaiming poetry long-distance to his sister in California—this was around 1990, before the era of cell phones and "free" minutes—I said to myself, "This schoolroom poetry means something to people."[1]

Part of that "something," it was obvious, lay in the memories of youth the anthology evoked, but a slip of paper my father inserted for my benefit when he passed the book on to me made apparent another aspect of its significance. His scrawled notation directed me to two pages: on one, a bit of paternal advice ("Gather Ye Rose-buds While Ye May"); on the other, a reference to a long-standing family joke—his rueful, wistful, and utterly incongruous fantasy of leaving the office for the open road ("The Vagabond"). That gesture entangled the poems he prized with dreams as well as recollections, and turned the volume into a token of relationships both past and present.

A few years later, when my father was dying of cancer, I read aloud to him from *Through Magic Casements* while sitting at his bedside. The drama of Samuel Taylor Coleridge's "Rime of the Ancient Mariner" and John Greenleaf Whittier's "Snow-Bound" furnished diversion and pleasure, but I acknowledged to myself that the poems had taken on a function unrelated to their subject and structure: they had given me a way to cope with my distress at not knowing, in those pained circumstances, what else to do. At my father's funeral I turned to the book one more time, choosing to read, in the setting of a twentieth-century Jewish synagogue, William Cullen Bryant's "To a Waterfowl," a poem of nineteenth-century New England that nevertheless expressed what I most wanted to say: "Thou'rt gone / The abyss of heaven / Hath swallowed up thy form; yet, on my heart / Deeply hath sunk the lesson thou hast given, / And shall not soon depart."

Although I fully recognized its implications only in retrospect, among the precepts I had learned in the "lesson" of my father's last years was one that had emerged from my role as witness to and participant in those acts of reading verse: namely, that the meanings of texts were inseparable from the associations, longings, and purposes they acquired in the hands of readers. That dawning realization coincided with my attraction, as a scholar, to the burgeoning field of the history of the book. The term encompasses efforts to chronicle not just individual writers or publishing firms, but instead the production, distribution, and reception of the entire range of written communication. With increasing momentum over the last fifteen years, book historians have tackled such subjects as authorship, access to knowledge, the circulation of texts, and the responses of readers in various times and places. Much of the early work in the field came from Europeanists like Robert Darnton, Roger Chartier, Carlo Ginzberg, and Natalie Zemon Davis, whose pioneering investigations of bookselling, cheap print, reading communities, and the like demonstrated the ways in which *l'histoire du livre* could reveal the *mentalités* of ordinary people. David D. Hall, uncovering the mental world that print created for ministers and laity alike in colonial Massachusetts, extended the Europeanists' enterprise across the Atlantic. Whether about Europe, America, or other parts of the globe, those pathbreaking studies and the best ones that have followed have contributed to what Hall has called a "social history of culture." That is, their common goal has been to situate print at the intersection of the material conditions, social structures, and cultural values that give the written word its forms and meanings.[2]

Because of my commitment, as a cultural historian, to exploring human aspirations, anxieties, needs, and beliefs over time, the promise of the history of reading seemed to me especially compelling: it might furnish, in Darnton's words, insights into how people "made sense of life." Equally exhilarating was the prospect of excavating the stories of actual readers (not just textual representations of them) to elucidate how categories of culture (the "high," the "popular") have worked in practice.[3]

I decided to contribute to such a history by turning to the genre my father had enjoyed: poetry. That focus, I have since learned by giving assorted public presentations, tends to elicit either high or low expectations. In the first category are poetry lovers, who hope to find in my work the same reverence—"Ah, poetry!"—with which they themselves approach poems. In the second are some historians who are, by temperament and training, inhospitable to the study of a literary form, especially one that has never commanded more than a small fraction of the book market. I have more affinities with the first group than the second: like many American teenage girls, I was a dreamy-eyed adolescent poet myself. (Once I bewildered my grandmother, who had asked to buy me a present, by telling her that all I really wanted was a slim paperback edition of Carl Sandburg's *Harvest Poems*.) Yet, my exposure to the power of *Through Magic Casements* aside, I chose to write about verse (a word that, for the sake of variety, I use interchangeably with "poetry") for largely practical reasons—namely, that the genre's public dimension affords scholars at least some access to the elusive evidence of reading's functions and effects. We may associate poetry with private or intimate occasions—lovers sharing sonnets with each other—but, especially in the late nineteenth and early twentieth centuries, Americans also encountered poetic texts at a number of public, or at any rate observable, venues: in school, at civic gatherings, in women's clubs, as parlor entertainment and bedtime routine, within religious ceremonies, at celebrity performances, and around Girl Scout campfires. Furthermore, the uses of verse in those settings gave the genre a cultural presence that publishers' sales figures do not measure: in school, for instance, everyone read poems every year. As I had noted in my father's case, poetry also survived in memory even when readers no longer confronted words on the page. Thus it offered the chance to see at close range the interplay between values, ideologies, and practices such as reading aloud, rereading, and reciting to oneself.

In addition, an exploration of poetry reading fit nicely with one of my ongoing concerns: the attempt, on the part of American critics, journalists, and others, to disseminate literature to a wide audience. In *The Making of Middlebrow Culture,* I had examined such activities for the interwar years.[4] Pushing the narrative back a decade or two led directly to poetry—specifically, to the early modernists (such as Edna St. Vincent Millay and Vachel Lindsay) who called themselves the "new poets," and whose emergence in the 1910s as a self-conscious avant-garde had made them central to literary histories of the period. Unearthing how both the "new poetry" and its successor, the "high" modernism of T. S. Eliot, found its way into the textbooks and libraries of ordinary readers seemed a worthwhile endeavor when I began my research.

I still think that is so, and I tell that story here. Nevertheless, as soon as I made my first foray into the records of early-twentieth-century readers, I was reminded of an often ignored fact: that nineteenth-century verse and non-modernist expression persisted alongside poetic innovation and experimentation. That is, for the reading public the 1920s were as much an era of Henry Wadsworth Longfellow as of Eliot. Furthermore, while poets, critics, educators, publishers, and readers alike frequently used the word "poetry" as if it denoted a single type of literature (and while I sustain that usage in representing their ideas), within that rubric there was always wide variety: canonized texts coexisting with "light" verse, political poems with children's rhymes, lengthy epics with four-line stanzas, English romantic effusions along with American ones.

A history of poetry reading thus allowed—indeed, enjoined—me to participate in the rethinking of American literary history that has engaged the editors of surveys like the *Cambridge History of American Literature* (2003). Older volumes that laid out American poetry's development—a classic example is Robert Spiller's *Literary History of the United States* (last reissued in 1974)—had depicted that process as a series of efforts to "make it new": while they described the social context of American thought and paid some attention to popular figures, Spiller and his colleagues followed a mainly linear progression from romanticism to realism (with its regional variants) to the "new poetry" and its successors. Since the 1970s, the canon debates and the impact of postmodern theory have altered that picture significantly. The third edition of the *Heath Anthology of American Literature* (1998), for instance, contains a "sheaf" of popular sentimental poems by late-nineteenth-century women. The *Norton Anthology of American Literature* (second edition, 1985) carefully specifies that modernism overlapped with traditionalist impulses. The *Columbia History of American Poetry* (1993) reclaims women poets as crucial makers of modernism. The monument to an American tradition that Spiller oversaw has given way, in David Perkins's words, to essay collections that "deliberately avoid consecutiveness and coherence." As Sacvan Bercovitch declared in his introduction to the newest *Cambridge History*, "The study of American literary history now defines itself in the plural, as a multivocal, multifaceted scholarly, critical, and pedagogic enterprise."[5]

One of my primary purposes in the pages that follow is to contribute to that more inclusive account of American literature (while retaining the historian's faith in chronology). At the same time, I intend to show how the social history of reading differs from projects that, however open to lost traditions, remain organized around authors and movements.[6] Such surveys and anthologies generally register the *results* of literary production. Even in their postmodern manifestations, they inevitably constitute exercises in canon formation by featuring selected works. In this book, by contrast, I emphasize the cultural expectations, economic demands, and ideological interventions that influenced the *circumstances* of both production and reception. The readers I discuss did not confront an expanded canon so much as multiple canons; these included religious verse, poetry for the home, and other groupings organized by thematic rather than aesthetic qualities. Often their reading was eclectic, mingling texts that varied in style, structure, craft, provenance and, by contemporary critics' measures, literary value. To restore to view the mixture of "steady sellers" and innovations, domestic products and foreign imports, "serious" art and "lighter" writing that Americans read and to recover their reading experiences in particular settings is to arrive at a more accurate as well as a more democratic portrayal of American culture than we have previously possessed.

I also depart from standard literary history in the periodization I have adopted. Although it ranges backwards and forwards in order to accommodate topics and themes with earlier origins or more recent echoes, this book focuses on the years between 1880 and the mid-1950s—dates that are "out of sync" with customary renderings of American poetry's development. I begin more or less at the time when the rise of the realistic novel seemed for contemporary critics and literary historians alike to spell the subordination of poetry to fiction, and I end (again, more or less) when Beat poetry is catching on. My contention is that the reading of verse flourished alongside realism even as its standing in "high" culture became precarious, and that the promise of the Beats' experimentation was less important for reading than the waning in the 1950s of rote learning in American schools.

My second major purpose is to connect the uses of literature to the untold chronicle of emotional life in America. Mine is a story of poetry as lived experience. The young Iowa woman who, in 1886, invested a volume of Wordsworth with the power to signify that the man she pined for cared about her; the turn-of-the-century immigrant who linked a classroom recitation with attaining acceptance in his new country; the teacher who, in the same period, recovered her mental balance after her mother's death by rereading lines affirming nature's goodness—these are among the many examples I adduce to show how poetry functioned to carry, shape, and serve the feelings of American readers. The so-called "New Critical" interpreters of poetry in the mid-twentieth century demonstrated what one might call the aesthetic work of poetic language (the way, for instance, sound and metaphor rendered beauty and insight). A later generation of literary critics has emphasized the "cultural work" of texts, particularly their role in constructing categories of race and gender. My effort, while it borrows from both of those approaches, documents for specific historical settings a third aspect of literature's power: the emotional work it has performed for the readers in whose lives it has been a vital presence.

Another of my goals is to document and elaborate in the American context three premises that have gained ground among historians of reading. The first of these is the one I had glimpsed in my brush with *Through Magic Casements*: that, as Roger Chartier has written, works "have no stable, universal, fixed meaning." Rather, their meanings arise in what Chartier has called a dialectical "encounter between a proposal and a reception." With regard to readers (the "reception" part of the dialectic), my fundamental assumption is one that, in Hall's words, had become a scholarly "truism" by the mid-1990s: "readers remake the text." They arrive at provisional meanings through the ways they understand and use print, "appropriating" it for ends that its creators may not have anticipated and cannot control. My decision to recite Bryant at my father's bedside and funeral was an example of appropriation, one that imputed therapeutic and ritualistic overtones to the text that it did not necessarily acquire in the schoolroom. In this study, I show

how late-nineteenth- and early-twentieth-century readers of poetry "took command of books, . . . gave them meaning, and invested them with their own expectations" by engaging in practices that derived from and served their personal requirements and historical situations.[7]

Yet I also show how the "proposal" that readers received—the other half of Chartier's dialectic—inflected and constrained their acts of appropriation. Readers are never free to construe works in limitless fashion, because the form of a text (for example, its adherence to certain literary conventions), as well as its cultural status, conditions readers to approach it in preconceived ways. Furthermore, texts do not arrive in readers' hands without the imprint of what book historians call "mediations"—those culturally specific activities, personal and impersonal, that construct a work's physical characteristics and content, affect its marketing and accessibility, and color the responses of readers. Darnton's famous construct of a "communications circuit" singled out such intermediaries as printers, booksellers, paper suppliers, shippers, and censors; for modern America the list would also include literary agents, editors, librarians, book clubs, reviewers, and mass-market retailers. While a poetry anthology like *Through Magic Casements* mirrors the selection principles of its compilers, it may also reflect the impact of copyright restrictions, the publishers' sense of what sells, the price of binding, or the fluctuating judgments of critics.[8]

A defining feature of this study is my close examination of two kinds of mediations. In the first part of the book I sketch the historical status of poetry as a "text genre"—a status forged by publishers and editors, anthologists and commentators, and poets themselves. These individuals established the market value (and place in the cultural hierarchy) of various kinds of verse; more than that, they conferred on the genre a shifting set of images and attributes on which readers could draw in making sense of poems. In the second part of the book, I affirm that reading is a practice "always realized in specific acts, places, and habits" by reconstructing the mediations that prevailed at particular sites where Americans encountered poetry. Implicitly, I argue that the meanings of texts are inseparable from the ideological and cultural tensions in play at sites for reading.[9]

The second of the premises of book history that I explore is the assumption that reading is a social act. It is social because texts are socially produced through the mediations just described, but also because readers employ texts for social purposes. As Elizabeth Long has stated, the "ideology of the solitary reader," buttressed for centuries through visual images of isolated male scholars and leisurely women in their boudoirs, conceals modes of reading that entail collective activity. Long's prime example is the group reading of the women's book club; in my study, poetry appears both in that public setting and in numerous additional ones. Moreover, reading is social because it generates relationships between authors and audiences that bear the mark of the reader's own social position. This book affirms that fact by exploring how individuals used poetry in the service of identity formation. It gives attention as well to the affective ties that poetry created not only between poets and readers but also between readers and parents, classmates, and lovers (among others). I emphasize the social nature of reading by discussing the employment of a literary genre often read in private to attain social ends: for instance, the use of verse as a tool for progressive reform. I also show how poetry (in the United States and elsewhere) created its own forms of sociability—ways of talking and commingling—that added to Americans' repertoire of collective behavior. Examples of these include the bohemian or theatrical poetry reading, the speaking choir, and the poetry club.[10]

Third, I adopt and apply the more controversial premise that there is no necessary correspondence between "cultural cleavages" ("high" versus "low" or "popular" literature) and "social differences." That is, as both Chartier and Hall have convincingly maintained, demarcations of class, gender, or race do not automatically enable the historian to infer what and how people in those categories read. Thus in the United States during the late nineteenth century, the plays of Shakespeare—a supposedly "sacralized" author—were not merely the province of an "elite," nor was the consumption of dime novels—a popular form—restricted to the working class. Rather, both kinds of printed works existed in what Hall has labeled "a middling social and cultural space in which many texts seem to have circulated widely." The status of poetry in the United States after 1880 is a good case in point. Although literary critics elevated the genre to a high station among the arts, the common school and the standardized curriculum undercut any aura of exclusivity it acquired by ensuring its distribution to virtually everyone. Publishers who issued inexpensive anthologies and other affordable volumes for classroom and home use did the same. To be sure, deluxe editions had their place, but so did pamphlets and magazines. Class, race, and gender thus figure in my account not so much as explanations of reading differences but as categories to be reckoned with in charting the many factors that shape dissemination and reception of a text. To my way of thinking, to reject "exclusive relationships between specific cultural forms and particular social groups" is to arrive at a fuller appreciation of the agency of ordinary people than the concept of an autonomous working-class culture permits. I should add that because of the available evidence, the readers I discuss are by and large white and middle-class, although I have tried to overcome that limitation wherever possible.[11]

The structure of this book follows from my determination to write a history of verse reading that recovers the interaction of proposal and reception and concentrates on poetry's social uses. Part I, "The Poet in American Culture," is designed to unsettle linear narratives of the genre's development in the United States while providing some basic information about production and dissemination. One of its central concerns is the status of poetry within the book trade and the periodical press. Thus it is about editorial choices and marketing decisions. It is also about the broad understandings of the poet's authority which—as both constraint and opportunity—influenced what texts got published, how intermediaries interpreted them to audiences, and how readers regarded them. Each chapter of Part I revolves around a pair of antithetical images that, upon closer inspection, signify complementary aspects of Americans' attitudes toward poets and their work. Although I introduce these pairings chronologically, as a device for displaying the cultural tensions dominating a particular era, it is not the case that new sets of images repeatedly displaced older ones. Rather, these figures should be thought of as actors who, once they take the stage, stay there—sometimes in shadow, sometimes brought forward for a reprise—while a shifting spotlight shines on other members of the troupe.

The first chapter briefly looks back to two familiar ideals of antebellum New England's literary culture, "Seer and Sage," in order to trace persistent, competing formulations of the relationship between the artist and society: the poet as lone visionary and as wise civic leader. Next, I juxtapose "Amateur and Professional" to suggest the ways in which the literary marketplace and the nineteenth-century trend toward professionalism could work both to increase readers' reverence for poets and to foster their sense of accessibility to them.

The third chapter, "Absence and Presence," brings us to the beginning of the period on which this study concentrates and provides an extensive look at the mediations of the book industry. Here I review the reasons for regarding the years between the 1880s and the 1910s as decades of decline for American poetry. I also show how the pessimism occasioned by the deaths of eminences such as Longfellow and Tennyson and the complaints of younger poets about the difficulties of publishing verse in the United States must be qualified by distinctions among kinds of poetry, by an examination of the actual output of various types of publishers, and by the amount of poetry reading and rereading in which Americans engaged.

Another pairing, "Sophisticate and Innocent," revolves around two popular poets of the early twentieth century: Edna St. Vincent Millay and Edgar A. Guest. Millay represents the poet as agent of a new kind of sociability—the urbane, bohemian style of social exchange endemic to New York's Greenwich Village, where early modernism thrived. At the same time, I describe Millay's participation in the contrasting phenomenon of the "girl" poet who, in cap-

tivating audiences during the 1920s, kept alive a conception of po-
etry as art uncorrupted by modern values. Edgar Guest embodied
similar contradictions. A poet of the domestic and the sentimental,
he was, in his own way, also a master of the modern. Because
Millay and Guest each combined elements of prescriptions for mas-
culinity and femininity, this chapter likewise permits me to point
out the complicated connections between gender and cultural con-
structions of the poet's roles.

In the fifth chapter, "Celebrity and Cipher," I extend the narra-
tive of poetry's cultural status by following its fortunes within the
book trade into the 1940s. The underlying question here is the ex-
tent to which the book industry's conviction that "poetry doesn't
sell" reflected publishers' priorities rather than readers' resistance.
Resistance is also one theme I address through the final set of fig-
ures in Chapter 6, "Alien and Intimate"—specifically, how, from
the early days of free verse onward, modernist obscurity formed a
barrier to engagement with poetic texts that certain readers would
not cross. But I also look at the activities of mediators who inter-
preted modernism to a less wary audience, and recover the stance
of those readers willing to tolerate the difficult or obscure in order
to remain conversant with the poet as friend and guide.

Following my overview of poetry's cultural status as a literary
form, I turn to my larger task: to elucidate the values and practices
that governed specific sites for verse reading in the United States
between 1880 and the mid-1950s. In Part II, "Poetry in Place and
Practice," my emphasis is on the enduring values and beliefs that
prevailed throughout that period at the sites where readers remade
texts, as well as on the shifts that altered poetry's uses. I consider
the experiences, for example, of schoolchildren, immigrants, moth-
ers, worshippers, and campers. Those groups, however, contended
with the results of other readers' interpretive acts: namely, the re-
sponses of teachers, "Americanizers," librarians, ministers, and the
like who were involved in dissemination as well as reception. The
ideological commitments of these intermediaries simultaneously op-
erated as limits for the readers they sought to influence and pre-
sented them with multiple avenues to meaning. I should add that

neither the five sites which I have selected for close inspection nor the sources on which I have relied are the only ones pertinent to my subject; given that I am treading on fairly unmapped ground, I regard my approach as suggestive rather than exhaustive of the possibilities for study.

The first chapter of Part II, "Listen, My Children," highlights the key site that mediated verse reading for young Americans: the public school. I explore various aspects of this site in relation to poetry: the continuities and disjunctions in the poetry curriculum between 1880 and 1950, and the rationales that educators put forth for its study; the several competing modes of reading, as well as the social needs those modes reflected and served; the history of the verse speaking choir; and, finally, the testimony of the students themselves about the presence of poetry in their lives and the significance they attached to schoolroom verse irrespective of educators' intentions.

The following chapter, "I Am an American," centers on both the school and the larger community. Here the social uses of verse are entirely explicit, and the figures of the poet as sage and seer reign. Poetry, I show, nurtured civic pride and unity (while allaying cultural anxieties) at commemorative events; in the hands of clubwomen and settlement house workers, it became a means to assist urban immigrants. The social ideals and hopes with which readers freighted verse reading are especially visible in the wider "Americanization" and "intercultural education" efforts of the interwar period. This chapter concludes with an assessment of the genre's uses in World War II and a look at one further alliance between poetry and citizenship, the successive editions of the *American Citizens Handbook*.

The home is the principal focus of "Grow Old Along with Me." I note the material forms in which poems for home use circulated and the moral imperatives they acquired in connection with the domestic setting. My greater interest, however, is in the emotional or psychological weight that poetry bore within the context of the family and other intimate relationships. Both working-class and middle-class readers called up the figure of the poet as innocent in trying to meet their needs for security, domestic order, and parental love. Yet the poet as sophisticate, or as prophet of personal liberation, can be glimpsed in individuals' recollections of their home reading as well. As they forged new social bonds outside the confines of the family, readers also assigned emotional work to verse, drawing on the capacity of the poet to serve as imagined companion and friend. This chapter ends by examining the correspondence between Carl Sandburg and his audience to reveal the emotional ties and putative intimacy that real poets and readers could mutually create.

Although I observe that poetry acquired religious resonances at several of the sites I investigate, "God's in His Heaven" deals with the genre's overtly religious uses: its presence in devotional exercises, anthologies, and denominational periodicals; in the contemplative and social lives of missionaries and ministers; and in congregational worship for both liberal Protestants and Jews. This chapter also moves ahead to the 1960s in order to look at the religious appropriation of verse from the viewpoint of a participant in revisions to the Reform Jewish High Holiday prayerbook.

The last locale I explore is the outdoors, the subject of "Lovely as a Tree." Here I consider a further set of cultural tensions: on the one hand, the American propensity to value action over intellection; on the other, the presumption (which publishers harnessed to a marketing strategy) that perusing verse "in the open" could enhance the reader's capacity to enjoy the "simple life" and to appreciate nature. As I demonstrate, that conflict between experience and print—between surrender to the sensory stimuli of the natural world and regard for the poet as companion and field guide— marked readers' perceptions of the poet-naturalist John Burroughs. Similar ambivalences about the relationship between poetry and nature conditioned the celebrity of cowboy poets at the turn of the twentieth century and the verse-reading practices of Girl Scouts and Camp Fire Girls.

The book ends with a forward glance at the poetry boom of the late twentieth and early twenty-first centuries. A sampling of responses to former Poet Laureate Robert Pinsky's "Favorite Poem

Project" allows me to suggest some of the similarities and differences between the values and practices of recent verse readers and the ones at the center of my study.

As American readers compounded meanings out of printed words and their social uses, they bridged a number of divides: not only between the high and the popular, but also between the secular and the sacred, the liberatory and the conservative, the modern and the traditional. Even after World War I, they preserved a large space for legacies of the nineteenth century, intertwining what Raymond Williams called the "residual culture" of the past with the "dominant order" of the interwar period.[12]

A case study drawn from William S. Gray and Ruth Munroe's *The Reading Interests and Habits of Adults* (1929) offers a preview of the examples to follow that bear out that point. The authors reported on a reader they called "Mr. M.," a middle-aged business executive from the Chicago area. A "mild sort of person," Mr. M. spent almost every evening relaxing by reading books. Although he devoted most of his time to recently published mysteries, once or twice a week he took down from his shelves "certain old favorites": Dickens, Robert Burns, Longfellow. "There has been almost no change," Gray and Munroe observed, "in his reading interests throughout his life." His choice of Longfellow and Burns, they speculated, was "perhaps a link with his early home and his mother." In any event, Mr. M's practice of rereading had added the "charm of old associations" to the poetry's "intrinsic appeal"; his "long habit of finding pleasure" in his favorites gave them "a pervading richness that no new books could have."

Mr. M's enactment of reading rituals that reinforced his "quiet, happy home life" and summoned continuities with his youth beautifully documents the contributions of site and practice to the construction of meaning. Yet his "rather old fashioned," unexciting "mode of living" (as Gray and Munroe termed it), into which an investigation of poetry reading allows access, has, for the most part, slipped from view. Together with the experiences of verse readers who did not share his gender, class, or aesthetic preferences, Mr. M's world deserves to be restored to the social, emotional, and human history of American culture. In carrying out that charge, the following pages confirm the tantalizing speculation with which Gray and Munroe closed their case. In America, they wrote, "there must be many Mr. M's."[13]

PART I

THE POET
IN AMERICAN
CULTURE

chapter one

Seer and Sage

WITHIN THE history of American poetry, certain scenes have become, in the retelling, almost mythic moments, marking a turning point in the career of a poet or symbolizing the genre's cultural standing. One episode that looms especially large occurred in 1855, the year Walt Whitman brought out the first edition of *Leaves of Grass*. Having received a copy of the book from its author, Ralph Waldo Emerson sent the poet a letter celebrating Whitman's achievement and hailing him as a kindred spirit. Although literary scholars have usefully questioned and redrawn the so-called Emersonian line which the letter implicitly established, the continuity that Emerson himself perceived lay chiefly in the conception the two men shared of the poet as prophet and seer.[1]

Emerson expounded on that conception in both verse and prose, but his fullest discussion of the subject appeared in his essay "The Poet" (1845). There Emerson famously depicted poets as "men of genius"—"liberating gods" whose perceptual gifts enabled them to transcend the obstacles impeding the ordinary person's consciousness of beauty. The task of the Emersonian poet was not only to apprehend messages hidden from plain view but also to "integrate" them, elucidating both their meaning and coherence. Able to command art and nature alike, poets grasped the unity between the real and the ideal. That special insight affiliated them with visionaries across cultures and throughout history. Emerson's emphasis on intuition and freedom, however, specifically allied him with the broad movement of European romanticism. From Coleridge in particular he absorbed the idea that the poet's extraordinary vision enabled him to discern spiritual laws and universal truth. In addition, Emerson's understanding of the poet as seer drew on the specific American context in which it developed, relying, for one thing, on the antebellum American's literal concern with enhancing the power of sight. The construct of the poet-prophet also met Emerson's vocational requirements—his desire to function as a preacher without succumbing to what he saw as the sectarian, morally vapid requirements of the institutionalized Christian ministry.[2]

Despite its cultural sources, Emerson's figure of the poet as seer was necessarily remote from those he served as interpreter. As Emerson explained, "He is isolated among his contemporaries; to realize his art, he must leave the world, and know the muse only."[3] In that respect, poets were supreme exemplars of "self-reliance," detached from the pressure for conformity to the expectations of others. The separation was not total; seers performed a social mission in the act of communicating, and their insight enriched culture overall. Yet standing above politics and self-interest, the seer Emerson imagined enlightened his readers from the height—and the distance—of his conscience and his ideals.

In 1842, the 23-year-old Walt Whitman heard Emerson deliver the lyceum lecture on poetry that Emerson later adapted for publication as "The Poet." Energized by the prospect of meeting the nation's need for "liberating gods," Whitman decided to become the American bard for which the lecture advertised. (Whitman in turn advertised Leaves of Grass by quoting without permission the sentence from Emerson's letter to him that declared: "I greet you at the beginning of a great career.") "Song of Myself" announced Whitman as the possessor of the "cosmic consciousness" and prophetic voice of Emerson's Orphic poet. Whitman's prophet-poet was also Emersonian in exemplifying the "superhuman" self, set apart from ordinary people by virtue of the ability to see the soul and the order of nature more clearly than they. "Finally shall come the Poet worthy of that name," Whitman wrote in lines from 1868 that later became part of "Passage to India"; "The true Son of God shall come, singing his songs."[4]

Versions of Emerson's and Whitman's poet as lone visionary routinely appeared in the prescriptive literature available to nineteenth-century American readers in search of literary guidance. Noah Porter's *Books and Reading*, subtitled *What Books Shall I Read and How Shall I Read Them?* (1871), declared that the poet's "genius impels him to employ a dialect of his own which no man can imitate." The American edition of *The Highways of Literature* (1890), a collection of advice about reading by the British teacher and popularizer David Pryde, portrayed poets as voicing ideas "too imposing and too vivid to be expressed by ordinary language." Both Porter's and Pryde's comments at once affirmed and justified a view of poetry as inherently distant from the average reader. As another commentator, Charles F. Thwing, insisted in the same period, "the elevated intellectual and emotional character of this noblest type of literature" not only originated in poets' special capacities, but also required the "special culture" and "training" of audiences. Although Thwing acknowledged that most readers had to overcome a natural reaction against the genre because it used unfamiliar diction, he and his contemporaries assumed that any seer worthy of the name would speak in exalted or mystical phrases. Even if one accepts the debatable premise that certain elements in American culture—Shakespeare, classical music—became sacralized in the course of the nineteenth century, the popular image of poetry which the Emersonian tradition promoted was not susceptible to that process because, from that romantic perspective, it was an inherently sacred form.[5]

Yet anyone who is familiar with Emerson, and who has thus learned to expect inconsistencies and contradictions in his thought, will not be surprised to discover that the figure of the solitary seer is only one of the representations of the poet that his work contains. Equally prominent is the sage, the dispenser of wisdom to the citizenry. In Lawrence Buell's phrase, the particular "bipolar mode of vision" governing "The Poet" juxtaposes the Orphic bard who "forgets" the "public" with a portrait of the poet as public man: "he will tell us how it was with him, and all men will be the richer in his fortune." In their capacity as transmitter of the moral laws embedded in the natural world, poets established a vital, active correspondence, to use an Emersonian term, between themselves and their readers. Furthermore, Emerson's efforts to reveal the divine elements in ordinary objects led him, as F. O. Matthiessen noted, to take "continual joy in the homeliest speech" even when his meaning remained abstruse. Whitman went even further in countermanding his own stance as isolate by devising the multiple identities of "Song of Myself." His theme of fusion with his audience, his concerted address of the working class, his "reinvention" of himself as "poet-comrade" during the Civil War, and his transformation into the Good Gray Poet at the end of his life all moderated his prophetic outsider's voice.[6]

The ideal Emersonian poet also participated in public life by virtue of involvement in the mid-nineteenth-century culture of oratory. Although the composition and delivery of eulogies, commemorative odes, and occasional verse are ancient cross-cultural practices, for Americans such forms, imported from eighteenth-century London, were hallmarks of civility. As David Shields has demonstrated, in the 1720s the printing of "state odes and elegies" in the colonies stimulated their increased use in public ceremonies, while a volume such as Aquila Rose's *Poems on Several Occasions* (1740) certified the existence of an American "market for polite letters." Throughout the new nation, anniversaries and holidays such as the Fourth of July necessitated declarations in verse. Joseph Bartlett, speaking in Boston's Exchange Coffee-house on Independence Day, 1823, finished his remarks by delivering both a poem and an ode he had written for the observance. Charles Sprague, a Boston banker and author of the city's "Centennial Ode" (deemed "a production destined to be revived on every Boston centennial celebration, to the end of time"), won six prizes in the 1820s for "the best poems for the American stage." Other kinds of ceremonial occasions also incorporated the recitation of poetry. In the nascent American colleges, graduates delivered valedictory verses at commencement. The Phi Beta Kappa chapter at Harvard routinely called out poets' talents. As Emerson's Harvard Phi Beta Kappa poem of 1834 attests, even geniuses were expected to write when the occasion demanded it.[7]

Furthermore, poets joined orators in forging careers as public lecturers. The editor Park Benjamin, for example, searching for a stable source of income after his marriage in 1848, became a "platform poet" on the lyceum circuit, then in its heyday. His narrative verse often served as an opening act for more "solid" lectures by Benjamin's friends Henry Ward Beecher or Horace Greeley. In addition, as the account of Whitman as Emerson's auditor has already indicated, Emerson, Lowell, Bryant, and other poets embraced the vogue of oratory by speaking about literature or other topics. Even when they employed prose sentences, they were giving writers of verse a public presence. More than that, as Emerson delivered his remarks on "American Character" or "The Philosophy of History," he constructed—and embodied—the figure of the poet as an engaged, civic-minded intellectual. As Buell has phrased it, in place of the "Romantic tendency toward privatism," oratorical culture enhanced the status of the poet as "a sayer, an announcer, a liberator, a lawgiver."[8]

That status held even when audiences had difficulty grasping the speaker's words fully. For perhaps the majority of Emerson's listeners, the sense of being in the presence of both celebrity and brilliance surmounted the temptation to dismiss the speaker as incomprehensible. "We do not go to hear what Emerson says," James Russell Lowell famously remarked, "so much as to hear Emerson." Nevertheless, for some nineteenth-century observers the genre's functions as didactic rite seem to have heightened the expectation that (in contrast to Thwing's acceptance of mysticism) poetic language should be transparent in every instance. James Spear Loring, the nineteenth-century chronicler of Boston oratory, lauded Sprague's freedom from "confused conceptions" and "incongruous images." Likewise, Benjamin's success as a reciter of verse derived partly from his decision to set aside his propensity for Wordsworth and instead give his audiences the more accessible rhythms of classical pentameter couplets. Among other things, those responses demonstrate that some American readers deplored obscurity in poetry long before modernism made such remarks habitual.[9]

By depicting the poet as seer and sage alike, one cultural effect of the Emersonian tradition was to affiliate poetry with the domain of the sacred and esoteric, while another of its consequences—whether by example or, for those such as Loring, by counterexample—was to reiterate the poet's worldly responsibilities. Again, those ideals were not diametrically opposed to each other, because commentators valued both the seer's exalted vision and the sage's homely wisdom as complementary aspects of poetry's didactic utility. Nevertheless, taken together, the figures of the poet that confronted American readers in the era of Emerson and Whitman encapsulated the broader tensions between individualism and community, self-expression and civic obligation, that marked the nation as a whole. Both the types and the tensions continued to define poetry's social uses in the United States well into the twentieth century.

chapter two

Amateur and Professional

❧ EMERSON WAS also an actor in a second pivotal scene in the history of American poetry: the dinner that Henry Houghton, the publisher of the *Atlantic Monthly*, organized at a Boston hotel in 1877 to mark the seventieth anniversary of John Greenleaf Whittier's birth. The purpose of the event was to sustain the prestige of the magazine by underscoring its association with four distinguished New England writers, all of whom were present among the fifty-eight guests. Three—Henry Wadsworth Longfellow, Oliver Wendell Holmes, and Whittier himself—belonged to the group that has come to be known as the "schoolroom" or "fireside" poets (along with Bryant and James Russell Lowell). The fourth writer was Emerson. Also in attendance was William Dean Howells, then editing the magazine, as well as Mark Twain, who had accepted Howells's invitation to deliver after-dinner remarks.[1]

The Whittier Day celebration attempted to consolidate the magazine's future by trading on its past. Except for Whittier's "Snow-Bound" (1866), most of the schoolroom group's most famous works had first appeared in print decades earlier. Bryant, the oldest, had written "Thanatopsis" in 1817, published a collection of verse in 1821, achieved belated recognition for it after he became a journalist, and reached the peak of his reputation as a poet in the 1830s.

Holmes's "Old Ironsides" (1830) and two poems from 1858—
"The Chambered Nautilus" and "The Deacon's Masterpiece, or
The Wonderful One-Hoss Shay"—had predated his later success
as a novelist and most of his tenure at Harvard Medical School.
Longfellow, the most popular American writer of the nineteenth
century, had contributed "The Song of Hiawatha," "Evangeline,"
"A Psalm of Life," and "The Village Blacksmith" to the nation's
collective memory by 1855. Lowell, the youngest, had done the
same with "The Vision of Sir Launfal" in 1848. Although all five of
the fireside poets were still living at the time of the Whittier Day
commemoration (Bryant died the next year), all had passed from
poetry's rank-and-file to become—as the commemoration testified—
icons of New England literary culture.[2]

That circumstance colored both the content of and the response
to Twain's now-notorious speech. Twain spun a tale of three "lit-
erry men"—Emerson, Longfellow, and Holmes—bumbling into a
miner's log cabin near the Sierras. Drunk, uncouth, and cantanker-
ous, the three spout "queer talk" consisting of lines of their own
verse. Emerson looks "seedy," Holmes is "fat as a balloon," and
Longfellow steals the miner's boots in order to leave "footprints on
the sands of time." At the end of the sketch, the narrator pro-
tests that the three must have been "imposters," but, according
to Twain, that subtlety escaped the shocked audience, which re-
sponded with "a desolating silence." Scholars have since argued
that Twain exaggerated his listeners' distress out of an impulse to
underscore the difference between pretentious Boston and the dem-
ocratic West. Be that as it may, Twain's Whittier Day message was
that the schoolroom poets were the objects of undeserved adula-
tion, and that the literary establishment was exploiting the credu-
lity of the unsuspecting public.[3]

Twain's depiction of the schoolroom poets as disreputable
drunkards was an obvious fiction, offensive because it was insult-
ing, not because it might be taken as true. But the send-up more
subtly attributed to its targets traits that were less easy to refute. In
Twain's sketch, Emerson, Longfellow, and Holmes appear inept at
dealing with day-to-day realities. For all of their skill at cards, they

play "on trust." Much of the speech's humor derives from Twain's juxtaposition of the westerner's down-to-earth language ("I started to get out my bacon and beans") to the poets' ethereal phrases ("Give me agates for my meat . . ."). The implication is that, despite their swagger, these "literry swells" are useless fools, their otherworldliness at odds with the practical outlook and energies that post–Civil War Americans prized. In that respect they were misplaced not only as easterners who had wandered west, but also as effete holdovers from an era that was fortunately vanishing.[4]

Twain's Whittier Day speech thus foreshadowed the problematic position that poetry would shortly occupy in the United States as the realistic novel gained ground. It also anticipated the customary judgment of the fireside poets—as against modernist voices—in the twentieth century. As more than one scholar has noted, in every poetry anthology from the late nineteenth century on, and in every history of American literature, "the space devoted to them shrinks."[5] Yet Twain's characterization, while prescient (as well as hilarious), was inaccurate in two respects: it misgauged not only the feelings that underlay the poets' popularity but also their participation in the nineteenth-century culture of professionalism.

As William Charvat observed in 1950, the modern tendency to devalue poets popular in their time "arises in part from our persistent neglect of the reader as a force in literature." As a guide to the reading public's regard for the schoolroom group in the postbellum period, no one is better than Howells himself. At the home of Representative (later President) James A. Garfield in Hiram, Ohio, one summer evening in 1870, Howells sat on the porch conversing about his life in Cambridge. "I was beginning to speak of the famous poets I knew," Howells recalled in *Years of My Youth* (1916), "when Garfield stopped me with 'Just a minute!' He ran down into the grassy space, first to one fence and then to the other at the sides, and waved a wild arm of invitation to the neighbors. . . . 'Come over here!' he shouted. 'He's telling about Holmes, and Longfellow, and Lowell, and Whittier!' and at his bidding dim forms began to mount the fences and follow him up to his veranda. 'Now go on!' he called to me, when we were all seated, and I went on, while the whippoorwills whirred and whistled round, and the hours drew toward midnight." In that anecdote, pathos derives partly from Garfield's humility in subordinating politics to literature. Yet it is Howells's account of the mood and setting of the assemblage—the neighbors' silent, willing compliance in the dark, the atmosphere of natural and domestic tranquility—that imparts to the scene most of its power and poignancy. The neighbors respond not out of concern for social formalities—the source, one may assume, of some of the Whittier Day guests' shocked reactions—but with a reverence that Howells likens to religious worship: "beautiful devotion" that, as the darkness deepens, shades into "mystical experience." The deference the schoolroom poets commanded—while reinforced, as the label suggests, in the hierarchical setting of the classroom—here appears founded on the meaning their works imparted to readers' lives, rather than merely on the stature the poets enjoyed as pillars of culture.[6]

At the same time, it would be naive to ascribe the sustained popularity of the group solely to the sentiments their poems voiced. Their reputations derived as well from their ability to capitalize on the rise of authorship as a profession in the United States. That development required a quality with which Twain did not credit them: savvy attunement to the rhythms of the print market as well as to the sound and meter of words. In contrast to the colonial period, transformations in that market in the years roughly between 1820 and 1850 permitted some Americans to think of themselves as professional poets—which is to say that they began to regard writing as a significant source of income, not simply as a labor of love. Several factors converged to shape the opportunities for poetry at a profit: the example of Byron's and Scott's commercial success in England; the growth of book distribution networks; the separation of printing from the retail trade; the perfection of more cost-effective production techniques; and the rise in the numbers of American periodicals and their circulation to a wider, national readership. The usefulness of short poems as magazine filler made editors willing to print them, but as the genre became popular they were also willing to pay for them: Charvat reported that by the late 1840s Bryant, Longfellow, and Nathaniel Parker Willis were receiving as much as fifty dollars a poem. In addition, by the 1850s both poets and publishers discovered that they could make money by reprinting magazine verse in volumes of collected works or in anthologies such as Rufus W. Griswold's *Poets and Poetry of America* (1873). The inclusion of poems in gift books beginning in the 1820s, and the manufacture of deluxe, illustrated editions as well as cheap ones for mass consumption, also encouraged readers to think of poets as producers of a valuable commodity.[7]

Within the fireside group, the master of the new conditions was Longfellow, who, in his choice of subjects and language, systematically instructed his readers to view the creation of verse as a career. Longfellow also made a concerted effort to establish the gender of the professional poet as masculine, undercutting the image of Byron and Shelley as sensitive, effeminate romantics even as he retained the sentimental plot devices and emotionalism associated with women. His career benefited enormously as well from his business relationship with James T. Fields, the Boston publisher whose firm, Ticknor and Fields, pioneered modern techniques of book promotion. Longfellow himself kept a sharp eye on the audiences for various editions of his works. "It is doubtful," Charvat asserted, "whether any other poet of the century was so resourceful in bringing his work before the public in so many forms and on so many price levels." In 1874, for example, Longfellow accepted $3000 from Robert Bonner of the *New York Ledger* in payment for advance publication in the newspaper of his poem "The Hanging of the Crane."[8]

That assiduous professionalism contrasts sharply with the silliness of the Longfellow in Twain's speech. Yet the evolving figure of the poet as professional—and, in Fields's hands, as marketable commodity—remained only one available model for conceiving of poetic production. Throughout the nineteenth century (and up to the present), it coexisted and overlapped with amateur traditions. It is impossible to tally how many lines of verse Americans created in this period, but many more individuals wrote poetry than regarded "poet" as their occupation. Lawrence Buell's statistical study of 276 New England authors between 1770 and the Civil War suggests that women were more inclined than men to define

Henry Wadsworth Longfellow, both icon and compan-
ion to American readers, in a Southworth and Hawes
daguerreotype of 1850. Courtesy of the National Park
Service, Longfellow National Historic Site.

themselves "primarily" as writers because they lacked alternative
sources of income and personal satisfaction. But women also sus-
tained amateurism because prescribed gender roles discouraged
their economic independence and because critics disdained the sen-
timental mode in which most women poets wrote. Furthermore,
even for men, the literary culture of the time did not support a
rigid distinction between amateur and professional. As Buell has
noted, after it became possible to make a living by one's pen, litera-
ture still continued to attract the energies of "well-educated gentle-
men" who saw founding periodicals as a form of public service and
viewed writing as a type of "refined accomplishment." In their
hands, occasional verse continued to flourish.[9]

More broadly, the same development that stimulated an ethos of
professionalism—the proliferation of print outlets for verse—en-
couraged amateur production. As formal schooling became democ-

ratized, the widespread inclusion of poetry in the curriculum entrenched its status as a sign of cultivation. The relative ease of working in the genre—compared, for example, with the composition of music—prompted both men and women with literary inclinations to write poems as a hobby. Print nurtured the fantasy that the hobby might turn into a career after one's talents came to light.

Amateurism also coexisted with the ethos of professionalism in the sense that not all of the schoolroom poets resembled Longfellow in the wholehearted embrace of commercial considerations. Whittier, for instance, continued to exhibit ambivalence about building an identity as a professional poet even as he assented to Fields's plan to include him in a series of Diamond Poets, volumes designed to be "cheap, cheap, cheap, so as to open a market far away among the unbuying crowd hidden away in the dust holes of our country." As a Quaker and anti-slavery agitator, Whittier insisted instead that his writings had been "simply episodical, something apart from the real object and aim of my life." He also repeatedly complained about the autograph seekers, honorary uses of his name, and similar invasions of privacy that attended his authorial triumphs.[10]

Such intrusions (as Whittier perceived them) are a key to an additional way in which the phenomenon of professionalization did not fully account for the cultural roles of the schoolroom poets any more than did Twain's depiction of them as incompetents. Insofar as the growth of a professional class went hand in hand with the development of a less personal, more bureaucratic society in the post–Civil War years, the figure of the poet could represent the opposite of that trend. Longfellow, Whittier, et al. were popular possessions as much as objects of veneration. As fixtures of the fireside, they were approachable and familiar. That much is evident from the anecdote concerning Garfield's neighbors: while, on the one hand, their hushed response conveys awe that they are in the presence of someone who has rubbed shoulders with the gods, on the other hand they experience access—at only one remove—to literary greatness. The autograph hunters who plagued Whittier overcame even that distance by going directly to the source.

An extended illustration of the same point—that to some of their readers the schoolroom poets seemed more approachable, and hence more emotionally available, than was consistent with the ethos of professionalism—appears in *The Americanization of Edward Bok* (1920), the autobiography of the influential editor of the *Ladies' Home Journal* at the turn of the twentieth century. Bok's narrative is a fascinating reassertion of faith in opportunity and the efficacy of individual action at just the point when the growth of urban, corporate America had decreased the possibility of controlling one's life by relying on face-to-face encounters. In Bok's Algeresque reminiscence, the fireside poets occupy the same echelon as generals and statesmen; what is more, all are equally within reach when, as a youth of sixteen, Bok decides to contact them. While working as an office boy and reporter for the *Brooklyn Eagle,* he had walked up to Rutherford B. Hayes and convinced the President to give him a copy of a speech. Subsequently, Bok, who had started collecting autograph letters from famous men— "it never occurred to the boy that these men might not answer him"—determined to pursue the same tactics with the poets he admired: Holmes, Longfellow, and Emerson.[11]

According to the autobiography, he simply showed up in Boston and asked to see Holmes, who invited him to the celebrated breakfast-table. Emerson, whose writings Bok kept in his pocket, was by then suffering from dementia, but favored his visitor with a signature. Bok's account of his visit with Longfellow, written in the third person like the rest of his book, is particularly telling for its portrayal of the poet as both god (or angel) and surrogate father (or chum), but not as a man engaged in writing for a living: "When Edward Bok stood before the home of Longfellow, he realized that he was to see the man around whose head the boy's youthful reading had cast a sort of halo. . . . 'I am very glad to see you, my boy,' were his first words. . . . Edward smiled back at the poet, and immediately the two were friends." During dinner, a walk, and an excursion to the theater, Bok and Longfellow discuss the poet's work, the latter revealing his unpretentious view that neither "The Song of Hiawatha" nor "Evangeline" was "'as good as it should be.'" Because Bok elsewhere lauds the "opportunities" that his pursuit of celebrities affords him, his wide-eyed innocence in recounting these episodes is hard to take at face value. But if Bok was somewhat disingenuous, his stance was consistent with his depiction of these poets as only tangentially connected to the business of publishing. Instead, Bok perpetuated not only the schoolroom poets' venerable stature but also their capacity to speak directly—literally and figuratively—to their readers as kindly parents or wise friends.[12]

A poem entitled "In a Volume of Lowell's Letters," published in the *Dial* (Chicago) in 1897, nicely summarizes the entanglement of amateur and professional attributes attending the figure of the poet at the end of the nineteenth century. The author, Frederic L. Luqueer, an amateur poet with a Ph.D. in philosophy, connected his own efforts to James Russell Lowell's by envisioning Lowell as both inspirational model and sympathetic equal. The first line of his encomium—"Lowell, I never met thee while on earth"—conveys both familiarity through direct address and distance arising from the stated absence of personal contact. The sense of the poet as a living, immediate presence pervades Luqueer's next lines: "Yet thou so livest in these words of thine / That thy rich nature friendly seemeth mine." The concluding images place Luqueer in a posture of deference ("grateful I took / The hand thou openedst here") while simultaneously expressing the wish that Lowell "knewest the winning of thy reader's heart." That conceit implies that, by reading and emulating the accomplished professional, the amateur has melded his identity with that of his mentor. The appearance of the text in print—which is to say the reader's entry into the author's milieu—symbolizes such a transformation.[13]

In this instance, it is true, the merging of poet with reader-disciple occurs through the medium of Lowell's letters, not his verse. Yet that reference accentuates the stature of the schoolroom poets as human beings, not simply as artists. Neither were they the all-too-human figures Twain had drawn. Amateurs and professionals, they inhabited schoolroom and fireside for nineteenth-century American readers as both icons and friends. The descendants of those readers would find the poet less godlike but equally companionable.

chapter three

Absence and Presence

ॐ ON AN October morning in 1892, fifteen years after the Whittier Day dinner, the poet Harriet Monroe took her place at the festivities marking the dedication of the World's Columbian Exposition in Chicago. As the author of the ode commissioned for the occasion, she watched with special delight as the actress Sarah Cowell LeMoyne ("six feet tall, handsome, and vocally magnificent") moved toward the platform to recite Monroe's lines. The performance—a third celebrated moment encapsulating the history of poetry in American culture—unfolded before distinguished statesmen, civic leaders, and other luminaries. Afterwards, Monroe accepted a laurel wreath from Vice President Levi P. Morton and assumed a seat of honor for the remainder of the ceremony, which included oratory, a 5000-voice rendition of the "Hallelujah Chorus," and prayers.

Although the event drew on what was by then the well-established national tradition of verse composed for civic observances, Monroe nevertheless insisted that the spectacle reflected not the poetic genre's exalted standing but, rather, its beleaguered position in late-nineteenth-century America. The legend of Monroe at the Columbian Exposition, which she actively fostered in her own memoirs, was, by her reckoning, a story of evanescent triumph and ongoing struggle. As the sister-in-law of John Wellborn Root, the exposition's consulting architect, Monroe had been well acquainted with preparations for the fair as early as 1890. As painters, musicians, and sculptors were busy executing commissioned works, however, poetry remained "neglected." Monroe's aspirations, combined with her Chicago society connections, led her to claim that the dedication ceremonies would be "incomplete" without a commemorative ode—a work, she proposed, that she herself was in the best position to write. Early in 1891, she convinced the fair's organizers that she was right. Soon afterwards, however, Monroe experienced a protracted nervous illness. What was perhaps worse, one of the organizers began lobbying to dump Monroe and commission a poem from Whittier or another famous figure instead. Monroe fought back and, in the end, she won, provided that the reading take "not more than ten minutes."

Monroe's victory, which she interpreted as an acknowledgment that poets deserved the homage of society, assured her jubilation on opening day. After the festivities, however, respect for Monroe's métier continued to prove elusive. First, the New York *World* printed the entire text of the "Ode" without securing her prior consent, forcing Monroe to sue the newspaper for copyright infringement. Second (and perhaps as a consequence of the poem's appearance in the *World*), visitors to the Columbian Exposition resisted purchasing either a pamphlet containing the ode or a more expensive "souvenir" edition. As Monroe sardonically remarked, "Evidently the public for poetry had oozed away since the happy day when Longfellow received three thousand dollars from the *New York Ledger* for 'The Hanging of the Crane.'" Thus, despite the thrill of her triumphal appearance, the entire "Columbian Ode" episode, in Monroe's view, revealed the poet's marginal role in American life, and exposed a corresponding need for a "planned and efficient program of propaganda" on behalf of poetry.[1]

In 1911, Monroe executed such a program by soliciting funds from socially prominent Chicagoans for a new magazine, which she called *Poetry: A Magazine of Verse*. As Monroe explained in an early publicity circular, her periodical was "the first American effort to encourage the production and appreciation" of the art. *Poetry* promised to set high critical standards, to improve the paltry remuneration most magazines offered poets, and to provide a venue for poems "of more intimate and serious character" than could be printed elsewhere. Monroe and her associate editor, Alice Corbin Henderson, announced that they would read "with special interest poems of modern significance." The early years of *Poetry* testify that they did so. In addition to Ezra Pound, whose stormy professional relationship with Monroe is well known, contributors between 1912 and 1915 included Vachel Lindsay, William Butler Yeats, William Carlos Williams, Amy Lowell, Robert Frost, T. S. Eliot, Edwin Arlington Robinson, Carl Sandburg, and Edgar Lee Masters, to name the more prominent experimentalists. To various degrees, and in tension with their desire to build an audience, those figures, the so-called (and self-identified) "new poets," shared the conviction, as Williams put it to Monroe, that poetry required a "tincture of disestablishment." By publishing such work, Monroe saw herself revitalizing the genre after thirty years of decline, a judgment with which scholars have often concurred.[2]

Three fin-de-siècle developments substantiate that story of lapse and rebirth: the deaths of the most beloved and accomplished nineteenth-century poets; the dominance of the realistic novel over poetic expression; and the reluctance of publishers to issue volumes of verse. The first of these phenomena is incontrovertible. Bryant died in 1878. In the 1880s and 1890s, not only the remaining "fireside" figures succumbed, but also Robert Browning (1889) and, even more significant, Alfred Lord Tennyson (1892). Reporting Tennyson's imminent passing, the *New York Times* gave the story more prominence than either the killing of the Dalton gang or the victory of the Democrats over the Populists in Georgia. For Americans, the magnitude of Tennyson's loss resulted from both his outlook and his accessibility. His poetry, as the Presbyterian minister and poet Henry Van Dyke commented in the *Century*, "has woven itself into the dreams of our youth. . . . Our closest bonds of friendship and love have been formed to the music of 'Enoch Arden' and 'The Princess,' 'Maud' and the 'Idylls of the King.'" Another eulogist noted that "no poet of our century has been oftener quoted in sermons by theologians of all schools." Moreover, thanks to the absence of international copyright protection, Tennyson's works reached "all classes, in every part of the country," at a lower cost than in Britain.[3]

Thus Tennyson enjoyed an influence among the American reading public that was "diffusive, pervasive, atmospheric." His demise was correspondingly calamitous. Many wondered whether adequate verse would emerge from the diminished ranks of its creators. As *Publishers' Weekly* queried in noting the deaths in the same year of Whittier and Whitman, "Who shall take their place? Not in this generation can the void left in literature by their loss be ever even partially filled." Ten years later, writing in his "Editor's Easy Chair" column for *Harper's*, William Dean Howells worried about the disappearance of the "lords of rhyme": what, he asked, would be the effect, especially on older Americans, of the reality that "there is no longer a Tennyson, a Browning, a Longfellow, to compel our allegiance"?[4]

The second source of the late-nineteenth-century perception that poetry had fallen on hard times was the rising prestige of the realistic novel. In the post Civil War era, the popularity of fiction of all sorts increased, far outstripping other genres in terms of new titles issued. Within that category, realism emerged as the style consonant with the massive economic and social changes of the period. Realistic fiction was both a protest against and a reflection of the disruptions that industrial capitalism brought to everyday American life. In its materials and in the circumstances of its production, realism faithfully exhibited the pervasive effects of urbanization, immigration, and modernization in the aftermath of brutal war. Its purpose, as Howells (the form's greatest champion) explained, was "to picture life just as it is, to deal with character as we witness it in living people, and to record the incidents that grow out of character." As Americans sought to make sense, in Lawrence W. Levine's resonant phrase, of the "new universe of strangers" surrounding them, that purpose gave "fictions of the real" an appeal that poetry—with its emphasis on the ideal, the symbolic, the atypical, or the sentimental—could not supply. Nor did the poet seem equipped to record the pace and scope of social change. As a reviewer commented in noting the weaknesses of E. C. Stedman's *An American Anthology* (1900), "The volume betokens the inadequacy of poetic literature to sustain a large and vigorous modern national life; it denotes the transfer of power from the Sayer to the Doer." The spirit of action, both in the air and on the page, instead made the realistic novel, in the words of Howells, the "supreme literary form."[5]

The argument that poetry in the late nineteenth century was in decline also drew on publishers' and poets' mutual disdain for each other's contributions to the genre. In decided contrast to Fields's boosting of his authors, between the date of the Columbian Exposition and the founding of *Poetry* the majority of the annual surveys of book production appearing in *Publishers' Weekly* deprecated the quality of most new books of verse. In 1897, for example, *PW* averred that the poetic "contributions" during the previous year were "scarcely worthy of notice." The trade journal's overview of poetry published in 1904 was even more strident in tone: "The majority of the original works [as opposed to reprints] was far below mediocrity." The *PW* editorialist conceded that the printing of poetry in magazines had the effect of siphoning off "the larger part of the output" that might have found its way into book form. Still, apart from the 1906 *PW* retrospective, which cited strikes and overproduction, the implication of the *PW* assessments was that poets had failed to offer the book industry enough manuscripts of literary promise.[6]

For their part, however, Monroe and her contemporaries blamed publishers and editors for devaluing their art. The continuing practice of allocating leftover space in periodicals to verse, Monroe believed, reflected editors' cavalier attitude toward poets' work; in many quarters, the term "magazine poet" became one of derision. Book publishers, Monroe thought, were equally culpable. The manifesto she wrote to publicize the launching of *Poetry* declared: "Leading publishers of England and America have told me that they 'almost never' publish a book of verse unless the expense of publication is paid by the author when the book is issued." Furthermore, poets seeking contracts from large, established New York houses for first books of verse reportedly encountered little enthusiasm for their efforts. The most famous case is that of Robert Frost, who did not find an American publisher for his collection *A Boy's Will;* instead, the book initially came out in England in 1913. Similarly, Edwin Arlington Robinson required the intervention of Theodore Roosevelt to win a hearing at Scribner's for a new edition of *The Children of the Night.*[7]

By the turn of the century, this state of affairs was prompting a number of writers in both the United States and abroad to debate the state of poetic expression. To assess the American situation, the editors of the *Critic* conducted a "forum" among poets, critics, and publishers, stacking the deck by asking why "poetry nowadays seems to attract so little attention." The results, published in 1905 as "The Slump in Poetry," identified additional factors contributing to the decreased stature of verse: contributors cited the rise of science, the pace of modern life, and the emergence of mass culture as injurious to the poet's craft.[8]

The reality underlying the comments in the *Critic*'s forum cannot be discounted. Neither can the poignancy that pervades them, which arises in part from the fact that poetry's fate symbolized to many the demise of a familiar and secure world. Yet the scenario of turn-of-the-century decline had origins and functions apart from the actual record of poetry's production and distribution. For one thing, the declension narrative, especially later, when it could be paired with resurgence, served to entrench a particular definition of poetry's "higher forms": one that equated evolution toward modernism with artistic achievement. Moreover, that narrative seems, at least in part, an artifact of the oppositional identities in which "new poets" were so self-consciously invested. (In Monroe's case, the complaints about publishers may also be traced to the series of rejections she received between 1895 and 1910.) American poetry in the period between 1890 and 1912 appears moribund only if the measure of health is the production of new, singly-authored volumes of verse exhibiting either the moral authority of Tennyson and Longfellow or the crafted language, formal complexity, and rejection of ideality and sentiment associated with the high culture canon by the early twentieth century. From the perspective of readers and amateurs, the history of poetry in these years had somewhat different rhythms.[9]

With regard to sheer quantity of output—and hence, the genre's capacity to "attract attention"—poetry was actually on the upswing. Apart from the pervasiveness of verse in periodicals devoted to everything from agriculture to religion, *Publishers' Weekly* calculated that the number of poetry and drama titles (unfortunately for the historian, the trade journal amalgamated those categories) issued by all American book publishers in 1911 was more than two and a half times greater than in 1892: 674 titles as compared with 259. To be sure, production fluctuated within that nineteen-year span; in 1893 and 1894 (during a severe depression), as well as 1897, 1900, and 1911, the number of new books of verse (as distinguished from new editions of older works) fell from the previous year (although the production of reprints offset the drop in 1894). Yet, as a contributor to the *Critic* forum pointed out in rejecting the idea of a "slump," between 1903 and 1904 alone new titles increased from 421 to 530. An even bigger jump—from 250 to 421—had occurred the previous year. Those statistics, moreover, underestimated production by leaving out both the high and low ends of the hierarchically structured marketplace as *PW*'s editors understood it. In the words of the *Bookman Year-Book* for 1898, *PW*'s tallies (at least up to that time) "include the better class of paper-covered books issued as periodicals, in order to secure postal privileges, but not the cheap five and ten cent 'libraries.'" Moreover, they omitted some self-published works emanating from printing companies. A comparison of *PW*'s 1905 totals with a list for that year gleaned from the *American Book Publishing Record* (organized by Dewey Decimal System number) reveals 56 titles that appeared only in the latter, almost all from publishers or printers on the margins of the trade. Instead of classifying them as "Poetry and Drama," beginning in 1901 the annual survey also swallowed up under "Literature and Collected Works" reprints in so-called "standard editions" of the oeuvres of canonical poets.[10]

In the face of poets' complaints about restricted access to publication, the upward trend in output suggests that generalizations about the state of the genre at this time require distinctions among the various forms of print in which poetry appeared: for example, between works by an individual poet and collections of verse; deluxe editions and cheaply manufactured pamphlets; books tendered by an established, for-profit New York or Boston publisher and a regional printer with few distribution outlets. Variations in physical makeup in turn created and reinforced differences in the cultural expectations surrounding a given poetry volume—whether it seemed ephemeral or carried an aura of permanence, whether it signaled spiritual weight or frivolous amusement.

Despite its undercounting, *PW*'s week-to-week record of volumes of verse published in 1905 (chosen because it was the year of the *Critic* forum) makes possible a rough determination of just who issued poetry—which institutions made it a presence for American readers—and what kinds of books they produced. The total output of 280 volumes emanated from four sources: mainstream commercial houses with national distribution networks, including religious firms and reprint houses (116); small, largely regional publishers (97); printing companies and self publishers (33); and (worth separating from the former category because of its large operation) the "vanity" press of R. G. Badger (28). Six more were unidentifiable by publisher. Within the output from mainstream publishing houses, half (58) were new original works; the other 58 consisted of reprints and translations. Men were the authors of 211 volumes, women of 51, with another 18 volumes unidentifiable by gender.[11]

These statistics demonstrate that trade publishers in 1905 continued to bring out substantial amounts of verse—more than 40 percent of the total volumes of poetry, and about 20 percent of original new works. To be sure, most poetry (especially non-reprints) came from other sources. Whether these numbers mean that commentators were right in insisting on the difficulty poets faced in getting published depends on what one means by "published." As Monroe would probably have conceded, access to print in the form of the locally or regionally distributed, limited, or author-subsidized edition was readily available. Furthermore, despite ongoing complaints that poetry was the province of sentimental women, it is obvious that men dominated verse publication.[12]

Each of these categories of publication, moreover, conceals a range of formats. Mainstream, commercial publishers between 1890 and 1912 were more likely to issue collected works or anthologies than the new poems of an individual, because the former were more profitable: given that most poets did not have a great enough supply of unpublished poems to fill a long book, and that the costs of printing, binding, and distribution did not increase in proportion to a volume's length, it was cheaper per page to produce a collection of several hundred pages than a "slim volume" of new verse. Moreover, the anthology's greater heft, adaptability as a gift or school book, and intrinsic variety made it a more saleable commodity to parsimonious buyers. An example in the 1905 sample is Houghton Mifflin's publication of *The Chief American Poets,* edited by Curtis Hidden Page, which contained 713 pages exclusive of front and back matter.

Nevertheless, certain firms undertook to promote both collections and singly-authored "slim volumes" of recent vintage, as well as reprints of classics. Macmillan (the American branch of the British house) built the strongest reputation for consistently doing so. In 1905, for example, it brought out Longfellow's *Courtship of Miles Standish and Minor Poems* and *The Song of Hiawatha* (both in its series entitled "Pocket English and American Classics"); it also published *The First Wardens,* a book of 99 pages by the relatively unknown (then and now) writer William J. Neidig. Macmillan's issuance of those works grew out of the house's professed ambition to foster literature; such an objective was economically feasible because the firm's international reach, large list, and energetic marketing generated enough revenue to subsidize its aesthetic commitments.[13]

Similarly, Houghton Mifflin balanced sales income against the desirability of sustaining the house's reputation as "publisher of the best in American literature," deciding that "poets were imperative" while making some of them assume the expenses of publication and pay the firm a commission. On its list in 1905 were both

Anna Hempstead Branch's *The Shoes That Danced* and a 312-page volume of *The Poems of Trumbull Stickney*. Like Macmillan, Houghton Mifflin was sincere in professing its high-minded motives, but its associates also understood the contribution of poetry to an imprint's appeal as a token of culture. As Horace Scudder argued in urging a contract (at no cost to her) for the poems of Josephine Preston Peabody, "As a mere matter of advertising, a book of genuine poetry has its value just as a Catalogue of Authors may." That is, even in the face of the perceived decline in quality and the challenge from the realistic novel, publishers in some measure continued to confer on poetry a mantle—and a market value—as the "noblest" literary form. Such firms as Harper and Brothers, Putnam's, Frederick A. Stokes, and the nondenominational Protestant concern of Fleming H. Revell did the same to a lesser degree, bringing out one or two volumes of contemporary poetry in a given season.[14]

Other sources of volumes of new poetry in the American market were the maverick editor and the "arts and crafts" house. In the former group was Mitchell Kennerley, who oversaw publication of numerous English and American poets as manager for the British-based John Lane Company before starting his own firm in 1906. In the latter category were the William Morris–inspired firms of Copeland and Day and Stone and Kimball (both with Boston connections), founded in the 1890s by figures whose independent wealth and passion for the decorative arts led them to enter the business for aesthetic rather than commercial reasons. Small, Maynard, another Boston house devoted to the arts, began by issuing an edition of *Leaves of Grass* (1897), then purchased Stone and Kimball's list in 1899, and acquired the poems of Bliss Carman that same year. In 1905, Small, Maynard published only a slight volume by William Frederick Kirk, entitled *The Norsk Nightingale*, but in 1910 it brought out Ezra Pound's first book in the United States.[15]

In sum, both within and outside the mainstream, trade publishers' sense of mission, along with the adaptability of poetry to treatment as art, created steady—although tightly circumscribed—opportunities for amateurs and professionals to gain audiences for their work. One sign that accounts of Frost's and Robinson's experiences may not be an accurate gauge of the new poet's access to commercial publication is a letter Alfred Harcourt wrote to Frost in 1915 when the former was an editor for the firm of Henry Holt. Observing that reviewers of Frost's *A Boy's Will* had harped on the poet's initial difficulty getting the book published in the United States, Harcourt voiced skepticism about whether the American marketplace was really as inhospitable as Frost's story implied. "Of course, I don't know the history of the manuscript," Harcourt wrote, "but wonder if its publication first in England was not the result of your being in England when it was finished. . . . Do you know whether it was regularly offered to other American publishers or not? In any event was it offered to an American publisher before it was offered to an English house?" An answer to those questions surfaced in an interview Frost gave in 1958. "It was more or less an accident that it happened over there," Frost remarked of his publication abroad. "I had never been discouraged in America, I had never been much encouraged."[16]

Among printing companies and vanity presses that facilitated self-publishing, the output at the turn of the twentieth century varied from professions of religious faith to lines celebrating family history, along with love poems and paeans to nature. This activity took place all over the country; representative titles for 1905 included *Seeds of Truth,* printed by a Seattle concern, and *After Noontide,* issued by the Nicholson Printing and Manufacturing Company of Richmond, Indiana. Some firms that offered private printing also participated in the commercial market: an example is A. C. McClurg of Chicago, which privately published Harriet Monroe's first book, *Valeria and Other Poems,* in 1892 and tendered it for public sale the next year.[17] The most active vanity press was the Boston firm of Richard G. Badger. In 1897, it brought out Robinson's *The Children of the Night* on those terms. Not everything Badger did was a "vanity" undertaking, however: for example, the firm printed and, later, published the magazine *Poet Lore,* which included plays by Strindberg, Maeterlinck, and Chekhov. Still, the number of poetry volumes on Badger's list that remained important primarily to their authors far exceeded those that presaged a major literary talent. Badger's twenty-one books of verse in the combined 1905 *PW* listing and the *American Book Publishing Record* included Edward Farquhar's *The Youth of Messiah* (about Jesus) and Edward Oscar Jackson's *Love Sonnets to Ermingarde.*

From the standpoint of *Publishers' Weekly* and Monroe, Badger and similar operations did not qualify as producers of "good" poetry; they deserved condemnation for contributing to poetry's "decline" by flooding the market with inferior works while exploiting men and women with embarrassingly limited talent. The term "vanity press" itself suggests self-indulgence. Two of Robinson's biographers, Hermann Hagedorn and Emery Neff, made no secret of their contempt for the way Badger, in Hagedorn's words, "fed on the ambitions" of poets by following a "formula" that was "enticing and glib." Yet, from the poet's perspective, the chance to see one's lines in print—to achieve the fixity, embellishment, and circulation that print seemed to afford—could feel like opportunity rather than exploitation. After a series of disheartening rejections, Robinson had brought out his first group of poems, *The Torrent and The Night Before* (1896), in an edition of 312 paper-bound booklets, for which he had paid fifty-two dollars to Houghton Mifflin's Riverside Press. For him, Badger's arrangement was a step up (especially because a friend agreed to foot the bill): a trade edition of five hundred copies, offering the promise of the audience for which Robinson was "desperately eager"; and a deluxe edition of fifty more, printed on and bound in vellum.[18]

The same point can be made about verse that authors carted off to printers for private or small editions. Books produced in that way lacked the certification bestowed by the editorial process; they evaded the "gatekeeping" function of the mainstream publishing industry. Authorial subvention also worked against the idea that the poet deserved the payment due any other professional. Nevertheless, while presumably they mainly considered themselves amateurs, the creators of such non-commercial texts did not necessarily see their position as that of unfortunates mired at the bottom of the publishing hierarchy. Rather, like self-publishers on the Internet more recently, they could experience access to print as a source of open-ended possibility.

In any event, the poetic output bound in the volumes originating from mainstream publishers, religious houses, decorative arts devotees, vanity presses, and author-financed printers between 1890 and 1912 supplemented magazines and newspapers in making contemporary poems a thoroughgoing presence in American culture during the ostensible period of "slump." Howells's concern about the absence of "lords of rhyme"—figures who commanded a place in the high culture canon—raises a different problem: that of quality. Given that in the "aftermath of modernism," to use Dana Gioia's phrase, the stature even of Longfellow may appear unwarranted, it may be difficult for twenty-first-century readers to see much aesthetic worth in the poetry of the 1890s. Critics and scholars who have done so have usually adopted one of two lines of argument. First, even as the "new poets" were depicting their predecessors as beleaguered idealists clinging to an "enfeebled genteel tradition," certain observers began moderating that view by discerning proto-modernist tendencies in turn-of-the-century verse. Jessie Rittenhouse, a poet, founder of the Poetry Society of America, and rival of Monroe's, declared in 1934 that there were signs of vigor in American poetry long before the supposed "*annis mirabilis* of 1912." Idealism, the literary historian David Perkins later wrote, was "obviously prevalent" in the 1890s, but "opposition movements were strong." More recently, feminist scholars have countered the charge that women poets of the era were awash in sentimentalism by arguing that some supposed sentimentalists, instead of impeding modernist experimentation, actually laid the foundation for it with their own bold departures from convention.[19]

Second, over the last several decades literary critics attentive to popular texts have questioned the criteria that gave rise to the presumption of a qualitative decline in poetry in the first place. Emphasizing the "cultural work" of literature has opened the way, for instance, to an alternative reappraisal of late-nineteenth-century women's verse. Conceding that figures like Lizette Woodworth Reese and Louise Imogen Guiney used domestic, religious, or nature motifs to evoke familiar emotions, feminist writers have shown how dismissing those poets as sentimental "scribblers" reflected the biases of male modernists desirous of clearing the field in order to assert their own preeminence as professionals. Similarly, Cary Nelson's effort to "recover" the politically radical poetry outside the canon of the interwar period suggests the possibility of regarding the abundant verse of social commentary in the late nineteenth century—the most famous example is Edwin Markham's "The Man with the Hoe" (1899)—as an indication of the genre's strength.[20]

Howells's contemporaries who defended poetry's continued vigor on qualitative grounds tended to adopt the second line of argument, bypassing canonical standards in favor of weighing the genre's significance for readers. In the *Critic*'s forum, for example, the poet Frederic Lawrence Knowles voiced optimism about the state of his art by observing that audiences unfailingly responded to poetry containing "genuine human appeal." Even though "we are tempted to look back upon the heyday of Longfellow's fame as to a lost golden age," Knowles added, in fact the poems of James Whitcomb Riley—the Indiana poet who used dialect to celebrate homey virtues—"sell far more widely than Longfellow's ever did." It was only the misguided critic, Knowles implied, who could not take heart from Riley's success. The public, Knowles concluded, "wants poetry of all kinds . . . and, what is more, is willing to pay good money for it." The addition of poetry to newspaper editorial pages, the expansion of the "reading world" through the telegraph and cable, and the rise in the income even of minor poets indicated to other *Critic* contributors a healthy increase in audience demand.[21]

The public posture of Will Carleton, the Michigan poet whose verse circulated widely from the 1870s through the turn of the century, illustrates the same assumption about the need to separate critics from readers. (Like Riley, he also provides a useful reminder that feminist defenses of sentimentalism do not account for the enormously popular writers in that vein who were men.) Born in Michigan in 1845, Carleton, a newspaper reporter, launched a literary career in 1871 after benefiting from the reprinting practices of the era: a poem he wrote for the *Toledo Blade* about a divorce case, "Betsey and I Are Out," caught the eye of *Harper's Weekly* editor George William Curtis, who republished it with illustrations. Carleton followed up with *Farm Ballads* (1873), which sold 40,000 copies in short order. That volume contained his most famous poem, "Over the Hill to the Poor-House," a narrative involving the abandonment of a widow by her selfish children. As if to assuage anxieties about the disappearance of traditional rural values, Carleton frequently depicted figures who, despite their plain clothing, lack of education, or mere age, triumphed over the seductions of the new. Carleton's own sense of his role echoed the same motif, counterposing the popular poet to the sophisticated but essentially irrelevant critic. He personified accessibility, touring the country to stage readings before the public five nights a week. In the prefaces to his books, Carleton disarmingly admitted his "literary faults" but credited his audience with greater wisdom and happiness than carping reviewers possessed. Such statements underscored and celebrated the existence of a reading population beyond the reach of those who shaped literary opinion in the columns of *Publishers' Weekly* and the *Nation*. Carleton alluded repeatedly to his "large family" of supporters—the "millions of readers" who, functioning as alternative cultural authorities, had "induce[d] him to believe that he has, to some extent at least, succeeded in carrying out his own theories" that the poet should speak to "the average mind and thought of the world."[22]

Carleton's explicit repudiation of the equation between good literature and complexity only made plain the basis on which his detractors judged his work beneath notice. Nevertheless, for many readers his position gave sentimental and un-modernist poetry a cultural presence that was at once subordinate to and independent of the "high" poetic traditions with which it coexisted. The introduction to *A Bookfellow Anthology* (1925), although from a slightly later period, is worth quoting at length because its author, George Steele Seymour, offers a striking confirmation of that point. The volume, which was printed in an edition of 700 copies at the

Torch Press in Cedar Rapids, Iowa, was, in Seymour's phrase, "an adventure in cooperative publishing," one based on the premise that "there is no reason why the minor poet should not be heard." Seymour acknowledged but simply refused to be constrained by terms such as "sentimental." Instead, in marked contrast to the assumptions of recent scholars (while anticipating their reliance on the concept of canon formation), he depicted a kind of literary free market that critics regulated but did not control: "Since there is no absolute canon of poetry, and so long as it is a thing that depends wholly upon the individual taste of the reader . . . there is no reason why the disapproval of this one or that one should doom the singer of the lesser strain to silence." Noting that Robinson's first book had been privately printed, Seymour speculated that fame might await one or more contributors to the volume. Yet, at the same time, he expressed skepticism about the standards of cultural authorities: "Once I read in a well-known poetry magazine an alleged poem addressed to a dead cat festering in an alley. . . . Never since have I been able to bring myself to regard its editor [quite possibly Monroe] as a discriminating judge of good poetry." Self-publication enabled Seymour to envision himself as a citizen of a "democracy of letters" in which individuals joined in "bookly fellowship" could freely exercise their own taste. His turn to that mode of print beautifully represents the multiple canons and parallel markets that defined American literary culture in the late nineteenth and early twentieth centuries.[23]

Contemporary defenders of poetry's vibrancy also overrode critical appraisals of newly written verse by emphasizing readers' demand for older poetic texts. Reprinting was at the heart of nineteenth-century book culture even in the antebellum period. By the 1890s, however, *Publishers' Weekly* and other observers regarded the American manufacture of "standard works and classics of literature" as a sign of improving public taste. While Macmillan and other trade houses were active reprinters, Houghton Mifflin was in an especially good position to profit from such "steady sellers" (as David D. Hall has termed them). In the 1870s, the firm had acquired the plates from James R. Osgood & Company of

Osgood's lucrative 130-volume *British Poets* series, edited by Francis J. Child. In the next decades it produced multiple, variably-priced editions of Edward FitzGerald's translation of the *Rubaiyat of Omar Khayyam*. Furthermore, as the successor to the firm of Ticknor and Fields, Houghton Mifflin enjoyed rights (though not exclusive ones) to the writings of the schoolroom group, which in the 1880s they began tailoring to the entire range of the reprint market. In 1886, the firm had in print nine different complete collections of Longfellow's poems; they included the six-volume Riverside edition (at five dollars a volume), which traded on the reputation of the firm's Riverside Press for excellent craftsmanship; the Cambridge, with its Harvard overtones; the Household; the "cheap, cheap, cheap" Diamond (priced at one dollar); and the three-volume, sealskin-bound deluxe Subscription edition, which brought in over ten thousand dollars. At the turn of the century, new Household editions appeared three years in a row, along with a Cabinet edition in 1908. Between 1900 and 1910, commemorations marking the centenaries of the schoolroom poets' births contributed to this reprint activity; in the case of Longfellow, a "Hiawatha" revival in film and performance at roughly the same time and periodic dramatizations of "Evangeline" likewise kept the poet before the public.[24]

Advocates for poetry's presence in American culture, despite the supposed "slump," also argued that two agencies of dissemination, public libraries and schools, sustained the place of the genre in readers' lives. As Knowles asked in his *Critic* response, what school or municipal library could function without the complete works of Longfellow, Lowell, and Whittier? The African-American poet Paul Laurence Dunbar was particularly instructive in this regard. "It may be the consensus of opinion that the love of poetry is declining," Dunbar stated, "but I for one don't believe it. . . . Go into any school on a Friday afternoon, in our Middle West, and I think after you have gotten through listening to the 'Friday afternoon exercises,' you will agree with me. Perhaps New York, Chicago, Philadelphia and Boston are too busy for it, but I do not believe that we of the great Middle West, and the people of the old New England towns, and the old dramatic Southerners have yet gotten past it."[25]

An "Evangeline" perpetuating Longfellow's presence in a pageant of the 1920s.
Courtesy of the National Park Service, Longfellow National Historic Site.

Two sets of questions—each posed by a well-known contemporary observer—may stand as a summary of the contest over poetry's absence or presence between 1890 and 1912. One formulation emerged from the work of the philologist Francis B. Gummere, whose book *The Beginnings of Poetry* (1901) charted "the rise of poetry as a social institution." Gummere's research enabled him to take the long view of poetry's situation in his own day. Although he granted that contemporary verse lacked the power that Tennyson and Longfellow had commanded, he thought the decline only temporary. In an essay of 1911, Gummere asked: "Why may not sterility simply mean the fallow season? And what age has not thought itself at the death-bed of poetry?"[26]

Yet equally provocative was the question Howells raised in his "Easy Chair" column after making known his decided uneasiness about the genre's future. "The really interesting and important thing to find out," Howells declared, "would be whether the love of poetry shares the apparent decline of poetry itself." Only a few readers took him up on his implied invitation to discover the answer to that query, and their letters were as mixed as the publishing record itself. His ambiguous findings prompted Howells to emphasize the significance of "that great reading world with which the small writing world is really so little in touch." As the record of persistent production and readership affirmed, in that world—the realm of "steady sellers" and schoolroom recitations, of audiences for sentimental, devotional, and political verse along with volumes of standards—poetry poured forth imagination, pleasure, and comfort even when "the sacred spring" appeared to be running dry.[27]

chapter four

Sophisticate and Innocent

🖎 AROUND 1906 the reporter R. L. Duffus, who had gradu-
ated from high school in Waterbury, Vermont, the previous year,
received an assignment from his boss at the *Waterbury Record* to
cover a poetry reading in the next town. The speaker was Will
Carleton, whose verse the young man had read in his grand-
mother's illustrated edition. Duffus, who later became a prominent
contributor to sociological studies of books and the arts in Ameri-
can life, had been steeping himself in the literature available at the
local public library. "I read the poetry of William Cullen Bryant,
Henry Wadsworth Longfellow and John Greenleaf Whittier," he
remembered, "partly because I liked it and partly because, like the
sulphur and molasses we used to take in spring, I considered it
good for me." Duffus supplemented those authors with Tennyson
and Browning, gulped doses of fiction by Dickens and Thackeray,
and tried writing his own poetry—all in an effort, as he recalled, to
fulfill a "dream of culture."

That dream was in his mind when, en route to Carleton's talk, he
recognized the only other passenger on the train as the poet him-
self. Too shy to speak to him, Duffus followed Carleton to the
Green Mountain Seminary, where thirty or forty people had as-
sembled for the reading. As Carleton recited by the light of kero-

sene lamps, he "touched the chords of life in New England small towns." At the same time, he had (over his career) "made poetry pay," and exhibited to his advantage "the instincts of the stage." Yet despite Carleton's successes, Duffus noticed on the return journey that the speaker seemed defeated. Gathering the courage to address him, Duffus remarked of the evening's program, "I'm sorry there weren't more people there." The poet thanked him, adding with a sigh, "I never know, these days." He looked, Duffus commented, "as though he had gone over some melancholy hill from which he knew he would never return."

Duffus cast the story of Carleton as an elegy for innocence—both his own and America's. He himself had believed, he noted, that "if words are arranged in regular lines in a printed book they are poetry." In a remark that incidentally captures the ability of readers to exercise eclectic taste by setting aside their awareness of aesthetic hierarchy, he characterized Carleton as skillfully redirecting the harsh light of adult judgment: "For one thing he had managed somehow not to disillusion that boy who had read Shakespeare and Milton so eagerly, who knew that 'Over the Hill to the Poor House' was not as good as Shakespeare or Milton, but who knew also that the man was real and honest at heart." Duffus's implied message was that such protection from the truth was temporary. When the poet sought "escape" on the midnight train "into a world where hundreds and even thousands of people waited for his slightest word," the cub reporter understood that he could only find such a place by fleeing the future.

Of course as a memoirist Duffus had the advantage of hindsight: he realized that the poets taking center stage in the years between 1910 and 1950 often would be purveyors not of "happy endings" but of despairing self-examination. Yet to draw a dichotomy between Carleton's (and Duffus's own) naiveté on the one hand, and a modern sense of complexity on the other, is to oversimplify the matter. For one thing, Duffus ascribed to Carleton the performance skills that were identifying marks of American consumer culture in the twentieth century. More important, Duffus's elegy overlooked the persistence throughout the next several decades of the form and themes of Carleton's poetry in an ongoing tradition of popular verse—one that relied on a well-honed appreciation for the exigencies of selling poetry as a commodity.[1]

Duffus's sense of an impending challenge to the poet as innocent has an odd echo in another journalist's portrait, almost thirty years later, of one of the chief challengers: Harriet Monroe. The vignette is a virtually unknown sequel to the famous appearance of Monroe at the Columbian Exposition: it concerns Monroe on the eve of Chicago's Century of Progress Fair in 1933. One of the officials in charge of the event had asked the founder of *Poetry* magazine if she would write an ode as she had done in 1893, but Monroe declined. It may be that she chose not to reprise her earlier role merely because of her age—she was by then seventy-three—although she may also have been discouraged by the planners' decision not to have a women's activities division and by their relative inattention to the arts. In August, however, Monroe relented. At a reunion dinner for members of the press who had covered the Columbian Exposition, she read a poem entitled "Chicago, 1933," which celebrated the technological advances the Fair itself commemorated. In place of the bestowal of laurel wreaths, the accompanying celebration for Monroe's second ode included what the Chicago *Tribune* called "a post-prandial survey of the Streets of Paris": the press veterans debated "just how Sally Rand [the risqué dancer] might stand up against Little Egypt [an 1893 belly-dancing show] from the standpoint of news interest." The occasion thus marked Monroe's fall from the grace she had tried so hard to achieve as a representative of the avant-garde. One pictures her in that men's-club atmosphere, a representative not of the "new poetry" but instead of the Victorian sensibility invoked by the humorist George Ade at the dinner when he was asked to compare the two expositions. "How would the puffed sleeve and long skirt compare with the present bathing suit?" Ade asked rhetorically. "The bathing suit is not as formally correct, but a good deal more of a show."[2]

The account of Harriet Monroe in 1933 makes a good companion piece to Duffus's description of Carleton because together the two scenes underscore the transience of the modern and the subjectivity of sophistication. Monroe represented (literally) the poets for whom Carleton had to make way; soon enough, however, she was in Carleton's unenviable position. More to the point, in the early 1900s, the poet's public persona was often simultaneously traditional and innovative, provincial and urbane. The continuing availability of the sage, seer, amateur, and professional as models likewise combined with a multifaceted literary modernism to produce even more varied figures of the poet than existed in the nineteenth century. David Perkins's distinctions are useful: the "popular" modernism of the "new poetry," which broke with the past but remained appealing to a large public, was one major strand; another— dominant among academic critics by the end of the 1930s—was the less accessible "high modernism" of Eliot, Pound, Wallace Stevens, Hart Crane, and William Carlos Williams.[3]

Yet in 1928, when the *Ladies' Home Journal* ran a page of photographs with the headline "Can You Name These Modern Poets?" the featured individuals ranged from Robert Frost, a "new poet" with high modernist leanings; to other "new poets" (Edna St. Vincent Millay, Vachel Lindsay, Sara Teasdale) who had fallen out of favor with academic canonizers; to older traditionalists (Edwin Markham, Henry Van Dyke); to Gelett Burgess, author of the ditty beginning "I never saw a Purple Cow / I never Hope to See One . . ." For the *Journal*'s editors and readers, the word "modern" encompassed them all—as did the word "poetry." Still, the overriding lesson of the 1928 *Journal* headline was its indication that, prescriptively, poetic expression remained an important part of the cultured American's repertoire, even if the image of the poet as a personality sometimes loomed larger than verse itself.[4]

If no single anecdote can do justice to American poetry's several facets in the period immediately before and after World War I, one picture of a "modern" poet is nevertheless more familiar than others. This is the image of the young Edna St. Vincent Millay as the darling of Greenwich Village in the teens and twenties. To the audiences that made her a symbol of liberation, Millay exuded sophistication—a quality that in this context was a composite of theatricality and bohemianism. Her work and her persona, indistinguishable from one another in the public eye, conveyed an intensity and de-termination to live passionately that made her, in Nancy Milford's estimation, the most popular writer of verse of her generation.[5]

One can view at closer range the elements that constituted Millay's reputation as a modern sophisticate by examining Edmund Wilson's slightly fictionalized portrayal of her as Rita Cavanaugh in *I Thought of Daisy* (1919). The narrator of the book, a young man Wilson both satirizes and resembles, first encounters Rita at a Greenwich Village party just after the war, where she is surrounded by admirers. Requested to speak her poems, she replies in "some-thing like an English accent": "Did you know I'd been asked to read in public?" Tellingly, the narrator's observations focus at this point on her voice and mannerisms: her accent seems "artificial," her handling of a cigarette "precise," her laugh an emission of "distinct, impish, economized notes." As Rita begins to recite, Wil-son's young man, who, as a reader, had been drawn to "the un-counterfeitable force of sincerity" in her verse, reacts when he en-counters her poetry in person as if he were hearing an actor; gradually, the "deep sonorities of sorrow and wonder began to move [him] as much as a play." Sound governs the scene—both Rita's lyrics, which are "a kind of song," and the competing music of a phonograph that the hostess turns on. Listening to the banter that follows, the narrator identifies two styles of talking—one of the Village, the other of Broadway—and confesses, "I do not know which, at that period, enchanted me more."[6]

The events of Millay's tumultuous personal life by themselves furnished ample material to shape the theatricality and disdain for convention that Wilson's novel caught so well. The episode that launched her career, the publication of "Renascence" in 1912, also launched a style of flamboyant performance that she employed re-peatedly in her sexual relationships with both men and women. Nevertheless, Millay's outlook and behavior took shape not only in a personal context but also in a cultural one. Among the larger his-torical factors that molded Millay's dramatic pose was the develop-ment of the theater itself. Of course recitation for any audience, regardless of its size, involves vocal emphases, the creation of a mood, and other properties of dramatic delivery. Starting in the 1890s, however, the association between the poet and the actor was heightened by a type of cosmopolitan demeanor that developed hand in hand with the growth of New York nightlife. The maître d'hôtel of the Waldorf, commenting on this changed social climate, noted: "It is not the sociability of friends, the intercourse of congenial people, but the looking on as it were at a pageant." The lights of Broadway were a tangible manifestation of the sparkle and conviviality that would-be sophisticates sought for themselves. Impressing others in this environment required mastery of gesture, voice, and appearance—precisely the qualities Rita Cavanaugh/Millay used to such great effect. Poets such as Vachel Lindsay, whose readings involved audience participation and whose rhythmic refrains ("Boom-lay, boom-lay, boom-lay, BOOM") made auditory sensation central to the poet's enterprise, also understood this new context. The poet had to speak louder, or more enticingly, than other forms of entertainment (such as Daisy's phonograph record) in order to win a hearing.[7]

Another facet of the urban milieu—the concentration of artists, writers, and radicals in the bohemian enclaves of Chicago and Greenwich Village—paradoxically provided a wider platform and an institutional base for the figure of the poet as rebellious free spirit. As Christine Stansell has phrased it, the Village was a "theater of contemporaneity" in which poetry played a starring role. The play which Millay joined when she arrived there addressed the power of the writer to live fully and, at the same time, to advance a set of political ideals. The promise of the bohemian setting was that, as Wilson wrote, it would bridge the "gulf between the self which experiences and the self which writes." In that respect the Village was, ironically, a venue for the performance of authenticity and commitment.[8]

Poetry—recited or invoked by an individual's demeanor—was an essential component of the informal public sociability that bohemia encouraged. To be sure, older forms of social exchange did not disappear. The salon tradition, nurtured in the late nineteenth century by men of letters like Edmund Clarence Stedman, contin-

ued to flourish after the turn of the century at the hands of host-
esses such as Mabel Dodge. So did the college literary society,
where Edmund Wilson's aspirations to the writer's life achieved
their early expression. In addition, the founding of the Poetry Soci-
ety of America in 1910 offered practitioners a chance to hear each
other's work at monthly meetings that were also opportunities to
see and be seen. ("Wonder if Witter Bynner will be at the Poetry So-
ciety meeting Tuesday night," Millay wrote hopefully in her diary
just after her arrival in New York.)[9]

The quintessential arena for the poet as urban sophisticate,
though, was the party: not the one arranged through the calling-
card summons of Stedman's milieu, but the casual mixer at which
Wilson's narrator, who shows up on the invitation of a friend,
meets both Daisy and Rita. As Wilson observed, it was there, in
the contrivance of Rita's recitation, that Broadway and the Village
fully merged. While it functioned as a medium of sociability, poetry
reading in the middle of a boozy Greenwich Village party also
inflected the genre with the ethos of freedom and pleasure that Vil-
lage rebels valued. As Millay demonstrated with seeming tireless-
ness, the most obvious way in which Villagers pursued that ethos
was in the area of sex. Yet the quest for liberation from repression
influenced the clamor for free verse as well as free love, and the
loosening of compositional strictures felt good, like the loosening
of moral prohibitions and corsets. Furthermore, sophisticated au-
diences could find in the act of reading verse an analogue of the sur-
render to the moment, of the desire for sensation, that they sought
less vicariously in sexual encounters.[10]

That message lies just below the surface of the social critic Max
Eastman's popular guide, *Enjoyment of Poetry* (1913). Eastman
posited a distinction between practical and poetic people—the for-
mer focused on achieving results, the latter on "intense experi-
ence." The poet "must receive the being of things with his whole
nature," he explained, in order to communicate to readers "imagi-
native realization" of objects or events. Eastman likened the poet's
state of mind to the freedom from rationality and restraint that
came from drinking wine; he charged poets with bringing audi-

ences into the same "sensuous" state of "exaltation" that baccha-
nalian revels induced; and he instructed readers to give themselves
over to a childlike impulse to love feelings and perceptions for their
own sake. There was room for ideas in Eastman's prescription for
"enjoyment," yet his approach was essentially romantic and un-
analytical. Laws of rhetoric were superfluous to the creative pro-
cess he envisioned, just as standards of respectability were. Such
restraints—like conventional sexual mores—were unacceptable if
poetry was to remain "unconditionally upon the side of life."[11]

When Millay, costumed in the flowing garments she hoped
would look "more like a negligee than a dress," swept onto the
stage to read her poems, she was thus acting out a set of values
with more than idiosyncratic sources. Nevertheless, Eastman's ref-
erence to the sensibilities of children is a clue that Millay's sophisti-
cated image was entangled with another construction of the poet:
one that connected authenticity to innocence, and particularly to
the ostensible attributes of girlhood. Wilson's description of Rita
Cavanaugh after the narrator has extricated her from the party and
taken her to his apartment similarly configures the poet as an inno-
cent. Alone with her, he perceives that she smiles in an "ecstatic
childlike way." Millay's small stature contributed to her girlish ap-
pearance, but it was a look of which she took full advantage. As
numerous reporters noted, she projected through her affect and
personality the qualities of an "elf." Her husband's reference to her
as "my child"—a striking phrase from a spouse who had sanc-
tioned her affair with a younger man—is only one indication of
the psychological complexities underlying Millay's recourse to that
role.[12]

Despite the depth of her psychic needs, however, it is likely that
Millay managed to sustain her childlike bearing because her audi-
ences reinforced that aspect of her self-presentation as much as
they did her stance as bohemian. As Bernard Duffey cogently put
the point, "Millay's appeal to the sophisticate lay in her ever-ready
naiveté." In considering why that was so, it is important to note,
first, that the term "girl" is sufficiently ambiguous to carry over-
tones of sexual freedom and availability, as in the phrase "It-girl"

(which the biographer Elizabeth Atkins applied to Millay). Another product of the turn of the century, the label "chorus girl," connoted a degree of wholesomeness but also called to mind sensuous women playfully entertaining men. Perhaps "girlishness" invariably conceals and evokes a fantasy of virginity about to be lost. As Sandra M. Gilbert and Susan Gubar handle the word in their analysis of Millay and gender, a girl is simply a youthful version of the "feminine" voice that Millay and other women poets adopted as an alternative to male forms of power.[13]

Among contemporary readers, however, were those equally receptive to interpreting the figure of the "girl poet" as presexual or asexual, and hence guileless. In 1922, the *Bookman's* "Literary Spotlight" feature commented: "When she is reading her poetry, she will seem to the awed spectator a fragile little girl with apple blossom face." That theme is even more striking in an article about Millay's upbringing that appeared in the November 1930 issue of *American Girl,* a publication of the Girl Scout movement. The author reworked the hardships Millay faced as a child into a Norman Rockwellesque idyll of "cheerful resourcefulness" nurtured in the virtuous environment of a Maine seaside village. Although Millay was by then nearly forty, it was "Vincent" the girl who emerged from this portrait as a model for Scouts to emulate: quiet and "delicately built," she was nevertheless "popular in school" and athletic. Despite her sensitivity and bookishness, the author noted that she had been, "as her mother characterized her, a regular girl, normal and healthy and full of fun."[14]

Especially with respect to women, the image of the poet as innocent, one may speculate, provided a mechanism for coping with several troublesome aspects of modern American life. It is not difficult to see that, in the context of an urbanized, mechanized, and increasingly bureaucratic society, such a free spirit could be a reassuring symbol of individuality's survival; so much the better if that figure also demonstrated the persistence of the fresh, authentic vision that youth ostensibly exemplified. While the city heightened the value of theatricality as a strategy for standing out from the crowd, it also increased the premium on discovering the real—in

Edna St. Vincent Millay as innocent. Library of Congress.

the person of the untutored child—among the standardized and the imitative. The "girl poet" ideal both held out the exciting prospect of a literary life and stripped it of risk: the understanding that the poet was not fully grown offered the comforting illusion that the girl in question would neither violate conventional sexual mores nor compete professionally with men. In addition, as World War I made manifest the human potential for rapacity and destruction, an art founded on naiveté might hold even greater appeal than it had when Millay first impressed audiences with her childlike features.

In the 1920s, the reassuring possibilities that coalesced around the "girl poet" informed a little-remembered but revealing chapter of American literary history: the publication and promotion of writers who (unlike the twenty year old Millay) actually were girls at the time of their "discovery." One of the most famous of these was Nathalia Crane. A Brooklyn resident, Crane began composing verse on a typewriter in 1922, when she was nine. At the suggestion of her father, an erstwhile self-published poet and former newspaper copy editor, she sent two poems to an acquaintance of his, the managing editor of the Brooklyn *Daily Times*. The editor dispatched a reporter to interview the child. For the next few weeks, newspapers around the country ran articles treating Crane as a literary prodigy. A short time later, Crane sent another poem to the New York *Sun*, which accepted it without knowing the author's age; subsequently William Rose Benét took two more for the New York *Evening Post*. Over the next five years Crane authored first more poems in periodicals and then two collections of verse. In 1925, eight hundred people attended her Christmastime reading in New York's Aeolian Hall. At the same time, controversy erupted over whether Crane's fans were the victims of a hoax. Edwin Markham, for one, declared that no child could have written the poems in her first book. The allegations prompted a flurry of interviews proving Crane's authorship, along with a threat from the girl's parents to sue their daughter's detractors.[15]

In certain respects, Nathalia Crane's story was a typical ploy to sell newspapers and books by harping on novelty or freakishness. Yet the hoopla it generated was the result of more than the well-developed state of journalistic exploitation. At precisely the moment when, as Robert and Helen M. Lynd's classic *Middletown* chronicled, Americans feared their children's "early sophistication," Crane demonstrated—counterintuitively—that innocence could coexist with mature insight. More interestingly, the Nathalia Crane phenomenon de-eroticized poetry, reasserting the genre's connection to women's disembodied spirituality even as Millay in her bohemian voice was propounding female sexual liberation.

From the beginning, the press emphasized Crane's age and appearance in terms that implicitly contrasted her not only with adult women but also with modern ones. In the era of the flapper, the *New York Times* found Crane "very simple and natural. . . . Just a little girl with large hazel eyes and light brown hair, dressed in a short blue linen frock." In the thick of the hoax debate, a *Times* reporter investigating her work's authenticity described Crane as sporting a "middy blouse, knickers, [and] tousled curls"—symbols of wholesome girlhood. As in the case of Millay, journalists also confirmed Crane's ordinariness: "Her manners are properly juvenile and pleasing," one wrote; "no sign of precocity appears." These observations—like the repeated references to the "child poet" and "girl poet"—served to underscore the distance between Crane's looks and her vocabulary. Much of the fascination with Crane, as well as the skepticism about her authorship, arose from her incorporation of what one reporter called "multi-syllabled words that might trouble even a sophisticate."[16]

The full meaning of Crane's image as a "normal" child emerges, however, in light of the themes of some of her verse. The "janitor's boy," who figures in the first seven poems of Crane's 1924 collection, is the object of the poet's "love": "He'll carry me off, I know that he will, / For his hair is exceedingly red; / And the only thing that occurs to me / Is to dutifully shiver in bed." A stanza of "The Flathouse Roof" reads: "And, oh! the dreams of ecstasy. Oh! Babylon and Troy. / I've a hero in the basement, he's the janitor's red-haired boy." Elsewhere, in "Jealousy," the object of the poet's affection is her father, who must be protected from a "big girl" wearing makeup. Such lines were not merely the lyrics of charming "songs," as Crane called her poems, but, rather, allusions to womanly desire. Coming just at the time when Freud's views of infantile sexuality and Oedipal longing were gaining popular acceptance, those texts contained enough material for a psychoanalytic field day. Yet, taken at face value, Crane's verse could alleviate anxieties about the power and pervasiveness of sexual impulses by permitting readers to regard her poems as "pranks" emanating from her "elfin" personality. The fact that reporters chose to solicit Crane's opinions about bobbed hair and love and then presented her ideas as "cute" likewise suggests that Crane's image functioned to neutralize, or ease adjustment to, changing morality. In other words, poetry in this instance (as in the context of Millay's own "elfin" persona) became a cultural location for an affirmation of innocence under siege.[17]

To go further, the deeper significance of Millay's and Crane's popularity lies in the challenge it poses to the claim that in the 1920s a masculine ethos superseded the feminization of American culture that had occurred in the nineteenth century. The large, approving audiences that these poets garnered by manifesting either womanly allure, girlish cuteness, or both, testify to the contrary. Likewise, the continuing power of the "poetess"—a relative of the supposedly deposed "titaness"—can be measured by the sales of Millay's work in the 1930s. The 33,000 readers who bought Millay's *Fatal Interview* (1931) in its first ten weeks in print and those who, despite mixed reviews, snapped up 66,500 copies of *Wine from These Grapes* (1934) in its first seven months were exercising a preference for the feminine that cannot be overlooked in characterizing the ethos of the interwar years.[18]

Yet the gender issues that underlay the poet's projections of innocence and sophistication are not as easy to sort out as the terms "feminization" or "girl poet" might suggest. For one thing, there is the inescapable fact of Millay's bisexuality, which, as her use of the name "Vincent" implies, made her both a masculine and a feminine icon. For another, Gilbert and Gubar have convincingly called Millay a "female female impersonator." That is, the femme fatale aspect of her self-presentation was a strategy that gave the poet the means to "expose the artifice and absurdity of romance." Similarly, Millay's reliance on rhyme and lyric rather than free verse—on stylistic devices that male high modernists deprecated as marks of female conservatism—enabled her to explore the constraining and liberating effects of the conventional feminine masquerade. Furthermore, she exhibited a decidedly unsentimental and, at the time, stereotypically unfeminine interest in building a career: calculating which of her poems would "make a bigger hit in a college full of women"; assiduously learning the characteristics of the niches in the magazine world in order to maximize her acceptance rate; inventing a pseudonym so as to sell short stories to *Vanity Fair* without compromising her standing as a poet; securing an unusually high royalty arrangement from the house of Harper. Such moves indicate that, along with childlike innocence, Millay evinced sophistication in a double sense—market savvy along with bohemianism—and that she confounded gender categories in doing so.[19]

Millay's simultaneous representation of these contradictory attributes defined one version of the figure of the poet as "modern" American. The ranks of popular poets also contributed another iteration, however, in the person of a man for whom the term "modern" seems—on the surface—anathema. This was Edgar A. Guest, a writer who, notwithstanding Milford's claim, amassed even larger audiences for his verse than Millay did. At the same time he drew far greater scorn, not only from high modernists but also from "new" poets.

Guest was Will Carleton's successor as the "poet of the people." As such, he refuted Duffus's view that the tradition Carleton typified was on the wane. Born in England in 1881, Guest, like Carleton, benefited from reprinting practices in the newspaper business. In 1898, three years after joining the *Detroit Free Press* as an office boy, he was assigned to clip verse from other papers for republication. Guest decided to submit lines of his own in addition to the exchange copy. When his poems met with his editor's approval, he turned out more. In 1910, with the help of his brother, a typesetter, he produced his first book of poems, *Home Rhymes,* a volume indistinguishable from the hundreds of amateur poetry collections privately printed in this period for limited distribution. The edition of 800 copies rapidly sold out. Guest and his brother also published his next compilation, *Just Glad Things,* which sold 1500 copies. By 1914, Guest had begun writing a daily column called "Edgar A. Guest's Breakfast Table Chat," which contained his verse. These poems formed the contents of a third collection, issued that year.[20]

The large following that Guest built among *Free Press* readers and Detroit Rotarians grew to nationwide proportions when his columns became syndicated in 1915. Subsequently, after Harper and Doubleday had both turned down the manuscript, the Chicago firm of Reilly & Britton (later Reilly & Lee) issued Guest's first commercially marketed book, *A Heap o' Livin'* (1916). The firm was a logical choice to promote works that, as one of its advertisements for Guest noted, "touch[ed] the heartstrings": it was also the publisher of the best-selling sentimental novelist Harold Bell Wright. Reilly & Britton's advertising campaign emphasized the accessibility of Guest's verse—its focus on "everyday things"—and called Guest "the poet of the home" and "a poet of human nature." Thanks to those appeals and to Guest's prior reputation, *A Heap o' Livin'* sold 2000 copies before publication and subsequently more than a million in thirty-six printings. Nine more books of Guest's verse appeared between 1917 and 1928, along with two additional ones in the 1930s and two more in the 1940s. By 1930, a first edition of 50,000 copies was a "ridiculously conservative" estimate of a Guest volume's sales potential. As an editorial in the San Francisco *Bulletin* declared when Guest was in mid-career, "There is more of Edgar A. Guest in the American scrapbook, and in the American head than any national poet since Longfellow."[21]

Guest's poems were unvarying in form and outlook over the course of his career. Like Carleton's, they rhymed, employed simple diction, and paid tribute to American middle-class domesticity. Many used a folksy dialect, eliding words and substituting colloquial locutions and spelling for standard English—rhetorical strategies that might be seen as sustaining Guest's aura of amateurism even as he became slickly professional. In Guest's world, friendship mattered more than money; men and women could assert control over their relationships with others; and natural beauty was a sign of a Christian God's goodness. Families lived in homes, ate "mother's" home cooking, and revered their home towns. Guest fully acknowledged life's difficulties: the import of many of his verses was that travails were inevitable. Even his most famous poem—the one beginning "It takes a heap o' livin' in a house to make it home"—contained, in the second line, a reference to "shadder" as well as sun. His view, however, was that optimism was the best response to personal disappointments, and that things tended to work out for the best.[22]

Like Millay, Guest thus exuded a kind of naiveté. His was an adult rather than a childlike innocence, although his ability to maintain a sense of a benign universe despite world war, scientific advancement, and social upheaval arguably offered comforts analogous to the ones that Millay's girlish free spirit provided to a largely different audience. The fact that he was grown and a man, combined with his explicit assurances that the past still survived, strengthened his authority. Guest's most compelling quality was sincerity, which he occasionally demonstrated by weeping at his public readings. Thus equipped, he became a sage for readers beset by the consequences of a modernizing, increasingly impersonal society. Innocence—in the form of openness and trust—also marked the relationship he established with his readers by means of his domestic subject matter. Both women and men responded to Guest's personal voice as if he were a wise companion. For example, after listing the friends and relatives whose deaths she had endured, a woman from Montana wrote Guest, "I was wondering just what you would council [sic] if you were advising me as you advise your boy, Bud."[23]

For that placidity, lack of skepticism, and accessibility, as well as for the banality of his style, Guest received nothing but opprobrium from critics and other observers who implicitly positioned themselves as literate, up-to-date, and cosmopolitan. Like the figure of Sinclair Lewis's Babbitt, he became a symbol of mediocrity, and responses to his poems a quick measure of the distinction between serious readers and the "illiterate" American. As the aspiring artist and Village rebel Eugenia Hughes noted in her diary for 1926, "Went to school to-day and surprised the teachers by handing in some work. Listened to a fool state that Edgar A. Guest was a great poet. What a damnable idea."[24]

Yet the innocence Guest projected in his verse cannot be equated with either his mentality or that of his readers. In the first place, Guest himself was more intellectual than his persona; he read modern poets even though, as one writer put it, they "seldom return the compliment." Second, he articulated familiar—and even shared—ideals to an audience whose experience, especially if they lived outside small town America, was presenting them with a reality disquietingly at odds with Guest's ideal milieu. For a population contending with dispersed families, greater ethnic and racial diversity, routinized work, and economic fluctuation, his poems might be more affirmations of hope than mirrors of belief. Furthermore, to call Guest "thoroughly nineteenth century in his views" is to miss the consonance between his rhyme schemes and the advertising jingles that touted the proliferating products of America's modern consumer culture. It was not coincidental that the man who introduced Guest to Reilly, his publisher, was the marketer who had reputedly coined the brand names "Uneeda Biscuit" and "Nabisco." Guest was also well aware of his predecessors in the tradition of American newspaper verse and of the lucrative possibilities with which that tradition presented him.[25]

In 1916, Guest capitalized on those possibilities by accepting George Matthew Adams's offer of national syndication for his poems. Guest had by then achieved some recognition outside Detroit, not only because of the exchange system but also because the *Free Press* sought circulation beyond its immediate region. (In addition, he had a greeting card contract with the Buzza company of Minneapolis.) The rise of syndicates in the late nineteenth century, however, fostered much greater non-local distribution. Although the system had more noticeable impact in disseminating fiction, it brought fame and wealth to poets as well. One example was Ella Wheeler Wilcox, the author of *Poems of Passion* (1883) and, by his own reckoning, Riley's "female counterpart." Guest, too, took full advantage of syndication's reach. In signing with Adams, he exhibited what his biographer called the characteristic "shrewdness" behind his unprepossessing facade: on the advice of the *Free Press*'s owner, he held out for top dollar. Adams, however, had no complaints: "It was the fastest selling feature I ever saw," he later recalled.[26]

More than the banalities they found in his verse, and more than his newspaper and greeting card connections, it was Guest's embrace of syndication—and the commodification it signified—that disturbed contributors to *Poetry* magazine in the 1920s. That is, Harriet Monroe and other proponents of the "new poetry" had greater objections to what they regarded as Guest's pernicious sophistication than they had to his relatively harmless innocence. The distribution system for Guest's verse turned the author into the proprietor of a "factory," Monroe charged, making him "like other wide-awake business men." Like the criticisms that accompanied the founding of the Book-of-the-Month Club just a few years later, that indictment implied that Guest's fatal flaw was his denial of the artist's remoteness from, and superiority to, the world of commerce.[27]

Finally, Guest was a skillful manipulator of the winning image that success in modern America required. His performances were calculated to look extemporaneous but were thoroughly planned. Guest usually began with an air of embarrassment and the remark that "speaking was not his regular business"—a statement that was completely untrue. More accurate was *Current Biography*'s observation that Guest was "a master of crowd psychology." Beginning in the late teens, Guest mustered those skills on innumerable speaking tours throughout the country, during which he addressed thousands of people. Not surprisingly, in 1935 he was willing to spend several months in Hollywood under a contract to Universal Studios, although this ultimate American image-making effort faltered when no one could devise an acceptable script featuring Guest. He also transmitted his personality over the radio, first locally and then, after 1932, on a series of nationwide broadcasts sponsored by Household Finance (which was attempting to profit from Guest's association with domesticity).[28]

In his own way, then, Guest constructed a "modern" American

A Mother's Day Gift Item

Edgar Guest's

Little Book of Verse
"MOTHER"

Makes a lasting gift for Mother
on Her Day, May 11th

Artistically printed in colors and handsomely boxed

Edgar A. Guest combining domesticity and business acumen. Print Collection, Miriam and Ira D. Wallach Division of Art, Prints and Photographs, The New York Public Library, Astor, Lenox and Tilden Foundations.

figure of the poet by forging an amalgam of innocence and sophistication. Guest's literally weepy sentimentalism on stage and his domestic subjects offer further testimony that nineteenth-century "feminized" values remained powerful. Again, however, gender categories become murky when one adds to the argument not only Guest's own male heterosexuality but also his insistence on a vision of tough-minded manhood that entailed the obligation to "buckle to the hard job." Furthermore, although he celebrated the private home, Guest also capitalized on a form of modern, public sociability that was decidedly male: the lodge affairs, club meetings, and golf games populated by the admen and industrialists who transacted the business of American consumer culture. Indeed, it may be more accurate to suggest that Guest represented not the "feminization of American culture" in masculine guise but, rather, a kind of masculinity that scholars have often overlooked: a male world of love and ritual analogous to the female one that Carroll Smith-Rosenberg identified as part of late-nineteenth- and early-twentieth-century American culture. In that male context, rituals included practical jokes (Guest was honored at a lunch where sportswriters and Shriners had "good fun" putting salt in his coffee) and father-son fishing trips along with Rotary songs and handshakes (secret and otherwise). Love was also present, expressed in the letters that passed between men who shared long-standing friendship and common values. Thus George Matthew Adams signed one letter to Guest, "My love to you, not as an incidental affair, but as one hanging tight to the strings of eternity itself." In other words, the male world of love and ritual—a world that was white, middle-class, Protestant, and full of 1920s "pep"—accommodated at least to a limited degree both masculinity and sentimentalism.[29]

Poetry could be compatible with both those qualities: in 1926, when the *Christian Science Monitor* surveyed the "poetic interest and taste" of Kiwanis, Rotary, and Lions club members in Salem, Oregon, it found that two-thirds of the three hundred respondents read verse; the poets they named cut across cultural hierarchy to include Kipling, Poe, Longfellow, Keats, and Robert Service. (As *Poetry* commented in reprinting the story, "A varied and highly suggestive assortment!") A letter Guest received in 1928 from E. V. Baugh, a railroad manager and president of the Rotary club of Baltimore, provides a closer glimpse of poetry's role in promoting a ritualized, domesticated masculinity. Baugh wrote Guest requesting that the poet write a few lines he could paste on the flyleaf of *Harbor Lights of Home*. Noting that the volume was among "the collections of your books that I have on a little table right by my easy chair," Baugh told Guest that he had had "many an evening's visit with you." He asked for the lines to be about an old baby's high chair. "Some of my family have felt it should be disposed of," Baugh explained. "I have maintained that it was just like giving away one of the babies, and so when we moved away from the home where we had lived for over twenty years," he took it along.[30]

These examples do not negate the fact that many members of the reading public in the interwar period (not just disgruntled high modernists) perpetuated the long-standing disdain for the figure of the poet as feminine. The poet and anthologist Louis Untermeyer testified to the persistence of that stereotype, and attempted to refute it, in a 1935 article for the *Rotarian* proclaiming the "essential manliness of the arts." Yet in trying to win an audience on that basis, Untermeyer was preaching to at least some men among the *Rotarian* readership who, like Baugh, were already converted— that is, who were comfortable expressing certain emotions, and reading certain types of verse, along with the pursuit of sports and business.[31]

In 1926, the poet Edwin Markham anthologized Guest together with Millay in a volume "collected from the Whole Field of British and American Poetry."[32] The juxtaposition would have affronted each of the poets, and even now may appear sacrilegious to their remaining readers. How could a perfectionistic fashioner of soulful lyrics, a practitioner of literature, have any connection to a writer of simple jingles? Yet, however different the two were in aesthetic and moral terms, the tensions and ambiguities they evinced in common amount to an unlikely but unmistakable resemblance culturally. Both figures were, in their own way, emblems of modernity.

Yet both collaborated with their audiences in preserving a space for the poetry of sentiment and even moral instruction, making available motifs of innocence to readers of both genders. Together they demonstrate that poets and readers could imagine themselves as modern in ways that mingled new styles and behaviors with those of the past.

A telling illustration of that larger point comes from an undated newspaper clipping in the 1921 diary of a Wisconsin librarian named Flora Neil Davidson, who was forty-three at the time. The clipping was an excerpt from a column signed "Anne Elizabeth" and addressed "To a Youth, Cynical." It read:

> Because I say 'damn' and use lipstick, you were sure that I was a flapper; however, the fact that I hated F. Scott's type of youth, and that I hadn't been kissed was inconsistent with flapperism. But when you found out that I subscribed to the 'Bookman' and read Huneker, you decided that I must be a 'Young Intellectual,' and were surprised that I hated 'Erik Dorn' and preferred Whitcomb Riley to The Benéts [*sic*]. . . . Now, why won't you believe that a person can be 20 and live in Chicago and yet have old-fashioned ideas? Please believe that I *do* hate studio parties and the 'new' literature and blasé youths, and that I can like organ music and lolly-pops and Thackeray and still be modern.

As if to demonstrate that possibility, Davidson's diary included lines from both Millay and Riley among its numerous transcriptions. In its placement of the Benéts in an innovative and even oppositional role, a position that preceded their consignment to the dustbin of middlebrow culture, the writer's entreaty is also notable for capturing the evanescence of the modern.[33]

Along with their versions of innocence and sophistication, masculinity and femininity, Millay and Guest shared an additional quality: the enormous celebrity they enjoyed before falling out of favor. By the 1920s, their fame reflected not only their ability to convey their mixed, functional images by commanding podium and press, but also the impact of certain other material conditions and mediating factors affecting the status of poetry for its American publishers and readers.

chapter five

Celebrity and Cipher

On a Sunday evening in the spring of 1927, Millay brought her penchant for the theater to an event that further displayed the entanglement of modern poetry, sociability, and cosmopolitan performance. The occasion was a reading at Manhattan's Little Theater of Edwin Arlington Robinson's long poem *Tristram*, which Macmillan was about to publish as a book. As a member of the audience, Millay joined the company of others who were stylish, well-connected, and at ease in the precincts of Broadway. The reader of the text, the actress Eleanor Robson, was in private life the society matron Mrs. August Belmont. The "reception committee" and group of sponsors consisted of fifty-three prominent individuals: such figures of wealth and power as Mrs. E. H. Harriman, Mr. and Mrs. Kermit Roosevelt, and the Thomas Lamonts. Edwin Markham, Hamlin Garland, and the popular novelists Fanny Hurst and Hervey Allen joined Millay in lending literary reputation to the affair. Other participants from the world of the arts included designers Norman Bel Geddes and Robert Edmond Jones, the composer Daniel Gregory Mason, and critics John Erskine, William Lyon Phelps, and Louis Untermeyer. The only dignitary notably absent for most of the night was the reclusive poet himself, who made a reluctant appearance toward the end. Robinson's aloofness, however, did not prevent newspapers throughout the country from hailing the brilliance and discrimination of the gathering's "invited guests," and may well have enhanced the announced purpose of the event: to pay homage to literary genius.

In fact, the *Tristram* evening, while based on sincere respect for Robinson, was essentially a marketing ploy for the Literary Guild, founded the previous year. Carl Van Doren, the guild's chief judge, had recognized that subscribers to the book club, like other middle-brow Americans in the interwar period, wanted to stand out from the mass of readers while at the same time putting themselves in the know. With the future of the guild at stake, Van Doren also knew he had to make a profit. His solution was twofold. Invitations printed like wedding announcements and specifying that Mrs. Belmont would recite Robinson's poem "in advance of publication" conferred the requisite tone of exclusivity on the reading. The guild then selected *Tristram* as an offering to its members, furnishing a full description of the Little Theater tribute and a list of its sponsors in its monthly newsletter. In order to charge subscribers a higher price than *Tristram* alone could bring, Carl Van Doren also enlisted his brother Mark to write a book about Robinson that the guild could package with the poem. Mark did so in three weeks. Marketing Robinson as a glitzy celebrity worked: although by 1924 Scribner's had printed fewer than a thousand copies of its 1921 edition of the poet's collected works, readers bought more than 75,000 copies of *Tristram* in the two years following its publication. "For the rest of his life," Van Doren noted with satisfaction, Robinson had "renown and tranquility."[1]

Unlike Emerson's pronouncement on Whitman or the debut of Monroe's *Ode*, the *Tristram* preview is not a particularly famous incident in the annals of American poetry. Yet it belongs among those revealing episodes because it captures the process by which a representative of the "new poetry" moved from the position of disaffected outsider to become a possession of the mainstream. Although Robinson had initially experienced difficulty gaining access to the imprint of a large commercial press, by the late 1920s various agencies of dissemination including book clubs, schools, and anthologies had enabled not only Robinson but also Millay and other "new poets" to migrate from an oppositional, "disestablishment" stance toward the cultural center. In addition, Van Doren's invention of an elaborate marketing strategy for *Tristram* points to the conditions with which publishers of poetry contended in the period roughly between the 1910s and the mid-twentieth century. Packaging the figure of the poet as celebrity, the strategy James T. Fields had pioneered at Houghton Mifflin, was one response to those exigencies, as was the book industry's experimentation with new forms of distribution.

It should be emphasized that in terms of publishers' total output during these years, poetry contributed very little more than a zero or cipher in the ledger books. Some of the same factors that limited its popularity before the renaissance of the pre–World War I era affected its production, dissemination, and reception thereafter. Fiction continued to dominate publishers' lists. The ongoing, pejorative association of poetry with women was evident in one bookstore owner's remark in 1924 that reading poems had become the "secret sin" of the "red-blooded American nation." Ironically, for some individuals works that epitomized the public voice of the nineteenth-century poet became the object of private, furtive reading in the early twentieth century. More recent developments also altered the cultural status of the genre: intensified competition from new media such as the movies, the sense that the "modern temper" precluded the contemplation of older poetic sentiments, and the relative inaccessibility of the high modernists all militated against the popularity of verse. As the anthologist William Stanley Braithwaite noted in 1929, "In spite of the widespread interest in, and appreciation of, poetry today, this interest and appreciation is tenuously supported by a machine age."[2]

Nevertheless, as Braithwaite's observation suggests, within publishing there were also countervailing trends. Between 1912 and 1920, the number of new titles and editions categorized in *Publishers' Weekly* as poetry or drama fluctuated between 902 in 1914 and 500 in 1919 (the latter attributable to soaring wartime production costs). In the second half of the 1920s, however, the totals were consistently between 800 and 991. (Despite a sharp downturn during the Depression, the total for 1940 came back up to 738.) The boom in production during the 1920s matched the overall pattern in the book industry, which benefited from several socioeconomic factors—among them a higher standard of living for the middle class, increased leisure time, and larger numbers of high school and college graduates anxious to present themselves as well-read individuals. The emergence in the postwar years of a new wave of young publishers, along with book clubs and other agencies for the popularization of the humanities, likewise contributed to the growth of literary markets. Vanity and small-press publication continued to provide a significant share of the amount of verse in print. The firms of Henry Harrison in New York and the Stratford Press in Boston engaged exclusively in bringing out poems at the author's expense. Private printing of a limited edition also remained accessible. In 1936, Scribner's editor John Hall Wheelock estimated that producing 500 copies of a 100-page book of poems by simply paying a printer to manufacture them would cost perhaps three or four hundred dollars.[3]

Contemporary analyses of the upward trend during the pre–World War I years ranged from Harriet Monroe's insistence that her magazine had created the necessary conditions for the "new poetry" to Louis Untermeyer's derisive suggestion that *Poetry* merely took advantage of a surge that crested just as Monroe's venture got under way. The truth probably lies in between. For poets themselves, the "little magazine" furnished a sense of community and made getting into print much easier. Moreover, during the debate over American entry into the war and then after the United States had joined its European allies, amateur and professional poets voiced both support and dissent by extending the traditions of popular political verse that had flourished during the Civil War and the era of populist reform. By the close of the 1920s, the tally of American poetry volumes reflected as well the centrality of poetry to the Harlem Renaissance.[4]

A less tangible but more pervasive influence on production was the legitimation of free verse, and the corresponding assumption that writing poems had come within easier reach of ordinary people. For prospective poets the freer style made the distinction between amateur and professional seem easier to transcend. Furthermore, as free verse gained acceptance, turning to that form was not necessarily the compositional equivalent of rebelling against middle-class mores. In 1922 Gladys Hasty Carroll, a young Maine woman about to start her first year at Bates College, made both those points clear in recording her jubilant reaction to Untermeyer's preface to *Modern American and British Poetry*. Confessing that she had excitedly read his words "at least a hundred times," Carroll quoted Untermeyer's statement that free verse "is capable of many exquisite and unique effects impossible of achievement in a strict, metrical pattern." Although throughout her journal Carroll expressed conventional loyalties to college, region, and family, from Untermeyer she seized on the reassuring understanding that innovation in poetic style had removed the limitations on self-expression which her nineteenth-century predecessors had faced. "What a wonderful, *wonderful*, WONDERFUL time this is to be young in America!" Carroll exclaimed. "What an absolutely, positively marvelous thing to know that, if you have something you want to say and can find out how to say it, you will be one of the springs bursting up through, and part of some rushing current, and representative of your age! . . . In this twentieth century in America one does not have to be Sophocles, or Shakespeare, or George Eliot, or Browning, or even Melville or Hawthorne or Walt Whitman to be read by his fellow citizens."[5]

In addition to the increased production of verse resulting from war, affluence, and the widespread perception of opportunity, there continued to be a steady demand for reprints of poetry books, as well as school textbooks and anthologies. The owner of the Hampshire Bookshop in western Massachusetts observed in 1931 that critics like Edmund Wilson, who had pronounced poetry out of favor, "will be surprised to know that Shelley and Keats are still best sellers in any college bookshop worthy of that name." Moreover, older poets who had established their reputations closer to the turn of the century and those who, like Guest, turned out topical rhyme, devotional or nature verse, and love poetry, maintained their following of readers.[6]

The proliferation of new titles and reprint editions should not be confused with either a rise in the number of copies per title or with an increase in the number of American readers who bought poetry volumes. The difference between writing, reading, and purchasing poems is especially clear in the World War I era, when the high cost of books created a vogue not of adding to one's library but instead of rereading works already on the shelves. *Publishers' Weekly* in 1924 nevertheless called "the increase in the sale of poetry in the last ten years" one of the "outstanding features of bookstore experience." As the article noted, "it may be that a large percentage of this sale has been in the form of anthologies." A few individuals—Millay and Guest among them—also contributed inordinately to the overall rise. Two other best-sellers were Kahlil Gibran's *The Prophet,* which has continuously made money for the firm of Alfred A. Knopf since its appearance in 1923, and, a few years after the *PW* article, Stephen Vincent Benét's *John Brown's Body* (1928).[7]

It is thus striking that, even in the prosperous 1920s, the conventional wisdom among commercial publishers was that poetry did not sell. As Roger Burlingame, an editor at Scribner's, observed, "There is probably nothing which scares a publisher so much as the manuscript of a volume of verse. Unless it is certain that the poet has a public of his own, built up with infinite difficulty through the years, the printing and distribution of the book are usually undertaken from a nonprofit motive." Yet, as was the case earlier, certain firms made more efforts to publish poetry than others. In 1932, *Publishers' Weekly* examined the list of the approximately five hundred volumes that Harriet Monroe and Alice Corbin Henderson identified in the updated edition of their anthology *The New Poetry* as the most important books of poems issued in the previous thirty years (excluding reprints). On that basis, the trade journal calculated that 60 percent of these books had come from twelve houses. At the top was Macmillan, followed by a mix of established and recently founded firms, including Alfred Knopf, Houghton Mifflin,

Liveright, Holt, Harper, and Scribner's. Certain publishers also continued to operate from a personal involvement in the genre. Benjamin W. Huebsch, for example, was known for paying the expenses of verse publication out of his own pocket. In 1936, when Wheelock gave advice to a woman in search of an outlet for her poems, he pointed her toward several publishers at which poetry lovers exerted editorial influence: Farrar and Rinehart (John Farrar being a poet); Viking (where Huebsch had gone after ending his own imprint); and the still-active house of Frederick A. Stokes. In addition, a few commercial presses accepted partial or full subventions from authors: according to Wheelock, these included Putnam, Houghton Mifflin, and Dodd, Mead.[9]

Between production and consumption was another factor: the interventions of publishers and other promoters to influence reception. "Little magazines" and anthologies were key influences on the construction of literary reputations. As Van Doren's strategizing so clearly demonstrated, however, such interventions also included the creation of events that showcased poets to the public. In 1914, Mitchell Kennerley held a series of Sunday gatherings in his publishing firm's offices for the press and others to meet authors and listen to readings of their work; the series opened with Vachel Lindsay. Georgia Douglas Johnson's Saturday night salon in Washington, D.C. during the 1920s brought Langston Hughes and other poets of the Harlem Renaissance into social contact with the wider community of African-American writers and intellectuals. On a larger scale were the nationwide lecture appearances of the sort that Millay and Guest made in the same period. These activities were extensions of the nineteenth-century Chautauqua circuit, but in their modern form they shared in the promotional techniques that advertisers were learning to develop for consumer goods at this time. As Untermeyer recalled, "In 1916 forums broke out in a rash of contemporary culture. Versifiers whose names had never been mentioned in any household were quoted as oracles; chairmen fought for the current best-selling poets; agents cajoled them with national tours and glittering percentages; the self-descriptive circulars grew suddenly and ever more superlative."

Tours both publicized books and generated them: the Irish poet James Stephens, who made nine American lecture trips in the 1920s, brought out *A Poetry Recital,* a collection of the works he found best suited to large theaters, after his 1925 season. Lingering American provincialism added a special glamour to the events honoring poets from Great Britain. William Butler Yeats's second American tour in 1920 was something of a disaster: the newspaper reviewer Burton Rascoe recalled that, at a reception in Yeats's honor, the Irish poet "so far forgot where he was as to begin chanting some verse" while another speaker was lauding him to the audience. Yet his absent-mindedness only added to the image of the poet as an unworldly seer. Another British visitor, John Masefield, traveled extensively in the United States during World War I; his assignment from his government was to build American support for Britain, especially in "the German-dominated areas of the Middle West." Named Poet Laureate in 1930, Masefield returned for two more tours in the 1930s, including the delivery of an ode at the Harvard Tercentenary in 1936.[9]

Lecture tours, teas, and gala dinners reinforced poetry's function as a source of status and sociability while bolstering assumptions about the genre's beneficial spiritual influences. For example, Amy S. Oppenheim, who went to hear Masefield in New York in February 1936, not only recorded that Masefield recited from "Fox-Hunting" and eulogized King George during the hour-long program; she also expressed her pleasure at exposure to celebrities by noting that Henry Goddard Leach, the president of the Poetry Society, had introduced the poet and that she "sat in a box with Clement Wood—poet." Similarly, although it is not clear whether she was present, Oppenheim had earlier clipped a newspaper story describing Edwin Markham's eightieth birthday celebration in Carnegie Hall, an event that must have struck spectators as a powerful statement of the poet's entitlement to treatment as a personage. The affair, attended by hundreds (including representatives of thirty-six nations), included an arrangement by the dancer Ruth St. Denis of Markham's "The Joy of the Hills." Even for people unable to encounter famous poets in person, the press coverage and promotional materials for such occasions made poets look like other "stars" of the period. Indeed, a 1922 *Literary Digest* poll querying editors, critics, and publishers about the "five leading American literary stars that have risen above the horizon in the past ten years" gave Frost fifth place, with Masters, Millay, Sandburg, Robinson, Amy Lowell, and Don Marquis tying novelists for various places in the top ten.[10]

The enhancement of the poet's image through the vehicle of celebrity may explain why Roger Burlingame, who noted that Eastman's *Enjoyment of Poetry* had "outsold almost any volume of poems on the Scribner list," concluded that in the United States "books about poetry are more popular than the poetry itself." But something deeper was also at work: the audience's desire to draw closer to the creators of texts they found meaningful. As the literary scholar Percy Boynton put it in 1919, "Not only have authors' readings taken the place of dramatic interpretations in the lecture market," but the audiences who attend them "go to listen to poems with which they are already familiar and to get that sense of personal acquaintance with poets which ten years ago they coveted with playwrights and, further back, with novelists." Modern sales techniques arguably fostered further professionalization of the poet's role by enabling authors to sell more books, but they also multiplied opportunities for readers to regard them as wise but accessible friends.[11] Beginning in the late 1920s, another source of celebrity—the development of radio programs such as A. M. Sullivan's "New Poetry Hour" or Ted Malone's "Between the Bookends"—contributed to the same effect by bringing the sound of poetry into the intimate setting of the living room.

In addition to harnessing the mechanisms of publicity and technology, publishers and their retail distributors—the nation's local booksellers—intervened to affect sales of verse by implementing experiments in format and promotion. Even in the early 1920s, when total purchases of poetry volumes were up, the booksellers understood their efforts as a rejoinder to the idea that the genre had limited appeal. Yet retailers also acknowledged that the key to selling verse was to treat it differently from other kinds of books. For

Fanny Butcher, who ran a bookstore in Chicago, that meant dissociating it as much as possible from the market by conveying to potential buyers that poetry was less a form of "merchandise" than a token of the mutual sympathy between purchaser and seller. "To sell poetry," Butcher explained, "one must love it." Another retailer recommended starting customers on "Guest, Service, or [Douglas] Malloch" and then giving them "light doses of Millay, Teasdale, Lindsay, Sandburg, or Lowell"; creating displays near high-traffic areas of the store; speaking about the genre before women's clubs; and including some poetry in every advertisement. By such methods, booksellers attempted to counteract the seasonal pattern of poetry sales—the concentration of purchases at Christmas and in connection with graduations—as well as to disprove publishers' pessimism about the genre's profitability.[12]

Publishers themselves also continued their attempts to reconfigure the market for verse by targeting multiple audiences. Under the leadership of George Brett, Jr., Macmillan issued school editions through its Educational Department that it promoted "as if the trade edition" of the same work "did not exist." In the mid-1920s, the firm also apparently concluded that high prices were a barrier to overall sales of poetry: it offered a cheap Modern Readers' edition along with its regular one. When the poet John G. Neihardt expressed his concern that the less expensive format would adversely affect his trade sales, Brett replied: "Actually they [the cheaper volumes] will strike an entirely new market with a new level of purchasers, and we do not expect to have any serious interference between the cheap and the regular editions. They will be promoted by different methods and kept quite distinct." In the late 1920s, Macmillan also linked format and market by backing away from multi-volume sets, which had not been selling; the firm surmised that families—the purchasers of sets in the past—lived in smaller apartments and were therefore more likely to buy one-volume editions.[13]

A more ambitious effort in the mid-1920s to capitalize on the perception of an untapped audience for cheaply printed verse was Simon and Schuster's "Pamphlet Poet" series. The source of the

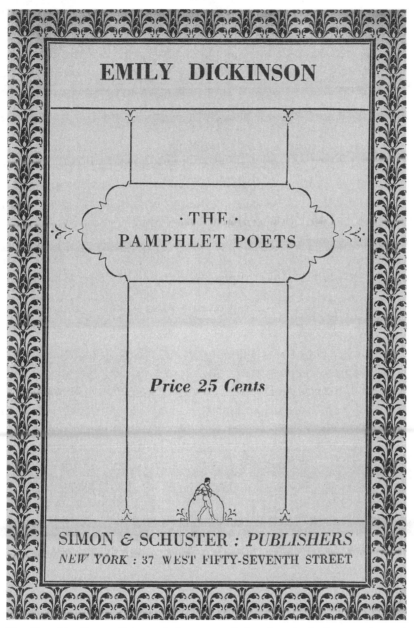

The *Pamphlet Poets* editions of the 1920s, designed to be both attractive and portable. Department of Rare Books and Special Collections, University of Rochester Libraries.

idea was the success, in England, of the "Six-Penny Poets," leaflets consisting of poems by a single, well-known British author. Max Schuster's description of plans for the project is a classic example of entrepreneurship combined with a genuine desire to improve public taste. The series was to include attractively designed pamphlets devoted to Whitman, Poe, Emily Dickinson, and leading contemporary poets (such as Millay and Nathalia Crane). Each volume would also contain commentary by an established critic like Untermeyer or the series' general editor, the educator Hughes Mearns. To secure reprint rights, Schuster promised not the usual permissions fees but instead a 5 percent royalty to be divided between the poets and their original publishers. He also held out a vision of an expanding readership that would find the low price appealing and would then go on to purchase the poet's complete works. In that way, the Pamphlet Poets would help to achieve the great audience which Whitman sought for America. Without access to the firm's business records, it is impossible to know how well the series actually sold, but between 1926 and 1928 Simon and Schuster expressed its commitment to the venture by publishing sixteen such pamphlets.[14]

At the other end of the price continuum, the deluxe edition aimed at collectors and patrons of literature permitted publishers to bring out certain volumes of poetry that they might otherwise have rejected. At Scribner's, for example, John Hall Wheelock, who usually told poets aspiring to be clients of the firm that they had better look elsewhere, recognized in 1928 that Louise Bogan deserved a response other than "poetry does not sell." (She had come to him and his boss, Maxwell Perkins, highly recommended by Edmund Wilson, and she had already published Body of This Death in 1923.) "What we set about to do," Perkins explained to her, "was find a way by which we could publish in a form that would bring more satisfactory results in a material sense than is generally to be counted upon with poetry." Their solution was "to issue a small volume of your poems in a distinguished format, not a limited edition, but with better paper, presswork and binding than is used in the ordinary trade edition. In this way we could charge a little more for the volume and get back our investment without the necessity for a sale larger than is customary in the case of verse." Even this plan, however, required attention to what the traffic would bear: Wheelock cautioned Bogan that the book needed to be at least fifty pages long. Otherwise, he insisted, a volume "runs the risk of appearing scant or precious and makes a difficult problem for the publisher, because it is hard to get a fair price for a book of so little bulk." Under the terms of that arrangement, the volume—*Dark Summer*—sold 400 copies by February 1930, and did not meet its $150 advance until five years thereafter (at 642 copies). Nevertheless, without provisions for the special edition Bogan's work might not have appeared with the Scribner's imprint at all.[15]

A different kind of publishing experiment aimed at increasing poetry sales was Viking Press's decision, in 1936, to put the full force of its promotional apparatus behind a first book of poems. The volume was *Landscape with Figures,* by a 20-year-old college student named Lionel Wiggam. Viking produced an attractive edition that included wood engravings. The firm then made an exception to its usual procedures by sending bound proofs out for comment, while instructing its sales department to plug the forthcoming book. Those steps generated an advance sale of more than 2,000 copies, and hence enough income to launch the sort of hefty advertising campaign in nationally circulating literary journals that unknown authors usually did not receive. At the end of the campaign, Viking realized "reasonably impressive results," selling a regular trade edition at the rate of a hundred copies a week during the first three weeks after publication. As *Publishers' Weekly* commented, "Viking's experiment would seem to prove that something can be done for new poets by commercial publishers when they put their minds to it."[16]

This observation underscores the point that the markets for verse—and the nature of the poetry volumes that found their way to those markets—were somewhat susceptible to the control of the same individuals who claimed helplessness in the face of readers' indifference to their wares. Publishers were not wrong to maintain that poetry sales were difficult to achieve. Yet whether the book industry could have altered its priorities to foster the genre is another matter. Decisions about formats, reprint rights, and publicity were always the product of a contest, on the part of both author and publisher, between artistry, ego, and profit. At Macmillan, for example, when Brett reassured John G. Neihardt about the viability of the school edition, he simultaneously refused to do an illustrated volume which the poet had requested—illustrations obviously being more expensive than plain text. "You will realize," Brett explained, "that the whole problem is one of markets, and on this we hope we can persuade you to accept our judgment." Similarly, in 1916 Brett squelched Edgar Lee Masters's idea for a "center table" version of his *Spoon River Anthology*, insisting instead on "a sort of small book, not much larger than the present edition, but gotten up in rather more ornamental form." Such judgments had consequences for an author's cultural location: in having the best of the exchange, Brett fixed the place of Masters's melancholy verse in a relatively rarefied literary universe, despite the poet's apparent vision of the book as a household treasure for a more popular readership. Brett also prevented Robinson from participating in the "Pamphlet Poet" series by insisting that letting another publisher issue cheap reprints of its authors would only erode Macmillan's profits.[17]

No one was more convinced that markets for verse were subject to book industry control than poets desirous of greater recognition from the public. Ciphers in search of celebrity, such figures repeatedly complained to their editors that their professional disappointments were the direct consequence of publishers' business decisions and practices rather than the fault of an indifferent audience. Advertising was a particular bone of contention. In 1916 and 1917, for example, Amy Lowell told Brett that she resented her omission from advertisements featuring Masefield and Masters, "as though you personally were not behind me." Before Brett severed Lowell's relationship with Macmillan in 1920, she was subsidizing her own publicity expenses. At the same time, Masters stipulated to Brett that he did not want to be advertised with Lowell, but also protested that "you do not advertise my books as you do Lindsay."

Ironically, however, when Masters accused Macmillan in 1928 of having brought out an edition of his *Domesday Book* without honoring the alleged provisions of his contract, he found Lowell a convenient ally: "All over America," he asserted, "is the story that your company tried these tactics on Amy Lowell . . . and that she bluffed you out, having plenty of money to hire lawyers." During a subsequent battle in 1931, Masters charged: "The main thing with your company is to sell a book and get the money." Sara Teasdale was more gracious but similarly concerned, communicating her disappointment at the lack of advertising for her work. Disgruntled poets on the Scribner's list—notably John Peale Bishop, Edmund Wilson, and Bogan—articulated the same perception that publishers defined markets and limited advertising to suit their own interests, at the expense of writers.[18]

Neihardt provided perhaps the most pointed observation about the publishers' role in constructing the poet as a cipher within the overall book trade. Still irritated, in the 1940s, by Macmillan's inattention, Neihardt asked the editor Harold Latham why the company wanted his books at all. He received a predictable response: "We publish books in which we believe. Sometimes we know that there is little hope of profit in them, and this is usually true of poetry. Yet, we wish to do this sort of book whenever conditions permit, as part of an obligation we feel to the reading public." Neihardt would have none of it. "As for the market," he shot back, "we all know that markets are largely a matter of contrivance in these days."[19]

Neihardt's comment of course overlooked the factors that publishers could *not* control on their own. In terms of poetry between the two world wars, the most important of those factors was the emergence of high modernism—"high" in the sense not only that it represented the greatest challenge to the verse forms of the nineteenth century, but also in that it occupied the pinnacle of the cultural hierarchy that literary critics allied with the avant-garde established and sustained. Perceiving isolation at the heart of human existence, and dissociating themselves from the market economy of industrial capitalism, high modernists venerated the artist as loner.

They sought as well to harden the line between amateur and professional, which they redrew as a marker not just of income from writing but also of authority and rarefied talent. As John Crowe Ransom put it in 1935, modernist poets were, to their satisfaction, "those whom a small company of adept readers enjoys, perhaps enormously, but the general public detests; those in whose hands poetry as a living art has lost its public support." An incipient version of this anti-popular attitude was present even among early modernists and their readers to the extent that they saw themselves as rebels and sophisticates.[20]

Thus what Neihardt did not acknowledge was that, especially after the mid-1920s, for publishers to invest their resources in the "contrivance" of markets for poetry would have required them to fight against some writers' fear of being tainted by popular acclaim. (Neihardt himself was obviously not in the latter group.) As Catherine Turner has shown, Alfred Knopf, Alfred Harcourt, and others did just that in packaging novels by Thomas Mann and John Dos Passos. Even so, Neihardt's suggestion that poetry could sell if publishers wanted it to prompts the question of whether the modernist aversion to popularity had a kind of self-fulfilling (if unconscious) effect on the commercial trade in verse. This hypothesis seems plausible at least in the case of Wheelock, who was both a poet himself and a traveler in high-culture circles. To be sure, Wheelock was not a fan of poets who wrote "for a small coterie by means of a sort of shorthand intelligible only to themselves." Nor did his own work fit the category of high modernist experimentation. Nevertheless, perhaps with jealousy as well as conviction, Wheelock did evince some disdain for the poet with a large following. His jacket copy for *The Collected Poems of Sara Teasdale* revealingly declared that she had become a "popular poet" in "the true and high sense of the word"—as opposed, presumably, to the base sense of celebrity without substance. To a correspondent who had written in 1937 to complain that Scribner's did not promote Bogan the way the house of Harper advertised Millay, Wheelock replied along similar lines: the comparison was inappropriate, he claimed, because Millay was "almost a popular poet in her appeal.

. . . Miss Bogan's art is of a very different order and the number of readers capable of appreciating her work is far smaller." What he did not say, although he seems to have believed it, was that, even if it were commercially feasible, turning Bogan into Millay would have sacrificed the poet's position as cipher—a position in which high modernists had their own sort of investment.[21]

Yet even those poets who valued marginality for the critical distance it permitted participated in aspects of American celebrity culture as public figures. Ironically, by the late 1940s and 1950s, that increased distance between poet and public was itself a source of celebrity, or at least of causes célèbres.

chapter six

Alien and Intimate

ON JANUARY 12, 1957, the *Saturday Review* carried an assessment of *The Unicorn and Other Poems,* a collection of verse by Anne Morrow Lindbergh. The reviewer was John Ciardi, a poet and editor of the magazine's Poetry Department. Well aware of Lindbergh's stature as the wife of flier Charles Lindbergh and the mother of their kidnapped baby, Ciardi nevertheless declared, "I am compelled to believe that Mrs. Lindbergh has written an offensively bad book—inept, jingling, slovenly, illiterate even," a book exemplifying "aesthetic and human failure." By way of evidence, Ciardi quoted some of the clichés, ungrammatical constructions, forced rhymes, and other instances of "violence against language" that Lindbergh frequently employed. ("Down at my feet / A weed has pressed / Its scarlet knife / Against my breast.") For such "miserable stuff," Ciardi could offer "nothing but contempt."[1]

That judgment unleashed what *SR* editor Norman Cousins subsequently called "the biggest storm of reader protest" in the periodical's history. Many disgruntled readers ascribed to Ciardi (somewhat erroneously) a preference for the formlessness, obscurity, and insensitivity to feeling they associated with modernism and academic criticism. "Maybe the arrangements of some of [Lindbergh's] ideas into poetry sound trite to the hardened ultra-sophisticate," a Massachusetts woman wrote, "but I am sure that to many these poems express what Mrs. Lindbergh intends them to without using a lot of double talk and futile phrases that mean nothing either to the reader or the writer. Why not take this book of poems for what it is, an expression of Mrs. Lindbergh's own thoughts. Don't dissect it for technique." Ciardi reacted by identifying an impassable rift between those readers who shared his commitment to discipline (many of whom eventually voiced their support of him) and those who, in their quest for poetry that was "pretty, vague, and easily effusive," belonged to a discredited "genteel tradition." For the better part of a year, the battle between the partisans of high modernism's aesthetic achievements and the detractors who called modernist poems "ridiculous nonsense" raged on. Eventually the controversy simply petered out, with neither side having altered the other's views.[2]

The Ciardi-Lindbergh episode provides one further point of entry into the tensions attending the figure of the poet in the United States up to the mid-twentieth century. While many features of the exchange reflected characteristics of post–World War II American culture, the exposure of a sharp disagreement within the readership for poetry over the language and form appropriate to the genre was in other respects part of an ongoing story of challenge and rebuttal. In the 1910s, the most strident opponents of free verse had contended that the "new poetry" desecrated the art. For certain observers, poets who eschewed rhyme abandoned their roles as sage and seer; they became defilers of the "sacred precincts of the muse" and saboteurs of civilization itself. Yet the "new poets" also possessed a more immediately disorienting emotional power: the ability to create feelings of outrage—what Stanton Coblentz called "cold fury"—or at least bewilderment by estranging readers from the familiarities of the text and the reading experience. As late as the 1930s, a St. Louis advertising man, while priding himself on adopting a stance of "tolerant amusement" toward literary "pioneers," betrayed that discomfort by referring to Sandburg as "strange" and placing him among the "freak followers" of Harriet Monroe. For such individuals, modernism created a dichotomy between the poet as intimate or friend and as alien.[3]

Ironically, what permitted these reactions against the "new poetry" was the accessibility of the language and imagery that most early modernists employed. When Sandburg, for instance, evoked the sights and smells of the packinghouse—or when Millay alluded to her lovers—there was no mistaking what they meant. Millay, for one, facilitated the reader's ready comprehension of her message by retaining traditional lyric structure and rhyme as the vehicles for her adventurous themes. Yet even Pound's and Amy Lowell's Imagist experiments were efforts to connect feelings to concrete objects the reader could visualize. By contrast, the major complaint against high modernists was the inaccessibility of the poet's meaning and purpose. As Babette Deutsch explained in 1935, "No charge is so frequently brought against current verse as its obscurity. Even those poets not moving, as many do, in the privacy of a dream-world . . . offer problems not readily solved. . . . [The poet of today] erects so many more hurdles for the reader to leap." Opponents of high modernist verse not only echoed earlier distress about the corruption of the genre's rules; they also resented what seemed to them a self-indulgent retreat from intimacy, a deliberate alienation of the poet's rightful audience.[4]

Nevertheless, strident denunciations of both "new poetry" and high modernism coexisted with more temperate reservations about poetic innovation. While the more accessible poets of the 1910s were easier to assimilate, even the later group could elicit reactions that fell between the extremes of wholesale rejection and whole-hearted endorsement—reactions situated instead on the middle ground of demurral, hesitancy, and accommodation.

These intermediate responses—although the tendency to depict cultural conflict in terms of stark opposites has clouded them—took several forms. First, in the context of the book review, some writers coupled their dismay over certain aspects of the "new poetry" with a willingness to acknowledge its positive dimensions. A case in point is the poet and critic William Aspinwall Bradley. Writing in the *Bookman* for October 1914, Bradley acknowledged that literature could not retain its power without periodic infusions of fresh perceptions and styles. Hence he had no quarrel with free verse, and voiced only mild skepticism about Pound's early poems.

Instead, he faulted experimentalists for failing to recognize the artistic lineage to which they belonged, and for their corresponding demand for a poetry devoted to contemporary issues instead of "timeless" themes. Bradley, in other words, objected more to the "new poets'" erroneous conception of a "dead past" (a position which in fact allied him with Eliot's affirmation of tradition) than to their vision of the genre's future.[5]

As readers, moreover, even the most ardent champions of high modernism might embed traditional understandings of poetry in their approach to poetic texts. A striking example of such commingling at the level of reading practices appears in the poet Louis MacNeice's account of his first brush with Eliot's work as an eighteen-year-old in 1926. MacNeice, who was English, identified his generation as a product of both the nineteenth and the twentieth centuries: born too late to espouse romanticism without perceiving its limited relevance to urban, industrial society, he and his peers were nevertheless "over-emotional" romantics "at heart." MacNeice's education had also prepared him intuitively to place some of Eliot's early poems within the canon of British literature. "The images, the rhythms, and the hypnotic, incantatory repetitions of *The Hollow Men*," he remembered, "were not too alien to anyone brought up on the Bible and on Shakespeare's tragedies and even on the autumnal Victorians." On first reading, "The Love Song of J. Alfred Prufrock" seemed to him more unconventional in structure, although in retrospect MacNeice remarked that his youthful attraction to "release" had probably misled him into considering the text free verse rather than grasping its rhythmic patterns. At the same time, MacNeice and his friends who aspired to be "modern" missed entirely Eliot's satiric distance from the character of Prufrock, instead regarding Prufrock's pronouncements as declarations of their own adolescent protest against the world. What MacNeice called "this egotistical (romantic, if you like) approach" inflected his peers' silent reading of the poem; perhaps it also accounted, he speculated, for their habit of reading it aloud "in an over-emotional booming monotone." Furthermore, when he turned to *The Waste Land*, MacNeice "still thought of poetry more as effulgence (Dr. Johnson's word) than as analysis." Thus, for all of his aspirations to join a disaffected avant-garde, MacNeice's mode of reading the quintessential high modernist manifesto, in terms of cadence, voice, and mood, kept him from making a complete break with the literary past.[6]

A more concerted kind of accommodation lay in the efforts of figures who joined publishers, booksellers, and literary entrepreneurs like Carl Van Doren as mediators between author and reader—individuals who, as anthologists and critics, established themselves as interpreters of apparently rebellious poets to bewildered or skeptical audiences. Some of those figures, such as Amy Lowell, were poets themselves who had sidelines as editors. Harriet Monroe and Alice Corbin Henderson fell into this category in assembling *The New Poetry*. By identifying the "new" with linguistic simplicity and thematic authenticity, rather than with radicalism in form, Monroe and Henderson extended the term to numerous examples of poetry that readers wary of departing too far from rhyme and meter could readily accept. Other mediators between modernist poets and their audiences were the authors of textbooks and critical studies designed for the general reader. Percy Boynton was one, as were the Van Dorens. So was Deutsch, although she was primarily known as a poet. The Harvard English professor John Livingston Lowes's *Convention and Revolt in Poetry* originated as a series of public lectures for the Lowell Institute in 1918. The most prominent of these popular critics of modernist verse, however, were Marguerite Wilkinson and Louis Untermeyer.[7]

Wilkinson, who was born in 1883 and emigrated from Canada to the United States as a child, wrote poetry herself but established a greater following as a reviewer for the *New York Times Book Review* and a lecturer on contemporary verse to college students, librarians, and women's clubs. In 1919 she issued the first edition of *New Voices*, a work that interspersed commentary and analysis of modern poetry with illustrative texts. The book is notable for Wilkinson's decision to organize it not around individual poets, like most anthologies, but according to poetic techniques and themes: diction and symbolism, democracy and nature. In her opening chapter, Wilkinson signaled her intermediary role by imagining herself clearing the jungle path that lay before readers struggling to approach poetry with "confidence, understanding and sympathy." The overgrowth she felt compelled to cut away consisted of a number of faulty assumptions: that modern poets dispensed with careful composition; that the beautiful must also be pretty; that great poems necessarily resembled one another. At the same time, she explicitly anticipated and counteracted the image of the poet as alien by assuring her audience that anyone imbued with "feelings we all share" could find in modernist verse the same consolation and pleasure which they derived from "a beautiful friendship." The key was to ignore the "abracadabra of critics" and to approach poetry as "natural," not as "an intricate puzzle game for sophisticated intellects." She combined an insistence on openness to both "conservative" and "radical" poets with a disapproval of novelty for its own sake, a fault she assigned to the Imagists and to Wallace Stevens, among others. Such judgments established Wilkinson herself as the reader's friend; they staked her authority not on her superior critical expertise but, rather, on her power to remake the alien as intimate by infusing the new with the comforts of the familiar. In 1928, she brought out a revised edition of *New Voices* that made space for figures such as James Weldon Johnson, Marianne Moore, and T. S. Eliot, but she remained protective of ordinary readers by remarking that modern poetry, having shed sentimentality, required a new infusion of idealism in order to achieve the large audience it deserved.[8]

Wilkinson's death by drowning in 1928 silenced her own voice as minister to that potential audience. Even during her lifetime, however, she was less audible in that role than Untermeyer, whose influence on ordinary readers has already been suggested by Gladys Hasty Carroll's experience. Born in New York City in 1886, Untermeyer forged a career that was itself the result of a series of mediations, bridging what he identified as disparate "worlds." His father, a jewelry manufacturer, was from a German Jewish immigrant family; his mother was Christian and a Southerner. At age sixteen, having dropped out of school, he began leading a "double life," shuttling between days spent in his father's firm and nights devoted to culture—classical piano, theater, and the composition of poetry. By his early twenties he had become a prolific writer of verse. According to Untermeyer, his perspective became less fragmented when he fell in with the Greenwich Village set in the 1910s. In the same period, he published what became his most famous poem, "Caliban in the Coal Mines," a brief for exploited workers. Yet Untermeyer, still in the jewelry business, was never fully a Village radical or avant-garde artist, but remained, instead, an emissary from the middle class with an eye on the literary main chance. In 1915, after establishing himself as a book columnist, he used his international connections to pave the way for Robert Frost's return to the United States.[9]

Assuming the mantle of the mediator as discoverer or impresario (rather than merely as friend) suited Untermeyer's temperament and ambition. Soon he was embellishing that self-concept in print. Untermeyer's volume of parodies of the "new poetry," *—and Other Poets* (1916), distanced him from the more alien poetic innovators, implying both his superiority to the individuals he lampooned and his sympathy with the discomfited reader. In 1919 he brought out *The New Era in American Poetry,* a set of essays that subsequently served as the basis for his *American Poetry Since 1900* (1923). These works, as Untermeyer noted from the perspective of the more self-deprecatory persona he adopted in old age, consisted of chapters which, "purporting to be critiques, were essentially pronunciamentos": his overriding tone was that of a confident literary authority spreading enlightenment to the public by means of what he later called "a series of zealous overstatements."[10]

After Alfred Harcourt, Untermeyer's editor at the publishing house of Henry Holt, left that firm to start Harcourt, Brace and Howe, he suggested to Untermeyer that he edit an anthology of recent American verse. The result was *Modern American Poetry.* First issued in 1919, the collection went through eight expansive revisions before 1965. In addition to seeking trade sales, Harcourt successfully marketed the volume as a textbook and library reference work. By one estimate, it sold at least 200,000 copies in its first decade and, together with Untermeyer's *Modern British Poetry*, over one million by 1967.[11]

For Untermeyer, the term "modern" in his title was a chronological rather than an aesthetic designation. Retrospectively, he noted that the publishers had "easily" convinced him to balance "strange new poets" with traditionalists in order to give the anthology broad appeal, especially in the Midwest. The result was, in the first edition, a roster that included Riley and Field alongside James Oppenheim and Pound, with no space at all for Eliot. While those initial commercial pressures presumably diminished once the anthology proved a strong seller, Untermeyer remained planted on a middle ground between "convention" and "revolt" even in the volume's subsequent editions. Later versions emphasized those modernists, such as Frost and Hart Crane, whom Untermeyer could assimilate to a Whitmanesque tradition of democratic speech. His selection principle, he conceded, was "that mixture of preference, prejudice, and intuition known as personal taste," a standard that encouraged readers to have confidence in their own judgments. By the 1942 edition, Untermeyer was explicitly disavowing the claim that "every poem in this collection is a great poem."[12]

Untermeyer's balancing act was partly responsible for his low standing among other critics. His denunciation of *The Waste Land* in 1923, followed by his grudging admission of Eliot's merits in the 1925 edition of *Modern American Poetry*, impelled Edmund Wilson to label him "merely an expert politician," bending in the direction of changing taste. Poets who felt maltreated by the financial or space arrangements that Untermeyer's anthologies entailed also railed against him. Yet, as Craig Abbott has argued, Untermeyer operated from the premise that offering American readers a "marketable product" meant privileging contemporary poetry that was accessible and affirmative rather than despairing. His attunement to that market overrode his desire to win the approbation of intellectuals and even poets themselves. His reward was instead a continuing influence, especially upon students and lecture audiences, as the "chief anthologist of modern American poetry" until his death in 1977.[13]

Certainly the activities of Wilkinson, Untermeyer, and other mediators reflected and contributed to the culture of celebrity, increasing the fame of poet and promoter alike. At the same time, however, the accommodations to modernism effected in book reviews, reading practices, literary histories, and anthologies preserved or restored at least the possibility of an imagined intimacy between poet and reader. In part because of such efforts, there emerged "a reading public," as Carl and Mark Van Doren observed in 1925, "which realized that both old and new forms had merit and that they could exist side by side."[14]

Even as they strove to widen the audience for contemporary verse, however, such mediations were always limited by the antipopular dimension of the high modernist outlook. That is, pulling against the figure of the poet as intimate was the modernist's own vested interest in being an alien, in relinquishing the public voice of sage and seer. T. S. Eliot's famous declaration in "The Metaphysical Poets" (1921) that poets "in our civilization" must be "difficult"— a dictum that implicitly defended the high modernists' reliance on erudite allusions, ambiguous symbols, and fragmentary structure to convey the disorder of contemporary life—directly challenged Wilkinson's assertion that one need only be natural in approaching the text. Readers complained in kind. "Why is it," a Michigan man wrote in a fan letter to Carl Sandburg in 1942, "that so-called good poetry must be so difficult? Why, when attempting the average poem in Harpers [*sic*] for instance, must I usually find myself up against a blank wall?"[15]

Earlier, Babette Deutsch had tried to head off that reaction by stressing that what readers found frustrating was simply "the elliptical diction" and "private jokes" that "we all use in commerce with our intimates." Her comment underscores the irony that the private language in which modernist poets spoke to their coterie about alienation and loneliness worked to create—within the modernists' own circle—the same kind of human bond that many general readers accused the poets of destroying. Yet Deutsch's effort at mediation on human grounds could not withstand the emergence, in the 1930s and '40s, of the New Criticism, which further valorized the poet's distance from a general audience. New Critics argued that poetry was indeed an intricate puzzle; by making the analysis of linguistic effects the key to that puzzle, they withdrew from readers who rejected their view that, as Archibald MacLeish had put it, "a poem should not mean but be." Furthermore, New Criticism's unspoken premise that only a masculine tough-minded-ness could ensure poetry's requisite "difficulty"—that, bluntly, men were better poets and readers than women were—dealt a blow to the mediators' presumption of a large, unified reading public. As New Critics moved into academic English Departments, especially after World War II, they institutionalized what, from the perspective of many ordinary readers, amounted to the poetry of divisiveness and confusion.[16]

Modernist poetry's limited susceptibility to mediation—or, alternatively, the modernist poets' success in consolidating their appeal to an avant-garde alone—became strikingly apparent in an episode of 1949: the dispute over the Library of Congress's decision to award its annual Bollingen Prize for Poetry to Ezra Pound. Pound's antisemitic and pro-fascist beliefs made his version of the modernist credo particularly repugnant to critics and readers who upheld the Emersonian ideal of the poet as a moral force; it is likely that even if Pound (or an Untermeyer) had translated his ideas into simple declarative sentences, the award would still have aroused protest. Nevertheless, the opacity of Pound's language was also at issue, fueling the hostility of those who valued poetic texts for their readily understandable meaning. Robert Hillyer, the most strident opponent of the Bollingen decision among professional critics, railed in the *Saturday Review* against both the "private unintelligibility" and the moral bankruptcy that he saw at the heart of the modernist aesthetic. Hillyer's comments prompted a large number of readers to commend his remarks as a long-overdue exposé of "overpersonalized art, so confusing and unrewarding and, finally, obscure to the point of worthlessness." Hillyer and the *Saturday Review*'s editors may be faulted (as they were at the time) for fabricating guilt by association, succumbing to conspiracy theories, and distorting aesthetic values. Still, the desire of Hillyer's supporters to reclaim a relationship with poetic texts that high modernism had seemed to preclude was genuine and affecting. The Bollingen Prize controversy, and the diminished prospects for mediation it signaled, furnished the immediate backdrop for the Ciardi-Lindbergh contretemps eight years later.[17]

In "The Obscurity of the Poet" (1950), Randall Jarrell compellingly argued that "difficulty" and "obscurity" in verse were not inevitable barriers to the genre's popularity. Jarrell pointed to the propensity of the Europeans and Latin Americans to make modern poets into national heroes, or the vogue, in England, of Dylan Thomas, "surely one of the most obscure poets who ever lived." In every age, he contended, critics lament their inability to understand new poetry; later, the new becomes old—which is to say clear in comparison to the poems that supersede it. The charge of obscurity, Jarrell insisted, was really a mask for deeper deficiencies in American culture such as anti-intellectualism.[18]

Still, Jarrell conceded that it would be "absurd to deny" the "truism" that "the poetry of the first half of this century often *was* too difficult." And the standoff that Jarrell depicted—between "poet and public [who] stared at each other with righteous indignation, till the poet said, 'Since you won't read me, I'll make sure you can't'"—oversimplified the public's responses. For one thing, the process of absorbing the new that Jarrell himself described continued in certain locales like the college classroom, where the professor embodied the mediator as specialist. By 1948, when T. S. Eliot received the Nobel Prize for Literature, he was surrounded by what Wyndham Lewis called a "bland atmosphere of general approbation." More to the point, the audiences who made Untermeyer's anthologies best-sellers *were* reading poetry prior to—and throughout—the heyday of high modernist obscurity. Like Gray and Munroe's "Mr. M.," such readers sustained (through rereading) the poems they had memorized in school; they may also have followed Wilkinson or Untermeyer down the jungle path of early modernism. Finally, as Jarrell himself implied, not everyone who balked at obscurity demanded word-for-word transparency in its place. The correspondent who complained to Sandburg about the poetry in *Harper's* revealed a high tolerance for partial grasp of a text. Moreover, he shifted the properties of an understandable poem from clear ideas to clear feelings. Sandburg's poetry was accessible, he remarked, "not as with an Eddie Guest because everything is said that need be felt, but because I get a meaning and its consequence without having the thing itself pointed out as a teacher might the a-b-c's." More important, this reader was willing to tackle high modernism in the same spirit: "T. S. Eliot may be mixed up. Yet I enjoy him. And think I understand parts of his poetry. At least, he partially explains the unexplainable. Not in what he says. Rather in what he suggests and in the impressions he leaves—thoughts to which I can cling." Such readers thus rebuffed not "the poet" in general but, rather, a *kind* of poet who appeared willfully to exclude them even when they relinquished the need for full comprehension of the "difficult."[19]

In short, while the Bollingen and Lindbergh episodes reveal that high modernism polarized segments of the American reading public, it remained possible for some readers to occupy positions along the spectrum between the modernist and the traditional. From the inception of the "new poetry" through the 1950s, Americans' aesthetic preferences diverged to a much greater extent than those categories imply: one individual might reject free verse and at the same time exhibit openness to sexual imagery or vernacular language; another might disavow Pound and, as Jarrell noted, applaud Thomas. Even after the canonization of high modernists, the figures of the poet as sage, seer, icon, companion, innocent, and sophisticate still influenced to varying degrees the understandings that readers derived from poetry at school, by the fireside, in church, out-of-doors. A reader could be traditional and modern simultaneously. Yet alongside those differences in taste, a shared regard for the poet as intimate created commonalities in the expectations and practices that disparate readers brought to the sites at which they encountered verse.

PART II

POETRY IN

PLACE

AND

PRACTICE

chapter seven

Listen, My Children

Modes of Poetry Reading in American Schools

☙ THE SCENE is familiar: a boy stands uneasily at the front of a classroom, eyes lowered, shoulders sagging. Beside him, the teacher, a spinster with a stern exterior and a heart of gold, instructs him to take his hands out of his pockets and stand up straight. The recitation begins. "Abou Ben Adhem (may his tribe increase!) . . .," the boy mumbles, continuing on in a monotone until, vastly relieved, he returns to his seat. The teacher summons the next victim, a be-ribboned girl who completes her far more poised performance with a curtsy.

So widely held is that image of the schoolroom poetry recitation, in fact, that Americans are prone to assume the transparency of the practice. One measure of its status as a stock feature of cultural memory is its passage into parody, as in "The boy stood on the burning deck, eating peanuts by the peck." Yet the recitation, for all its predictable associations, may still yield important lessons about American culture. The school was the site at which the figures of the poet as sage and seer exerted their greatest influence. Furthermore, of all the public venues for poetry reading in the late nineteenth and early twentieth centuries, the school was the most consistent and predictable: despite the vicissitudes of production and marketing, every student read verse every year. Those traditions of youthful reading also generated lifelong traditions of memory. As Oliver Wendell Holmes wrote to James Russell Lowell in July 1881, "When the school-children learn your verses they are good for another half century."[1]

It might be objected that most of the materials related to poetry reading in school—courses of study, essays on pedagogy—are merely prescriptive, that they do not capture classroom realities. In fact, this was not always the case; many of these materials do indicate how instructors implemented lesson plans. Some also reveal how students responded. A more serious limitation is that the authors of curricular materials tended to be innovators, and hence atypical teachers. Nevertheless, it is important to remember that the educators who intoned, with Longfellow, "Listen, my children" were themselves a population of readers. They have as much to teach us as they did their pupils.

Lessons of the Recitation

In the late nineteenth and early twentieth centuries, learning poetry in the American school entailed both silent reading and speaking. Much of the former consisted in acquiring "a body of facts" about authors and literary movements. Reading a poem also meant studying it: deciphering unfamiliar vocabulary, attending to technicalities of meter and rhyme, mastering the spelling and grammar lessons the text provided. Writing in 1925, for example, the progressive educator Hughes Mearns observed: "For a half century [Sir Walter Scott's] *The Lady of the Lake* . . . has been almost a sacred book. . . . For the whole of the eighth school year it was studied word by word, memorized, scanned, and parsed." After 1890, high schools preparing students for college entrance requirements also routinely subjected to intensive scrutiny Bryant's "Thanatopsis," Gray's "Elegy," Lowell's "The Vision of Sir Launfal," Longfellow's "Evangeline," Coleridge's "Rime of the Ancient Mariner," and several works by Milton. At the same time, students read verse aloud. The recitation took place with varying frequency: at the beginning of each day, once a week, biweekly, every month. A fa-

A *Harper's Weekly* illustration from 1874 of the school recitation. Library of Congress.

vored time was Friday afternoon; the scheduling suggests an ideal of oral performance as end-of-the-week festivity and release from routine. By contrast, disciplinarians sometimes employed memorizing and reciting poetry as a punishment for misbehavior. One public school teacher required students to recite Bible verses before she would dismiss them for the weekend. Delivering poems "by heart" was also a feature of classroom holiday observances, commencement day "exhibitions," and elocution contests, which parents were often invited to attend. In some schools, recitation at "school closing" was an honor reserved for the most talented pupils. Both schools and civic organizations sponsored competitions that offered prizes to children who could recite the greatest number of lines or perform with the most finesse.[2]

A number of sources supplied teachers with poetic texts. The latter volumes of the famous McGuffey and Hillard readers reprinted brief poems like Felicia Hemans's "Casabianca" and the shorter works of Whittier and Longfellow. Anthologies such as Francis T. Palgrave's *Golden Treasury* made lengthier verse available. Early surveys like Julian Hawthorne and Leonard Lemmon's *American Literature* (1891) scattered poems among literary commentary. Universities published editions of the works that applicants needed to know. Along with those forms of print, beginning in the late 1870s educators relied on one which compensated for deficiencies in school libraries: the "memory gem" collection. These were predominantly excerpts from poetry, together with some prose selections, ranging from two to fifteen lines in length and usually classified by grade or subject. Many teachers in both elementary and high schools devoted ten minutes a day to individual or group recitation of an assigned quotation.[3]

Underlying the use of "memory gems" were assumptions about the role of reading in child development. The term in one sense referred to the fact that the quoted lines represented the essence of a longer work. Yet the phrase, with its connotations of preciousness and rarity, also suggested that the mind could function as a repository of "riches" acquired in youth that would remain stable in value. The title page of one volume contained this injunction from the British essayist Sir Arthur Helps: "We should lay up in our minds a store of goodly thoughts in well-wrought words, which should be a living treasure of knowledge, always with us, and from which, at various times, and amidst all the shifting of circumstances, we might be sure of drawing some comfort, guidance, and sympathy." Such language locates memory gems in the tradition of the commonplace book, into which readers copied beloved passages so as to preserve them for future reminiscence or inspiration.[4] It reflects as well the influence of faculty psychology—the view, popular among humanistic educators by the early nineteenth century, that memory and other components of the mind, although inborn, were expanded and perfected only through active learning.

Helps's imagery elaborates the connection between reading poetry and acquiring capital. (His own books included *Essays Written in the Intervals of Business*.) In particular, the phrase "goodly thoughts" encompasses both the idea of "the best" literature and a reference to commodities or "goods." In a society where the fluctuating fortunes of the nouveaux riches and the influx of immigrant "strangers" enhanced the need for stability, the figure of the reader as prudent banker could be particularly appealing. Yet that analogy (one thinks as well of the phrase "memory bank") also conveys the enticements of acquisitiveness, as if the mind, rightly furnished, could become, in Jackson Lears's image of the marketplace, a dazzling Ali Baba's cave.[5]

At the same time, memory gems and other collections of verse reflected the widely shared belief that the reading of poetry, even more than fiction and biography, promoted the creation of a "higher" self. To convey that idea, the proponents of memory gems employed a different vocabulary: the language of cultivation. Untroubled by the mixed metaphor, the authors of the prefatory material in a 1907 collection explained that memory gems were "seed-thoughts" which were "gleaned from the fields of literature." Like the term "culture" itself, this organic imagery drew its force from traditional notions of agrarian virtue. In the garden of the mind, a space that was tamed yet free from the corruptions of society, the "higher self" could flourish. Robert Louis Stevenson's choice of title for *A Child's Garden of Verses*, which became the most popular book of poetry for youth in the American market after Scribner's published it in 1905, shifted the garden imagery to the poems themselves but no doubt reinforced the link between intellectual "growth" and nature.[6]

Both of these understandings of the mind—as storehouse and as garden—connected the reading and memorization of poetry in school to the development of specific mental qualities. The first of these was moral sense. For that purpose, teachers had at hand the work of the schoolroom poets, whose verse was, in Lawrence Buell's phrase, "prevailingly a regulated poetry of moral statement." As authoritative sages and seers, Longfellow, Bryant, Whittier, Holmes, and Lowell dispassionately dispensed guidance on ethical conduct, through either lines that furnished maxims to live by or images that functioned to transmit "moral exempla." In consequence, their poems invited their audiences to read for theme or message (as distinct, for example, from symbol or sound): readers were to grasp the "moral" of the text. Given the erosion of widespread familiarity with their writings by the late twentieth century, a brief reminder of the lessons these New England figures offered in some of their most popular poems is in order. All the values they endorsed were at least loosely, and more often overtly, grounded in Protestant belief.[7]

In terms of tone, the moral authority of the schoolroom poets is perhaps sharpest in the words that begin the oft-quoted last stanza of Bryant's "Thanatopsis": the biblically phrased commandment to "So live" in a way that will permit one to face with a clear conscience the inevitability of death. With respect to the ratio of moralism to quantity of verse, however, the front-runner in the schoolroom group was Longfellow. In "Evangeline," for instance, the sentimental story of lovers uprooted and separated by the French and Indian Wars, Longfellow preached at length the virtues of patience, forgiveness, and what the poet identified as "the beauty and strength of woman's devotion." Awaiting eviction from her Acadian village after her beloved Gabriel has fallen captive to the British, the "maiden" Evangeline recalls "the tale she had heard of the justice of Heaven" and resigns herself to her fate. That turns out to consist of repeated near-misses as she searches Louisiana and the Ozarks for her lost fiancé. Yet Evangeline exemplifies what Longfellow calls "abnegation of self" and resolute good cheer despite her grief, eventually undertaking to assist the poor and sick in Philadelphia. There, in Longfellow's notoriously sentimental ending, she finally encounters the dying Gabriel and the two regain, for a moment, a glimpse of the happiness that had infused the pastoral existence—the "forest primeval" of the prologue—from which, tragically, they had been wrenched. The conclusion of the poem thus affirms the value of simplicity (as opposed to the fevered activity of the city) and of a world enriched not by goods but by purity of affection.[8]

Another Longfellow staple, "The Courtship of Miles Standish," also celebrates love, while weighing fidelity to oneself against the importance of loyalty in friendship. In the narrative, John Alden carries a proposal of marriage from his friend, Captain Miles Standish, to another "maiden," Priscilla, despite his own feelings for her. When she utters her famous query, "Why don't you speak for yourself, John?" he wrestles with the conflict between "passionate cries of desire, and importunate pleadings of duty." As the sea churns "like an awakened conscience," Standish stalks off to war against the Indians. Only when rumors of his death reach Priscilla and John do they decide to marry. Standish, still alive, turns up at the wedding, proffering an apology that allows both friendship and love to survive. Alden's ambivalence mirrors Longfellow's own struggle to espouse restraint despite the subversive pull of personal emotion; it stands as well for the tension between the poet's role as the voice of individual experience and as regulator of communal behavior. A third Longfellow schoolroom favorite, "A Psalm of Life," concludes with the lines Twain would mock at the Whittier Day dinner: "Lives of great men all remind us / We can make our lives sublime, / And, departing, leave behind us / Footprints on the sands of time. / . . . Let us, then, be up and doing, / With a heart for any fate; / Still achieving, still pursuing, / Learn to labor and to wait." In that poem the moral prescription is again, as in "Evangeline," one of self-sacrifice, cheerfulness, and service to the community.[9]

To the values of selflessness, self-trust, earnestness, and service, other schoolroom poets appended additional strictures similarly grounded in Protestant teachings. Holmes's "The Chambered Nautilus" explicitly identified the "heavenly message" which the nautilus shell communicated: namely, the importance of lifelong striving for spiritual improvement ("Build thee more stately mansions, O my soul"). James Russell Lowell's "The Vision of Sir Launfal," excerpts from which appeared in virtually every memory gem compilation, used the tale of a knight returning from his quest for the Holy Grail to stress the virtue of Christian charity toward the poor. The knight, once callous toward a leper begging for alms, learns through his own misfortune to see Christ in man and to give to others in Christ's loving spirit. "He gives only the worthless gold / Who gives from a sense of duty," Lowell admonishes the reader before depicting Sir Launfal's transformative dream. To take one more example, in Whittier's "Snow-Bound," the narrative of a rural family's determinedly cheerful response to a blizzard, the poet emphasized the warmth that resulted from sharing the "homestead hearth" with others. Among the lessons of the text was Whittier's comment on the capacity of selfless love—"the Christian pearl of charity"—to erase sectarian division between the Calvinist doctor and the Quaker matron who both respond to the claim of duty to the sick. Like "Evangeline," "Snow-Bound" also constructs an idyll of youth spent in bucolic surroundings, as against the care-laden "city ways" that arrive with adulthood.[10]

The British Victorian poets on whom American educators relied augmented the moral instruction of the schoolroom group with their own narratives of sacrifice and heroism (such as Rudyard Kipling's "Gunga Din"). Two of the most frequently excerpted and anthologized British texts—Leigh Hunt's "Abou Ben Adhem" and William Ernest Henley's "Invictus"—celebrated the virtues of brotherhood and self-reliance, respectively. Abou Ben Adhem, who is evidently not a Christian, unknowingly practices Christian love of his fellows and thus leads the names of those "whom love of God had blessed." Perhaps the most popular of the schoolroom staples stressing a morality of individual integrity rather than concern for others, "Invictus" plainly echoes Emerson's "Self-Reliance" in asserting "I am the master of my fate: I am the captain of my soul." Sir Walter Scott's "Lochinvar," who "rode all unarmed" and "all alone" in pursuit of his goal (marriage to Ellen), contained the same lesson.[11]

The appropriation of New England schoolroom poetry and that of British Victorians to foster moral sense in schoolchildren was thus consonant with the ethical purposes the poets themselves conferred on their work. The construction of poems that served such moral functions often aided their didactic uses in more subtle ways than mere reliance on commonplace diction: as Dana Gioia has argued in the case of "A Psalm of Life," Longfellow's achievement in part consisted of his ability to draw on "the colonial tradition of aphorism" to create a work of "extraordinary memorability." As accessible as the schoolroom poets and their British counterparts were to silent readers of their unabridged lines, however, the use of memory gems enhanced such texts' utility as vehicles for ethical instruction. "As a means of moral culture," W. H. Lambert wrote, memory gems were "of inestimable importance." By the same token, the repetitiveness of the recitation exercise, instead of boring students, ostensibly made such lessons more effective. Compilers invoked another, less prominent metaphor—that of fabric—to underscore the value of drill in strengthening "the warp and woof of character": "The pupil should not only be able to say the selection, but he should repeat it so often that it becomes inwoven with the very fibre of his mind." Borrowing from the ideology surrounding elocution, and sustaining traditions of oratory by importing them into the classroom, teachers associated vocal training with producing an eloquent citizenry possessed of high principle and judgment. Social success was a not unwelcome by-product of that process.[12]

The idea of buttressing morality by memorizing and reciting poetry affiliated those activities with traditions of religious instruction, not only in the echo of Protestant virtues the poems supplied but also in the similarity between speaking poetry and reciting Bible verses in Sunday Schools. In addition, the expectation that even poetry memorized in the public school could, as Helps put it, furnish "comfort, guidance, and sympathy" endowed the reading of non-biblical texts with the consolations of faith. It is tempting, of course, to view that assumption solely as evidence of the waning of religious orthodoxy. The British romantic poets whose work loomed so large in the curriculum were partly responsible for the conflation of the sacred and the secular. In attempting to reconcile belief and doubt, Wordsworth, Tennyson, Browning, and others had blurred the boundary between God and man. Emphasizing the divine nature of human love, such figures diminished the importance of "penitence and penance, the way of the Cross." In the context of this "Christianity without tears," as Hoxie Neale Fairchild called it, literature that explored mankind's goodness assumed a standing equal to actual Bible study. Readers undergoing their own crisis of faith were relieved to learn, from critics, teachers, and ministers alike, that poetry could substitute for prayer, and that the poet could serve as spiritual guide.

Yet, granted that the practice rested on a liberalized theology, the congruence of the form of the recitation in both church and public schools is a signal that, from the student's perspective, poetry reading might strengthen rather than weaken religious authority. To stand before a hushed class and speak edifying lines on Sunday, and to do the same thing on Monday, could make both experiences seem forms of devotion. (In fact, because the psalms remained a part of public school English, the lines might be the same.) Moreover, as romantic poets, with ministerial sanction, made the center of Christian belief its function as an antidote to psychic turmoil or ethical confusion, the cultivation of moral sense through the study of "inspirational" verse could seem an extension of, rather than a replacement for, religious teaching. As the educational reformer Charles A. McMurray explained in 1899, "What depth and beauty do we find in Snow Bound, . . . Evangeline, The Psalm of Life, The Village Blacksmith . . . The Chambered Nautilus, Vision of Sir Launfal. . . . To drink in these potent truths through poetry and song . . . is more than culture, more than morality; it is the portal and sanctuary of religious thought; and children may enter here." It is questionable whether the term "secularization" is adequate to encompass these practices.[13]

In "The Day Is Done," Longfellow himself acknowledged the weight of the moral instruction to which he and his colleagues devoted their verse: asking for someone to read him a poem to repel his sorrow, the narrator cautions that the text must be "Not from the grand old masters" because "like strains of martial music, / Their mighty thoughts suggest / Life's endless toil and endeavor; / And to-night I long for rest." But, in any case, for late-nineteenth- and early-twentieth-century educators the ability of poetry to serve religious purposes by shaping moral sense was only part of the rationale for its study. Educators attached another aim to read-

ing verse: cultivating aesthetic sensitivity. Drawing on their under-
standing of the figure of the poet as seer—as a person equipped
with special sight—they hoped students would learn to identify
and to prize both the beauty of language and that of the natural
world as described by poets' unusual vision. The wealth of British
romantic poetry offered many opportunities to fulfill that hope, as
did American nature poems. (Gioia has rescued "Evangeline" from
modernist contempt in part by observing that it contains "breath-
takingly beautiful" passages, beginning with the prologue.) Words-
worth's portrayal of "golden daffodils" as dancers who turn loneli-
ness into "bliss" and Emerson's description of "The Snow-Storm"
that is "announced by all the trumpets of the sky" are representa
tive of teachers' favorites.[14]

For some pedagogues and critics, of course, the goal of fostering
attentiveness to beauty was inseparable from morality. As the Rev-
erend Noah Porter observed in 1870, possessing a "poetic sensibil-
ity" did not ensure "poetic taste"; an appreciation for the beautiful
resulted only from training in the recognition of "choice and pure
words" (as opposed to "the sewerage of modern poetry"). Yet with-
in that framework Porter made ample room for poetry as a delight
to the ear and imagination. Most memory gem compilers likewise
mingled moral didacticism and aesthetic pleasure. "These gems,"
one editor explained, "are presented with the hope that good may
result to the children from the mastery of such a range of strong
and beautiful quotations." On occasion, the stress on beauty even
overshadowed moral objectives—or obliterated them entirely. One
prolific Indiana textbook author confined the rationale for his 1889
compilation to the goal that pupils would "gradually learn to love
the beautiful in language, and to discriminate between classic and
mediocre writing." Wilbur Cross, the future literary scholar and
governor of Connecticut, recalled that when he was teaching high
school in 1885, he altered the usual focus on grammar and compo-
sition in high school English courses at that time by urging "the
boys and girls to commit to memory something from every poem
they read." In that way, he hoped that they might "feel the rhythm
of the words." One young woman far surpassed her classmates by

learning the entire first book of Milton's *Paradise Lost*. "The beautiful verse often bogs down into lists of heathen divinities," Cross wrote, "but the music of their names carried her on."[15]

Poetry reading in the American classroom of 1890 or 1910 also aimed to instill patriotism. Before each holiday, students recited appropriate commemorative verse, such as Holmes's "Washington's Birthday" or Longfellow's "Paul Revere's Ride." Like the goal of fostering appreciation for beauty, the enhancement of patriotic fervor was not entirely separable from moral instruction, because patriotism was a subset of "love for that which is good and ennobling." When L. C. Foster and Sherman Williams assembled *Selections for Memorizing* (1892), however, they gave poems that "teach patriotism" a standing equal to those that "are good literature" and "inculcate good morals." Their choices included Emerson's "Concord Hymn" ("By the rude bridge that arched the flood . . .") and, for younger children, Holmes's "Old Ironsides" ("Ay, tear her tattered ensign down! / Long has it waved on high . . ."). In addition, as teachers knew, rousing stanzas praising national heroes addressed the gender expectations that surrounded the poetic genre. As the discussion of Edgar Guest has already indicated, the assumption that poetry was a feminine pursuit did not enjoy universal acceptance; neither did it entirely prevail in the school setting. Thus in 1890 the historian William E. Woodward, then a sixteen-year-old cadet at the Citadel who had "never cared for poetry," became an avid reader of verse when his literature instructor, a major in the military, gave him a volume of Shelley as a gift. Yet to the extent that boys faltered in the recitation because they were reluctant to excel publicly in an activity they associated with women, references to war and leadership ostensibly made the experience more palatable to them.[16]

In short, in the years roughly between 1880 and 1910 prescriptive pronouncements about the reading of poetry in school exemplified the educator William Torrey Harris's vision of humanistic study as a whole: students would thereby acquire "knowledge of truth, a love of the beautiful, a habit of doing the good," particularly for one's country. These benefits were said to derive from an analytical mode of reading that entailed line-by-line dissection, the drill of the memorized recitation, explication of theme, and attention to style. The structure of the memorization exercise itself reinforced the virtues of diligence, hard work, and thoroughness. In that respect it was well-suited to the requirements of industrial capitalism. The analytical mode of poetry reading thus captured the tensions inherent in public education from the start: between the classroom as a refuge from competitive individualism, and as a site of preparation for it. In addition, speaking a poem by heart promised to expand the student's sensitivity to well-crafted language. At the same time, such practices discouraged emphasis on the reader's "personal affinities, likings, and circumstances," which, in Matthew Arnold's words, had "great power to sway our estimate of this or that poet's work, and to make us attach more importance to it . . . than in itself it really possesses."[17]

To be sure, the dimension of the curriculum that consisted of British or American romantic poetry could work against the ideal of self-discipline, encouraging instead the outpouring or even indulgence of feeling. In that way it mirrored the assumption that Ruth Miller Elson detected in nineteenth-century schoolbooks generally: that moral virtue arose from training the heart more than the intellect. Moreover, the parsing and so on tended to fragment the text and could actually obscure its moral message. As a set of abridgments, the memory gem anthology may even be seen as a kind of cheating on discipline.[18]

Yet, despite these cross-currents, the structure, content, and ideology of schoolroom poetry reading remained strikingly stable as the twentieth century unfolded. While the term "memory gem" began fading in the 'teens, the memorized recitation and its accompanying rationale did not. In his influential *The Teaching of Poetry in the High School* (1914), Arthur H. R. Fairchild reiterated that "to store the mind with the noble thoughts and the lofty sentiments of great poetry is to repel vulgar and commonplace views," as well as to provide consolation in later life. The *Report on the Reorganization of English in Secondary Schools* (1917), which the National Council of Teachers of English and the National Education Association issued jointly, agreed. Courses of study for the next three decades reflect the persistence of the practice: fifty lines a year memorized in Kansas (1927) and at least one hundred lines a year in Rochester (1929); selections by "popular vote" of the class in Des Moines (1931); one poem for each tenth grade unit in Chicago (1933), including Longfellow's "The Builders" and Emerson's "Concord Hymn"; passages chosen for "sheer beauty of thought and imagery, or for expression of universal truth" in New Orleans (1946).[19]

Furthermore, the poetry curriculum in the interwar period displayed notable continuities in prescribed texts. Juxtaposing Melvin Hix's *Approved Selections for Supplementary Reading and Memorizing* (1905, 1908), which anthologized the poetry taught through grade eight in New York, Philadelphia, Chicago, New Orleans, and "other cities," and *Required Poetry for Memorization in New York City Public Schools* (1925)—a comparison spanning the period of the "new poetry"'s emergence—reveals that approximately two-thirds of the works on the later list appeared on the earlier one as well (with some grade levels varying more than others). Both collections relied for the primary grades on poems expressly for children, with even more Robert Louis Stevenson and Christina Rosetti selections in the 1925 curriculum. Both contained, for grades five through eight, the following: Longfellow's "The Arrow and the Song" and "The Builders"; Bryant's "To the Fringed Gentian" and "To a Waterfowl"; "Abou Ben Adhem"; Robert Browning's "The Year's at the Spring"; Ben Jonson's "It Is Not Growing Like a Tree"; Emerson's "The Rhodora"; Wordsworth's "I Wandered Lonely as a Cloud"; Tennyson's "The Charge of the Light Brigade"; and Shelley's "To a Skylark." Moreover, the major changes in the later requirements (notably the addition of numerous patriotic poems) seem more the product of World War I and the "Americanization" movement than of innovations in poetic technique.

Likewise, Nebraska schoolchildren in the lower grades during the mid-1920s learned almost the same works as their counterparts in New York. The Nebraska syllabus differed in including verse by midwestern "favorite sons" James Whitcomb Riley and Eugene

Field (although these poets appeared in abundance on a 1924 Connecticut list of suggestions for memorization). The New York and Nebraska curricula also varied in some individual titles (for instance, different choices from Longfellow and Lowell) but not in the character of the poems. All but one of the works "to be memorized" on the Nebraska syllabus had appeared in Hix's *Approved Selections* twenty years earlier, the exception being Oliver Wendell Holmes's "Union and Liberty." This picture of standardization modifies the historian's conventional portrait of the rift between rural and urban America in the 1920s. "Everyone knows," Mearns complained, "that [the best poetry] for the fifth year of school life is Longfellow, for the sixth year, Bryant; for the seventh year, Whittier . . .; for the eighth year, Poe and Holmes"—everyone, that is, regardless of where they lived.[20]

The state and local courses of study for high school English that proliferated beginning in the late 1920s reveal similar continuities over time and place. In the thirty curricula sampled, the titles for reading prescribed most frequently throughout the period 1917–1939 indicate the tenacity of nineteenth-century culture: the top choices included Matthew Arnold's "Sohrab and Rustum," "Snow-Bound," and "The Rime of the Ancient Mariner" (still prominent on college entrance examinations in 1935), as well as "Evangeline" and "To a Waterfowl," with "Sir Launfal" and "Thanatopsis" close behind. Students also still regularly read—and universities demanded—"The Lady of the Lake" (often in ninth or tenth grade rather than eighth) as well as excerpts from Tennyson's "Idylls of the King." More recent favorites were Masefield's "Sea Fever" and Alfred Noyes's "The Highwayman," while Robert Browning loomed large for college-bound students. Among contemporary American poems, however, only Frost's "Birches" (treated as a description of New England) appeared as often as the most widely assigned older works.

Apart from noting the deeper anxieties about changing values that permeated the interwar period,[21] one might explain that pattern, at least for the elementary grades, by citing the difficulty of recent verse. A striking feature of the required selections prior to

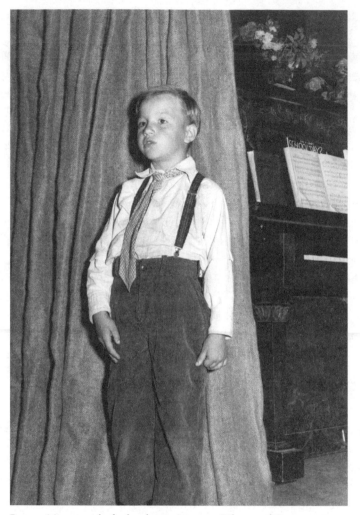

Boy reciting at end of school term in 1941. Library of Congress.

1925, however, is that, by the standards of today, many are hard to read. Nevertheless, the belief that younger children should build a basis for broad study did make the pre-secondary classroom a less logical place for the introduction of new writing than the high school. Another constraint, presumably, was that the perception of twentieth-century poetry as amoral or crude, in contrast to the tried-and-true nineteenth-century vehicles for moral uplift, made it less likely to win school board approval at any grade level, although the failure of most readers to detect an underside of despair (as in the case of Frost) might have counteracted that concern. The educators' assumption that students would find narrative poems the most engrossing also biased their selections toward classic epics. A more tangible factor sustaining the status quo was the cost for school districts of newer teaching materials. Finally, the dissemination of recent verse depended partly on publishers' success in securing permission to reprint copyrighted work.[22]

In any event, the "steady assignments" documented by these various lists constitute a graphic illustration of the discrepancy between literary production and consumption at any one time: despite the ferment the "new poetry" created and its practitioners' self-image, it did not much infiltrate American classrooms for two decades. In many schools, the moral and aesthetic framework of the earlier era held as well. Charles and Frank McMurray's 1921 lesson plan for Longfellow's "Excelsior" (still required for memorization in Nebraska in 1925) remained committed to fostering "enjoyment" and "appreciation of a certain moral idea." The dominant techniques for achieving those ends were repetition, equation of theme with meaning, and structured extraction of an ethical principle. Deciphering "difficult words and phrases" and retelling "the story" preceded a "figurative" reading: "Since the story is not to be taken literally, let us see how it should be interpreted." Although that strategy of distinguishing symbol from fact would become a *sine qua non* of reading modernist poetry, the latent content it unearthed here "pointed the moral" that persons with "high ideals" must show "unselfishness, courage, determination, energy." On the aesthetic side, courses of study in the interwar period reiterated that students should learn, as educators in Long Beach, California, put it in 1932, "to appreciate the beauty of the verse and the skill apparent in its structure." In some parts of the country, poetry also continued explicitly to augment religious instruction. The same Long Beach students were also supposed to read "The Ancient Mariner" to "discover the moral of the poem—love for all

God's creatures." In Fort Worth, high school students in 1939 were taught to read Longfellow to develop "awe for Him who is the creator of inanimate wonders and of human beings." The Fort Worth educators not only perpetuated nineteenth-century texts and outlooks but also appropriated "new poetry" (Sandburg and Frost) for the same religious purposes. To hear such echoes of older pedagogy is to appreciate more fully how the culture of the genteel tradition remained an integral part of the culture of modern America.[23]

Educational Theorists and the Implications of "Experience"

Continuity is not the whole story, however. Diffusion of the new occurred readily in sporadic locales. In the late 1920s, English teachers in Rochester high schools actively advocated modern poetry. So did progressive private institutions, such as Mearns's Lincoln School, affiliated with Columbia's Teachers College. In the 1930s, many high school juniors and seniors spent a week on contemporary poets. "Tracking" made a difference: the 1933 "enriched" course of study for Chicago tenth-graders incorporated four of Pound's poems and three of Eliot's, along with numerous examples of early modernism. Twelfth-grade elective courses covered recent verse, supported by a section on the "new poetry" in the fourth volume of the textbook *Literature and Life*.[24] Works that appeared to be about nature found favor more quickly than others: in addition to "Birches," other popular recent poems were Frost's "Stopping by Woods," Sandburg's "Fog," Millay's "God's World" and "Afternoon on a Hill," Bliss Carman's "A Vagabond Song," and Joyce Kilmer's "Trees." Although older verse decidedly predominated, by 1940 limited eclecticism within the bounds of standardization was the hallmark of the poetry unit in places scattered from Norfolk to Fresno.

Moreover, even the longevity of the nineteenth-century curriculum concealed a process of change. To explore poetry reading in the American school is to see, first, that literary canons do not evolve only within the high culture circles inhabited by critics or

members of an academic elite. But it is also to note the suscepti-
bility of canonized works to multiple approaches and uses. Even
while generations of students were reciting "Evangeline," discom-
fiting social phenomena were (however unevenly) altering the ra-
tionale and the procedure for doing so.

The big change was in the population of the American high
school. By the eve of World War I, enrollment and graduation rates
had entered a period of expansion, with even sharper growth be-
tween 1920 and 1935. Although their relative importance is a sub-
ject of some debate, several factors account for the increase: the
collapse of the demand for youth in manufacturing; the assimila-
tion of immigrants; high agricultural income per capita (outside
the North); the proliferation of white-collar occupations; and, in
the Depression, the disappearance of work opportunities that com-
peted with school attendance. Whatever its sources, this burgeon-
ing high school population created anxieties for teachers accus-
tomed to instructing the children of educated parents. As one writer
lamented, "Great numbers of students now come to the classroom
without a single tendency favorable to a literary interpretation of
life; and they go forth to a commercial and industrial existence
which is devoid of poetic feeling." Moreover, new types of popular
entertainment tempted both working- and middle-class students to
embrace the easy amusement of the "soda-fountain or moving pic-
ture show" rather than the "higher pleasure" of books.[25]

Roughly speaking, the responses to these developments among
teachers of poetry can be sorted into two categories: those that
sought to precipitate poetry's moral and social effects indirectly
through innovation in the mode of instruction for all students, and
those (discussed in the next chapter) that zeroed in on promoting
the genre's social utility as a tool for the "Americanization" of im-
migrants and for citizenship training. Both approaches were as-
pects of progressive reform, broadly defined.

The responses in the first category evolved gradually, as educa-
tors absorbed pedagogical theories promulgated even before the
demographic and cultural trends of the 1910s made new objectives
and methods seem imperative. One influential theorist was Johann

Friedrich Herbart. Beginning in the 1890s, Herbart's American followers popularized his belief that the elementary school should embody the "culture-epochs" through which the developing child passed. That outlook coincided with wider developments in anthropology; it infiltrated poetry instruction in the form of an emphasis on verse that either described primitive behavior or dated from a supposedly less advanced civilization. Thus it strengthened the justification for reading English ballads during the first year of high school, as well as for including certain staples like "Hiawatha." As the notes to Longfellow's poem in a 1925 Nebraska textbook explained, "These early peoples, compared with the peoples that live now, are like children compared with grown persons. . . . And just as children now believe fairy stories, these early peoples believed the wonder-stories of their heroes."[26]

The most important American educator to come under Herbart's influence was of course John Dewey. Dewey shared the view that schoolwork should derive from children's natural interests, but rejected the use of a text such as "Hiawatha" to recapitulate "savagery" because it filtered developmental stages through literary representation. Instead, he advocated a curriculum based on two general principles: fidelity to the child's experience and organization of subject matter around the needs of a democracy. The emphasis on experience, the focus of much that went under the name of progressive education in the early 1900s, implicitly rejected the concept of the mind as a storehouse. As Dewey's disciple William Heard Kilpatrick phrased it, education should be "considered as life itself and not as a mere preparation for later living." At the same time, however, other reformers advanced their own version of the connection between education and democracy by arguing that schooling should transmit practical skills geared to producing a society of efficient adults.[27] These competing outlooks both emboldened advocates of poetry in the classroom and threw them on the defensive. The tensions evident in the resulting pedagogical materials nicely illustrate that, at the level of application, discrete developments in educational theory disintegrated into approaches as eclectic as the poetry reading lists themselves.

Although they displayed little explicit engagement with philosophical controversy, among the first educators to exhibit the impact of the new theories were several experts who registered the changing climate by simultaneously moderating and reinscribing poetry's traditional moral functions. For instance, Arthur H. R. Fairchild and the Harvard professor of education Charles Swain Thomas, aware of the drawbacks of rote learning, urged English teachers to nurture a child's emotional as well as intellectual understanding of a poem. Yet Fairchild claimed that great poetry stimulated only "elevated and refined" feelings, rather than a "weak sensuousness." Christianity went unmentioned, but the purpose of reading verse remained the realization of life's "eternal laws and of its enduring ideals." (That vision of philosophical unity had an analogue in Fairchild's remark that the classroom "makes a social unit to be brought into a common state of feeling.") His advice for tackling the words of a text paralleled his repudiation of weakness: "The true enjoyment of poetry demands effort, steadiness of purpose, sometimes even pain, to achieve it." Taking account of changing conditions, Fairchild maintained that those precepts applied regardless of a pupil's background. Similarly, Thomas insisted on intensive interrogation of texts in order to elucidate a poet's message; he told students to "check every word that was not perfectly clear, master every obscure reference, and determine the grammatical relationship of each word, phrase, and clause to its neighbors."[28]

In a parallel development, by the end of World War I speech professionals had begun rejecting elocutionists' preoccupation with gesture and display. Critical of what they saw as the excesses of elocution, their goal was less moral cultivation than the stimulation of speakers' minds and emotions through exposure to texts as a whole. Still, advocates of "expression" and "oral interpretation" retained a belief in the values of discipline and control, both of which, in their view, the recitation enforced especially well. As one "expressionist" explained in 1917, oral performance precluded "superficial attention and 'snap judgment.'" The same writer noted that because poetry was "the highest and finest type" of literature, proper verse recitation was "one of the most effective means of bringing the voice under control and of making it responsive to thought, imagination, and feeling."[29]

The 1917 *Report* by the National Council of Teachers of English/National Education Association performed still another balance. Its authors' three "fundamental reasons" for studying literature renamed the moral, aesthetic, and patriotic justifications of the nineteenth century but did not depart very far from them: now the goals were cultural ("To open to the pupil new and higher forms of pleasure"), vocational, and social and ethical ("To present to the student noble ideals . . . and make him more efficient" in his "service to others in the community and in the Nation"). Cognizant of the transformed high school population, the authors declared hopefully that reading was "still the chief recreation of many people." Especially for the new "vocational pupils," literature might "be of great assistance in building character and may provide a good antidote for the harmful pleasures that invite the weary workers in our cities." Fears of deteriorating taste and behavior thus skewed the list of recommended poems in the 1917 curriculum toward nineteenth-century verse free of "the morbidly introspective, the vicious, the mentally abnormal." Yet the *Report,* in part the result of a movement to broaden the curriculum beyond college entrance requirements, conceded that "the admission of a large foreign element into our schools" justified including some "modern" books about daily life because they would more easily sustain pupils' attention.[30]

If many educators in the 1910s thus cautiously distanced themselves from their predecessors while affirming much of past practice, the curricular discussions of the 1920s and '30s reveal the full effects of pedagogical reform on the mode of reading prescribed for poetry instruction. By that time, poetry's advocates knew they were fighting a rear-guard action. Not only did the numbers of high school students continue to swell, but something had "come between poetry and boys and girls." A Minneapolis document mournfully reported that "a class of girls of higher than average intelligence when asked to tell which they would rather be, Gertrude

Ederle, who swam the English Channel, or Edna St. Vincent Millay, voted almost unanimously in favor of the champion swimmer. In their eyes hers was a more notable achievement than to have written The King's Henchman [*sic*]."[31]

For one cohort of progressive teachers in the interwar period, the key to reversing that trend seemed to lie in the idea that their predecessors had already begun to pick up from Dewey and Kilpatrick: experience. As the Deweyite educator Sterling Andrus Leonard declared in 1922, the goal of reading was "not arousing appreciation of literature itself," but, rather, "an achievement of realized, true, and significant experience." In that formulation and elsewhere in the writings of Leonard and his colleagues, the term had two definitions: it referred both to the personal history that readers could bring to bear on their understanding of texts, and to the effects on readers of being led to re-enact the behaviors and emotions an author evoked. That is, the way to read a poem, these theorists collectively argued, was simultaneously to draw on and to create experience. Allan Abbott's description of "The Imaginative Element in Poetry" (1926) captures the first aspect of the progressive educators' usage in language that is remarkably close to the reader-response criticism of the late twentieth century: "Reader and poet together produce the poem, like the strings and body of the violin; the poet plays on the strings, but the real music comes from the resonance of the body of the instrument, which is the mind of the reader. The response to such provocative words will be just as varied as the experiences, actual or imaginative, of the reader; no two persons will give back the same echo." In the second sense—as the contribution of literature to life—"experience" appears in statements like this one from a 1934 pedagogy textbook: "Only when the teacher learns that poetry and prose were written chiefly to be re-experienced or relived by the reader can we begin to hope that children will learn to like to read excellent things." A corollary of the emphasis on verse reading as the enhancement of experience was that poems lacked stable meanings. As Abbott went on to note, "No one response is necessarily better or truer to the poet's meaning than some other." Along these lines, John Hooper, the author of *Poetry in the New Curriculum* (1932), advised teachers choosing a poem for classroom use to make sure that it was "interwoven with suggestions that give it as many different meanings as there are minds to hear it."[32]

Several consequences followed from such premises. The first was the eradication of the overtly moral aspect of poetry instruction. As Leonard declared, "It can hardly be stated too often that no conventional and formal 'pointing of moral' is for a moment considered here as a function of literature. Insistence on the final quatrain of *The Ancient Mariner* rather than its amazing, varied pictures, or on the tacked-on last lines of *Thanatopsis* . . . cannot be too strongly condemned." The author of *Enjoying Poetry in School* (1931), Howard Francis Seely, likewise dissociated poetry reading from "the search for 'lessons' or 'morals'": "Personally, I wish that every English teacher would bury these two words 'deeper than did ever plummet sound.'" A second consequence was a heightened concern with discovering reading materials of "immediate interest to children," so that students could respond "freely, spontaneously, honestly." That position led to a flurry of Columbia Teachers College doctoral dissertations designed to determine what children "liked" in poetry, in order to adapt the curriculum accordingly. (This was precisely the subjectivity against which Matthew Arnold had warned.) By the same token, the memory gem and the forced memorization exercise fell from favor; instead, as one pedagogue insisted, "the teacher must do everything that can be done to get the child to memorize a poem because he likes it." The advocates of reading for "experience" also often endorsed what Leonard and others called the "'demolition of teacher supremacy.'" Citing a standardized test of the capacity to judge poetic quality (a stunning, if ludicrous, example of E. L. Thorndike's followers' view that educators could measure anything), Leonard observed that only the exceptional teacher would "fail to discover in his class pupils with distinctly better judgment than his own in matters of literary appreciation." Similarly, Seely announced, "We teachers are hosts. The poet and pupils are our guests. As we introduce our guests to each other we shall linger with them a moment to help them get acquainted before we leave them to develop their relationship alone." In that role, teachers relinquished not only the burden of ethical instruction but also the obligation to foster the "technical" command of form, or even full comprehension of meaning. Quoting the efficiency proponent Franklin Bobbitt, Leonard averred, "'One of the most mischievous superstitions of education has been that when a thing is presented it must be completely understood.'"[33]

This perspective in turn implied teaching students an alternative approach to the printed page: instead of dissecting a text, the reader was to embrace it. As Leonard phrased it, "'The literature of power' is rarely to be 'chewed and digested,' in grades [*sic*] and high school at least it is mainly to be 'apprehended'—taken hold of, that is, as genuine and living experience." Similarly, Hooper condemned teachers who, when they "emphasize the element of comprehension, and fail to recognize the existence of apprehension . . . preclude any possibility of encouraging feeling without knowledge." Thus he lauded the "experience" of a student who, when reading Samuel Taylor Coleridge's "Kubla Khan," mistook the name of the "sacred river" Alph for "elf," but nonetheless "although misunderstanding the poet's words . . . understood the poet; and one creative artist inspired another."[34]

An implication of this view was that there was "nothing inherently hard" about poetry. Paradoxically, submission to the text— "revel[ing]" in its "music," "idea," or "artistry"—was the key to the appreciation associated with the integrated self that teachers hoped to engender. Mearns approvingly reported that a student editor, reading a classmate's poem, had commented that the author was "'too fine for thinking; she is great when she's herself.'" This subservience to accessibility and feeling led certain teachers not only to minimize the discernment of moral truths but also to avoid introducing poetry containing figurative imagery, because such linguistic devices introduced "reading difficulties" that tended to "obscure the meaning [of a poem] and to interfere with the enjoyment" that it should provide. "Pay very little attention to the symbolism," the 1927 Long Beach senior high school curriculum advised teachers about Tennyson's "Idylls of the King," adding that it was "too intricate for the average youth to comprehend." In other words, the premium on "experience" displaced both the canonical status of poetic texts and the transmission of aesthetic standards.[35]

One of the most appealing accounts of reading for "experience" appears in the autobiography of the poet May Sarton, who attended the Shady Hill School in Cambridge, Massachusetts, between 1917 and 1925. (As one of the nation's earliest and most innovative "co-operative open air" schools, Shady Hill came to the "experience" curriculum before its public school counterparts.) Agnes Hocking, Shady Hill's founder and its head until Sarton reached the fifth grade, made poetry "centrally active" there. As Sarton recalled, Hocking taught poems "all day long, by bursting into spontaneous prayer when the spirit moved her, by those sudden noble angers, and, more formally, by meeting with each class for a scheduled hour. No doubt there was method, but to us it was heavenly madness, was delight. . . . She did not tell us about poetry; she made us live its life." Memorization occurred not through reading or "study," but through listening to Hocking's repetitions of texts. One spring, Sarton's class was reminded that verse was "not something told, it was something happening to us all the time" when a rain shower drenched the students while they were reciting Sir William Watson's lines about April's "weep[ing] thy girlish tears!" It would not have surprised her, Sarton remarked, if Hocking had arranged to "summon that cloud herself." Another day, learning a stanza referring to a "weary wee flipperling . . . Asleep in the arms of the slow-swinging seas," the students "became seals, a thing rather easy to do if you are already sitting in a gray woolen bag." Hocking, Sarton added, "also in a gray bag on the floor, was the Seal of Seals." In this way, Sarton and her schoolmates found that they "had become whatever it was [they were reciting] long before we guessed we were learning it."[36]

More conventional teachers who perpetuated the analytical mode of reading might have protested that lying on the floor dressed like a seal would weaken their moral authority. Yet the "experience" method had its own moral and social dimension, on which its proponents banked: namely, the prospect that in the long run the emphasis on equal participation and ease would boost readership. Hence the new curriculum promised to stabilize high culture despite the influx of students (many of them "boys of coarse fibre") who came from homes without "somebody reading beside the lamp." At the same time, some observers also hoped it would redress the association of poetry with femininity. Seely welcomed the avoidance of "elocutionary vocal tactics" in order to quell boys' fear that poetry was "'silly and sissy stuff.'" One mother informed Mearns that she "rejoice[d] that the Lincoln School has made poetry one of the manly sports. My boy and his boy friends talk and dispute over poetry as they would over any other natural healthy interest." In addition, Mearns and others specifically linked poetry instruction to defending or promoting the purity of American young people. This was true despite, or, arguably, because of the sexual sophistication that surrendering to "experience" connoted; Mearns's effort can be seen as preserving innocence by idealizing and hence containing the sexual impulses of adolescents. Thus, by entitling his account of his poetry classes at the Lincoln School *Creative Youth* (1926), he implicitly refuted the scandalous portrait Samuel Hopkins Adams had drawn in *Flaming Youth* four years earlier.[37]

In 1935, the "experience" model became the basis for another NCTE-sponsored project: *An Experience Curriculum in English*. "The class," its authors recommended, "should be a rather informal literary club in which the teacher is simply the most experienced member." Sharing "moral sentiments" (as in both "Abou Ben Adhem" and Sandburg's "Prayers of Steel") and "worthy expressions of patriotism" (Emerson's "Concord Hymn") remained objectives, as did the discernment of technique and rhythm ("Sea Fever"), but all reading experiences that fostered the "enlargement of the individual" carried equal weight. Throughout the interwar period, this curriculum filtered into state and local courses of study in a number of ways. Thirteen years after Fairchild's paean to hard work, Kansas educators—still assigning in high school "The Lady of the Lake," "Evangeline," "The Vision of Sir Launfal," "Sohrab and Rustum," "Rime of the Ancient Mariner," and "Snow-Bound"—recommended that "nothing hard or technical should be attempted" and "nothing should be burdensome." In some classrooms "The Courtship of Miles Standish," "Evangeline," and "Hiawatha" became either undemanding narratives or simply the source of exposure to history. "Evangeline," the devisers of Berkeley's 1939 curriculum for junior high schools noted, should be included but was "not to be studied intensively." The course of study for Kansas City elementary schools in 1932 captured the essence of the change: "Too often we have selected poems unrelated to the experiences of children and thus beyond their comprehension. We have also tried to explain the meaning of difficult phrases, allusions, and finally have asked the children to state the poem in their own words, thus killing all love for the poem." The Rochester innovators warned against concluding that "even the selecting of certain words or phrases for comment in some way violates the spirit of the poem," but sought to have pupils "experience the quickening and intensity of the emotions" from a "surrender" to the "mood" of a poet. The most florid formulation came from Montgomery County, Maryland, in 1939: "Literature is not the written expression in the form of the essay, novel, poetry, or drama, but rather is the living growth experienced by a person as he cooperates with the realities of life. . . . It is the expanding living made possible for him through the symbolized representation (words)." By 1946 the Florida state curriculum declared succinctly that "the old analytical process . . . seems to be gone."[38]

Nonetheless, there were ties between the "experience" curriculum and the approaches that both preceded and survived alongside it. Given the similarity between conversion and submission to feeling, the religious dimension was not entirely absent despite the erosion of moral instruction. At the same time, the method of "apprehension" magnified the sensory delight buried in the conceit of "gems." The imperative to surrender to the text likewise echoed nineteenth-century Transcendentalist or romantic conceits of escaping the bounds of the rational self. In that respect, the "experience" curriculum was the classroom equivalent of the emotional and sensual mode of reading that carried both innocence and sophistication to Edna St. Vincent Millay's audiences. The critic and writer John Erskine identified poetry reading as a locus for the persistence of romanticism in early-twentieth-century American culture by declaring in 1920 that the genre, "by romantic definition and by assiduous practice, has become an emotional experience without coherent meaning."[39]

Connected to past literary traditions and practices, the "experience" curriculum was also perfectly adapted to the changing cultural circumstances of the early twentieth century. First, the abandonment of "storage" and preparation was well-suited to a society in which spending was replacing delayed gratification. Similarly, the premium on ease of apprehension may measure the pervasiveness of Americans' expectations about the ability to assimilate sound and images quickly and effortlessly, resulting from the influence of movies and radio. In addition, the progressives' curriculum further illuminates the extent to which the pursuit of intense experience gripped middle-class Americans who were contending with a bureaucratized, impersonal society. The attachment of that quest to poetry reading is fraught with irony, because it was the distance of print from "real life" that so troubled figures such as Randolph Bourne and Jane Addams. At the same time, "reveling" in a text as a means of "self-integration"—like other manifestations of the search for experience—might deflect attention from social change. The progressives' deliberate avoidance of direct moral instruction was in a sense the first step down a road that dead-ended in self-absorbed individualism. It was on just this score, in fact, that Dewey and others eventually challenged the Progressive Education Association, arguing in the 1930s that the preoccupation with personal liberation was obstructing genuine reform.

That critique, however, should not lead to the conclusion that conceiving poetry reading as experience was the brainchild of an elite bent on social control. For one thing, submission to the text could subvert not only reform impulses but also the discipline necessary to sustain a capitalist economy. (Cary Nelson's contention that genteel critics, operating from class interest, defused poetry's revolutionary potential by encouraging the reader to escape through Keats's "magic casements" to another realm is open to the same objection.) In any event, the language of escape was not the progressive educators' primary vocabulary; connection to immediate life was. Moreover, despite the heavy component of individualism, community and democracy had a place in the "experience" framework. Seely, for example, specified that discovering "kinship with the lives of others" through reading would enable students to "grow" not only as "individuals" but also "as members of the social group." Although the latter phrase may betray a fear of conflict, on its face it reflected the progressives' overt commitment to "tolerance" and open discussion. Mearns, invoking Dewey, went further, pleading that the "spiritualization of public education" was the "hope of civilization" and relying on poetry instruction to nurture that hope. Yet if he did not encourage escape, Mearns, by appropriating some "new poetry" (Amy Lowell, Robinson, the early Pound) to those particular social purposes, arguably stripped it of the "tincture of disestablishment" which William Carlos Williams had identified as part of modernist poetry's essence.[40]

The Promise of the Speaking Choir

In the interwar period, some American educators imbued with a similar vision of personal and collective growth began promoting a third mode of poetry reading which they deemed more advantageous than either analytical study or the individual "experience" method: group recitation by means of the verse speaking choir. The product of several related efforts, the idea of the speaking choir originated in Great Britain shortly after World War I. The playwrights Gordon Bottomley and John Drinkwater, mindful of Greek choruses, began experimenting with unison voices in stage productions. In addition, a British speech teacher, Mona Swann, embraced the tenets of the French music instructor Jacques Dalcroze, who insisted on regarding artistic performance as a personal experience instead of a "task"; the result was Swann's propagation of a poetry reading technique she called "language eurhythmics." Most important, however, was the inclusion, after 1919, of solo verse recitations at national music festivals. These presentations, by students of a speech instructor named Marjorie Gullan, prompted the poet John Masefield also to envision a revival of the Greek chorus and to put choral selections from *The Trojan Women* on the program of the 1922 Glasgow Festival. Gullan took up the challenge, formed the Glasgow Verse Speaking Choir, and three years later organized a similar group in London. Many of the participants were teachers, who saw choric speech as a way of revitalizing poetry lessons in school. In the same period Masefield founded the Oxford Recitations, a verse speaking contest for adults, in order to enhance appreciation for the "British poetic inheritance." By the early 1930s, the vogue of the speaking choir had spread to other locales, including Germany, France, Canada, Russia—and the United States.[41]

The American movement flourished in settings ranging from fourth-grade classrooms to state universities; it thrived particularly on the campuses of private eastern women's colleges. Because progressive educators were especially enthusiastic about it, the speaking choir was concentrated in schools, although it turned up in other venues such as churches, men's and women's clubs, scouting organizations, summer camps, and settlement houses. Two types of popular drama—the pageant (discussed in the following chapter) and the Little Theater production—overlapped with and gave impetus to the phenomenon. As verse choirs spread across the country, their proponents invested the mode of oral group reading with diverse hopes and purposes, which they disseminated in numerous writings designed to clarify the "art" of choral speaking and to make available texts suitable for "concerts." Many such works were published by a Boston firm called Expression Company (its motto was "Expression is but Revelation"), the existence of which testifies to the perception—or perhaps the wish—that the movement had created a substantial American market for expertise on the subject.

Indeed, one unstated goal animating choric speech manuals and anthologies was the choir directors' desire to consolidate the professionalization of speech as an academic discipline. Commenting that she frequently received inquiries from English teachers and from "people with no training," Cecile de Banke, a British-educated member of the Wellesley College speech faculty, insisted on "the seriousness and difficulty of the proposed undertaking." The goal of the professional choir conductor, she and her colleagues insisted, was to produce a controlled sound that conformed to pre-existing standards of appropriate diction.[42]

These standards, certified by professionals, served a second aim of the movement: to assist the disadvantaged in overcoming the perceived liabilities of their backgrounds. Specifically, choir leaders strove to help people to lose their foreign, lower-class, or pronounced local accents. As scientists of speech, they prescribed instead the speaking style "common to the best-educated people in the region of the speakers." As the California teacher Elizabeth E. Keppie observed, "Many little children come from homes where baby talk or foreign speech has been encouraged"; the choir could reverse that influence. Advocates of choric speech in the United States particularly condemned nasality, which de Banke pronounced an "almost nation-wide handicap." To the extent that choirs followed directives to eradicate such traits, they continued to define the cultured American in terms associated with nineteenth-century genteel strictures: as a person who was native-born, cosmopolitan, and middle- or upper-class. Their appropriation of "new poetry" for this purpose thus had the effect of recoupling to the values associated with idealism works written in protest against those values.[43]

Improving pronunciation, however, was only one of the contributions that speaking choir advocates thought the activity could make to individual growth. Drawing on the burgeoning field of psychology, which they invoked as an allied science, they gave to group poetry reading a third, more sweeping purpose: the achievement of "personality adjustment." Part of that process entailed channeling aggression; for that reason the technique found favor in schools. Yet older individuals could also benefit. Although "various fears and complexes and lack of self confidence have paralyzed their efforts," Keppie remarked of shy adults, the "association and support afforded by the choir has given them courage. . . . Thus a new self has been discovered and revealed through the means of choral interpretation." The same term that Louis MacNeice had employed—"release"—was central to this therapeutic vision. In Keppie's words, "The inhibitions, the diffidence, and the self consciousness which have bound" the maladjusted person "will fall away when he experiences the joy of speaking poetry in this cooperative way. By the abandon which must come to one thus released of his self-consciousness, there comes an ease and relaxation which leads him on to braver and bolder undertakings. Something which he thought lost in his childhood has come back into his life." That language, connected in a general way to various forms of "mind cure," reflected in particular the spread (and the misinterpretation) of the Freudian concept of repression.[44]

In 1931, two influential popularizers of psychology—the husband-and-wife team of Harry and Bonaro Overstreet—added their imprimatur to the concept of poetry reading as a catalyst for adjustment. Writing under her maiden name, Bonaro Wilkinson published that year one of the more intriguing artifacts of the dissemination of modernism, *The Poetic Way of Release* (1931). Wilkinson argued that verse originated in intensified emotion "which finds no ready release in activity"; this pent-up feeling "quicken[ed] one's sense of rhythm and tend[ed] to express itself in a manner of speech adequate both to the thought and to the pulsing motion of that thought." By appreciating and reliving that transfer of "release" to poetic expression, readers gained heightened "power" that allowed them to substitute "unity" for frustration, routine, and "the boredom that comes from emotional poverty." Although connections to the choric speech movement here remained only implicit, H. A. Overstreet contributed an introduction to the book explaining that its purpose was to show the promise of poetry for grown readers in the way Mearns had for younger ones.[45]

Speaking choir advocates also endowed the practice with the potential to promote social as well as psychic harmony. In *A Guide to Civilized Leisure* (1934), H. A. Overstreet declared that "to join with others in the rendering of a great poetic experience" as a choir member was "to feel oneself swept into a oneness of life that is well worth the having." As in the case of folk dance, which he also recommended, Overstreet saw the "sociability" inherent in "communal" reading as representing an alternative to the "frenetic demands" of "our economic civilization." Verse choir leaders, who gratefully cited Overstreet's endorsement, described the social value of their enterprise in similar terms. As the affiliation of the anthropologist Gilbert Murray with the British speaking choir movement suggests, some proponents conflated primitive ritual and recitation with a salutary folk culture, which they saw themselves as perpetuating. From that perspective, the practice of oral group reading appeared an even more wholesome alternative to movies and jazz than silent reading or the lone memorized recitation.[46]

During the Great Depression, a belief in the potential of choric speech to enhance community affiliated it with other efforts that linked an interest in the art of the "people" to the renewal of American life. As de Banke explained, "Certain prevailing tendencies in modern men and women are found to be anti-social; they are for the most part introspective preoccupation, and exclusiveness resulting from diffidence or from a sense of class distinction. There has been a general move to combat these unhappy tendencies by gathering people together for the object of group enjoyment and experience in such forms of expression as community singing and country dancing, and to these we now add verse speaking in choirs." One Vassar faculty member classified choric speech as "oral arts and crafts" and also identified it as instrumental in national recovery: "The unemployed may well profit from the experience and the employed will find themselves stimulated by this cooperative work. Such a united choir or group may live equally well within a fashionable club or in a settlement house, in urban or rural districts. . . . The fireside may once more become a center for small groups whereas the settlement, mission, parish house, or village hall may become the working center for the larger and more ambitious groups." That vision not only reflected the writer's desire to secure federal aid for such activities but also addressed the need for

New York City teenagers in a speaking choir of the mid-1930s. From *All the Children: Thirty-Ninth Annual Report of the Superintendent of Schools, City of New York, 1936–37.*

a sense of belonging that animated many Americans in the aftermath of economic collapse. Group reading even promised global unity. In 1937, de Banke pointed to a performance at the foot of the Acropolis, ironically by the speaking choir of the University of Berlin, as evidence that the "welding influence of mass artistic achievement" could create international understanding.[47]

All of the perceived individual and social benefits of choric speech derived from overarching assumptions about the relationship between reading and "life." Speaking choir advocates, concerned about a shrinking audience for silent verse, stressed that speech uniquely bridged the gap between cold type and human emotion. Endowing the practice with the power to create an additional form of unity, they argued repeatedly that reciting poetry aloud (provided speakers steered clear of the mechanical techniques of elocution) invigorated otherwise "dead language on paper." As one observer exulted, "It is amazing to see a poem grow into life when the whole choir recreates it."[48]

Even so, choir leaders sharply delimited the aspects of life that the verse speakers expressed by declaring certain types of poems inappropriate for performance. Sound and structure influenced judgments of suitability. Speech teachers favored selections that incorporated different parts for high- and low-pitched, or what they termed "light" and "dark," voices; they also preferred repeated lines or passages permitting antiphonal reading and solos. Works too long for easy memorizing fell outside the repertoire unless they could be cut. Younger students, Keppie noted, required verse with "a robust and definite" beat. Poetry "inspired by" the "Negro rhythm and Negro dialect" seemed to work especially well, as did those built upon the tempo of the machine age. In de Banke's view, free verse had its place as long as speakers became attuned to its "circular movement" and "authentic" beat. Gender stereotypes inflected the criteria applied to selections for men's choirs: poems with a "virile, hearty appeal" promised better results than those replete with "rheumy-eyed intellectualism." The most significant distinction governing the choice of pieces, however, was between "objective" and "subjective" verse. The goal of psychological growth notwithstanding, choric speech advocates assumed that introspective, "purely personal" poetry ought to give place to works that "contained a feeling of universality of experience." Thus their compilations and lists tended to exclude poems that recorded a "mood," however full of "life," in favor of narratives or lyrics with vivid, contrasting images.[49]

These stipulations fostered the dissemination of much "new poetry" beyond the obvious "boomlay, BOOM" refrain of Vachel Lindsay. Sandburg's "Jazz Fantasia," "Grass," and "Four Preludes on Playthings of the Wind" became standard offerings; as Gullan noted, Sandburg's "very impersonality" made his poems especially suitable for the chorus, "perhaps more so than that of any other American writer." In *The Speech Choir* (1937), a collection of mainly American verse she compiled after spending a term on the faculty of Teachers College, Gullan also highlighted Robinson's "The House on the Hill" and Harriet Monroe's "Supernal Dialogue" as examples of two-part texts; Sara Teasdale's "There Will Come Soft Rains" for "sequence work"; selections from William Carlos Williams, Louis Untermeyer, and Léonie Adams for unison performance; and excerpts from Pound, Frost, and Millay to encourage individual training. Another choral reading teacher of the late 1930s singled out Millay's "God's World" as an example of the rare "objective" sonnet. Amy Lowell's "Patterns" frequently appeared on lists of recital possibilities. Even later and less accessible modernists, although more controversial, reached a wider public by means of the speaking choir. While one director advised, "I should avoid at all times the intricately geometrical and fanciful outbursts of some of our modern self-expressionists" because no one "knows what they mean," others championed Eliot's *Collected Poems, 1909–1935* with equal fervor, recommending choruses from "The Rock," "Sweeney Agonistes," and "The Hollow Men" as well as "Triumphal March" (which fairly demanded a choral rendition).[50]

Here again one may note the double implications of a reading practice with respect to the fate of the rebellious, anti-idealistic impulses that engendered the "new poetry." If oral group techniques affirmed and disseminated the spirit as well as the words of "God's World" or Lindsay's incantations, in other instances—"The Hollow Men," or Sandburg's grim meditations on industrialization, or Robinson's bleak observation of "ruin and decay"—the message of the text, however "objective," belied the assumptions about individual and social progress brought to bear on its performance.

The history of speaking choirs is instructive in two further respects. First, constrained only by a bias against the "subjective" and by the need to mix "light" and "dark" voices, eclecticism had free reign. Especially suited to school programs, Whitman (for example, "I Hear America Singing," "O Captain! My Captain!," "Pioneers! O Pioneers!") appeared even more frequently than Sandburg in Gullan's anthology, together with selections from Shakespeare,

Longfellow, Tennyson, and English ballads. De Banke's suggestions mixed Eliot, Conrad Aiken, Edgar Lee Masters, and Amy Lowell with Blake, Ben Jonson, Keats, and Dryden. "Masculine" poems, one teacher counseled, included Byron's "Ocean," Kipling's "Boots," and three works by Lindsay. As Gullan reported, some choirs may at one time "present a program of old and modern ballads and, at another, seventeenth-century verse or modern and modernist poetry, or nonsense verse, or all combined." Choir programs spanned poetic structure as well as chronology, while amalgamating the high and the popular. In short, even though choir directors retained "modernism" in their critical vocabulary, it was less useful as a category than psychological potential, sound, virility, and objectivity.[51]

Second, the development of the choir repertoire along lines of "objectivity" reflected and reinforced certain premises about public art. The idea that poetry ought to be readily understandable was at the core of the "experience" curriculum. The emergence of verse drama and other poetry on the radio strengthened that assumption as it transformed poets into celebrities. As Milton Allen Kaplan put it, the "heterogeneity of the audience" required that the language of radio be "lucid to the point of transparency." In addition, radio encouraged the consignment of brooding reflection or subtle emotion to private sites for reading. The medium disseminated diverse poetic texts, from "Sohrab and Rustum" to works of Frost, Sandburg, and Masters to the choral speech of Norman Corwin's plays. Yet "in gaining his audience," Kaplan noted, the "poet of the air has presented a 'public' poetry that is hopeful and affirmative in spirit. . . . The positive element in radio poetry supplies the balance which keeps poetry in equilibrium and prevents it from becoming detached or distorted, criticism that is often made of modern poetry." That characteristic became even more evident as the propaganda needs of World War II increased the demand for patriotic and inspirational verse. Thus the speaking choir movement helped to shape a set of expectations about culture's smiling public face, of which controversies in the 1990s over the self-critical aspects of the

National History Standards and museum exhibitions were later manifestations.[52]

Readers' Uses of the Recitation

The grandiose visions pedagogues attached to the reading of verse up to the mid-twentieth century did not come to pass with respect to either education or civilization. Still, the moral, aesthetic, and social benefits which the proponents of discipline, experience, and collectivity assigned to the poetry curriculum were not merely examples of wishful thinking on the part of educators. A sample of 479 readers queried in 1995 about their participation in school poetry recitations between 1917 and 1950 partly confirmed the efficacy of their teachers' objectives. The responses also documented the persistence of late-nineteenth-century practices and assumptions well into the twentieth century, and their entanglement with innovative approaches. Yet informants revealed as well that the school recitation served a number of purposes only tenuously connected to the pedagogical foundations on which it rested. T. S. Eliot's comment that for most people "such taste for poetry as they retain in later life is only a sentimental memory of the pleasures of youth" does not begin to cover the many functions that the genre fulfilled.[53]

A word about the sample, which derived from a query inserted in the *New York Times Book Review*: readers were invited to describe the poems they had learned in school between 1917 and 1950, as well as to comment on what the task meant to them at the time and later in life. The respondents obviously reflected the audience of the *Times*. their current residences were concentrated in the northeastern United States. The biggest single group (forty or so) had attended New York City public elementary and high schools. Nevertheless, many had been educated elsewhere: in one-room North Dakota schoolhouses, California parochial institutions, midwestern state teachers' college laboratory schools. As a consequence of the dates in the query, respondents were predominantly between 65 and 85 years of age. The loneliness from which older people often suffer may partly explain the volume and detail of most responses; while a handful wrote postcards, many more sent three or four single-spaced pages, and two recorded tapes. Jews (to judge from surnames), pre-collegiate English teachers, and academics were disproportionately represented. Yet the sample was sufficiently diverse that the largest subset (the New Yorkers) represented less than ten percent of the total. Given the teachers' supposition (and the cultural expectation) that girls were better at reciting than boys, the number of men who answered the query (206) was surprisingly high compared to the number of women (273)—both groups exhibiting the same enthusiasm. To be sure, 22 respondents condemned poetry reading in school, about equally divided by gender. Within the negative group, almost a third blamed the teacher's approach—both mindless drill and the "apprehension" that had been progressives' point of pride—for their disaffection. "Poetry was stuffed down our throats," a woman exclaimed. "I hated having to spend Sundays memorizing something I thought of as pretty stupid, uninteresting, and meaningless."[54] Like the authors of fan letters, however, the overwhelming majority of the people who took the trouble to write relished learning poems, attending school, reminiscing about those activities, or all three.

In terms of titles cited, the letters document the emphasis on texts written before 1900. A reader educated in rural Michigan observed that in some grades she realized that her poetry book had belonged to her mother when she had attended the same school before the turn of the century. The letters also substantiate the eclecticism that governed curricula to varying degrees. One informant, for example, leafing through a tattered copy of *My Poetry Book* (1934), commented on the presence of Longfellow, Sandburg, Whitman, Field, Edward Lear, Wordsworth, Tennyson, and Emerson. Another, a parochial school student in upstate New York in the early 1930s, called Frost an "especially great favorite," but noted as well his fondness for Robert Service, Grantland Rice, Kipling, Kilmer, and Shakespeare.[55] In addition, the letters reveal a developing consciousness of the processes of canonization. A respondent who, between 1931 and 1934, had relied on a compilation entitled *One Hundred and One Famous Poems,* was forcibly introduced to categories of taste when a university professor gave him a lower grade for performing a section from James Whitcomb Riley in a recitation contest. A reader from Massachusetts who eventually earned a Ph.D. in English literature observed, "I realized that the poems [the teacher] had made us memorize were considered second rate . . . and sentimental." For a student at Detroit's Edgar A. Guest School, whose "lower-middle-class immigrant family . . . knew the difference between art and kitsch," the recognition of hierarchical distinctions came early.[56] Nevertheless, as Victor Nell has put it, because "earlier tastes do not wither and die as more refined appetites develop," such readers became, over time, repositories of both the high and the popular—aware of, but not constrained by, a shifting boundary between them.[57]

To turn from content to classroom procedure, respondents confirmed that oral poetry reading occurred in a range of formats reflecting both the older approaches and the progressive innovations educators mandated: memory gem books, spellers, and, in the 1940s, "personal growth leaflets" issued by the National Education Association. These materials often sustained the moral lessons that educators strove to impart. In the 1930s, an Illinois father repeatedly quoted Edwin Markham's "Outwitted" to remind his son "of ways to foster tolerance." The much-taught "Abou ben Adhem" developed in many readers a similar mistrust of zealotry. One reader who became a high school teacher reported that when he learned "Invictus" around 1935, he gained "the courage to face whatever has come my way these seventy-two years of my life." The same poem helped a young girl hold her head up when her father, "a Jew in KKK land," went to prison for a crime he did not commit.[58]

In particular, several respondents revealed that they perpetuated the curricular affiliation between poetry recitation and religion by endowing certain texts with the properties of scripture or prayer. A Methodist woman who grew up in rural Georgia learned Longfellow's "Psalm of Life" in fourth grade; it "put to rest the

nagging questions of what life was about." Poetry, she added, sup-
plied the "simplicity, the certainty, the lyricism" which "answered
some need for guidance, for assurance, for relief from existential
angst." Another reader described her first exposure to Wordsworth's
"The World Is Too Much with Us" in terms akin to religious con-
version: her seventh-grade English teacher wrote the entire sonnet
on the blackboard, and "at that moment my world changed. . . .
All that I knew on that day was that I felt my mind awaken." The
88-year-old daughter of Italian immigrants to New York astutely
perceived the Christian ideals within her elementary school assign-
ments, which were studded with Longfellow: "Without being
taught religion to children of different faiths, we all imbibed the
religious teachings." Overtly religious applications tended to cut
across canon boundaries, resulting in another example of eclectic
reading: for instance, a Baptist minister chronicled his reliance on
British and American works ranging from Kipling's conventionally
pious—and conventionally rhythmic—"Recessional" to Robinson
Jeffers's disillusioned, unrhymed "Shine, Perishing Republic."[59]

For such individuals, poems were "treasures" and "possessions"
cherished over time for their wisdom and solace. As several letter-
writers indicated, they also signified the status of the poet as com-
panion or intimate. "The poems have remained friends thru the de-
cades," a Texas resident wrote. "At changing times in my life they
have said different things to me, and similarly I to them. Now I'm
retired and we don't need to say much to each other; but I remem-
ber them lovingly, and the parts of our relationship which I can ver-
balize and also the parts which I cannot." That language coexisted
with a deeper response: the acknowledgment that poetry mitigated
a perception of cosmic isolation. "The poems I keep with me," a
woman who finished high school in 1941 confided, "all seem to en-
capsulate certain moods, or seasons. I do say them often to my-
self—they give me great comfort or an awareness of the universal
human condition (in other words, 'I'm not alone')." Even as chil-
dren, some readers came to that conclusion: "I was able to identify
with the poet and know I was not alone or unique in my feelings,"
wrote one man. "Not a bad thing for a twelve-year-old boy to
know."[60]

Several respondents also testified that they attained the aesthetic benefits that teachers ascribed to the recitation, explicitly mentioning rhythm, sound, and imagery as a source of delight. Some appreciated the "precision" of well crafted lines; others drew analogies to the satisfactions of listening to music. "I still enjoy the measured rhythm of it," wrote a man who learned "Paul Revere's Ride" as a sixth-grader in 1948 or 1949. Certain readers, perhaps influenced by progressive pedagogy, counterposed enjoyment of the "tune" of verse to engagement with meaning. "I must have had some dim idea," explained one who completed eighth grade in 1933, "that poems do not need to mean anything, that poetry was . . . a kind of incantation." Yet others declared, "I loved the sounds and the ideas." The singer Julius LaRosa reported a "never-ending memory" linking "Invictus" with a damaged World War II aircraft carrier; from his teachers, he learned to relish both "the beauty and power" of language.[61]

Thus both mainstream and progressive educators would have been gratified to know that, as their students remade the texts they transmitted, at least some of them grasped and valued the moral ideals and aesthetic content which the teachers' own remakings had privileged. Both instructors and pupils embraced the figure of the poet as sage, as guide to conduct and belief. A few students even re-enacted a favorite text: two individuals described taking the Staten Island ferry in order to reproduce Edna St. Vincent Millay's innocent exuberance (being "very young and very merry") and sophisticated behavior (staying out all night). That activity was perhaps the most literal demonstration that, in keeping with pedagogical expectations, for many readers the message and form of a poem were intrinsic to its meaning and significance.[62]

Yet just as the procedures for learning verse in school served ends not necessarily connected to the genre as literature, the most striking facet of the responses to the query was the frequency with which respondents ascribed to the recitation consequences unrelated to a particular poem's moral or aesthetic properties—effects that one might call not intrinsic but extraneous to its substance, import, or sound. That is, some readers remade texts by assigning them social and personal uses that derived more from the act or site of reading than from the words on the page. The term "recitation exercises" itself suggests an instrumental function. The speaking contests mentioned earlier are a case in point: people who recalled competitions such as the one sponsored by the Texas Interscholastic League during the 1930s located the importance of the event in the fact that it enabled participants from different regions to mingle with one another. As a man who attended a small-town Wisconsin high school in the early 1940s reported, the state contests in "interpretive reading" and "choral reading" helped "lead me to a world beyond the backwater slough in which I lived." Something of the same effect resulted from joining the Literary Explorers Club, a venture of the 1930s that linked students to a national network of members, each of whom was required to memorize twenty-five poems from a "Treasure Chest" in order to advance through "degrees." In other words, for those informants the primary significance of reciting verse—and in a sense the meaning of the text—lay in the benefits conferred by the act of reading itself.[63]

Similarly, despite the progressive educators' concern with spiritual growth, readers retrospectively judged the recitation to be a useful lifelong aid to getting ahead in the business world. The notion that memorization provided "mental training," a secondary goal for many educators, assumed primary importance for both men and women, who reported deriving "confidence" from the process as well. "I have never in subsequent years," one prize elocutionist asserted, "felt any reticence or undue nervousness about addressing large or small audiences." (His reward was a solid brass bust of Shakespeare which his mother used as a doorstop.) Hamlin Garland's lines about manly triumph ("Do you fear the force of the wind?") would "flash into my thoughts," a company president indicated, both as a newspaperboy and, years later, "before going into a corporate boardroom."[64]

Respondents mentioned other applications of poetry learned in school—some practical, some more contemplative—that were ambiguously related to the poet's sentiments, if not entirely severed from them. Before charting such additional uses, however, it is worth pausing to consider how even the instances just cited defy easy classification. In the Garland case, the poem's message about being a man seems integral to its function as executive weaponry; by contrast, for the cultivation of mental agility or confidence, almost any lines will do. In any event, the distinction between intrinsic and extraneous meaning is unavoidably fuzzy, because one may sometimes invoke a poem in a setting which seems utterly at odds with its manifest content but which nevertheless permits the reader access to its emotional impact. For example, a woman who reported that recalling "The Daffodils" ("I Wandered Lonely as a Cloud") helped her endure an abortion was not primarily engaged in considering the delights of nature, yet the image of dancing flowers may have furnished her the same solace, on the operating table, that the poet achieved on his "couch."[65] That is, the poem may have served as more than an anesthetic, although it is impossible to tell from the reader's circumscribed remarks how much Wordsworth's language mattered. More generally, while the words of a text might seem irrelevant to readers' responses, the apprehension merely of mood and feeling, as progressive educators had recommended, could remain a pertinent aspect of its meaning. Furthermore, even when a poet's words appear to have been entirely unrelated to their use, respondents were never completely indifferent to what they were saying; although a few conceded that they could achieve an intimate relation to the text through "lulling" or "stirring" rhythms without understanding a poem's sense, in this sample more readers indicated that modernist obscurity defined alien territory.[66]

To proceed cautiously, then: in the category of extraneous effects belong several more instances of recitation as anesthetic or diversion—among them, to fall asleep or stay awake,[67] provide relief from dental or medical procedures,[68] offset "gloom" or stress,[69] alleviate boredom,[70] break obsessive rumination,[71] get through a plane ride,[72] overcome a stutter,[73] deflect anxiety,[74] or "block out unpleasant life circumstances."[75] "As a lonely young adult in a remote mining camp," a 90-year-old man reported, "I found myself recalling [certain] poems on restless nights as a sort of soothing pastime."[76] The recourse to poetry under these conditions attests to the continuing life of the educators' "storage" or "treasure" model of reading verse (although in these cases the value of the memorized lines lay in their instrumental provision of "comfort" rather than in the "guidance" they offered). The "treasure" metaphor, in addition to appearing in the description of the Literary Explorers Club, turned up explicitly in ten readers' letters and gave shape to many more. As one soldier, educated in the 1940s, recalled about walking guard duty years later, "where one found oneself totally alone for two hours at a stretch, without being able to speak or read, this lode of memorized poetry was mined for pleasure and as a means to overcome boredom. I have always been grateful for this mental treasury that . . . is still a part of me."[77]

Readers reported a second set of largely extraneous uses that revolved around the family. That subject is discussed in a later chapter in the context of poetry reading at home, but it is worth noting here that the school was the source of much of the verse that one generation of a family recited to another. In fact, the school recitation supplies a vivid instance of the interpenetration of the school and the domestic realm. As Clarence Poe, the longtime editor of the *Progressive Farmer,* put it in his autobiography, "The mothers and fathers of my day did not deride Longfellow's 'Psalm of Life' as being too 'moralistic.' Thus when my mother had me 'learn by heart' . . . Longfellow's lines, 'Lives of great men all remind us, we can make our lives sublime,' it was not strange that I included the phrase in one of my original compositions for Friday evening recitation, adding, 'I want to make my life sublime; don't you?'" Yet when parents attended assembly programs featuring their children's performances, the emotional tenor of the familial relationship between speaker and listener could outweigh the sagacity of the poet. One of the respondents in the sample, for instance, the son of a New York City police officer, most vividly recalled not what poem he read at a school assembly but rather "catching a glimpse of my father and mother in the throng" as he finished saying it; "the look of approval on my father's normally stern face," he explained, "spoke a volume to me that day." Another reader poignantly expressed the way in which a text imported from the classroom could signify the bond that constituted the family unit. "In 1939," she wrote, "I remember coming home from the fourth grade determined to memorize the poem about Columbus that begins, 'Behind him lay the gray Azores . . .' As I was stumbling through the first few lines, my father began saying the poem, and said it to the end. With feeling. That glimpse of continuity and linkage between my father and me has stayed with me these fifty-six years."[78]

That example discloses as well the contribution of schoolroom poetry reading to the formation and maintenance of identity. Regardless of a work's content, several readers echoed this theme by conceptualizing poems not only as "treasures" or "possessions" but also as virtually physiological attributes; poetry, these individuals remarked, "had become a living part of" their being. Even verse assigned as punishment became "imprinted on the mind" and "a part of" one reader, a biologist. A great-granddaughter of Nathaniel Hawthorne, 82 years old at the time of the query, quoted a phrase from "I Wandered Lonely as a Cloud" to convey the bodily sensations that memorized lines seemed to create: "They flash upon that inward eye / Which is the bliss of solitude." Those effects were consistent with the progressive educators' prescription for apprehension of the text.[79]

The role of memorized verse in self-definition was particularly evident in respondents' remarks about the ways in which poetry highlighted the stability of identity over a lifetime. "The depth of feeling in these poems," a New Jersey woman explained, "moved me then—at sixteen or seventeen—and still do [*sic*] at sixty-eight." On this point, one reader's anecdote is especially powerful. When cancer drugs disoriented her father, she brought him back from dementia in part by reading Kipling: "The rhythm and old familiar words were beloved, reassuring and confirming of some sense of continuity of self and self's concerns. . . . Memorized poetry played a part in helping his death to be a human one." Less dramatically, schoolroom poems were "triggers to the past" that enabled individuals to see themselves whole, while engaging the facility for long-term memory that often functions in older people better than short-term recall. Frequently, a lover of Longfellow announced, picking up a poetry book allowed him to feel himself back in the world of his youth. Although this reader employed it, the word "nostalgia" does not fully capture this mood.[80]

In addition, as was true for the "poetry meets" described earlier, the recitation contributed to identity formation by placing the self in wider contexts. Writing about her education in Ithaca, New York, from 1933 to 1946, one respondent saw performances of "Abou Ben Adhem," "Old Ironsides," and Lindsay's "Abraham Lincoln Walks at Midnight" as aspects of her school's "great emphasis" on "community-building ritual." Others mentioned the "common cultural grounding" the curriculum supplied. The sense of belonging which the recitation could create was not part of every reader's experience in the classroom: a few informants found speaking verse an "agony" that isolated them from their peers; one referred to the "devastated feeling of aloneness" when standing before an assembly. Yet many remarked that the practice fostered closeness among classmates who sweated through each other's nervous delivery. (It also drew together scoffers who taunted a high school boy for his love of the genre.) More important, the lines readers retained in their heads furnished the opportunity, long after graduation, for social exchange on the basis of shared experience. As a testimony to the national curriculum, readers described striking up friendships in retirement communities and tourist groups after impromptu unison recitations of "The Lay of the Last Minstrel" or "I Wandered Lonely as a Cloud."[81]

It would be simplistic to interpret those episodes of mutual discovery only as moments when members of the middle class implicitly signaled their shared power to one another, because it is equally possible to see the text overriding class barriers by providing a common language. Yet something of what Roger Chartier has referred to as reading that offers "ways to signify difference" seems to be at work in such encounters, in which the "shock of recognition" both enables former strangers to form new bonds and perforce excludes others. In some cases, schoolmates rekindled attenuated relationships by quizzing each other—with much laughter— about texts learned decades earlier. Like the banter surrounding a request to watch home movies, even the negative language in which readers characterized their current performances—"boring" their friends, "indulging" themselves, committing "recitation crimes"— suggests a conventional and hence reassuring pattern that confirmed individual and social identity. In all those instances, again the literal meaning of the lines on the page seems secondary to the transactions encompassed by the readers' behavior.[82]

Finally, a half-dozen readers explicitly claimed that the recitation shaped collective identity by buttressing certain shared values that did not necessarily permeate the text. One informant announced that in hindsight poetry reading seemed a behavior that resembled taking tea—that is, a sign of class pretensions. Less pejoratively, a woman educated in Indiana from 1935 to 1948 declared that memorizing poems in school was not only a "civilizing and unifying experience"; the task also reinforced "the idea that poetry was something that an educated person should be familiar with and enjoy." Some readers were aware that this definition of "civilization" carried gender expectations; one man confessed that he studied poems to "impress girls," while a feminist respondent averred that the speaking choir taught young women the "loyalty and obedience" that society demanded.[83]

Whether they experienced the schoolroom recitation as confining or broadening, however, these individuals understood that their youthful engagements with poetry helped to define them in relation to others. Even those who emphasized the moral or aesthetic dimensions of the practice recognized themselves as part of a community of readers. The sense that they belonged to a vanishing era reinforced that communal bond. Overwhelmingly, the respondents displayed both distress that students today no longer memorized verse and regret about the attendant loss of commonality. This result—a diminishing population reading beside the lamp— was not the one for which educators in search of cultural stability had hoped, but it partially explains the numerous expressions of gratitude for the chance to answer the query: "I have been waiting all of my adult life," one woman declared, "for someone to ask the question you pose."[84]

Competing Modes of Reading in the 1940s and 1950s

In the years during and immediately following World War II, new pedagogical trends partially reshaped the practices that had governed poetry reading during the period when most of the query respondents were in school. One was the trickle-down effect of the New Criticism's infiltration into college-level English courses. The hallmarks of the New Critic's mode of reading—precision, rigor, careful attention to the workings of poetic form and language, and an insistence, with Eliot, on poetry's "difficulty"—were a direct reaction to the unsatisfying premises of both the analytical and "experience" approaches. New Criticism was itself a type of close analysis, but its partisans rejected their predecessors' emphasis on dissection of a text to discover a message or moral that could be separated from the poet's means of expression. They also disavowed the idea that a poem possessed as many meanings as it had readers. An early, influential articulation of this position was I. A. Richards's *Practical Criticism: A Study of Literary Judgment* (1929). Richards, a British scholar, attacked the "misleading" consequences of "the reader's being reminded of some personal scene or adventure, erratic associations, the interference of emotional reverberations from a past which may have nothing to do with the poem." To counter that outcome, he systematically surveyed undergraduates' responses to a series of poetic texts, interrogating and refuting the students' interpretive assumptions. Richards distinguished between two types of meaning—"what seems to be said" to the reader and the "mental operations of the person who said it"; his goal was to improve techniques for comprehending the latter, which he saw as a prerequisite for evaluative criticism. Notably condescending toward his subjects, Richards condemned both "careless, 'intuitive' reading and prosaic, 'over-literal' reading"— that is, both "experience" and moralism—while exposing the sources and perils of sentimentality. Animated by the New Critical doctrine that "poetic rhythm" was inextricably bound to "sense," he also discouraged classroom recitation of verse on the grounds that it drowned out the "rhythm of the mental activity" through which individuals arrived at "not only the sound of the words but their sense and feeling." Poetry reading, Richards insisted throughout, was a "craft" requiring "instruction and practice," the evidence of which his student sample largely failed to exhibit.[85]

In 1938, two American poets in the forefront of the New Criticism, Cleanth Brooks, Jr. and Robert Penn Warren, sought to rectify that situation in the United States by issuing *Understanding Poetry: An Anthology for College Students*. In a prefatory "Letter to the Teacher," Brooks and Warren differentiated their recommended mode of reading verse from those they identified as in common use: paraphrase of content, biographical and historical study, "inspirational and didactic interpretation," and (overcorrecting for the first three approaches) treatment of a poem's technical elements in isolation from the poet's "total intention." The word "experience" remained important to their critical vocabulary, but only in the sense that "the poem itself is an experience," not as a term denoting the contribution of readers to meaning. Furthermore, while detection of theme, emotion, and meter all had a place in the interpretation of a poem, Brooks and Warren argued that teachers should never discuss these matters without taking into account the "organic" relationship of these qualities to one another. On a "scale of ascending difficulty," they organized their volume around a series of poems which they subjected to the New Critics' trademark close reading. In that way they strove to equip students with the "critical apparatus" necessary to grasp poets' purposes and assess their skills. They also revitalized the study of symbols and images, which some advocates of the "experience" curriculum had set aside.[86]

Within that framework, the editors pointed out not only misguided or commendable reading practices but also "bad" and "good" verse. Thus Longfellow's "A Psalm of Life," which they referred to as "very bad," figured in *Understanding Poetry* only as an occasion to describe the pitfalls of "message-hunting" without attending to the poet's form and language. "If the advice is what the poem has to offer," Brooks and Warren queried, "then we can ask why a short prose statement of the advice itself is not as good as, or even better than, the poem, itself." (They were equally dismissive of the idea that poetry entailed "pure realization" or a "beautiful statement of some high truth.") In a memorably devastating inspection of Kilmer's "Trees," Brooks and Warren took apart each of the poet's metaphors—the tree's roots are a human's mouth, the branches are "leafy arms," the tree is a "sucking babe," a "girl with jewels in her hair"—to indict Kilmer for failing to think clearly about the "implications" of his imagery. (It was this procedure that Ciardi would follow in condemning Anne Morrow Lindbergh.) All of Brooks and Warren's explications rested on their determined effort to focus on the good poet as an artist in control of the text—as one who has "assumed a particular view to the exclusion of other possible views," adopted certain words and rhythms for particular purposes, "developed the implications" of images—rather than on the reader as recipient of either precept or impression.[87]

Both Richards and his American successors implicitly faulted English teachers for lengthening the distance between modernist poets and ordinary readers by failing to convey how to read for complexity (although Richards's tone in particular also suggests the modernists' embrace of alienation). *Practical Criticism* differed from *Understanding Poetry,* however, in clearly enunciating the social implications of its author's findings. Richards attributed the widespread "decline" in mental agility he inferred from his subjects' responses to a too-rapid diffusion of print among heterogeneous cultural groups, which led in turn to pressures for homogenization at an "inferior" level. "It may well be a matter of some urgency for us, in the interests of our standard of civilization," he remarked, "to make this highest form of language"—that is, poetry—"more accessible. . . . As the other vehicles of tradition, the family and the community, for example, are dissolved, we are forced more and more to rely upon language." In that regard, Richards circled back to a version of the same justification for poetry reading that had prevailed before the influx of progressive ideas: the view that individual and social benefits would accrue from the genre's capacity to shape and discipline the mind. Brooks and Warren, by contrast, replicated in their editorial remarks the tendency of New Critical analysis to pull away from social context toward exclusive preoccupation with the workings of the text: "Even if the interest is in the poem as a historical or ethical document, . . . one must grasp the poem as a literary construct before it can offer any real illumination as a document." Echoing the concern of Richards and others in Britain about the distinction between scientific and humanistic cultures, Brooks and Warren introduced *Understanding Poetry* with an exposition of the ways in which poetic speech differed from the communication of information. In addition, they argued for the importance of verse as a means of expressing and satisfying "common human interests." Yet beyond those vaguely social considerations they did not venture. It remained for a subsequent generation of scholars to indicate the institutional and political uses that the New Criticism's purportedly apolitical orientation served: its suitability to the increased size of university English courses in the 1950s; its masking of gender and class biases; its reassertion of the critic's power as arbiter of taste.[88]

By the late 1950s, teachers who had learned to read poetry in college under New Critical tutelage had begun to import close reading practices into the English curricula of better American high schools. Nevertheless, for all the later reaction against the dominance of New Criticism in literary studies, elementary and secondary school materials of the years surrounding World War II also reveal a different trend that took shape despite the New Critics' best attempts to oppose it: namely, the renewed effort to reduce poems to their instrumental content and to classify them thematically. Such categories included not only "The Happiness of Home-Keeping Hearts" but also, for example, "Extending our Experience with Respect to Community Living" (under which the 1939 Montgomery County curriculum placed both "Paul Revere's Ride" and "Evangeline") and "Developing a Feeling of Pride and Appreciation for the Nation of Today" (which encompassed all the examples of early modernism in the 1933 Chicago course of study). As the United States faced the rise of fascism and, later, the Cold War, the themes adopted by educators and textbook authors once again invested poems that had long occupied a place in the school curric-

Student at the Lincoln School, New York City, in 1942 reciting an original poem about Brazil to foster Pan-American understanding. Library of Congress.

ulum with new messages. "America may be in danger of becoming smug and gullible and materialistic," the 1939 Fort Worth course of study declared by way of introduction to a section entitled "Spirit of the Western World," but "there is as yet within her the leaven of democratic and religious principles which will protect her from the various 'isms' that threaten the world." The poems that followed included Carl Sandburg's "Prayers of Steel" as well as excerpts from *The Bay Psalm Book* and Whitman's *Leaves of Grass*. The same curriculum listed "Abou Ben Adhem" as an example of "World Fellowship," while "Sea Fever" served to ingrain this lesson: "England has been the democratic leader—meeting the challenge of the sea. The future distribution of the air and sunshine may need such leadership." More generally, the assembly program recommended in 1945 for high school students by the state of Oregon linked poetry to similar ends: proposals for the theme "The American Way of Life" included "choral reading, individual reading of poetry, short talks on the theme, and music which represents America." In the same period, the St. Paul educators planning for students on the regular track regarded "Evangeline" as a contributor to the United States' "good neighbor" policy," assigning it under the heading "Know Your Neighbors in the Americas." These uses resuscitated the patriotism prominent in nineteenth- and early-twentieth-century poetry instruction, but gave it the internationalist twist the 1940s and '50s seemed to require.[89]

The postwar assumption that most American children required schooling for "life adjustment" further strengthened the reduction of poems to theme. The proponents of the "life adjustment" curriculum, convinced that education should entail "social efficiency," lobbied to revamp schooling to emphasize vocational training and preparation for family and civic life. With the "pure" study of the humanities thus under siege, a thematic treatment of literature linking it to "knowledge of, practice in, and zeal for democratic processes" provided the justification for teaching it at all. For "life adjustment" advocates, memorization and drill, already modified by progressive prescriptions, were further marginalized as the aim of fostering inward discipline receded even more. (The irony was that the nineteenth-century educators who had endorsed memory gems thought that *they* were preparing students for life.) Yet in some respects, older pedagogical rationales reappeared in new guises. As the St. Paul curriculum writers observed in 1946, the importance of helping pupils to cultivate "self-integration" (a need heightened, they implied, by the atomic age) made Henley's "Invictus," Browning's "Pippa Passes," Emerson's "Self-Reliance," Anna Hempstead Branch's "The Monk in the Kitchen," or Henry Van

Dyke's "Work" valuable as sources of the "personal philosophies" that students would ostensibly require as adults.[90]

The curricular innovations of the mid-twentieth century thus dissolved into the same sort of uneven, mixed picture of actual practice that had characterized the introduction of the "experience" mode. A 1946 Columbia Teachers College dissertation entitled *A Critical Study of a Group of College Women's Responses to Poetry* underscores the point. The author, Allys Dwyer Vergara, tried to identify the factors that shaped readers' reactions to poems. As enamored of social science methods as previous investigators had been, she devised a series of tests revealing responses to verse, which she administered to three groups of women undergraduates. Vergara's project is of interest partly because of her own assumptions, which indicate both the evolution and the constancy of curricular content and interpretive methods since the late nineteenth century. She also framed her experiments by reiterating a premise that might have been extracted from the pages of a memory gem compilation: that verse should be "studied for moral, social, intellectual, and aesthetic values." Regarding the contributions of "experience" to meaning, she conveyed mixed messages, resembling the transitional figures of the 1910s: on the one hand, her major (and hardly remarkable) finding was that "a rich experience"— by which she meant, for example, travel, knowledge of the arts, "maturity"—increased the comprehension of poetry; on the other hand, like the New Critics, she insisted that the wide variability in the personal histories readers brought to poems did not legitimize equally wide variability in interpretation. Some meanings that students formulated were "far-fetched" and unacceptable. If the American school curriculum as a whole was, by the mid-twentieth century, a "hybrid" of successive theories, Vergara's dissertation (an exercise, after all, that certified her to train English teachers) exhibited the effects of that process in microcosm.[91]

Vergara's book also offers a hint of the mentalities her subjects brought to her investigation. Although some of her interviewees revealed that they regarded modernist poets as alien obscurantists, most were comfortable with the idea that understanding poetry involved puzzling over texts. A striking facet of her study is the frequency with which the students remarked that they assumed poems contained symbols, even when they could not explain how the symbolism functioned. That is, by the early 1940s (when Vergara conducted some of her research) the diffusion of modernism had attuned undergraduates to expect linguistic complexity in literature and the absence of a readily accessible message or moral. As one of the young women, a devotee of T. S. Eliot, remarked, "I love this new trend in poetry. It says so much in terse, piquant phrases. Those who say one must dig for meaning are not, perhaps, so learned as they should be, because so much of this poetry is dealing in universals and symbols." Vergara observed that this reader also tended to praise the "modern" because she thought it "culturally correct" to do so. In that respect, the student resembled those about whose "general approbation" of modernism Wyndham Lewis had complained.[92]

Nonetheless, such bows to what they perceived as their teachers' expectations did not prevent Vergara's subjects from making poetry their own. Because her questionnaires did not ask readers to comment on their attachment to particular poems over time, one cannot say whether metaphors of storage or cultivation remained salient for them. Yet in Vergara's report one occasionally glimpses the basis for the same uses—both intrinsic and extraneous to the text—that respondents to the *New York Times* query described more fully, in that one can see the students appropriating verse to suit their own thoughts and feelings. Hilda, whose replies to the questionnaire incurred Vergara's observation that her preoccupation with romance and marriage "distorted" her judgment, found insights into love in almost every poem she read. Harriet apologized for being "so taken up with the vividness of [Wilfred Owen's] description [in "The Show"], the horror of it," that she "failed to grasp his point." She liked best one of Walter de la Mare's poems containing a mermaid because it made her "think of the various times [she had] watched the sea from a battleship deck or from the shore and just longed to have been born a boy like my brothers and to have followed the lure of the sea." Marion, writing about

H. D.'s "Song," declared (to Vergara's dismay), "There may be some symbolism in the poem relative to a captured bird, although I think it is just a beautiful nature poem." Taken together, Vergara's assumptions and the young women's comments summarize two lessons from the schoolroom about poetry reading: first, that the cultural values and social functions with which educators inflected poetry at that site colored the meanings their students derived from reading verse; and second, that neither poetic nor pedagogical fashion could contain the responses of the children whom teachers invited to listen.[93]

chapter eight

I Am an American

Poetry and Civic Ideals

❧ ON JANUARY 21, 1961, the 86-year-old Robert Frost stepped up to a lectern outside the United States Capitol to read a poem he had written for the presidential inauguration of John F. Kennedy. The invitation to participate in the ceremony was the outcome of Frost's particular circumstances at the time: he was serving as Honorary Consultant in the Humanities to the Library of Congress (having finished a term as Consultant in Poetry); he had publicly hailed Kennedy's New England fortitude; and he had established relationships with several prominent members of Congress. The story goes that Kennedy, hearing the idea for including Frost in the inauguration, worried aloud that the poet would upstage him, and that is exactly what happened. Frost began reciting the first lines of "Dedication" (the draft title of the poem he had composed for the event), found that the glare of the sun prevented him from continuing, and then recouped by joking about Vice President Lyndon Johnson's effort to come to his aid. When the audience's applause and laughter subsided, he movingly delivered from memory his 1942 poem "The Gift Outright," with which he had planned to follow "Dedication." The next day the *Washington Post* reported that Frost "in his natural way" had stolen his listeners' hearts.[1]

While the quirks of Frost's unassuming persona were what made the episode memorable—"I'll just have to get through as I can," he had mumbled upon realizing that he could not see—his appearance on the inaugural program nevertheless drew upon several long-standing traditions affiliating poetry with civic ideals. Although Frost had initially declined to write anything new for the day, he changed his mind, and the result (later titled "For John F. Kennedy His Inauguration") belongs to the corpus of American occasional verse as much as Emerson's Phi Beta Kappa poem. Moreover, Frost's text served the multiple purposes that poetry reading at civic sites had often carried out since at least the late nineteenth century. As Kennedy well understood, Frost's appearance lent prestige to the ceremony, permitting politicians to take on the aura of sage and seer. (Had Frost continued reading "Dedication," the crowd at the inauguration would have heard him make that association explicit: the poem identified the first four American presidents as "founding sages" and "consecrated seers.") In addition to transforming public officials into bearers of high culture, the reading reiterated the poet's standing as a figure of national importance. As Frost wrote in the first lines of "Dedication," "Summoning artists to participate / In the august occasions of the state / Seems something for us all to celebrate. / This day is for my cause a day of days." (In the case of Kennedy, Frost's presence underscored the interest in the arts shared by the President and his wife, which was good both for poetry and for Kennedy's image.) Most important, Frost's performance, like virtually all verse reading as a civic act, aimed to arouse in the listener feelings of loyalty and pride. "The Gift Outright" was a patriotic poem conveying, in the words of Frost's biographer Jeffrey Meyers, "a nation's spiritual and physical union with the land and its manifest destiny to complete the conquest of the continent."[2]

Frost's execution of those functions connects his participation in the Kennedy inauguration to still another tradition governing the civic uses of poetry in the United States: the repeated (if unwitting) expression of two abiding tensions in American culture. The first of these is easy enough to see in the lines of "Dedication" expressing Frost's gratitude for the invitation, as well as in Harriet Monroe's

"Columbian Ode" crusade: it concerns whether the arts, and po-
etry in particular, are marginal or central to national life. That is-
sue, which influenced decisions in the late nineteenth and early
twentieth centuries about the structure of civic events, forms a sec-
ondary theme of the discussion that follows. The other tension lies
buried in "The Gift Outright" and relates to the assertion of a na-
tional creed. The text's reliance on the first person plural—"The
land was ours before we were the land's"—presumes a shared alle-
giance to a single entity, as does the image contained in the poem's
title: the "people" giving themselves wholeheartedly to their coun-
try. Yet as both historians and political scientists have recently
pointed out, American invocations of democracy and equality for
all have often clashed with the exclusionary and discriminatory
policies enshrined in the Constitution and in statute books. Fur-
thermore, immigrants to the United States (in part responding to
those policies) did not always surrender "outright" to their adopted
nation.

That second set of complexities, embedded in Frost's language,
becomes more apparent in considering another patriotic text, one
that remained a staple of the memory gem repertoire in the year
Frost published "The Gift Outright": the sixth canto of Sir Walter
Scott's "The Lay of the Last Minstrel." Scott asks: "Breathes there
the man with soul so dead / Who never to himself hath said, / This
is my own, my native land!" Those words, and the ones that fol-
low, associate patriotic fervor with religious faith by locating its
source in the living "soul," and condemn as patriotism's antithe-
sis the individualism of a person "concentrated all in self." On
grounds of ahistoricism alone, one might argue that the canto was
problematic in the American milieu. Published in 1805, "The Lay
of the Last Minstrel" rests on local Scots legends and deals with
themes of chivalry, feudalism, and sorcery, not the obligation to up-
hold democracy. Yet Americans could—and did—read the sixth
canto in a way that evoked what Michael Ignatieff, Gary Gerstle,
and others have called American "civic nationalism": the belief
that they belonged by consent to a nation of free and equal citizens,
and that they owed to that nation their primary allegiance.[3]

Despite that potential of the text, however, Scott's poem can also prompt reflection on whether the ideal of a national community predicated on the absence of racial, gender, or ethnic hierarchies fully encompassed American concepts of citizenship. Even leaving aside the gender issue ("the man") to which modern readers have become sensitive, Scott's rhetorical question invites a number of challenges. Was "land" a reference to locality, region, or nationhood? In addition, what did the concept of one's "own land" mean to the descendants of slaves, whose experience often did not include land ownership? For urban workers, the double meaning of land as terrain and land as nation (on which "The Gift Outright" also depended) might be similarly dissonant. And for immigrants, "This is my own, my native land" might conceal the persistence of both the newcomers' divided loyalties and the nativism that prevented them from achieving their rights as Americans. Although most readers remained unaware of such ambiguities, thinking about Scott's poem can thus bring into view the existence of various shadings of civic nationalism—some more dependent on assimilation than others—as well as the "ethnic" or "racial nationalism" that made being American a consequence of possessing (or masking) the inborn traits constituting descent.[4]

The same tensions about national unity that Frost's and Scott's lines evoke in microcosm characterized Americans' appropriations of poetry for civic purposes generally. This was true even when the poems so employed made no mention of patriotic sentiments or of the United States. In the years between 1880 and 1950, verse transmitting civic ideals took many shapes, from the commemorative ode to the wartime radio broadcast; the tensions broke through most powerfully in the multiplicity of Americanization activities that reformers directed at immigrants in the early twentieth century. But whatever their form, civic uses of the genre were not simply empty ceremonials. Neither were they only expressions of the secular faith in a democratic creed that scholars have called American "civil religion," although that is part of their significance.[5] Rather, what those diverse practices had in common was their function as carriers of the competing assumptions from which Americans derived their understandings of themselves as citizens.

Poetry and Commemoration

Nineteenth-century Americans were prone to public ritual. To assure themselves of their noble past and glorious future (especially after the divisiveness of the Civil War), they bound themselves together through community observances that—in oratory, ceremony, and verse—sounded what Lincoln called "mystic chords of memory." Festivities for Arbor Day, Decoration Day, and presidents' birthdays spilled out of schools into municipal settings, and with them the recitations that characterized such holidays in the classroom. Crowds of residents might listen to speakers intoning the same texts as the ones students memorized—thematically suitable poems already in circulation. Alternatively, on civic anniversaries or at dedication ceremonies for buildings or monuments, audiences would customarily hear a poet or dignitary deliver lines commissioned for the event. In the latter case, the poem was often an ode (in title if not in Horatian or Pindaric structure)—that is, an example of the lyric form that, since the days of ancient Greece and Rome, had inspired exalted feelings at public celebrations. Other compositions were simply called, for example, "Centennial Poem." Typically, poetry reading occurred as part of the "literary exercises" that constituted the formal or official aspect of a community commemoration. Additional speakers at such exercises sometimes augmented the presentation of an ode or other rhyme by interpolating favorite poetic quotations into their orations and addresses.

Commemorative verse written expressly for localities assumed the audience's receptivity to the power of place; such texts were paeans to the history and promise of a village, town, or city. As one speaker explained in introducing the poem written in 1893 for the centennial of Bath, New York, the aim of the occasion was "to live over again, as it were, the years which have passed." Some poems singled out particular episodes in local lore. The centennial of Geneseo, New York, in 1890 featured a reading of "Red Jacket's Story," verses which retold the brave deeds of a Native American leader. Other poems offered panoramic views of a municipality's progress since its establishment. In nearby Mt. Morris, the 1894 centennial celebration centered around a parade arranged to highlight the improvements residents had witnessed over time: early on, a cart with a spinning wheel; later, a boy carrying a mailbag on horseback and an "Indian Chief," also on a horse; near the end, a "modern binder and reaper." Subsequently the townspeople gathered in the opera house, where they heard a poem by Mrs. Eunice H. Hall that metaphorically replicated the parade by describing the "march of progress" in unrhymed iambic pentameter. Still other commemorative verse strove for a more philosophical message by contrasting human accomplishments with the unchanging natural landscape. In Rochester, a 1912 centennial day event included a "Centenary Ode." The text centered on a dialogue between the city's statue of Mercury, identified as the god of commerce, and the Genesee River, symbol of timelessness. In addition to these local artifacts, texts appropriated to commemorate events of national significance—the 1889 reading of Whittier's "Vow of Washington" in New York at the one hundredth anniversary of the first president's inauguration, for example—could also work to cement loyalty to place, the place in such instances being the United States as a whole.[6]

As several historians have noted, by the 1890s parades and civic festivities that promoted local pride and national patriotism had acquired a larger strategic function: to foster social cohesion in the face of divisive ethnic, racial, and class affiliations. While holidays such as the Fourth of July had been occasions for raucous working-class entertainments since the antebellum period, the planners of later civic celebrations inflected these programs with their anxieties about growing immigration and urban disorder. This process of reconfiguration was gradual and widely variable, not only because of regional differences but also because business leaders were neither monolithic nor all-powerful; hence, in John Bodnar's words, "commemorations in some places excluded celebrations of patriotism and progress completely." Furthermore, especially after the turn of the century, leaders in some communities concluded that civic order required paying homage to ethnic diversity rather than suppressing it. A good—and relatively early—example of that approach comes from the Bi-Centennial Celebration of Richmond

County, held on New York's Staten Island in 1883. A parade representing "firemen, military, mechanics, civic and other organizations" signaled the mix of class and ethnic identities among the participants. A poem by James Burke cemented the point that all belonged to the community through ties of "Love": "Refuge from dangers, both natives and strangers, / Black, white or red, or the sons of Cathay, / All here abiding, in Friendship confiding, / Find welcome and weal in our Isle of the Bay!"[7]

Whether they mustered poetry to enshrine sameness or difference, the question remains why Americans felt compelled to include a patently literary form in commemorations at all. What did a poem add that a parade could not supply? One answer is that, along with the sermon or the oration, poetry could be reprinted in souvenir booklets or newspaper accounts; it could be saved and revisited. In that way, it gave weight and at least the promise of permanence to events that often went by in a day or two—with savvy publishers the immediate beneficiaries. As the Springfield (Massachusetts) *Daily Union* remarked in its coverage of the 1883 centennial in nearby Longmeadow, "It was remarked as a fine instance of journalistic enterprise that copies of the *Union* containing . . . reports of the forenoon addresses and poem, were on sale at the tent before the close of the afternoon exercises."[8]

Other advantages arose from the unique properties of the genre. Its capacity to disseminate images in brief, concentrated form made it an efficacious method of ingraining shared values. Moreover, the practice of the recitation enhanced the sacred overtones of holiday observances, sustaining both Christianity and civil religion. That function is particularly evident in Arbor Day programs, where the connection to nature often endowed the proceedings with an explicitly Protestant character. A mainstay of the public school calendar by the 1880s, Arbor Day intersected with wider civic projects such as the "City Beautiful" movement of the late nineteenth century. As Leigh Eric Schmidt has reported, in 1882 fifteen thousand residents of Cincinnati participated in a procession and "appropriate ceremonies" to plant and dedicate trees in a city park. The tree itself evoked biblical symbols like the tree of knowledge; it

An Arbor Day recitation in 1908. Library of Congress.

called up associations with God as creator of life; more than that, as Schmidt has put it, "Arbor Day could enact a ritual of repentance; the tree, like the cross, became the atonement." Verse on these themes frequently reinforced the holiday's religious dimension. Popular examples included William Cullen Bryant's "Forest Hymn" ("The groves were God's first temples . . .") and Joaquin Miller's poem declaring "In penitence we plant a tree." Yet the content of the text that tree-planters spoke aloud or heard recited was only one aspect of the way poetry served religion on Arbor Day. The ritualistic, prayerful quality of the act of recitation—especially when it demanded memorization on the part of the speaker and silence on the part of the audience—itself fostered civil religion even in the absence of theological allusions. The constancy of form integral to the recitation's ritual character also strengthened participants' sense of tradition and human connection by evoking recollections of the past—of schooldays, family gatherings, or previous public observances, perhaps, on Arbor Day, in the same grove of trees.[9]

One can make a similar point about Memorial Day (formerly Decoration Day) rites. The holiday's ubiquitous icon—the red poppy—derived from John McCrae's poem "In Flanders Fields"; Robert Haven Schauffler's 1911 anthology of selections suitable for the day included dozens of poetic texts honoring the nation's war dead. Many of these (Thomas Bailey Aldrich's ode on the unveiling of the Robert Gould Shaw memorial is a prime example) likened righteous sacrifice in wartime to Christian martyrdom. What W. Lloyd Warner famously described as Memorial Day's evocation of a "sacred symbol system" resulted, however, not so much from the language the day called forth but from the ceremonies—poetry reading among them—that organized that language publicly year after year.[10]

A poem also surpassed a speech or a parade in conferring an aura of refinement on commemorative events, and hence on the residents who attended them. By invoking a tradition that stretched back to ancient Greece and Rome, an ode implicitly reiterated the belief (or the hope) that American civilization resembled those classical repositories of both republican virtue and aesthetic achievement. The impressment of local "professors"—personifications of erudition—into service as reciters of verse could also help to certify refinement. This function of civic poetry was most visible at sites with ties to well-known authors. At the 1907 centennial festivities in Cooperstown, New York, for example, numerous readings of verse—including a poem Julia Ward Howe had composed for the occasion—fulfilled the planners' desire to "signalize the unique position" of the town in "the development of American literature."[11]

The same symbolic function attended the multiple references to poets and their works in the programs of the Boston Tercentenary in 1930. In this instance the relationship between schoolroom and civic forum was especially close: during the academic year students in English classes read prose and poetry "appropriate" to the commemoration; the following summer, so many people attended a series of "historical presentations" that headlines exclaimed "The Public Now at School in City Celebrations." The audience's education included tableaux with poetic accompaniments—for example, readings of excerpts from Bryant's "Thanatopsis" and Longfellow's "Hiawatha" while figures dressed as Native Americans appeared on stage. That and other frequent recourse to verse throughout Boston's Tercentenary—lines composed for exercises at Bunker Hill, Robert Grant's reading of his poem "The Puritan" on Boston Common, two odes published in newspapers, poetry and folk songs on "Ukrainian Night"—cumulatively proclaimed literariness an essential component of the city's identity.

At the culminating ceremony of the festivities, the dedication of a memorial to Boston's founders, Edwin Markham ("the poet of the occasion") delivered his official Tercentenary Ode. Markham had recited a revised version of his "Lincoln, the Man of the People" at President Warren G. Harding's dedication of the Lincoln Memorial in Washington eight years earlier; perhaps the note of culture momentarily offset Harding's reputation for corruption and vulgarity. In Boston, Markham's rhymed review praising "All you have been and all that you will be" made Poe, Longfellow, Lowell, and Emerson no less heroic than John Winthrop, James Otis, or Wendell Phillips. As if to act out and perpetuate the poet's role as exemplar of Boston's achievements, Markham himself took a place in the "Court of Honor" at the Boston Day parade.[12]

Despite the Boston planners' determination to recognize the "genius of our foreign-born citizens," one might contend that the cultured sensibility which the literary exercise symbolized was simply another sign of middle-class determination to stifle the disorderly behavior of workers and ethnic minorities. Yet to equate the refinement conferred by commemorative poetry merely with the repression of working-class exuberance would be to overlook a key aspect of the context in which the evolution of American holiday observances occurred: namely, the growth of commercialism along with social control. By the late nineteenth century, enterprising business owners had discovered that civic events offered ready access to potential customers, either directly by means of hucksters on the scene or indirectly through the sponsorship of entertainments. Thus the souvenir publication distributed as part of the Fourth of July celebration during Buffalo's semi-centennial in 1882 ("Fifty Years of Progress") amounted to a compilation of adver-

Edwin Markham at the dedication of the Lincoln Memorial in 1922. Library of Congress.

tisements for local companies. On Staten Island, the reading of the poem hailing Richmond County's diverse inhabitants competed with a procession of wagons promoting a grocery, brewery, and plumbing establishment; the famed editor and civil service reformer George W. Curtis (a local resident) was present along with George Ross, "the awning king." Commercial amusements exerted wide appeal. At the Cooperstown centennial, the afternoon literary exercises gave way, at night, to demonstrations of moving pictures on Main Street. While the reformers who complained of the "carnival atmosphere" on Patriot's Day in Lexington were the same individuals who sought to stabilize their own moral leadership, their advocacy of poetry reading as a commemorative practice was more than a ploy to preserve elite power; it also preserved a space for art that commerce threatened to obliterate. In that respect, the centennial ode might even be regarded as a small act of resistance to the consumer culture that surrounded and impinged on it.[13]

At the same time, with respect to the enhancement of prestige, the relationship between spoken verse and public taste was reciprocal: as Frost would later suggest at Kennedy's inauguration, civic celebrations dignified poetry as much as poetry elevated the occasion. In the earlier period, when technological innovation and mass production were rapidly expanding the material progress of which commemorative parades, orations, and odes themselves boasted, a public demonstration of Americans' spiritual and artistic attainments could seem superfluous beside a display of their practical knowledge and specialized skills. Those circumstances added to the challenges that the aging of the schoolroom poets and the rise of realism posed to poetry by the late nineteenth century.

In addition to Harriet Monroe's exertions prior to the Columbian Exposition, a fine symbol of the precariousness of the ode tradition comes from the celebration marking the one hundredth anniversary of the Battle of Concord in 1875. The event epitomized both the cultural power poets could exercise and their vulnerability to displacement—in this case literally. On the one hand, James Russell Lowell prevented Boston and New York newspapers from printing the ode he had written for the day so that it could appear first in the *Atlantic Monthly* (and presumably thus acquire the high culture cachet it deserved). On the other hand, the speakers' platform collapsed during the reading of the ode, "causing a momentary disorder and providing the newspaper reporters present with an opportunity for witticisms."[14]

The tensions attending the role of poetry in public life illuminate Bayard Taylor's reaction following his delivery of "The National Ode" at the Philadelphia Centennial the same year. Although most literary critics judged the poem a failure, the audience of 10,000 people responded warmly, first listening quietly and then bursting into shouts of approval. Taylor's and his wife's accounts of the event mingled pride, relief, and astonishment. "I never before saw the common people silenced, then inspired, by poetry," Taylor wrote George Boker. "As we went out through the mass, hundreds

of hard hands were stretched to me, and there was a continual suc-
cession of 'three cheers for the Poet!' It was simply amazing, and I
can yet hardly comprehend the effect." Some of Taylor's amaze-
ment may be attributed to the low expectations with which he had
undertaken the centennial project: he disliked writing occasional
verse, felt generally underappreciated, and knew that the ode com-
mission had invited him to compose the poem only after each of the
schoolroom poets had turned it down. (Whittier instead wrote lyr-
ics for a "Centennial Hymn.") But his comments, and especially his
wife's observation that the performance was a "real victory for Po-
etry," also suggest that his surprise proceeded from an awareness
of the commemorative ode's place as both a venerable and a threat-
ened ritual.[15]

Poetry as Pageantry

In the first decade of the twentieth century, a new kind of civic com-
memoration emerged alongside ceremonies and parades: the his-
torical pageant. Initially modeled on British reenactments of medi-
eval and Renaissance events, pageantry in the United States became
a project of progressive reformers intent on enhancing community
spirit and democratic citizenship. In particular, progressive educa-
tors who advocated organized play as a means to child-training,
and who had endorsed dramatics—including dramatized verse—as
an outlet for self-expression, welcomed the pageant as an opportu-
nity to extend the play philosophy beyond the school. Charles A.
McMurray, who had prescribed poetry as a "portal" to religion,
likewise endorsed pageantry for the active approach to history in-
struction it provided to students dressed as Pilgrims, presidents,
and the like. The format also seemed to offer all members of a com-
munity a collective ritual that would supply the unity and partici-
patory activity which industrialization had eliminated. Reformers
who, around 1908, sought to counter commercialism, reduce inju-
ries from fireworks, and maintain social order (in the name of de-
mocracy) by advocating a "Safe and Sane Fourth of July" were
early proponents of the movement. Subsequently, William Chauncy

Langdon, Percy MacKaye, Thomas Wood Stevens, and other "pageant-masters," working in small towns and urban centers, turned historical pageants into elaborate spectacles that affirmed continuity and a sense of heritage while celebrating progress.[16]

Pageantry was also one of several guises for the various Americanization campaigns directed at immigrants in the early twentieth century. (Other sites at which poetry became a resource for such campaigns included the women's club, the settlement house and, most elaborately, the school, as discussed in the following sections.) Although the term may suggest merely a coercive program to strip foreigners of their ethnic heritage, support for Americanization actually took both nativist and pluralist forms. Pageant organizers usually stressed tolerance and respect for immigrant cultures while striving to inculcate an overarching allegiance to the United States. That version of civic nationalism led them to see in the pageant format the opportunity for immigrants to merge their own folk traditions with representations of significant episodes in the nation's past. Integrating dance, music, and speech, pageant-masters thereby hoped as well to integrate, or submerge, class, ethnic, and racial tensions into a harmonious whole. The 1914 "Pageant and Masque of St. Louis," led by Stevens and MacKaye, did so in grand fashion: it involved a cast of 7,000, many from the city's immigrant groups, who staged the evolution of "social civilization" in a "model community." Up to 100,000 spectators at a time witnessed the "Pageant and Masque"'s five-hour performances.[17]

In certain respects, historical pageantry was a substitute for the practice of reciting poetry at commemorative festivities, and hence another indication of public ambivalence toward the genre. In a fictitious anecdote that incidentally highlighted the connection between the school recitation and its civic counterpart, Mary Master Needham (writing in 1912) introduced the benefits of pageants by depicting a young girl, Pollie, who lived in a southern Michigan town. Faced with preparing for the town's upcoming "anniversary" celebration, Pollie balks: "We don't want to learn any more pieces." Nothing kindles her enthusiasm until she and her schoolmates hear of the town's plans to personify its history through a pageant. In Needham's view, the participatory dimension of dramatic commemorations made them appealing alternatives to what she saw as the passivity inherent in recitation practices, for speakers as well as audiences.[18]

Yet in other respects pageantry was simply a new vehicle for poetry as civic speech, and hence a sign of the poet's tenacious cultural presence. To some observers, the pageant's structure and purpose—its epic proportions and "heroic" message—made it an inherently "poetic" form. Percy MacKaye's "lyric dramas" reflected that assumption, as well as his lifelong sense of himself as both sage and seer. Born in 1875, MacKaye was the son of Steele MacKaye, an actor and dramatist who once wrote that poets were "among the greatest benefactors of mankind." By the time he was a teenager, Percy had become a poet himself. In 1897, when he graduated from Harvard, he delivered a commencement address that assigned the playwright the obligation to create poetry in order to reveal fully the subtleties of the human condition. That identity—poet *and* playwright—governed all of MacKaye's subsequent professional activities. MacKaye frequently accepted commissions to write commemorative odes. At Carnegie Hall in 1914 he read his verses celebrating the builder of the Panama Canal, prompting a member of the audience—Walter Lippmann—to affirm MacKaye's role as sage by writing him the next day "that *poets are absolutely vital to the nation.*" As if to symbolize his greater willingness to sustain traditional forms than his early modernist friends possessed, in 1925 he even picked up at the last minute Frost's assignment to produce a poem commemorating the Battle of Concord when Frost declared that "he could not think of one."[19]

As his career developed, MacKaye increasingly found the genre of the drama more congenial to the expression of his visionary or seer-like tendencies, but his plays and masques remained founded on the conception of the poet as public servant. MacKaye's poems and lyric dramas were linked as well by his conviction that both drew their democratizing, reforming power from the delivery of the spoken word, whereby the texts became "intimately a part of the vital, throbbing, varied reactions of many thousands of people." The introduction to his St. Louis masque cast the "poet-dramatist" as "engineer," charged with coordinating "large rhythmic mass-movements of onward urge, opposition, recoil, and again the sweep onward" toward "an harmonious socialized state of human society."[20] MacKaye's effort to promote democratic ideals through the reading of poetry coincided with uses of the genre in two other settings: the women's club and the settlement house.

The Poetics of Reform: Clubwomen and Settlement House Workers

In 1898 Jane Addams, the founder of Hull House, and Martha Foote Crow, a clubwoman and authority on poetry who taught at the University of Chicago, participated together in a program at the Illinois Federation of Women's Clubs' annual meeting. From their distinct vantage points, Crow (whose subject that day was "the drama") and Addams addressed the "Interdependence of Progressive Influences in the Community." Their joint appearance nicely symbolizes not only their shared commitment to social reform but also how both the club and settlement house movements relied on literature and the arts to realize that commitment. Especially as each organization turned its attention to the Americanization of immigrants after World War I, verse reading was among the forms of cultural expression that seemed especially effective in bringing about their vision of society.[21]

Women's clubs had incorporated both literary study and social service into their programs since their inception in the late nineteenth century. Sarah Decker's famous pronouncement upon her inauguration as president of the General Federation of Women's Clubs in 1904—"Dante is dead . . . and I think it is time that we dropped the study of his Inferno and turned our attention to our own"—imposes too neat a separation between the educational aims of clubs in the 1890s and the civic-mindedness of subsequent ones. It is true that early women's clubs and reading circles were important institutions for disseminating literature in the name of self-culture, and that Dante as well as Tennyson and Browning loomed large among the subjects women tackled for that purpose.

Women's Literary Club of the Evening Recreation Center, PS 137, Manhattan, c. 1905. Milstein Division of United States History, Local History & Genealogy, The New York Public Library, Astor, Lenox and Tilden Foundations.

Yet the members' objectives were never entirely divorced from social improvement, because, as Jane C. Croly put it in her *History of the Woman's Club Movement in America* (1898), self-education entailed acquiring an understanding of "the working of a spirit of human solidarity" and "interdependence." Thus the "Longfellow evening" to which the African American Charleston (West Virginia) Women's Improvement League invited the public in 1900 fostered what Barbara Sicherman has called "vital engagement with the world . . . by uniting women temporally and physically." In addition, some African-American clubwomen regarded the production and dissemination of "race literature" as a key strategy for reversing racial stereotypes.[22]

By the same token, until 1920 (when it ceased publication) the General Federation's magazine, while reflecting the organization's greater interest in social work, regularly featured, along with verse by members, essays about poets and other literary figures that highlighted the aesthetic rewards of reading and writing. In 1917, well after community and philanthropic activities had come to outweigh literary study on women's club agendas, Martha Foote Crow, by then the Federation's "advisor on poetry," urged every club to read a poem at each meeting, "just as we have a selection on the piano." Her instructions about how to approach the text underscored the way in which women's groups provided a space that offered an alternative to academic or professional modes of reading: "Just read it off—let anybody read it—not with elocutionary effect at all, but like simple reading matter—reading it for what it says, not to make it sound grand!" Implicitly stressing poetry's accessibility, Crow further recommended that the poem be read twice and discussed to elicit "all the meanings that the lines have suggested to different members of the club." Throughout the 1930s, clubwomen also encouraged the creation of new verse by selecting poet laureates for their State Federations, with local clubs paying the traveling expenses for the laureates to give statewide readings.[23]

Nevertheless, in her didactic role Crow also aligned poetry reading with the more explicit civic concerns of the women's club at the height of the Progressive era. For the Federation's biennial meeting in 1917, Crow distributed lists of living American poets that she had helped prepare under the auspices of the Poetry Society of America; accompanying the lists was her declaration that present-day poetry commanded the clubwoman's attention because it expressed "our national mind and character." Her description of the qualities in contemporary verse that mirrored American traits included "love of native land," a "new attitude toward various important problems" such as immigration, and "intense sympathy for the oppressed." In the Federation magazine during the same period, Crow especially urged her constituency to read the works of present-day poets who wrote about the dispossessed—what Crow called "our great social burden." What is striking about Crow's outlook is that her sense of poetry's civic utility coexisted with affirmation of both "philosophical idealism" (her phrase) and innovations in form such as free verse. Instead of corroborating the view that, until assaulted by the vernacular diction and cold stare of modernist verse, a genteel, idealist poetry blocked the expression of what Andrew DuBois and Frank Lentricchia called "the impurities of experience," Crow's position represents a middle ground between "genteel" and "modern" extremes: her description of the "new movement" then engaging American poets looked backward to the seer enunciating "Absolute Truth" and forward to a "revolt" in form to transmit the plight of the working class.[24]

In the late 1910s and early 1920s, with the Red Scare, immigration quotas, and the achievement of nationwide women's suffrage on the horizon, the civic activities of women's clubs became another agency for Americanization. Clubwomen mustered poetry in support of that priority. The all-too-appropriately-named Mrs. True Worthy White, Chairman of the Federation's Department of Literature and Library Extension, called on members to brush up on their knowledge of "The America of the Poets" so as to pass their ideals to "resident aliens." In 1919, the New York State Federation sponsored a contest for the best poems on the theme of Americanization, with separate prizes for submissions by immigrants, children of immigrants, and Americans by both birth and parentage. The judges (who included Crow) received 212 entries. Although the nationwide General Federation reorganized its departments in 1920, Crow remained in charge of a Committee on Poetry and dedicated it to Americanization through the discussion of poems written in English about various nationalities.[25]

That same year Crow also approached friends and fellow writers about organizing a poetry festival in western Massachusetts. One of her contacts was the poet Anna Hempstead Branch, whose lengthy profile by Edwin Markham had been included by Crow in the Federation magazine. Branch was lukewarm about Crow's festival idea, but she shared the clubwoman's belief in poetry's civic possibilities. Born in 1875, Branch came from an old Connecticut family active in law and politics. Her mother, Mary Bolles Branch, wrote and illustrated children's books; her mother's father had been a poet. In 1897, upon graduating from Smith College, Branch attended the American Academy of Dramatic Arts in New York, from which she received a degree in dramaturgy in 1900. Over the next decade she published three books of poetry: *Heart of the Road* (1901), *The Shoes That Danced* (1905), and *Rose of the Wind* (1910). At the same time, she began volunteering at Christodora House, near Tompkins Square in lower Manhattan. Her activities there included reading verse to immigrant women and children and encouraging them to write their own poems. Within a few years she had become the most prominent advocate among early-twentieth-century settlement house workers of poetry's centrality to the nation's welfare, and particularly its utility in meeting the educational and spiritual needs of urban immigrants.[26]

The sensibility Branch brought to that work placed her firmly in the tradition of the seer: throughout her life, she exhibited strong mystical tendencies, which were intertwined in her case with Social Gospel Protestantism. Influenced by the Brownings and Christina Rosetti, Branch made attunement to the spiritual aspect of the universe essential to her concept of the poet, and hence to her own mission. In "Songs For My Mother," she explained: "God wove a web of loveliness / Of clouds and stars and birds, / But made not anything at all / So beautiful as words." Elsewhere (in drama and verse) Branch invoked the image of a female deity or "great mother," a beneficent Lady with "long golden hair and a bright blue dress" who comforted her children with "singing thoughts" while remaining "unseen." Apart from its Christian origins, that conceit of the poet-angel as beautiful woman may have had other sources. It suggests, first of all, Branch's familial ties and maternal longings. Extremely close to her mother, with whom she lived off and on after her father's death in 1909, Branch lost her only sibling (her brother) when she was thirteen, never married, had no children, and was romantically attached to other women. The Lady thus could be seen as capturing Branch's fantasy of mothering the next generation. Moreover, the angel with poetic gifts was, in a sense, an idealized version of what Vachel Lindsay, in a letter to Branch, called the product of the "truly cultured women's college." The graduates of institutions like Smith (or, somewhat later, Millay's

Vassar) participated in numerous activities—processions in white dresses, traditions such as Ivy Day and the Daisy Chain, nighttime outdoor dramatics featuring woodland sprites—that, at least rhetorically, reinforced and ritualized the assumption that women possessed a strong spiritual nature. Branch's editorship of Smith's literary monthly drew her closer to that aspect of college culture even as it enhanced her worldly skills.[27]

Yet Branch's seer-like qualities did not wholly define her frame of mind. Rather, her Christian mysticism was anchored in, and consistent with, another perspective fostered at Smith—one that enabled Branch to cast the poet as reformer as well as prophet. Like its sister campuses at the turn of the century, the college encouraged its students to apply their appreciation of beauty and of transcendent human emotion to the task of improving the lives of others. In contrast to the experience of Jane Addams fifteen years earlier, Branch did not have to endure a period of restlessness and turmoil before discovering a way to turn her college training to useful ends; her mentors taught Branch and her classmates that educated women were obligated to undertake social reform.

A letter Branch wrote to her mother in 1899 suggests both the visibility of her Smith loyalties in her work and the way in which the immigrant girls who frequented the settlement could bridge without apparent self-consciousness the distance between their economic circumstances and those of the volunteers. "Thursday evening," she reported, "I received a pressing invitation to go to . . . a meeting of the Sangster Club [named for the novelist Margaret Sangster], as guest and it turned out to be a 'Branch evening' that the girls had gotten up themselves. They read and recited some of my poems and . . . sang "Here's to Smith College" and "Here's to Ninety Seven" and "Here's to our Miss Branch" and I had to make a speech and tell them how it was that I began to write." Branch's "Sonnets for New York City," published in *The Shoes That Danced,* exemplified the translation of Branch's reform commitments into verse; their subject matter included a weary shopgirl who deserved compassion even though she flouted modesty and decorum.[28]

In the 1910s, Branch combined her ideals of spirituality and service in a series of projects that expressly made poets agents of social change. One of these was an effort to achieve international peace through an exchange of games by the world's children, for whom (echoing the imagery of the poet-angel) she imagined staging a "celebration of the Loved and Unseen." If that scheme sounds impossibly impractical, Branch herself regarded it as a move away from aestheticism and abstraction. "I believe the time has come," she explained, "when the poet is to be identified not merely as a man of vision but also a man of action and that poetry . . . is to be not only a thing of beauty, but of immediate and obvious usefulness." Poetry's promise of spiritual growth was not an alternative to reform, deflecting attention from the here and now; in Branch's view, it was a way to ameliorate social conditions.[29]

At Christodora, Branch pursued that promise by taking charge of a neighborhood newsletter and soliciting "College women" to underwrite publication expenses. She also operated the "Wonder Wagon," a traveling miniature theater that dramatized stories for children about the "Faery Man." Periodically, she read her own poems at the settlement, some of which she wrote for that purpose. In addition, she sponsored readings by Edwin Markham, Vachel Lindsay, Margaret Widdemer, and other "new poets" with whom she had forged connections. (Of Markham, she declared to her mother: "The east side audience goes wild over him.") Discerning the popularity of the readings, she thought at first of trying to mentor "the occasional real talent" among those in regular attendance. With some uncertainty, Branch subsequently adopted a less individualized approach: she started a club at Christodora dedicated to nurturing "lyrical expression" in boys and girls whose time for reflection often occurred on the subway after a hard day's labor. Then she enlisted Josephine Preston Peabody in setting up a second such club. Her underlying premise, she later remarked (borrowing from William Butler Yeats), was that poetry was the most practical of the arts, possessing an untapped "organizing value."[30]

As the turnout increased at presentations, club meetings, and classes in verse, Branch concluded that the genre was demonstrably

more than a "private spiritual experience"; it had been "proved to
be a communal interest." In 1919, she decided to strengthen that
interest by proposing the Poets' Guild, an autonomous entity based
at and coordinated by Christodora House. Its central feature was
that poets would act as "councillors" to the settlement's youth
clubs. Margaret Widdemer and her then-husband Robert Haven
Schauffler (mentioned earlier as the compiler of literature for holi-
day observances such as the Memorial Day collection) pronounced
Branch's plan a "lovely" one. Edwin Markham replied with char
acteristic effusiveness: "Joyfully, I join the lyric procession. Write
my name upon your roster in eternal ink—black ink long brewed
in some deep Vesuvian crater." Just before Christmas, Branch con-
vened the Guild's first official business meeting, consisting of
Markham, Peabody, Widdemer, Schauffler, and two other poets,
Witter Bynner and Gertrude Hall. As Branch put it in a letter to
John Masefield, the resultant Poets' organization was "in no sense
an ordinary poetry society or 'literary group.' We meet because we
are interested in social service, and in poetry[-]loving young peo-
ple of limited opportunity." In addition to those present at the
first meeting, Branch and her colleagues added to their ranks sev-
eral other poets "whose writings have shown an especial interest
in social conditions," eventually signing on, among others, Percy
MacKaye, William Rose Benét, Hermann Hagedorn, Sara Teasdale,
and Robert Frost. The only poet who initially declined on principle
was the loner Edwin Arlington Robinson. Three years later, how-
ever, he was listed in an article about the Guild as a club coun-
cillor.[31]

Like Crow's mixed messages about idealism and modernism,
Branch's emphasis on the Guild members' concern with "social
conditions" is an especially clear indication of the way the vary-
ing uses of verse confound the customary divisions scholars have
drawn in writing late-nineteenth- and early-twentieth-century liter-
ary history. Branch's efforts to recruit councillors tacitly endorsed
the lyrical transmission of ugliness, the questioning of convention
in conventional language, the spiritually inflected glimpse of pov-
erty or despair. The appearance of her own reform-minded poems

in Jessie Rittenhouse's *The Little Book of Modern Verse* (1913) likewise undermines Andrew DuBois and Frank Lentricchia's observation that nothing in Rittenhouse's collection was modern because all her selections "sustained an innocent ideal of sweetness, the voice of unadulterated song." (Neither, one might add, was Branch the epitome of innocence in her personal life: her posthumously published poems to her mentor Edith Thomas are bold evocations of sexual love.) The combination of romantic otherworldliness and realist social awareness is particularly evident in Branch's account of Josephine Preston Peabody's and Angela Morgan's role as Guild councillors. When Peabody, "standing behind the tall red candle which was called hers," recited one of her lines about the life-force represented by a flame, Branch wrote, "the beauty of her voice, that wonderful voice that carries within it those deep and singing sounds by which poetry is itself enriched, gave her share in the brief ceremony the solemnity of a ritual." Members of another club, which "rever[ed]" Morgan "as a sort of goddess," bragged to their friends that Morgan "belong[ed]" to them, that "she is our poet." The result was the beginning of a wider interest in poetry throughout the students' high school, and thus, Branch implied, the start of an improvement in the girls' lives.[32]

In 1920 the Poets' Guild embarked on its most noteworthy project, the distribution of previously published poems in a format first called the "Unbound Anthology" and, later, "Looseleaf Poetry." The idea was to make poetry readily affordable to workers and students by selling reprints of texts one leaf at a time, at a price of pennies per copy. In that way, Branch noted, "it is possible for everyone to make up his own anthology, and have a little personal collection of favorite poems." The low price was feasible because the strategy of keeping the sheets unbound circumvented several of the costs of republication in book form. The difference between loose-leaf and bound pages not only did away with the expense of binding but also convinced most authors and publishers to waive the usual permissions fees charged for reprinting. Out of support for the project's social service agenda, authors also agreed to forgo any income from sales; all revenue went back to the Guild to fund additions to the "anthology." The strategy of publishing poems singly likewise permitted the Guild to seek contributions toward publication costs from donors with a special interest in a particular poet. (Around 1922, by which time the Guild had obtained its own printing press, Branch reported that it cost ten dollars to fund one thousand copies of a poem.) Here again the presumption that college women had an affinity with both poetry and social service comes into view: Wellesley graduates subsidized the production of a series of individual poems (some by their fellow alumnae, such as Katherine Lee Bates) and then sold the leaves in the campus bookstore; Smith graduates underwrote Branch's own work. The project won support as well from women's clubs, church groups, and the American Library Association.[33]

Although Branch herself did not use the term "Americanization" in describing her work at the settlement, preferring the rhetoric of service, the "Unbound Anthology" was particularly suited to the Americanization activities of Christodora House. The accessibility of the anthology furthered the Guild's aim to "bring poetry to the greatest possible number of people—so that through it, the American tradition may be passed on." That statement of purpose was broad enough to accommodate many definitions of the nation's legacy. Swayed by Branch's speech at their statewide conference, however, the Connecticut Daughters of the American Revolution interpreted the potential of the "Unbound Anthology" in a way that made no room for immigrant traditions. Endorsing the Guild's judgment that there was a "popular demand for poetry in an inexpensive form," the Connecticut DAR assembled a selection of verse in three categories: miscellaneous "standard" poems "of real merit" such as "Abou Ben Adhem" and "O Captain! My Captain!"; poems with some connection to Connecticut; and patriotic texts. As the leader of the organization explained, the patriotic choices offered "teachers of Americanization, leaders of night-school classes, and of children's clubs" a "convenient" array of "splendid verse suitable to their purposes." Those choices included Edgar Guest's "United States," which was "in itself a liberal education to a newly made citizen"; Richard Watson Gilder's "On the Life Mask of Abraham Lincoln"; and Emerson's "Concord Hymn." The DAR leader especially noted the value of reprinting Whitman's "I Hear America Singing," which, she averred, "should undoubtedly be presented in quantity to the I.W.W. et al. for careful study." DAR chapters in Ohio, Michigan, and other states sponsored poems or series as well.[34]

The "Unbound Anthology" illuminates once again the presence of poetry in the interstices of print culture—away from the hard light and measurable space of commercial sales figures and distribution channels. The juxtaposition of disparate material—Guest and Emerson, "Abou Ben Adhem" and paeans to Connecticut—demonstrates that the anthology was unbound not only in the sense that it lacked stitching and covers but also because it exhibited no allegiance to the hierarchical classification schemes that differentiated poems on aesthetic grounds. Instead, the Poets' Guild project is further evidence of how social purpose can override distinctions between popular texts and those that literary critics deem canonical. It permits a glimpse as well of the fluidity that exists between high and low culture before a figure becomes ensconced in the academic canon. In 1924, when a Michigan DAR leader affiliated with a settlement house wrote Branch about underwriting a Poets' Guild series, she stated, "We have talked over having a committee of the right sort for working up the Anthology and have thought of Mr. Robert Frost [writer-in-residence at the University of Michigan] and one of the history professors . . . with perhaps Mr. Edgar Guest of Detroit." If Frost actively sought to win for himself the mass audience and public stature of the fireside poets, this reader's aggregation of him with Guest may signify his ultimate success—as well as his failure in this instance to gratify his simultaneous desire for readers who understood him as a literary radical struggling against the market that created Guest's fame.[35]

Throughout the 1920s the Poets' Guild continued to hold readings, classes on verse writing, and poetry appreciation programs at Christodora House. In addition, the Guild arranged holiday observances and participated in special events such as the 1927 Poetry

Week sponsored by the New York State Federation of Women's Clubs. That same year, the Guild moved into its own quarters, complete with fireplace and playhouse, in the new sixteen-story building the settlement house opened near its original site. Late in the decade, Branch renewed her effort to use poetry in the service of world peace. Soliciting contributions of verse for an exhibition aimed at international cooperation, Branch stipulated: "The poem should be lofty in thought and universal in feeling. . . . It should not be patriotic in a war like sense. A poem expressing simple devotion to the Mother Country would not be refused—but it would be better to have the poem express some universal mood, some spiritual reflection." At first glance, that directive appears to epitomize everything of which modernists accused their genteel predecessors: the exclusion of genuine emotion, the emphasis on uplift, the feminine sensibility (here symbolized by the condemnation of war). From one perspective, Branch's stipulations corroborate the survival of genteel strictures well into the 1930s. Yet the purpose behind them was not to keep poetry on the safe ground of disengagement with the troubling aspects of reality; it was, rather, to make the genre serviceable for the attainment of social ends by untried means.[36]

Branch sustained that sense of herself throughout her career. The Guild's activities by 1935 included a twenty-member speaking choir; some of its classes carried university extension credit from New York University. Poets who gave readings at Christodora House in the mid-1930s included Countee Cullen, Joel Elias Spingarn, Babette Deutsch, and Jean Starr Untermeyer—a diverse roster aesthetically and sociologically. The Guild also sponsored "Fireside Poetry" recitations on Sundays, for which participants memorized such works as Millay's "Ballad of the Harp-Weaver," Frost's "The Runaway," and other early modernist texts. The Guild's various programs did not entirely spare it, however, from perennial efforts to marginalize the arts in American culture. In 1936 a Christodora House board member, with his eye on taking over the Guild's (and the music program's) space, declared that Branch's project did not belong in a "normal Settlement program" and in any event failed to "attract the membership," which was more interested in a "good time" than in literature. Branch's rejoinder reinforced her stance as a risk-taker. "All Settlements of first caliber," she insisted, "consider it part of their vocation to engage in a certain amount of social experiment. . . . Is there any reason why poetry should not be investigated and utilized as a *social lever?* Isn't it just as good a form of experiment and extension as any other? It is an adventure—but the normal Settlement House stands for adventure." The board member seems to have prevailed to the extent that the Guild's international outreach effort was relocated outside Christodora House shortly after he issued his report. The Guild itself did not long outlive Branch, who died in 1937. The settlement still survives, with an emphasis on environmental programming. (Ironically, its website now touts its illustrious history as a source of inspiration for aspiring poets, including Ira Gershwin.) Yet the uses of poetry to realize what Branch called "plans and social dreams and adventures" continued, particularly in the form of other projects aimed at assisting immigrants in their adjustment to the United States.[37]

Americanization in the School

Emma Lazarus's lines engraved on the base of the Statue of Liberty—"Give me your tired, your poor"—made poetry integral to the nation's official outlook toward immigrants (even as the unwelcoming attitudes that many newcomers encountered in reality contradicted the statue's message). As already noted, however, pageants, club programs, and settlement house projects directed at Americanization gave poems more than symbolic functions. In the setting of the school, the genre achieved its fullest use as an instrument for acclimating immigrants to their new homes and transforming them from strangers to citizens.

Like MacKaye and Branch, educators who advocated poetry as a means to assist the foreign-born generally came from the pluralist wing of the Americanization campaign. That is, they differed from the conservatives allied with the North American Civic League, an association founded in 1907 "to change the unskilled inefficient immigrant into the skilled worker and efficient citizen." At the core of the League's activities to promote naturalization and English language instruction was its members' fear of subversive radicals and other agents of disorder. Thus while the League offered new-comers a range of services and publications, its governing aim was to ensure the productivity of the nation's industrial workforce by assimilating immigrant laborers as quickly and completely as possible. When the outbreak of World War I precipitated both greater nationalism and a stronger sense of crisis, the Committee for Immigrants in America, an offshoot of the League, intensified efforts to make immigrants shed their native language in favor of English and to promote naturalization through inculcating loyalty to "America First." In the immediate postwar period, the National Security League emerged to carry on the crusade against "Bolshevism and other un-American tendencies" through the training of English teachers and the dissemination of anti-foreign propaganda.[38]

Given the rhetoric of "super-patriotism" that many conservative Americanizers employed, it is easy to forget that their position was broad-minded in comparison to the nativist alternative of immigration restriction for which some of their fellow "progressives" were agitating. (Thomas Bailey Aldrich's "The Unguarded Gates," first published in 1892 and widely reprinted, had enlisted poetry in that cause.) Yet, especially after the war and the Red Scare subsided, re-formers also developed more amply the liberal version of Americanization that strove for respectful assistance rather than whole-sale transformation. In 1919 Frances A. Kellor, a veteran of the North American Civic League, assumed charge of a new organization, the Inter-Racial Council. With the stabilization of industry still her foremost concern, Kellor moved the drive for Americanization in the direction of tolerance and understanding of foreign-language speakers. In a reversion to the consciousness that Jane Addams and other early settlement house workers had exhibited in the late nineteenth century, teachers, social workers, and public policymakers increasingly stressed the contributions of the foreign-born to the United States and the importance of helping immigrants to preserve their ethnic traditions. Even labor unions that had protested what they saw as Americanizers' "alien baiting" endorsed the postwar campaign as potentially beneficial to workers.[39]

Proponents of both pluralist and nativist Americanization ideology relied in part on the public school system to implement their goals. There, in theory, poetry reading could be harnessed to either set of objectives. The reformers primarily concerned with safeguarding the interests of industry, however, generally dismissed the importance of studying poetry, literature, or, for that matter, any of the liberal arts. Instead, they made education synonymous with the acquisition of practical skills. For first-generation immigrants, these Americanizers emphasized rudimentary English classes, lessons in civics and hygiene, and vocational training, acquired through evening programs for adults and special tracks for school-age children. Poetry seemed irrelevant when the intent was to eradicate "alien" influences and inculcate conformity to workplace discipline. Furthermore, even certain Americanization advocates who, at least in their own eyes, evinced sympathy for the immigrant's predicament cautioned against using poems in language study. Insisting that people deserved to learn English from texts appropriate for their age, the author of a 1916 survey of Americanization activities in Cleveland was distressed to come upon a class of young men reciting Mrs. J. A. Carney's "Little drops of water, Little grains of sand," sometimes classified as a nursery rhyme, and another poem about a baby.[40]

More pointedly, M. Catherine Mahy, the supervisor of English at a high school in Providence, asserted that teachers who treated immigrant youths (or even second-generation students) in the same way as their non-foreign classmates were doing them a disservice, and she made the reading of verse her chief example. Adopting a purportedly scientific view, and presenting herself as an iconoclast, Mahy urged English instructors to foster "efficiency" and "economy" by avoiding those classic poems "in which the simplest figure of speech presents to the foreign mind a perfect maze of difficulties." Noting that her school already contained two divisions—one comprising "heirs of the priceless heredity of English

Immigrant children photographed by Lewis Hine at Boston's Hancock School in 1909, with "Lady Moon" on the blackboard. Library of Congress.

culture," the other entirely composed of the "foreign element"—she suggested instead a separate curriculum for each group. Out of what she saw as her awareness of immigrants' special needs, Mahy declared: "Think of it! Think of asking the Jew from Russia to read *The Courtship of Miles Standish* with the same zest and appreciation as is felt by the little girl in I A in whose veins runs the blood of Miles Standish; of asking the child whose religious experiences have been those described by Mary Antin [that is, Jewish ones] to respond to the serene Christian faith of *Snowbound*." In place of those works, Mahy substituted "simple" stories such as Dickens's *Christmas Carol* for the immigrants; while she hoped eventually to introduce more "of the simplest sort [of verse, such as] narrative poems like Browning's *How we brought the Good News,* or Alfred Noyes's *Highwayman*," the only poetry on her initial list of readings for the immigrant track was "Evangeline." "This quarter," she added, "we are making a special study of the business letter." Mahy was careful to remark that the innovations she prescribed were "only for the alien not capable of taking the classical course," but she did not indicate that she had run across any such exceptions. The same assumptions govern the schoolroom reading scene in Myra Kelly's *Little Citizens* (1904), in which the teacher abandons efforts to convey Wordsworth, Longfellow, Browning, and Shelley's impressions of nature to Jewish immigrant children who confuse "lark" with "lager" beer.[41]

As liberal Americanizers in the late 1910s and '20s began attributing the failures of the movement to their predecessors' disrespect for the foreign-born, however, they made a greater place for poetry in their model curricula. One line of argument stressed the importance of verse in demonstrating and developing the immigrant's aesthetic sensitivities and human qualities that nativists had refused to recognize. The people who came from countries "where song, poetry, architecture, and sculpture are part of their daily life," announced Peter Roberts, the YMCA's director of Americanization, in 1920, "are refined, no matter if they are unskilled workers." Roberts's interest was not in the distinctive character of poetry from other lands but, rather, in the universality that such literature made evident—its indication that "the human heart in its sorrow and joy is pretty much the same no matter in what clime or tongue it finds expression."[42]

Similarly, Huldah Florence Cook and Edith May Walker, the authors of a 1927 book on elementary education for adults, saw the study of language as a prerequisite for achieving and sustaining "adequate and sympathetic human relationships." Noting that the population of evening schools included those who wished to become as fluent in English as they were in their native tongue, the writers made a place for students' "higher development" in the instruction they prescribed. Like Branch, they welcomed poetry in achieving that end because of the genre's affiliation with spirituality. Their acknowledgment of immigrants' spiritual and intellectual capacities implied a civic nationalism that saw the foreign- and native-born as equal members of the American citizenry. Yet, like the pageant-masters before them, they turned away from the celebration or even acceptance of diversity, emphasizing instead poetry's power to encourage assimilation by tapping into a realm of human existence that transcended differences of background and circumstance. With the "illiterate native-born white" and the "American Negro" in mind along with the "foreign-born," Cook and Walker insisted that the "average man and woman" could "experience great emotions," and that poetry—"unconditionally upon the side of life"—was an effective means for transmitting "love, hate, joy, sorrow, patriotism" and other sentiments that united all people. At the same time, the authors approvingly noted the trend in the verse of their day to raise the "social consciousness" of readers.

Cook and Walker nevertheless dropped much of their universalizing rhetoric when they recommended and reprinted in their volume specific texts of value to adult students. Instead, they looked to the content of poems to convey the particular "ideals" they wished to impart, in the areas of "nature, home, patriotism, and philosophy." For Cook and Walker, those ideals continued to lodge primarily in the Anglo-American works that had formed the core of the school curriculum before the influx of immigrants—for example, Longfellow's "The Arrow and the Song" and "Paul Revere's Ride," Shelley's "The Cloud," Wordsworth's "I Wandered Lonely as a Cloud," Hunt's "Abou Ben Adhem," and Tennyson's "Crossing the Bar." Cook and Walker depended on such works for the same reasons teachers of non-immigrant children had long done so: not because a poem exhibited formal artistry or belonged to a high culture canon—their recommendations also included selections from Ella Wheeler Wilcox and another newspaper poet, Berton Braley—but because of the moral and social benefits it promised to confer on the reader. "The chief aim in presenting a poem to a class," the authors remarked, "is *to teach the meaning of the poem.* The teacher must discover the thought or ideal embodied in the selection and then prepare the group to grasp the thought." Here, however, all the chosen texts—not just the ones that explicitly concerned the American nation—acquired the additional function of promoting a distinctively American creed, even as the authors professed their belief in the immigrant's embodiment of a common humanity. Thus, despite Wordsworth's and Hunt's British background, they identified the daffodil's beauty and Ben Adhem's virtue with American values. By learning such texts, students would become closer to the white Anglo-Saxon Protestant and consequently more fully American.

The sample lesson they provided to illustrate their precepts, a class devoted to Joyce Kilmer's "Trees," focused on a series of questions that allowed the poem to bolster both brotherhood and nationalism. Instead of reading Kilmer's lines as a religious or nature poem, emphasizing God's role as the creator of beauty, or analyzing their symbolic features, the teacher was to use them to raise matters of civic obligation. The phrasing of the first question, "How may we make the world more beautiful?" erased national boundaries and presumed a universal appreciation for aesthetic values. At the same time, it alluded to the citizen's duty to make the earth more "lovely" (Kilmer's word) for the sake of all people. Subsequent queries may have reflected Cook and Walker's realization that the poem relied on the device of personification; they suggested employing the text to stress the differences which the natural environment (and perhaps, by implication, human society) accommodated: "Do all trees look alike?" "Do we find the same kind of trees in all parts of the world?" The culmination of the lesson, however, dropped globalism and pluralism alike in favor of questions designed to instill knowledge of and pride in the policies of the United States. "Is our government interested in trees?" the teacher was to ask. "How is the United States Government trying to protect trees?" In this context, the poet's literal subject became the occasion for a message entirely extraneous to the text: that the immigrants' adopted country deserved their gratitude and allegiance for being on the side of beauty and for its beneficent, sheltering activities. The last two questions continued the movement from the "world" to the United States by inquiring about the trees found locally and nationally.[43]

Other educators and reformers went beyond the interpretation of the immigrants' receptivity to poetry as a sign of both their spirituality and their malleability, arguing not just for the possibility of transcending difference but also for the merits of the particular literary traditions the newcomers brought with them. That is, such individuals participated in the conceptualization of immigrant identity as the "creative fusion" of "descent" and "consent" relations—of ethnic and national allegiances—that Werner Sollors has delineated. Put another way, they promoted a more "progressive civic nationalism" than Americanizers who sought total assimilation. These observers often grasped that immigrant parents, as their children grew up, experienced a "'vague uneasiness' that a delicate network of precious traditions is being ruthlessly torn asunder." Hence they contended that Americanization instruction ought to address the student's "two great interests—his vocation and his past cultural life." Several writers arrived at that position by extending the concept of American values or Americanness. In 1919, remarking that "America is no longer afraid of the word culture," Frances Kellor augmented the definition of Americanization to include "a recognition of the cultural forces in the various races as expressed in their literature and institutions." In an essay entitled "Teaching American Ideals Through Literature" (1918), the educator Henry Neumann marshaled a number of frequently assigned poems to instruct pupils that American democracy entailed prizing diversity instead of seeking "flat uniformity." Neumann read Whittier's "Snow-Bound" as a revelation of the "greatness latent in the commonest of persons," Lowell's "The Vision of Sir Launfal" as a testimony to "the truth that democracy respects the divinity in men," and Edwin Markham's "The Cup of Pride" as a way to point out that the "democratic principle of respect for merit bears with special significance upon the relations between our native stock and our foreign born." (He also directed teachers of "Evangeline" to emphasize that in that poem Longfellow, a Protestant, voiced "hearty admiration for a Catholic community," an attitude the writer hoped students would emulate.)[44]

For perhaps most such individuals, the standing they awarded European traditions remained instrumental to the paramount goal of inculcating loyalty to the United States. In an image evoking the regenerative qualities of the "melting pot," Roberts, the YMCA director, reasoned, "The Russian who knows that you appreciate Russian music and the poems of Pushkin . . . will open his heart and his mind and become as clay in the hand of the potter"— which is to say less Russian and more white Anglo-Saxon Protestant. Some progressive educators were less manipulative, however, prescribing acceptance of immigrants' culture because they discovered attributes in the foreign literature itself that made it equal or superior to its American counterpart. "I believe that we in the public schools have better 'material to work with' . . . than have private school teachers," one teacher wrote in describing the students at New York's Evander Childs High School, whom she had encouraged to read and write verse. "The very foreignness of our pupils is a great asset. The Irish and the Jews . . . have older and deeper poetic traditions than have indigenous Americans." Even Roberts noted that "if the ideals of the seers of these several [European] peoples were interpreted to America, we should all be better and nobler."[45]

Although presumably it became easier to adopt that attitude after 1924, when passage of the National Origins Act limited the threat to the Anglo-Saxon Protestant mainstream, a notable instance of this early multiculturalism prior to World War I appears in the ghostwritten memoir of Leonard Covello, himself an immigrant from Italy to New York. By 1910, Covello recalled, he had become convinced that he and his fellow immigrants needed "to know as much as possible about ourselves before we could feel that our people and their culture were not inferior—only different." A friendship with a poet persuaded him of a way to serve that end: by organizing East Harlem residents to study Dante. Later, as a faculty member at De Witt Clinton High School, Covello was adviser to a club of native Italian speakers that also made Dante one of its projects. The purpose of the group, Covello reported, was to "help create a sympathetic bond" between Italians and non-Italians by enabling people to "learn from each other." The outlook that Covello espoused as a young teacher also governed his response to the tensions among his students in the 1930s and '40s, when he was principal of Benjamin Franklin High School in another East Harlem neighborhood, one that had become racially mixed. A white student, he reported, "thought twice" about taunting African-Americans after listening to a recitation of Countee Cullen's "Incident" ("Once riding in old Baltimore . . .") in English class; another boy recalled hearing at the funeral of a black classmate a poem written by a Jew that repudiated racial and religious prejudice. For Covello, at least in retrospect, poetry was thus both the carrier of ethnic identity and the agent of a social harmony founded on mutual esteem. Imputing those functions to the genre idealized it in a double sense—both in terms of its ability to instill ideals and with respect to its power to alter social arrangements.[16]

Another immigrant writer and New York City public school principal, Elias Lieberman (1883–1969), advocated the fusion of ethnicity and Americanness through the medium of verse by writing his own poems on that theme. A Russian Jew who emigrated to the United States at the age of seven, Lieberman graduated from City College in 1903, where he wrote the lyrics for the school's alma mater. Thereafter he began his teaching career, which lasted until he was appointed to head Thomas Jefferson High School in 1924. He held the post until 1940, when he became an associate superintendent of schools. In these years Lieberman also served as an editor and contributor to *Puck, The American Hebrew, Current Literature,* and the *Scholastic.* In 1916, he submitted his most famous poem, "I Am an American," to the popular periodical *Everybody's;* it was accepted with a note indicating that it was precisely what the magazine wanted. The text consisted of two symmetrical stanzas, each beginning and ending with the declaration that furnished the poem's title. The first represented the voice of a Revolutionary War soldier's son, a native-born American whose ancestors had been statesmen and pioneers. The second stanza proclaimed the gratitude of a Russian immigrant whose forebears were victims of the Czar. The descendant of the founders, Lieberman imagined, was "proud" of his past; the immigrant, taught by his father that the United States was "the hope of humanity," was "proud" of his future as a defender of the "promised land." Both young men, the poet suggested, possessed equally noble backgrounds despite the differences in their fortunes, and both were equally loyal to the American dream of liberty. In contrast to the definition of "American" as "white" or Anglo-Saxon that had prevailed in the early nineteenth century, Lieberman thus self-consciously repudiated the attachment of a racial or an ethnic meaning to the word; that is, he rejected an emphasis on Americanness as a natural or genetic attribute of "descent." Instead, the poem furthered the work, in which Irish and Italian immigrants desirous of "whiteness" also participated, of recasting "American" as a national, and "volitional," designation. At the same time, even as Lieberman's lines demanded respect for the sacrifices ethnicity had exacted from minorities in Europe, the poet's insistence that the Russian would "live for" and "die for" his adopted country assured readers that former aliens posed no more threat to the social order than did their Anglo-Saxon compatriots.[47]

"I Am an American" was reprinted in Lieberman's verse collection *Paved Streets,* issued in 1917 by a small Boston publishing house, Cornhill. The book received mixed reviews ("Most of the things he says have been said before, and said much better by such men as Louis Untermeyer . . .") and appeared in only one edition. Like Branch's "Unbound Anthology," however, "I Am an American" circulated outside the channels of the book trade for the next three decades. The format and dramatic language of the poem were well suited to performance, by either one speaker or two different ones personifying each of the voices. Just after the fighting ended in World War I, for example, a professional elocutionist who billed herself as a "Reader" included Lieberman's text in an evening program she put on at the Waldorf-Astoria; her other selections— among them Whittier's "In School Days," Kilmer's "Trees," a scene from Shakespeare, and a story of the Liberty Loan campaign— interwove the values of liberal Americanization with refinement as well as patriotism. In the school setting, "I Am an American" was a frequent choice of participants in declamation contests. Sometimes entire schools memorized the poem. In 1920, graduation ceremonies all over New York City featured recitations of it. During one commencement at a Bronx elementary school, a Russian Jew who had experienced the persecution chronicled in the second half of the poem won a silver cup and medal for speaking, as well as intangible benefits: "It seemed to thrill my audience," he wrote Lieberman, "as much as it did me." Almost thirty years later, an Irish and a Jewish student staged a similar reading at New York's city-wide oratory competition, where their performance was a "highlight" of the finals. Religious groups also appropriated "I Am an American" for worship services and devotional reading, a gesture that affirmed the emphasis, in the interwar period, on tolerance as an expression of Christian ethics.[48]

In the late 1930s and early 1940s, the sites at which readers encountered "I Am an American" extended from settlement house work to an American Legion "New Citizen Rally." A Brooklyn woman, declaring that she knew the President and his wife "love poetry," gave one of Lieberman's volumes to the Roosevelts. Her description of incorporating "I Am an American" into "Tolerance Programs" in schools reflects the shift in the political uses the text supported—from cementing immigrants' loyalty by validating their past to admonishing them for failing to relinquish their foreign ideas. In a variant of the generational fears that Sollors identified as integral to the "cultural construction of descent," Lieberman's correspondent wrote him that his poem "can't be read too often to children of immigrant parents, especially of Fascist persuasion, of whom unfortunately, there are a vast number" in the neighborhood. During the 1950s "I Am an American," still frequently reprinted, continued to find an audience in activities connected to naturalization. All of these reiterations of Lieberman's poem suggest its almost inescapable presence, at least for young people in New York City. Yet most of the poem's appearances occurred without the (more than nominal) republication fees or other payments to author and publisher that signaled the commercial value of the text. Instead, it repeatedly exhibited its unquantifiable value in cultural and ideological transactions.[49]

Alongside the rhetoric of Americanization, another vocabulary developed that also had repercussions for the civic uses of verse: the reformulation of the language of citizenship. As Michael Schudson has argued, the concept of the good citizen underwent redefinition

Girl reciting at an Americanization program in 1940. Library of Congress.

in the Progressive era, shifting from an equation of civic virtue with party loyalty to an expectation that the full exercise of citizenship required intelligence and training. As early as 1919, some Deweyite educators pursued the latter goal by employing poetry to promote "civic traits and habits" such as "organized cooperation" among both foreign and native-born students. Citizenship training took a more elaborate form, however, in an effort of the 1930s and '40s: the intercultural education movement. Rachel Davis DuBois, the teacher who was the movement's central figure, believed passionately in the dissemination of knowledge about America's constituent minorities to promulgate civic nationalism and ensure peace at home and abroad. The device she promoted to accomplish that task—a series of school assemblies devoted, each time, to a different ethnic group—seems commonplace in retrospect, but was innovative in its day. Dubbed "separate" study because of its focus on a single ethnicity at a time, DuBois's plan grew out of her predilection for psychologizing the experience of discrimination. Immigrants who were made to feel inferior, she explained, suffered "personality maladjustments" that impeded their "integrity and creativeness," at a cost to "our common civilization." Former techniques of Americanization could not adequately achieve "cultural adjustment" because they tried to eliminate, rather than to accept, heterogeneity. The solution was to nurture in students "a justifiable pride in their cultural backgrounds—a pride, however, balanced by appreciation for the cultural backgrounds of other groups and by a feeling of the oneness of the human race."[50]

DuBois's most famous effort along those lines was her creation, in 1938 and 1939, of the 26-part radio series "Americans All—Immigrants All," with sponsorship from the United States Office of Education. Within the school setting, however, she designated poetry recitation in assemblies and classrooms as a stimulus (along with music, drama, and the importation of guest speakers) for producing both of those emotional results. In the category of generating pride, she devised a program on "the Negro" that included a pageant entitled "Two Races," in which the "Spirit of Poetry" appeared alongside characters representing "Progress," "Adventure," "Science," and other endeavors. To create "oneness," DuBois recommended a "brotherhood day program" such as the one held in an Englewood, New Jersey, junior high school and summarized in her *Build Together Americans* (1945). The script for the event associated verse with religious as well as therapeutic and moral functions: it coupled a prayer jointly written by a priest, minister, and rabbi with a "Civic Creed" that began "God hath made of one blood all nations of men"; it then presented as "responsive reading"—a technique borrowed from worship—a poem by Denis A. McCarthy entitled "The Land Where Hate Should Die," which preached a national orientation superior to bonds of "faith" and "race." DuBois placed her hopes as well in interactions that amplified the construct of identity beyond awareness of one's own ethnicity. The visit of a "Negro poet" along with a "German refugee professor" and a "dancer of Jewish themes," she explained, did more than strengthen a minority student's feeling of attachment to the products of a racial or ethnic group; in her view, it permitted a process by which students outside those groups could actively "identify themselves" with oppressed individuals, lessen their sense of "superiority," and gain "a greater respect" from their newly-proud minority classmates. It was this same outcome that Covello (acknowledging DuBois's influence) sought in championing an English course for Franklin seniors called "American Social Problems in the Light of American Literature."[51]

For all of her concern with mutuality, however, DuBois's scheme was controversial from the beginning. Although the American Jewish Committee financed its implementation in fifteen New York–area schools in 1934–35, the Progressive Education Association, which had endorsed DuBois's plan in 1936, shortly withdrew its support. The equilibrium implicit in the phrase "Americans All—Immigrants All" was unacceptable to educators who feared the divisive consequences of DuBois's failure to subordinate "group enthusiasms" to national loyalties. Despite DuBois's limited success in the 1940s, the full flowering of intercultural education—a term still in use—had to await the more receptive climate which the civil rights movement created in the postwar years.[52]

Verse Reading and the Promise of Rebirth

How did the recipients, or targets, of the various Americanization efforts in public schools between 1900 and 1940—the immigrant students themselves—respond to their teachers' attempts to apportion or balance the double consciousness they possessed as foreigners and Americans? Occasionally such students revealed the answer to that question directly (if retrospectively), commenting in particular about the impact of poetry reading and recitation on their sense of identity. Like the autobiographies in which they are usually embedded, their accounts conform to the myths Americans have relied on in constructing their understandings of immigration and assimilation. That is, they present an especially pressing case of the need to recognize the role of both convention and fantasy in shaping how individuals perceive and report experience. Within that framework, the recitation emerges as a ritual that melded varying proportions of consent and descent in the act of performance.

The most common such myth was that of rebirth as a new self, a process that reciting verse enabled and embodied in microcosm. Leonard Covello captured one version of that drama in *The Heart Is the Teacher* (1958). At an assembly in the New York City elementary school where he attended fourth grade, Covello recalled, he recited Eugene Field's "Wynken, Blynken, and Nod." As Covello related the event, it marked his transformation from alien to American-by-consent. "Waiting with my classmates to march into assembly," he wrote, "I was overwhelmed with fear"—a sentence that encapsulates not only the schoolchild's anxiety about speaking in public but also the immigrant's acute sense of difference from the mainstream. When the principal called his name (the Americanized "Leonard" he had adopted in place of "Leonardo"), he was at first "unable to move." Eventually, however, he made his way (one might say migrated) to the front of the room. "In a voice which I could not recognize as my own," Covello remembered, he introduced Field's poem and delivered it. Afterwards he returned to his seat, "bewildered, but with a wonderful feeling of exhilaration." He had "overcome a fear that had haunted me for weeks—fear of facing my more 'American' classmates, fear of mispronouncing some of the difficult words, fear of my accent or of forgetting my lines. To my amazement, what had seemed so difficult was easy, much easier than I had ever dreamed—an experience which has repeated itself often during the course of my life."

In that vignette, the recitation of an American text (a poem itself representing a dream) fulfilled Covello's fantasy of becoming a new person, in the process losing his old voice and acquiring accentless speech. Yet Covello's narrative of attaining national identity by consent contained a subtext that preserved his ethnic loyalties. Tellingly, he reported fortifying himself for the recitation by practicing before a mirror while pretending to address his uncle, Zio Prete, "sitting in his huge armchair with his cane at his side." Thus he carried with him, almost as protection, the homey image of part of his Italian family circle. Furthermore, despite his overt wishes, he was presumably unable to shed his accent entirely, so that reciting a poem publicly announced his ethnicity while simultaneously enabling him to transcend it. In the context of his autobiography as a whole, which charts Covello's gradual re-embrace of Italian culture, the recitation likewise appears as a kind of second-generation phenomenon (albeit within a single life), a renunciation of descent before the achievement of a balance between old- and new-world loyalties.[53]

As some liberal Americanizers had understood, among Jewish immigrants from Eastern Europe, traditions of Yiddish poetry persisted in the New World, creating multiple opportunities for individuals to imagine themselves anew. The poet and Lithuanian immigrant Solomon Bloomgarten translated "Hiawatha" into Yiddish in 1910; as Alan Trachtenberg has described it, this was a way of fully achieving "entry into the literary culture of the United States." Take-offs on the Longfellow text also appeared in Yiddish-laced vaudeville skits, providing comedic occasions for audiences to grapple with the tensions surrounding assimilation. Like their Italian counterparts, however, Jewish participants in classroom recitation typically saw poetry as conferring Americanness through the embrace of English. In *An American in the Making* (1917), M. E. Ravage recorded that the love of "the poets" he acquired by reading them in Yiddish led to his decision to improve his English by attending evening school, where he memorized Milton. As a result of this experience, he decided to forgo the counsel of his Jewish friends, enroll in a large state university, and reconceive himself as merely "human" (which he equated with "American").[54]

The poetry recitation as the agent and embodiment of rebirth figures even more prominently in the narrative of the most famous Jewish immigrant autobiographer, Mary Antin. Antin introduced the governing trope in the first paragraph of her memoir *The Promised Land* (1912). "Is it not time to write my life's story?" she queried. "I am just as much out of the way as if I were dead, for I am absolutely other than the person whose story I have to tell." Antin's "earlier self" was born in Russia in 1881. As a child, she felt her horizons expand when she traveled from her village to her uncle's home in the provincial capital. There she first encountered "secular literature" in Russian and Yiddish, including poetry that she recited by "walking up and down," in imitation of her worldly cousin Hirschel. After her father wrote her from Boston, where he had emigrated in 1891, America came to stand for the place where she could realize her "dream" of a richer life. Three years later, Antin and the rest of her family became immigrants to Boston themselves. Unlike her older sister, whom their father placed in factory labor, Antin was allowed to go to school, a decision that, in her view, bespoke her father's reverence for the education and culture he never attained himself. In grade six, she came under the wing of her most beloved teacher, Mary S. Dillingham, who set to work improving her pupil's command and pronunciation of English. She also invited Antin to stay after school and study poetry, an act that both associated the genre with a quality of specialness and confirmed Antin's potential to become like her native-born classmates. By reading and repeating poetic texts, "mostly out of Longfellow," Antin learned the meaning of meter in verse and proceeded to write her own lines. When Dillingham subsequently presented her with a volume of Longfellow's poems—the first book Antin had ever owned—the book betokened not only the pleasure of reading but also the "sense of possession"—one might say of self as well as of objects—that America offered her.[55]

Antin's exposure to printed verse, in Russia as well as Boston, set the stage for the culminating episode in her rebirth: her composition, performance, and eventual publication of a poem about George Washington. Antin recounted these developments in the section of *The Promised Land* she called "My Country," which

Mary Antin, with inscription to one of her teachers. Courtesy of the Boston Public Library, Print Department.

first appeared in the *Atlantic Monthly*. Despite the pronoun in the title, in the first paragraph of the chapter Antin (like Ravage) allied herself with "us foreigners" and spoke of "your country" to an audience she envisioned as consisting of "born Americans." From that beginning, she narrated the tale of what she called the "miracle" of her remaking as a "Fellow Citizen." Having read about the life of Washington, she voiced her admiration for him in rhymed stanzas that celebrated his virtues. More than that, the poem expressed Antin's newly discovered feeling of kinship with the first president—"he who e'er will be our pride . . . our Washington." Writing those lines, Antin explained, had involved struggle and then catharsis, when "inspiration perched on my penpoint, and my soul gave up its best." But that scenario was only a kind of rehearsal for the ultimate emotional drama of reciting her creation to her classmates at a celebration of Washington's Birthday. Antin stood before them looking and sounding palpably different and, by implication, un-American: her dress was out of place, her "pronunciation was faulty," her body suggested illness or weakness. (Antin heightened the contrast by implying here that there were no other immigrants among the forty "Fellow Citizens" in her audience, although elsewhere she indicates that there were.) Yet when she spoke, the effect was almost magically to release her from her former self: "Even the bad boys sat in attitudes of attention, hypnotized by the solemnity of [her] demeanor." The applause and praise that followed dissolved all of the gracelessness Antin felt she had exhibited before the performance. Later she repeated her poem to several more classes.[56]

As she presented it, Antin's verse recitation set in motion the chain of events that ultimately resulted in her career as a writer. (Nonetheless her family's respect for literature was already in place, as was one prior publication that Dillingham had arranged.) Perhaps encouraged by her father, Antin decided to submit the poem on Washington to a Boston newspaper. Making her way to her destination, she was already distanced from her previous self: in her account, "Jews, hurrying by with bearded chins on their bosoms and eyes intent," merely "shrugged" when she sought directions, and she could communicate no better with Italians. Though turned down on her first try, at the *Transcript,* she wandered into the offices of the *Herald,* had "instant good luck" in seeing an editor, secured the poem's acceptance, and left with a sense that she had crossed the boundary from amateur to professional. At the same time, the entire adventure highlighted Antin's experience (like Edward Bok's) of easy access to the literary culture that poets and poetry represented. When the poem appeared in print, Antin found that she read it as if it were the work of another person, "not at all as if somebody we knew had written it"—that is, it was the product of the new self she identified as both "author" and "American." As Antin said of the "My Country" incident in "How I Wrote *The Promised Land*" (1912), "every child awakens to a sense of self, of friendship, of patriotism; but while normally these things come gradually, obscurely, in my case they came spectacularly." Thereafter Antin began a "new life" by entering Boston Latin School; she then achieved fame by bringing out, to wide acclaim, several versions of her autobiography, as well as a series of short stories and further nonfiction works.[57]

Those triumphs coexisted with Antin's own recognition that she could not shed the influence of the Old World, that her transformation would never be complete, that she was—inside—always a Russian Jew, and that she was to be the "tongue" of "those who lived before" her. Thus, in contrast to her description of her mesmerizing power over her classmates during the recitation, she remarked near the end of *The Promised Land* that she "learned at least to think [but apparently not to speak] in English without an accent." Two chapters after her summary of the Washington's Birthday poem, in a description of the Saturday evening entertainments at the evangelical Morgan Chapel, she situated herself once more as an outsider catching "glimpses of a fairer world than ours . . . through the music and the poetry." Furthermore, Antin's memoir exists in the context of her unrealized educational plans and troubled later years, when the sense of self she had constructed fell apart in a protracted nervous breakdown. Yet despite those countercurrents, throughout her life Antin's public persona continued to affirm the volitional nature of Americanness and the "simple" opportunities by which an "outcast" immigrant could evolve into a "privileged citizen."[58]

The role of Longfellow in Antin's "miracle" shows how wrong M. Catherine Mahy, the Providence English teacher, was in assuming that "the Jew from Russia" could not fully understand schoolroom verse (although no doubt Mahy regarded Antin as exceptional). Instead, Covello's, Ravage's, and Antin's mythic remembrances at least obliquely fulfilled progressive educators' hopes that Anglo-American poetic traditions could assist immigrants in arriving at an American civic nationalism that subsumed (even as it preserved) their ethnic identity. The educators underestimated, however, the extent to which that outcome derived more from the act of performance than from the impact of the text performed. Moreover, except in Covello's account, the persistence of ethnic ties appears in these memoirs not in the celebratory mode of intercultural education but as a submerged or uncomfortable vestige of the past.

The dominant motif in published immigrant autobiographies— the depiction of the recitation as a site of rebirth—also appeared in the reminiscences of ordinary readers replying to the *New York Times* query. The daughter of an Italian immigrant warmly described a 1909 photograph of her mother standing on a pedestal, bouquet in hand, after winning a school prize for recitation. As in Antin's case, the event signaled the woman's entrance into the American mainstream; subsequently, her daughter reported, she "passed as Irish" to get a job, and ultimately "made it." Another child of immigrant parents echoed Antin's view of the Morgan Chapel programs by reporting that poetry reading allowed him to glimpse the sphere of the "attractive, well-groomed rich." He explained, "I perceived everything about my life as ugly—the drab tenement apartment in which I slept on a sofa in a cluttered dark parlour, the scarred furniture, the worn clothes we wore." Lowell's "The Vision of Sir Launfal" made him "think 'I, too, could experience beauty.'" The almost formulaic quality of that response may measure the trickle-down effect of the published regeneration narratives on second-generation readers making sense of their family's experiences—that is, it may calibrate the extent to which the story became a widespread cultural convention. In any case, like the moviegoers in the 1920s who welcomed the chance to submerge difference by joining the mass theater audience, these individuals mainly regarded their participation in a national, standardized American school curriculum as liberating rather than as oppressive.[59]

Nevertheless, some of the query respondents, unlike Covello, Antin, and the others, revealed that poetry reading in school could also heighten the tensions between consent and descent, instead of subordinating the latter to the former. A number of replies confirmed that, for all of Mahy's prejudices, her observation that the Pilgrims' history might not resonate with newcomers contained a kernel of truth. The best (and funniest) response documenting that fact came from a St. Louis man who remembered with "love and reverence" his teachers' dutiful efforts "to inculcate us with American values, culture, ideas." Yet he confessed that he brought to his reading of Whittier's "Barbara Frietchie" an awareness of the disjuncture between his lower-middle-class Jewish household in St. Louis and the "rather determinedly Protestant" women who taught him. Hence in the lines "The clustered spires of Frederick stand / Green-walled by the hills of Maryland," he substituted what he "fancied to be a Jewish hero": a character named "Greenwald." It may be that, before her sudden acquisition of reverence for her "country," Antin found the sentiments and settings in Longfellow's lines similarly alien to her experience, but that her investment in carrying a positive message to non-immigrant audiences impeded her saying so. It is also possible that the assertions of pride in descent among query respondents reflected the cultural approval of that emotion in the 1990s, when they were writing. In any event, their replies suggest that, for some immigrant readers, the school recitation entailed not the substitution of a new self for an old one but, rather, more of a struggle between competing selves than the narrators of rebirth recorded.[60]

The use of dialect poetry in school also furnished a special instance of the way in which reading and performance practices could galvanize tensions surrounding ethnicity (here understood to include race). Although this perspective is hard to recover today, from one vantage point verse in dialect offered an opportunity for inclusion; if one assumed that it faithfully represented the speech of a minority group, it could call attention to—and legitimate—the culture of Americans outside the white Anglo-Saxon Protestant mainstream. Thus the Italian immigrant Constantine Panunzio reacted with sympathy to Thomas Daly's poem "Da Little Boy," which seemed to him to represent effectively a widowed mother whose child has died. "Had [Daly] known this woman's sorrow?" Panunzio asked. "It seemed as if he was uttering her very words." Similarly, James Weldon Johnson admired Paul Laurence Dunbar's ability to use the dialect medium "for the true interpretation of Negro character and psychology," arguing that Dunbar surpassed the previous (and mainly white) practitioners of the form by refining its conventions. Dialect, Werner Sollors has noted, permits diffusion of the idea of ethnic culture; it also allows minority writers to exert power over their non-ethnic readers by treating them as outsiders. Yet Johnson, who had tried his own hand at writing dialect poetry, saw it differently: as a subgenre that subjected the African-American poet to the dominance of "a section of the white American reading public." After immersing himself in the "formless forms" of *Leaves of Grass*—he recalled being "engulfed and submerged by the book"—Johnson concluded that dialect constrained poets by permitting the expression of only the "pathos and humor" associated with "a happy-go-lucky or a forlorn figure." Thus the device often bore "no relation at all" to "actual Negro life," but instead merely served the image of the African-American that whites demanded.[61]

For Johnson, the consequence of those perceptions was an attitude toward his literary audience that alternated between racial advancement and universalism (a position that arguably paralleled Johnson's activism within the integrated National Association for the Advancement of Colored People). On the one hand, he fought against the poet's submission to white stereotypes. On the other hand, the means for doing so turned out to be the language of the educated white population; he noted "the need for Aframerican poets in the United States to work out a new and distinctive form of expression," but urged such poets not to "limit themselves" to the material of race. "The sooner they are able to write *American* poetry spontaneously," he insisted in the preface to *The Book of American Negro Poetry* (1922), "the better."[62]

This double vision colored Johnson's statements about the creation and diffusion of his most famous poem, "Lift Ev'ry Voice and Sing," which his brother J. Rosamond Johnson set to music. He wrote the text at the turn of the century, after deciding that the time had come for "a great poem on Lincoln" (that is, an American national hero) from an African-American viewpoint. Invited to participate in a celebration of Lincoln's birthday, Johnson resolved to write such a poem for the occasion, but directed that impulse toward a song instead, to be performed by five hundred schoolchildren. His description of devising the lyrics is not unlike Antin's account of writing about Washington: "feverish ecstasy was followed by . . . contentment." The result, Johnson noted, was a mixture of Anglo-American ("Kiplingesque") style and African-American experience, in which the "American Negro was, historically and spiritually, immanent." Johnson's observations about the performance of the work—which, in a phrase perpetuating ethnic nationalism, became known as the "Negro National Hymn"—struck a similar balance. (They also revealed a process of dissemination that, like the one that popularized "I Am an American," occurred outside the channels of commercial publishing.) "Within twenty years," he wrote, "the song was being sung in schools and churches and on special occasions throughout the South and in some other parts of the country. Within that time the publishers had recopyrighted it and issued it in several arrangements. . . . The publishers consider it a valuable piece of property; however, in traveling round I have commonly found printed or typewritten copies of the words pasted in the backs of hymnals and the songbooks used in Sunday schools, Y.M.C.A.'s, and similar institutions; and I think that is the method by which it gets its widest circulation." Johnson was "always thrilled deeply" when he heard "Lift Ev'ry Voice" sung by

"Negro children." Yet he was also "surprised" and gratified that the white students at the Bryn Mawr Summer School performed it "fervently" and had it in "their mimeographed folio of songs."[63]

For Johnson, the unstated problem that public poetic speech epitomized was thus how to sustain the competing claims of Americanness and ethnicity, how to appeal to white audiences without betraying one's own people in the act of "passing." If Johnson held those tensions in equilibrium (while Antin, for example, celebrated release from them), there was nevertheless a third (albeit less frequent) meaning that immigrant and minority writers attached to poetry recitation: in certain accounts, it neither prompted rebirth nor provoked conflicting allegiances, but functioned instead as a symbol of impassable social barriers or as an instrument of exclusion. That is, it fostered the ethnic nationalism that made full American citizenship commensurate with white Anglo-Saxon Protestantism. Although the episode took place outside the school setting, it is worth mentioning one such moment that occurs in Rose Cohen's *Out of the Shadow: A Russian Jewish Girlhood on the Lower East Side* (1918). Cohen, who worked in the garment industry during her first years in America, developed a love of reading in Hebrew and then attended night school to learn English. At the same time, she was acutely conscious of the anti-semitism surrounding her. Gradually, as she came into contact with well-meaning reformers like Lillian Wald, she stepped "out of the shadow" of oppression. Yet that progression was temporarily reversed when she visited a sanitorium-like farm to recuperate from illness. The episode Cohen described was the mirror image of the rebirth scenario. As she, a friend, and Miss Farley (the head of the house) were gathered around a cozy fire reading, they at first felt "friendly and congenial." Then Miss Farley "picked up a large new volume . . . and began to read to me a poem right from the beginning of the book which appeared to be a sort of introduction or opening poem." It told the story of a fair-haired boy killed by Jews as a Passover sacrifice. Through guilt by association, Miss Farley implicated Cohen in the slaughter. The upshot was that Cohen became "dumb with horror and was silent." Instead of facilitating partici-

pation in a larger national community, the reading forcibly ex-
cluded Cohen from becoming American by consent: "That night
Miss Farley and Irene and the two coloured women and all the chil-
dren were together and I felt alone, a stranger in the house that had
been a home to me." Falling back on an affirmation of her Jewish
identity, she "longed for my own people whose hearts I knew."[64]

Fuller examples of spoken verse as a sign of or catalyst for exclu-
sion appear in two beautifully wrought stories by the African-
American writer Charles Chesnutt. Both of them precede the Ameri-
canization movement but prefigure it by examining, with respect to
the color line, the same tensions that attended immigrants' access
to full citizenship. In "The Wife of His Youth," the main character,
Mr. Ryder, leads a social organization located in a Northern city
and composed of upwardly mobile African-Americans who look
and act "more white than black." Ryder's goal is not passing, but
instead preparing for the fact that the white race "doesn't want us
yet, but may take us in time." To that end, he cultivates not only
a "refined" demeanor and "irreproachable" manners but also a
"passion" for poetry; his favorite poet is Tennyson, and the library
at his "handsomely furnished" house on a "respectable street" is
"especially rich" in volumes of verse. Chesnutt's description of
Ryder's recitation style is, however, among the story's first clues
that, for African-Americans, mimicking the white social elite can-
not succeed as a basis for re-inventing the self: the author couples
Ryder's ability to "repeat whole pages of the great English poets"
with a reference to the "sometimes faulty" pronunciation that re-
veals his former condition as an uneducated slave. The plot turns
on Ryder's decision to give a ball notable for its "exclusiveness," in
honor of the woman he hopes to marry. As he practices reading
Tennyson aloud for the remarks he plans to deliver there that eve-
ning, another woman—subsequently revealed as the "wife of his
youth"—appears; speaking dialect, looking "very black," and de-
cidedly unrefined, she explains that she is searching for her hus-
band. Chesnutt signals her invasion of the protagonist's poetic rev-
erie—his fantasy of whiteness—by having Ryder write his visitor's
address on the flyleaf of the Tennyson book. When he later ad-

dresses his guests at the ball, he resumes speaking "in the same soft dialect" of the Southern slave. The only poetry he recites is Shakespeare's "to thine own self be true," a message he enacts by publicly acknowledging his wife, accepting his blackness, and relegating Tennyson to the white world that is closed to him.[65]

Chesnutt's tone in "The Wife of His Youth" conveys his disapproval of his character's aspirations and his endorsement of the "honor" with which he ultimately behaves. The loss of Tennyson, Chesnutt suggests, is not to be mourned, because it symbolizes an illegitimate desire at odds with Ryder's genuine identity. In a second tale involving verse recitation, "Cicely's Dream," Chesnutt's sympathies are more ambiguous, although the role of the practice in enforcing racial distinctions is even sharper. Here again the culminating scene is a public entertainment, this time in the school setting, and the action turns as well on a figure of mixed race, an escaped Confederate prisoner-of-war named John. The "Cicely" of the title is "a tall brown girl, in a homespun frock," whose speech reveals her Southern rural origins. Cicely discovers the wounded John lying in the underbrush and helps nurse him back to health.

Suffering from amnesia, John forms an attachment to his rescuer, who sees in her patient the fulfillment of her romantic hopes. "She taught him to speak her own negro English," Chesnutt writes, so that "his speech was an echo of Cicely's own." After the Civil War ends, Cicely attends a Freedman's Bureau School to "acquire the new and wonderful learning" that would make former slaves "the equals of white people." Her teacher, the white Bostonian Martha Chandler, earns Cicely's imitative devotion; while Martha selflessly instructs her pupil, Cicely teaches John to read. She also sets a date to marry him and thus to realize her "dream" of happiness with a light-skinned man. Before the wedding can occur, however, Cicely must participate in an "exhibition" marking the close of the school term. Having memorized one of the "half a dozen poems that her teacher had suggested," she dresses for the occasion with a style that emulates Martha's. Cicely speaks her lines so well that she wins first prize, an outcome that comes close to certifying her rebirth in the image of her teacher—that is, as white. But Cicely's dream falls to pieces at the moment that poetry permits her "triumph": while Martha stands "on the platform," John recovers his memory and recognizes her as the fiancée he had left to join the war. He, not Cicely, is the white one. Reading verse thus exposes the actuality that underlies Cicely's fantasy of escape from descent; it is the way she discovers that blackness must remain her lot. With more compassion toward her misplaced longings than he accorded Ryder, Chesnutt's story makes the recitation a symbol of the Americanization that his protagonist cannot fully undergo. That outcome was the antithesis of the reform agenda that many pageant-masters, clubwomen, settlement house workers, teachers, and students attached to the reading of verse in school and society.[66]

Wartime Poetry Reading and Its Legacy

Despite the ongoing reality of social divisions and racial or ethnic nationalism, periods of war strengthened the conception of poetry as a reminder of shared ideals and a source of national unity. During World War I, more than ninety anthologies of poems about war and peace appeared while the fighting was in progress. One representative volume, George Herbert Clarke's *A Treasury of War Poetry* (first series), went through sixteen printings and sold 42,000 copies between 1917 and 1920. In the same way that the category of "religious" verse overrode distinctions between modernism and its romantic or "genteel" antecedents, so the publishers of wartime anthologies saw, in Mark Van Wienen's phrase, "no particular contradiction" in issuing thematically coherent collections that juxtaposed rhyme and free verse, explicit moralism and allusive symbolism. The writings of martyred soldier-poets such as Kilmer and Alan Seeger were best-sellers; Seeger's *Poems*, published by Scribner's, went through eight printings in its first year, 1918, and sold more than 28,000 copies in that period. Van Wienen emphasizes the mustering of poetic expression to popularize dissent— its "deployment" to build support for the antiwar position of the Women's Peace Party or advance the anticapitalist protests of the Industrial Workers of the World. The great value of that argument, like Cary Nelson's in *Repression and Recovery,* is that it shows how even conventionally "genteel" forms of verse, far from fostering an "ethereal poetic realm," made the figure of the poet a sage who was also an activist.[67]

But the predominant uses of poetry in World War I, as Van Wienen concedes, were to consolidate support for American intervention and victory. For instance, he demonstrates how poets who contributed to newspapers and magazines—including Edwin Arlington Robinson, Alice Corbin Henderson, and other early modernists—"played the role of a chorus" by affirming government-sponsored initiatives such as food conservation. In addition to the activities of those professionals, amateur poets celebrated and sentimentalized wartime sacrifice. Van Wienen revives the story of how one such amateur text, "The Volunteer's Mother," which was first published in the *New York Times,* passed among women whose sons were either in military service or eligible for it. "I carried copies of it while traveling last Summer from the Canadian border down to quaint old Waynesboro, Ga.," the woman who circulated the poem remarked. "And no matter where I've read it tears have come into the eyes of those who heard, and comfort to aching hearts was given." Van Wienen adds that the "acts of reciting, hearing, and sharing the poem" provided an opportunity for "building unanimity for the U.S. war effort. . . . Through local, informal gatherings, the patriotic war poem promotes the kind of group self-definition and unity needed to delineate a 'patriotic' citizenry and mobilize the nation for war."[68]

The history of Elias Lieberman's "Credo" exemplifies that same phenomenon, not only in World War I but in the work's ongoing utility during and after World War II. First published in 1916, the poem is a first-person declaration of loyalty, "utter, irrevocable, inviolate," to the "truths" on which American democracy rests. It proclaims the speaker's connection to the soldiers who had defended the United States throughout its history by wielding the "white sword of God," and those who might defend the nation in the future. Significantly, that religious reference and a subsequent one to "the Almighty" reveal nothing of Lieberman's distinctly

Jewish beliefs; "God" here is an acceptably Judeo-Christian being. The poem likewise lacks any mention of Lieberman's foreign birth. It is as if the exigencies of war required the suppression of the ethnic differences to which Lieberman had drawn attention in "I Am An American." Despite what the poem did not say (or perhaps because of it), one correspondent, a Brooklyn history and civics teacher, praised "Credo" in 1916 for voicing "sentiments of my own which I never expected to see in words." In 1944, with war again raging, another reader displayed an "illuminated" version of the poem, along with a flag, in her window; "total strangers" asked for permission to transcribe it. The reader herself sent "numerous" copies to friends and to men in the military. As was the case with "I Am an American," the poem subsequently circulated in the 1950s as a devotional text suitable for church youth programs and Protestant worship services.[69]

"Credo"'s longevity nevertheless points to a key difference between the uses of verse in the two world wars. In the World War I era, the creation of poems such as Lieberman's overshadowed appropriations of older texts for the patriotic needs of the present. World War II called forth less heroic lyricism and, in the wake of modernism, more personal, pained reflections. As a British observer put it, "Perhaps the present generation, with the experience of their fathers behind them, are more conscious of the grimness of the thing." Thus, although certain contemporary poets—notably Stephen Vincent Benét—reprised the role of their counterparts in 1917, rereading acquired greater prominence as a civic activity than first encounters with newly composed works.[70]

The reinterpretation of extant poetry in World War II was especially visible at the site of the school. In pursuit of "education for victory," pedagogues increasingly stressed the importance of teaching skills that would serve military needs, at least by creating support on the home front. English teachers could not supply the practical benefits of learning radio operation or first aid, but they did their part for the war effort by insisting on a curriculum of literary study that helped "young Americans to realize the great values for which America is fighting." Presuming agreement about what those values were, the National Council of Teachers of English in 1943 recommended teaching literature that emphasized individual freedom while fostering "personal adjustment." The NCTE also advocated exposing students to works that advanced both "understanding of the diverse elements in our society and of the world" and "national unity through the democratic integration" of various "cultural groups." Those aims mirrored and reinforced the stance of the liberal idealists in the Office of War Information, whose propaganda depicting the war as a struggle for freedom and democracy ran up against the proponents of military expediency and political compromise with regard to colonial and occupied territories such as North Africa and Italy. That tension between ideals and realities—and even the potential conflict between individualism and unity—did not surface, however, in the official pronouncements of school leaders.[71]

For educators already imbued with the "experience" curriculum, poetry could be especially useful in defending freedom, diversity, and democracy because of its evident capacity to enrich the reader's emotional life, a process that would meet "wartime needs" by "deepening convictions" and "heightening sensitivity." The particular texts to which teachers turned to attain those ends were a mixed bag of venerable British imports, nineteenth-century schoolroom verse, and more recent examples by both canonical and popular American poets. For example, the NCTE offered its constituents a reading of Frost's "Mending Wall" that applied it "to illustrate the principles which underlie any peace program, for it stresses the necessity for human understanding" and relied on characterizations of "common people." Although a more accurate interpretation than the characteristic misreading in which the line "Good fences make good neighbors" signals Frost's approval instead of his dismay, the use of "Mending Wall" as a vision of the world after America defeated the Nazis was at odds with Frost's own statement that the poem elucidated "the impossibility of drawing sharp lines and making exact distinctions between good and bad or between almost any two abstractions."[72]

To encourage the understanding of minorities that would ostensibly strengthen the social cohesiveness war demanded, teachers turned to two types of verse: popular celebrations of American diversity and the poetry of African-Americans. In the first group were efforts that continued from the prewar period, such as Rachel Davis DuBois's. But educators also introduced students to poems in the manner of "I Am an American" which World War II itself had sparked. Such works explicitly paid homage to the distinct ethnic, class, regional, and racial groups the United States comprised but defined the nation as an entity welded together by common ideals, including acceptance of difference. One widely disseminated example was "Ballad for Americans," written by Earl H. Robinson and John LaTouche in 1939. Robinson, the composer as well of "I Dreamed I Saw Joe Hill Last Night," was a musician with strong working-class sympathies. The text, which became available to readers as both a poem and song lyrics, contains a figure who "represent[s] the whole"; he is "the nobody who's everybody." Asked if he is an American, he replies: "I'm just an Irish, Jewish, Italian . . ." as well as a representative of a dozen religious perspectives. The poem makes the Civil War a struggle for African-American freedom and specifies "belief in liberty" as the national faith. "Ballad for Americans" was first performed on the radio in 1939 with Paul Robeson as soloist. In 1942, the NCTE's pamphlet on literature in wartime recommended either Robeson's recording or the print version as a stimulus for instilling in schoolchildren "a respect for the dignity and worth of the individual." Another popular text with similar resonances was Hal Borland's "Creed," first published in the *Saturday Evening Post* in 1942. An explication of the words "I am an American," the poem became a resource for teachers in search of materials underscoring "the obligation to respect" religious choice and other elements of the American "covenant."[73]

The second wartime strategy for achieving "understanding of the diverse elements in our society," at least as prescribed by liberal-minded educators, was a heightened attention to African-American culture. The NCTE recommended that English teachers assign "collections of Negro verse" so as to "replace ignorance with knowledge and prejudice with fair-mindedness." To that end, an instructor in a Chicago-area high school, cognizant that "wartime heightens the need for certain values that reading can give," focused her lyric poetry unit on assignments that would enable the class to "enter emotionally" into the work of Countee Cullen and other African-American poets. She also arranged discussions among black and white students on integration. In the end, she felt confident that she had equipped her charges to assist in "solv[ing] one of the problems which remain the 'unfinished business of democracy.'"[74]

In addition to supplying the didactic content that "education for victory" made imperative, poetry became in some classrooms the catalyst for enactments of the ideals which the war jeopardized. In Madison, Wisconsin, a group of seventh-graders was intrigued to learn that books of verse were in high demand among soldiers stationed nearby; according to the report of the local library, the men wanted "something you can quote." Together the class arrived at the conclusion that "poetry means more to people when their lives are in danger and their thoughts on serious things." To fulfill the soldiers' requests, the students compiled an anthology, selecting its contents by interviewing not only military personnel but also ministers, public officials, parents, and other adults. All the pupils also created personal scrapbooks of verse; many committed favorite lines to memory. The "workshop" activities, which brought together "Invictus" and "Renascence," Tennyson and Robinson, allowed the class to live the Allied war aims by engaging in democratic choice, cooperation, and community service. In Highland Park, Illinois, another seventh-grade class listened to "Ballad for Americans." Their teacher reported that "it stirred them as it has stirred hundreds of others. They wanted to hear it again and again." Borland's "Creed" was also "inspirational." After these exposures, the students worked collectively on producing a ballad about freedom and diversity themselves. The result was a "composite work of the entire group," mirroring the unity necessary to combat democracy's enemies. A verse speaking choir performed the ballad at an evening of poetry for the public.[75]

In all the foregoing examples, educators cast poets as people whose unusual vision enabled them to clarify American ideals under threat, and whose sensitivity to language allowed them to reveal the sanctity of the common man. Yet by and large the educators themselves were blind to the strains which the accommodation of both consensus and difference lent to their wartime objectives. Most did not question whether marshaling literature to unify Americans—that is, extending the tradition of civic nationalism—necessitated devaluing texts that registered grievances against ethnic nationalists who regarded whites and Anglo-Saxons as superior. Even the teacher who showcased Cullen sponsored an African-American guest speaker who told students that "much of the poetry written by Negroes was too bitter to be read to young people." The only exception to that avoidance of conflict was an educator who complained that anthologists made little space for the "literature of freedom," preferring Whittier's "Barefoot Boy" to his anti-slavery poems. Can it be, that writer ventured to ask in 1943, that "the literature of freedom is still controversial in 'the land of the free'?"[76]

Outside the school, the assumption that poetry reading could serve the United States' victory in World War II took several forms. With respect to the recasting of older works, the educators' effort to reassert the importance of literary classics had its equivalent in the publication of anthologies and editions for adult readers. As Paul Fussell has argued, and as perhaps the Madison schoolchildren sensed, the anthology format exerted strong attraction in wartime partly because the "principle of variety" underlying its arrangement was "a way of honoring the pluralism and exuberance of the 'democratic' Allied cause." Norman Cousins, the editor of the *Saturday Review* starting in the 1940s, underscored that point by bringing out two such volumes: a compendium of brief excerpts from both prose and poetry entitled *A Treasury of Democracy* (1942) and, with William Rose Benét, *The Poetry of Freedom* (1945). Drawing together verse from nations around the world (including the Allies' enemies), the latter collection explicitly cast the poetic sage as "a major figure in the fight for freedom." The "leaders of both America and Great Britain," the editors explained, have "turned to" poetry "not as a matter of literary decoration, but because it delivers a message that can be conveyed in no other way." On a more personal level, John Kieran, famous as a writer and radio personality, assembled *Poems I Remember* (1942), a fine example of the survival of the fireside poets in memory as well as in the curriculum. Kieran's introduction to the volume did not address World War II directly (although Kieran did remark that as a soldier in the previous world war, he had walked through devastated France with "miniature collections of Burns, Browning, Swinburne, and Tennyson" crammed into his pack). Nevertheless, the fact that Kieran chose to gather (among others) "In Memoriam," "Breathes There the Man," "I Wandered Lonely as a Cloud," and Longfellow's "A Psalm of Life" at this time, and that Doubleday, Doran agreed to issue the collection, suggests that an insecure present may have influenced readers' desire to reclaim both the purported innocence of childhood and the ideals they had learned through poetry when they were young.[77]

Books of poetry specifically designed for members of the Armed Forces exhibited a similar emphasis on older texts, with some exceptions. Of the poems printed in Armed Services Editions, a line of paperbacks created for portability and distributed by the Council on Books in Wartime, most were canonized British works, examples of schoolroom poetry, and popular verse, although the series made room for several "new poets" as well. Its list included collections of Lindsay, Millay, and Sandburg, along with Longfellow, Wordsworth, Keats, Shelley, and Browning. Two anthologies edited by Louis Untermeyer also appeared as Armed Services Editions: *The Fireside Book of Verse: Favorite Poems of Romance and Adventure* (1945) and *Great Poems from Chaucer to Whitman* (1944). The latter compilation, 161 pocket-sized pages long, drew on Palgrave's *Golden Treasury, The Oxford Book of English Verse,* and Untermeyer's own *A Treasury of Great Poems* (1942) to present what the volume's back cover billed as primarily lyric poetry that had survived "the changing fashions of schools, movements, and generations." Thus the anthology represented a solidity and continuity that soldiers facing the uncertainties of warfare might find comforting. *Great Poems* also exhibited the upbeat attitude

Poetry for Americans fighting in World War II. Department of Rare Books and Special Collections, University of Rochester Libraries.

(again, a kind of innocence) which, as Fussell has argued, differentiated American anthologies for the military from their counterparts in the British market. For example, although the poem did not appear in his 1942 anthology, Untermeyer added "A Psalm of Life" to the Longfellow section of the Armed Services collection; probably he did so because the lines exhorting readers "In the world's broad field of battle" to "Be a hero in the strife!" could take on literal meaning for soldiers who were not only "in the bivouac of Life" but in a bivouac at the front. Likewise, Untermeyer's inclusion of Browning's rebuff to fear of death in "Prospice" and Arthur Hugh Clough's "Say Not the Struggle Naught Availeth" seems calculated to boost troop morale.

But Fussell's observation is not quite right with respect to the other anthologies widely disseminated to soldiers in World War II: *The Pocket Book of Verse* (1940) and Alexander Woollcott's *As You Were* (1943). *The Pocket Book of Verse* was one of the opening guns in the paperback revolution that continued after the war.

"Surprisingly popular," in Fussell's words, it went through nine reprintings in its first eighteen months. It, too, contained "A Psalm of Life" and other tokens of earnestness, sentiment, and stability. Furthermore, the volume omitted antiwar poems of the World War I period. Yet optimism and human indomitability were not the collection's only lessons. The armies in Matthew Arnold's "Dover Beach" are "ignorant" rather than triumphant; Emily Dickinson's lines "Parting is all we know of heaven, / And all we need of hell" precede Christina Rosetti's "Song" about death; Robinson's "Richard Cory" blows his brains out; and Sandburg's "Grass" offers his image of battle casualties piled high. Those somber choices belie Fussell's contention that the book "posed no danger to morale," but they arguably enriched the volume aesthetically and as a record of human experience. As one soldier reported, "I knew I would find in the volume the companionship I was not getting in the barracks and that the poetry would help to compensate for the beauty that was lacking in my life."[78]

As You Were, which had a first printing of 30,000 copies, accorded greater space to popular verse such as Eugene Field's "Little Willie," with the result that it encouraged sentimentality over irony; yet Frost's ambiguous "Mending Wall," Millay's "Lament" (beginning "Listen, children: Your father is dead"), Robinson's portrayal of "Mr. Flood" as isolated and futureless, and James Weldon Johnson's shudder, in "My City," at "the stark unutterable pity" of death were a counterweight to the "sentimental nostalgia" that Fussell detected. The more important point is that both *The Pocket Book of Verse* and *As You Were*, in assimilating the "new poetry" to older American literary traditions, demonstrate how thoroughly early modernism, once a locus of rebellion, had become by the early 1940s what Woollcott called "a fond, familiar voice" from home that spoke to the ordinary soldier.[79]

The Celebrity as Propagandist: Stephen Vincent Benét

As Anglo-American poetic classics became, for students, civilians, and military personnel alike, a point of access to the ideology undergirding the war effort, the figure of the patriotic sage simultaneously achieved renewed vigor in the careers of certain established contemporary poets who joined popular verse writers in turning their attention to war. Millay created the verse drama *The Murder of Lidice* (1942) to protest fascist brutality. Sandburg hailed the work of Hal Borland and produced his own poems extolling freedom. Archibald MacLeish was a key leader in the early days of the Office of War Information. The most prominent and influential individual to make poetry a weapon to aid the Allies, however, was Stephen Vincent Benét.[80]

Benét was born in 1898, the son of an army officer who, with his wife, placed books and reading at the heart of family life. When he arrived at Yale in 1915, Benét already thought of himself as a poet, in part because of the model supplied by his older brother, William Rose Benét. He evinced as well an earnestness about both his calling and his country: as his friend MacLeish later observed, "Steve was more conscious of being an American than any other man I ever knew." Although he participated in the artistic renaissance that emerged at Yale in the late 1910s, Benét shared with the writers who clustered around New Haven's version of an avant-garde less insistence on the merits of modernism than the editors of most of the period's little magazines expressed. That outlook is connected to what Benét's biographer has identified as his "nonportentous" quality—his distance from "erudite disenchantment." Benét maintained that stance, which amounted to another variant of innocence, even during two periods as an expatriate in Paris during the 1920s.[81]

Benét's early work was diverse and prolific, consisting of poems, novels, literary journalism, and short stories turned out to pay the rent. By the mid-1920s, his name was familiar to American readers of popular magazines. Benét then wrote the book that conferred on him his lasting fame: *John Brown's Body,* composed during his second stay abroad between 1926 and 1928. The long narrative poem, which Benét described as "an epic told in a new way" and a "cyclorama," recounted the experience of the Civil War from just before John Brown's raid to shortly after Lee's surrender. Its main characters mingled fictional creations, such as the New Englander Jack Ellyat, his Georgian foil Clay Wingate, and Wingate's slave Cudjo, with historical figures. The action of the poem included both battle scenes and lovers' trysts, forays into the mind of Lincoln and Lee, and the hardships of Andersonville prison. John Brown himself appears as a "fanatic," in keeping with his reputation among historians of Benét's day, but also as a heroic individualist destined to "change the actual scheme of things" by following his conscience. In form, the text mainly encompassed what Benét referred to as "a rather rough blank verse combined with a dactylic or anapestic pentameter that . . . binds the whole project together"; it also included rhymed quatrains and occasional prose passages.[82]

The critical reception of *John Brown's Body* was decidedly mixed; a number of reviewers thought the poem uneven and overreaching. Nevertheless, it was among the best-selling nonfiction books of 1928 and the only sustained work of poetry to attain a wide popular audience in the early twentieth century. Although reviewers frequently compared Benét to Whitman because of their shared scope and subject, readers' responses to the poem, as Benét's biographer has pointed out, resembled the enthusiasm the public had shown for Longfellow. Edited by Benét's close friend from Yale, John Farrar, and published by the fledgling firm of Doubleday, Doran, the book sold 130,000 copies in the first two years after publication; even in the depths of the Depression, Americans bought an average of 6,000 copies a year at the volume's original price. The Book-of-the-Month Club, whose board of judges was headed by Benét's former Yale professor Henry Seidel Canby, chose *John Brown's Body* as its main selection. Later it named the volume a bonus book for subscribers who had made at least four purchases a year. A high school edition, first issued in 1941, had sold 91,000 copies by 1957; in the same period a college edition, for which Canby wrote an introduction, sold 87,000 copies. Parts of the poem were broadcast on the radio for occasions like Lincoln's Birthday; the actor Raymond Massey recited it on the air in the shadow of World War II. It was also dramatized in England as well as the United States. In sum, *John Brown's Body* reasserted the figure of the poet as both sage and intimate at a time when high modernism had eroded those roles for many American publishers and readers.[83]

Farrar and Dan Longwell, the promotion manager for Double-day, Doran, contributed to the book's popularity by launching a systematic advertising campaign, complete with endorsements from literary luminaries. (Longwell sent proofs of the book to Edwin Arlington Robinson, who wrote back that "parts of it are very fine and parts of it are as bad as possible.") *John Brown's Body* also capitalized on the surge of interest in American culture during the 1920s, and particularly the Lincoln boom of the period. As count-less fan letters of the period attest, various qualities of the text itself judiciously appealed to a range of readers: Benét acknowledged the suffering of both North and South, balanced depictions of "virile" action with passages of feminine emotion, and tempered modernist devices such as Eliotic allusions with old-fashioned narrative clar-ity. The result of all these factors was that Benét's best-seller re-centered poetry as an American medium suitable for transmitting an American message. *John Brown's Body* seemed especially sus-ceptible to rereading. "I have no way of telling you the place in my life your [book] has found," a Texas man declared in a letter to Benét. "Let me say this—it is the book I pick up when I am frayed out, disgusted, exhausted—and it always brings back my balance."[84]

The response to the work by Benét's readers shaped his cultural function after 1940, as first the threat of fascism and then the out-break of World War II engaged the country's attention. One con-crete result of the persistent popularity of *John Brown's Body* was its issuance in 1943 in an Armed Services edition. In the wartime · context, the principle of freedom from slavery for which Brown had sacrificed his life became the basis for battling the Nazis and Japanese. More generally, the consensus Benét had forged about the centrality of the Civil War for all Americans served as the foun-dation for his stance as champion of national unity to further the Allied cause. On the air and in print, Benét rallied his audience to hear a single message: American citizens must defend their dem-ocratic traditions against the enemies threatening their free way of life.

Among the writings in which Benét expressed that view were those reprinted in *A Summons to the Free,* a pamphlet in the series "America in a World at War" which Farrar and Rinehart published in 1941. The pamphlet, containing both prose and verse, concluded with Benét's "Nightmare at Noon," a poem that had first appeared in the *New York Times Magazine* in June 1940. The text depicts Nazi occupation of northern Europe and prods complacent Americans into envisioning what their own cities would be like if fascism prevailed. One passage succinctly reiterates the principle of civic nationalism: "You can be a Finn or a Dane and an American. / You can be German or French and an American, / Jew, Bohunk, Nigger, Mick—all the dirty names / We call each other— and yet American." Acknowledging that American ideals did not always correspond to reality, Benét nevertheless affirmed that "as a country, we try." Still an exemplar of balance—here between isolationists and left-wing ideologues—he thus earned praise from a reader who told him that she wanted to send copies of the text both to "every official in Washington" and to "careless-thinking young radicals" contemptuous of "the American way of living."[85]

Benét's other contributions to the war effort included numerous radio scripts. "Listen to the People," a long narrative poem first published in *Life* magazine, originated as a radio broadcast commissioned by the Council for Democracy in observance of the Fourth of July in 1941. Because the program aired just prior to an address by President Roosevelt, Benét's biographer noted that his audience was larger than that for "any other serious writer in the history of the United States" (up to 1958). In the poem, ordinary men and women—the "people"—submerge their ethnic and racial differences to speak as "one nation" on behalf of "liberty and faith" and "the proud walker, Democracy." Shortly before his death in 1943, Benét articulated that belief in prose: his work *America,* commissioned by the Office of War Information, traced the history of the United States by highlighting the development of its commitment to "an experiment in life and government and the rights of man." Posthumously published by Farrar and Rinehart and sent abroad in an Armed Services Edition, the book also earned Benét a place as one of only five American authors included in the

New World Bookshelf distributed to Germans in stateside prisoner-of-war camps.[86]

All those wartime writings made Benét a prime representative of the qualities that Paul Fussell has derogated as "high-mindedness": the belief that the Allies were noble, moral crusaders for goodness against evil. In Fussell's estimation, "high-mindedness," and its corollary, "niceness" (which Benét also exemplified), were pernicious for several reasons: they intensified the vagueness surrounding America's actual war objectives; they left unexamined the exploitative possibilities inherent in concepts such as "freedom"; they obscured both the petty annoyances of military life and the grim reality of death in combat; and they created a climate conducive to bland, unadventurous literature. In support of the last point, Fussell put Benét at the top of his list of writers "persuaded that the war effort required the laying aside of all normal standards of art and intellect."[87]

Fussell may be right about the cultural consequences of trumpeting the nation's moral ideals during the war, especially the "ultimate disappointment" resulting from the failure to achieve a more just postwar world. Yet Benét's position, and the uses readers made of his poetry, were more complicated than "high-mindedness" implies. On the one hand, Benét himself was critical of documents about democracy and rights written in the "pianola-English" of the academy. His own work, he hoped, reversed rather than perpetuated "high-sounding and far-off" ideas about American government by showing that the founders' vision "meant something." In that respect, Benét saw his later poems and prose as serving a public that wanted writers to furnish "the succour and fortitude great work can bring to the troubled spirit in troubled and dissolving days." On the other hand, he understood his wartime verse as propaganda and therefore as an exercise of civic obligation.[88]

Even so, readers in the 1930s and '40s often reacted to Benét's work not as if he had produced it in order to strengthen opposition to fascism but, rather, as if his poetry were a transcription of the convictions and emotions the public already possessed. "It seems to me, Mr. Benét," one woman explained after reading and hearing

"Listen to the People," that "[you are] putting into words what [Americans] feel in their hearts almost to the bursting point yet lack the gift of expressing. To do this for them is a great thing. People want words sometimes—they want to say what they feel, they want others to know and understand." Perhaps this response amounts to the "self-satisfaction" that Fussell claimed "high-mindedness" provided the reading public, although it also suggests that public's need for the poet as sage and companion.[89]

Furthermore, such close identification between poet and reader permitted Benét's audience to embrace the idea that they themselves (and not inaccessible modernists) represented the "civilized" populace. One radio scriptwriter made clear that possibility in pleading with Benét to work with her: the times demanded poetry, she declared, from "the real writers, not the pseudo-intellectuals" whose "falsification of the purposes and ideas of poetry have given it a somewhat uncomfortable name in the mouth of the average American. Pure unembarrassed[,] unembarrassing poetry has as much place in American life as have our country's traditions of life themselves." Readers also responded to Benét's use of poetry as propaganda not by arguing that he had debased the genre but rather by concurring that the ability of poets to wield vivid, "thrilling" language gave them special importance in the war effort. Benét's commitments to a morally accented civic nationalism, his accessibility, his sacrifices for his country, and even his "niceness" meant that he not only articulated what the famous OWI films termed "Why We Fight," but also personified what Americans (thanks in part to educators, anthologists, and contemporary poets) came to believe they were fighting for.[90]

Poetry and Citizenship at Mid-Century—and After

On the eve of Pearl Harbor, one more anthology designed to clarify the civic ideals of the United States found its way to readers' bookshelves. Entitled *The American Citizens Handbook*, the volume further reconfigured the vocabulary of citizenship training that had gained currency in the interwar period. The book was a project of the National Education Association; its editor, Joy Elmer Morgan, was a prominent figure in the movement for adult education. By Morgan's account, the *Handbook* sold out in two early editions, went out of print because of wartime paper restrictions, and reappeared in 1946 in an expanded United Nations Edition more than six hundred pages in length. It then became a steady seller for the next two decades, with one last revision appearing in 1968. Its ongoing life even after that date provides a final commentary on the appropriation of poetic texts to support competing visions of the values that have defined American national identity.[91]

The intended audience for *The American Citizens Handbook* was the new citizen—not primarily the older immigrant but, rather, the student (of whatever national origin) who was attaining the voting age of twenty-one. To mark that milestone, the NEA had successfully lobbied Congress in 1940 to designate the third Sunday in May as "I Am an American Citizenship Day"; the volume, they hoped, would serve as a token of the occasion that school boards and other community officials could present to young people at appropriately dignified ceremonies across the country.

The designation of the publication as a handbook implied the editor's and publisher's hopes for the utility and longevity of their project: Morgan's vision was that both the physical book and the texts it bound together would "grow in value and usefulness as a lifelong possession of the American citizen." In his foreword, Morgan specified the reading practices—careful study of documents, memorization of poems and songs—that would facilitate that vision. Noting that literacy by itself was no guarantee of "intelligent citizenship," Morgan saw the handbook as representing the "wisdom in the choice of reading" that Americans required. By repeatedly referring to its contents, the nation's citizenry could "keep ever alive in [its] hearts the purposes and ideals which make for true greatness."[92]

In the 1946 edition, those contents ranged from Elbert Hubbard's anti-labor missive, "A Message to Garcia," to a page (complete with an aphorism from Poor Richard) headed "Planning Your Budget." They included as well selections that equated American and Christian beliefs, such as New Testament quotations and Harry Stillwell Edwards's "The Tenth Generation," a paean to schooling based on the tenets of Jesus. More predictably, a large number of items in the volume related to the government and laws of the United States: the Declaration of Independence, the Constitution, the addresses of Lincoln and Washington, advice about making contracts and purchasing property. In addition, under the rubric "Heroes of American Democracy," *The American Citizens Handbook* included photographs of 76 busts in the "Hall of Fame for Great Americans" sponsored by New York University, together with a biographical sketch of each figure portrayed. The grouping is notable for its assumption that "authors"—among them the poets Emerson, Longfellow, Lowell, Whittier, Bryant, Holmes, Poe, Whitman, and Sidney Lanier—could be democratic "heroes" whose achievements offered "strength" to new citizens.[93]

The most distinctive aspects of the 1946 edition, however, were two sections added after the end of World War II. One consisted of a history of the United Nations, together with statements arguing for the necessity of world government in the atomic age—a position that Morgan favored and that continued to earn him the opprobrium of the political right years after his death. The other was "A Golden Treasury for the Citizen," an assemblage of poetry (intermingled with a few prose pieces) arranged alphabetically within topical sections and indexed by grade level—through four years of college—to facilitate learning by heart. Its purpose, Morgan remarked in a headnote, was to promote a "common mind," a set of shared religious, patriotic, and aesthetic values to be implanted in children before they took their place in the ranks of responsible Americans. That formulation, like the rationale governing the book as a whole, largely reversed the stand of DuBois and other liberal Americanizers who highlighted multicultural contributions, although the category "Sacred Writings" included a token bit from Confucius, some "Proverbs of Hindustan," and a few "Sayings of Mohammed."[94]

Under such rubrics as "Life and Aspiration," "The World of Nature," and "Historical Selections," the "Golden Treasury" reproduced dozens of poems, many of which had appeared in earlier anthologies for school use such as *Through Magic Casements*. Here, once again, were Henley's "Invictus" and Milton's "On His Blindness"; classroom staples like Miller's "Columbus" and Holmes's "Old Ironsides"; excerpts from Keats's "Endymion," Lowell's "Sir Launfal," and Millay's "God's World." Lieberman's "Credo" appeared in the section called "Love of Country." Like Cook and Walker's exemplary texts, Morgan's choices also accommodated Wilcox, Braley, and lesser-known authors of popular verse, because his selection principle, too, concerned the theme or moral of the poem, not the degree of literary skill it exhibited. Stripped of the emphasis on feeling or apprehension underlying the "experience" curriculum, these works reasserted their didactic function as repositories of sage advice about living. This is not to say that the handbook omitted texts that promised to enhance self-expression; on the contrary, the source for much of the poetry that Morgan reprinted was the series of *Personal Growth Leaflets* which the NEA had previously issued. As that title suggests, the ideal of self-development resounded throughout the "Treasury"—in Phoebe Cary's lines urging persistence ("All that's good and great is done / Just by patient trying"), Langston Hughes's instruction to "hold fast to dreams," Edward Rowland Sill's imprecation to make the best of "Opportunity," and numerous other examples. Moreover, the "Treasury" took shape against the backdrop of the NEA's "Goals of America—And What Schools Can Do To Achieve Them," a document that Morgan reproduced earlier in the volume. Drafted in the 1930s with the consultation of Dewey and the sociologist Edward A. Ross, the "Goals"—formulated as a set of "rights"—identified an "active, flexible personality" as a national priority.[95]

Yet despite the guidance it proffered with respect to personal growth, the most striking facet of the *American Citizens Handbook* was its subordination of individual interests to collective ones. Morgan's editing transformed the transmission and mastery of literature, and particularly "treasured" verse, into a communal obligation as well as a private possession. In Morgan's hands, reading poetry became more than a means to nurture civic pride, as was the case with Benét; it was a civic duty. The NEA's "Goals" framed that obligation in the psychological parlance of progressive educators: reading and language study were "necessary for the enjoyment of group culture"; literature served to spread the "cultural values necessary for proper social adjustment." But reimagining mastery of the "Treasury" as a civic responsibility simultaneously imparted to the poems within it something of the intensified "sacred aura" that had surrounded the Constitution and other national icons since the interwar period. As a result, religious overtones accrued not simply to the rituals of recitation but also to the texts on the page. Moreover, packaging the poems in the *Handbook* as the expression of American democracy invested reading, recitation, and memorization with the same potential that, as Michael Schudson has demonstrated, reformers attached to voting in the first half of the twentieth century: such practices became "a performance of individualism oriented to the nation." In that respect even solitary reading could become a civic as well as a social act, and the living room as well as the town hall or the classroom could be a "locus of civic participation."[96]

Several ironies attended this reconception of verse reading as the citizen's duty. One is that Morgan's designation of the "Treasury" as a wellspring of the "common mind" necessary to fortify "order and government" was at odds with one of the most prominent themes of the collected poems, the importance of resisting pressures for conformity. For example, while Sam Walter Foss's frequently anthologized hymn to community, "The House by the Side of the Road," appeared in the "Life and Aspiration" section, so did his narrative poem "The Calf-Path," which made explicit the "moral lesson" that people should not blindly "follow in the beaten track." Kipling's "If" more famously sounded the same note, equating manhood with the ability to "trust yourself when all men doubt you." That was essentially the message of "Invictus" ("my unconquerable soul") as well. A reader who took seriously Morgan's imperative to strive for like-mindedness might well wonder how to accommodate those assertions of self. Another source of dissonance was the adaptation of texts that initially sought to challenge the moral or aesthetic conventions of nineteenth-century verse—specimens of the "new poetry" by Sara Teasdale, Edna St. Vincent Millay, Robert Frost, Carl Sandburg, and others—to deeply traditional purposes. In this context, the reprinting of an excerpt from "God's World," a poem that advanced Millay's career as Greenwich Village gamine, recovered and reiterated the innocence that also attached to her persona; here again the "tincture of disestablishment" with which "new poets" sought to infuse their art became undetectable.[97]

A further irony in a volume predicated on the uniqueness of American democracy was that it perpetuated the tradition, visible as well in Americanization materials, of treating British authors as part of the American heritage. In fact, nothing better underscores the pervasiveness of an Anglo-American culture, buttressed by 1946 with the alliance between Britain and the United States in World War II, than Morgan's failure to identify Tennyson, Wordsworth, Kipling, and Shelley's connection with the target of the Declaration of Independence. By the same token, the appropriation of British poets as American emphasizes that immigrants from England required no Americanization and presumably not much citizenship training either.

Finally, perhaps the greatest irony of the *American Citizens Handbook* has been the twist in its political fortunes since its first appearance. Emanating from the NEA, the 1946 volume bespoke a liberal outlook: in addition to its progressive educational philosophy and endorsement of the United Nations, the book also urged workers to organize and asked consumers to "patronize only industries which play fair." Despite those characteristics, however, the handbook's recent support has come from the right. In the 1980s, as Secretary of Education, William Bennett proposed that the NEA or some other group reissue the book; during his presidential campaign, Lamar Alexander pronounced it a "virtual user's guide to America." In 2000 Jay Nordlinger, writing in the conservative *National Review,* praised the collection's "thoughtful" patriotism and rejection of "special privilege" (that is, affirmative action). Nordlinger especially commended the book's "Golden Treasury" section. While he alluded to the persistent tensions surrounding poetry's place in American culture, he lauded the "Treasury" as "evidence of a nation, and a civilization," the awareness of which had been obscured by the misinterpretation of pluralism as a mandate for a divisive politics of difference. What had disappeared since the mid-twentieth century, in Nordlinger's opinion, was a liberalism that had championed reading's "assimilative power" for the sake of "our cultural and spiritual nationhood." In endorsing the civic hopes that Morgan had attached to verse, Nordlinger sought to enlist the older forms of the genre in a related crusade: the effort to cast off what modernist poets had helped to fashion, the "suffocating cloak of irony" itself.[96]

Nordlinger was wrong, of course, in implying that Morgan was typical of all liberals in his endorsement of total assimilation. Commemorative ceremonies and pageants, women's clubs and settlement houses, Americanization and victory campaigns accommodated liberals—and conservatives—with divergent convictions about the knowledge and sympathies that full citizenship required. But Nordlinger's response to discovering the *Handbook* underscores what one might call the pluralistic possibilities of poems themselves—the capacity of "Invictus," "The Arrow and the Song," or "Mending Wall" (none of which overtly addressed "Americanness") to support various conceptions of American civic ideals, depending on how and where readers read them. The history of poetry reading among family and friends, in religious settings, and outdoors reveals the same resilience and versatility of text and practice.

chapter nine

Grow Old Along with Me

Poetry and Emotions among Family and Friends

~ A POEM, Robert Frost famously remarked, "begins as a lump in the throat." Frost's pronouncement referred not only to a physical sensation but also to an upwelling of emotion in the poet. Yet poems produce feelings in the reader as well, a premise that the explorations of poetry in school and civic settings have already confirmed. In the late nineteenth and early twentieth centuries, Americans experienced the emotional weight of a particular text—its impact on their mood and sensibility—in a variety of ways.

One kind of reaction depended on the perceived correspondence between the mentalities of poet and audience. As the editors' introduction to *Through Magic Casements* explained, poets have always endeavored "to make us see what they have seen, feel what they have felt, grasp what they have learned."[1] The middle phrase in that formulation obviously denoted shared emotion, but the vision and knowledge to which the editors referred were not matters of intellect alone. In 1900, when the 25-year-old aspiring poet Ormeida Curtis Keeler preceded a quotation in her diary by remarking that "the truth of these words of Whittier [is] being demonstrated to me these days, and it is sad, very sad," she acknowledged both assent to the poet's views (her "grasp" of what Whittier had "learned") and her consequent emotional state. For the Methodist scholar Oscar Kuhns, Browning had the opposite effect: "I have found in his poetry," Kuhns reported, "A help and comfort, an antidote to the moods of sadness that come upon all men at times. . . . He has cheered and braced me with his unconquerable spiritual optimism."[2]

The serenity, comfort, and guidance that readers derived from verse were in turn sources of another emotion: pleasure. Lee De Forest, the "father of radio," made evident the connection between delight in sound, emotional acuity, and inspiration in thanking his family for their Christmas gift in 1899, a "fine edition" of Tennyson's *Poems*. De Forest invoked the treasure metaphor with particular fervor: "I shall enjoy to the utmost searching among that mine of jewels, renewing acquaintance with many precious thoughts, reawakening the echoes of many melodies heard before but forgotten. I need this inspiration now more than ever; for the engrossing work and the rush of the crowds dull the sentiments and the finer life, and muffle the notes of song."[3]

Instances in which poems implanted in readers the sense that they were reliving writers' feelings (not just discovering solace in their outlooks) carried additional emotional weight. "I never got so fully into sympathy with [Robert Burns's] poetry as today," Charles Keeler wrote in the diary he kept during his voyage by ship from San Francisco to Sandy Hook in 1893. "How it reveals the simple, gentle, warm hearted nature of the man, every line of it." Especially at times of illness or grief, as well as in courtship or love, particular poems enabled readers to feel better—in the sense of possessing heightened affect, if not greater well-being. "I was sorry—on Grace's account," the narrator of a short story written around 1915 remarked after he and his wife had lost an opportunity to adopt a child. "A day or so afterward, she opened a book of poems, and I found her crying over it as if her heart would break. She had come to a poem of James Whitcomb Riley's, addressed to a couple who had lost their baby." Omar Khayyam's allusion to "a book of verses underneath the bough" along with "a jug of wine, a loaf of bread, and thou" is perhaps the most succinct evocation of this mimetic way of reading. Like a painting of a room containing a

The solitary poetry lover, whose reading experience was always socially influenced. Courtesy of the Boston Public Library, Print Department.

painting of the same room, the verses in Omar's conceit stimulated sensuality and intimacy between poet and lover, creating a mood that American readers, well acquainted with Omar's lines, in turn self-consciously sought to replicate in their own private moments.[4]

Yet the comforts and pleasures of instruction and inspiration, the joy of sound, and the heightened sympathy arising from identi- fication with the poet's feelings do not fully account for the emo- tional valences that reading verse could carry, because all of those effects depended on the inherent message of the text. As the *New York Times* respondents suggested, pleasure and satisfaction might also derive from the laughter prompted by sharing memories; from the competence and mastery that a filled "treasure chest" afforded; and from the attainment of a clear sense of identity—sources that might be extrinsic to the poet's message, theme, or style. Poetry evokes feelings, in other words, because of the needs and purposes with which readers imbue poems at the site of reading, uses which can intersect with, but also obviate or transcend, the lines on the page.

Although various emotions attended poetry recitation in school, church, and camp, no setting for reading verse aloud entailed a stronger sustained affective dimension than the home. There the genre became entwined with relationships between parents and children, and with the vicissitudes of growing up. There, too, the figure of the poet as innocent was interwoven with desires for domestic order and safety, while the poet's attributes of sophistication found echoes in the quest for freedom from domestic bonds.

Poetry Volumes for Home Use

Several of the forms in which poems circulated to American readers reflected the presumption that poetry had a place in domestic routine. Memory gem collections, as already noted, were frequently identified by their titles or subtitles as suitable for home as well as school use. The children's book illustrator Margaret de Angeli recalled her father's reading to her a collection called *Gems for the Fireside* around 1900; the volume mingled "all the nineteenth-century poets[ ]Longfellow, Lowell, Tennyson" with stories in German dialect that de Angeli found especially amusing. Another locus of verse was the cookbook. Rollo Walter Brown, the son of a commercial potter in the clay country of Ohio, recounted discovering Byron's "Fare Thee Well" and "The Destruction of Sennacherib" in the back of a cookbook that his mother asked him to borrow from a neighbor: "Beyond the recipes for foods were useful hints on poison ivy, felons, cows with caked udders, . . . and the like. And beyond these was a clean-looking section of 'great poems of the world.'" The reprinting of poetry amid practical advice implied that reading verse was as commonplace and obligatory as preparing meals. Furthermore, the accessibility of the genre in a book kept close to the kitchen enabled some women to sneak a moment of reading between chores. Brown reported that his mother, whose household tasks began at 4:30 in the morning, "never worked at anything as if it were the only thing she had in mind. She would pick up a volume from the table when she was tidying the living room, see something that interested her, drop into a chair, read the shortest possible section that would enable her to understand," and then go on with her work. When readers extracted poetry from periodicals and pasted or copied it into scrapbooks, moreover, they inflected those texts with domestic ideals. Jock Wilson, who grew up in an Indiana coal mining family at the turn of the century, connected his mother's "efforts to keep a neat home" that was "beautiful to live in" with her compilation of verse from the *Toledo Blade and Ledger* and *Capper's Weekly*. Memory gem volumes, cookbooks, and more ephemeral formats adaptable to use in the home thus made poetry available to both working-class and middle-class readers, on terms that were antithetical to the sacralization of the genre.[5]

The most ambitious publishing venture linking domesticity and verse was the comprehensive poetry anthology designed for home libraries. Although widely disseminated, these compilations have generally escaped the notice of literary scholars who have treated anthologies as artifacts of canon-formation. For all the contributions of such studies, they have presumed a single, though changing, canon bearing the imprimatur of high culture. Hence, for example, Alan C. Golding has claimed that a defining feature of twentieth-century anthologies is the equation of the "good" with the "oppositional." Like compilations for Americanization classes, the collection for home reading testifies to a different reality: the existence of multiple canons, made up of texts deemed "good" because they conserved the values governing the conditions of their use. For nineteenth-century Americans, the two standard anthologies for the home were Charles A. Dana's *Household Book of Poetry* (1857) and William Cullen Bryant's *A Library of Poetry and Song* (1870). Although the firm of D. Appleton brought out a "thoroughly revised and greatly enlarged" edition of the Dana volume in 1906, six years later the publisher Henry Holt tapped the same market by issuing *The Home Book of Verse*, compiled by Burton E. Stevenson, a Princeton graduate and public librarian in Chillicothe, Ohio.[6]

Holt envisioned the readership for *The Home Book of Verse* as the population he described as the "ordinary bourgeois family," with possibly a child in college. To make the book at least relatively affordable to prospective buyers, the firm priced it at seven dollars and fifty cents (Holt had even pressed for five dollars). The venture was so successful that, when the book appeared, Holt congratulated his editor, Alfred Harcourt, on having correctly "felt the pulse of the trade." In 1923, *The Home Book of Verse* was twelfth on a list of two hundred books selected by the National Council for Better Homes in America to comprise the "Ideal Library." Stevenson subsequently edited an anthology for children and then *The Home Book of Modern Verse* (1925). In the 1930s, he lobbied against an offer from Blue Ribbon Books to issue a cheap reprint of the 1912 volume on the grounds that it would diminish the anthology's stature; the Holt firm went along with Stevenson's objections, indicating its confidence that the reading public would continue to acquire poetry for the home even without the lure of a bargain. As if to corroborate that fact, as late as 1959 Harper and Brothers signed the newspaper book reviewer Lewis Gannett to edit still another collection, *The Harper Book of Family Verse.*[7]

The Stevenson and Gannett volumes, geared to what Evan Thomas, the director of the Harper firm's general book department, identified as the "family" (as well as the "institutional") market, may be distinguished from Untermeyer's *Modern American Poetry* in the fact that their compilers did not aim to educate readers about a particular period or style of verse. In their contents, these household anthologies bore the cumulative weight of their predecessors. Holt, discussing potential inclusions with Stevenson, recurred to his boyhood encounters with Bryant's and Dana's collections. Decades later, after Harper's editor Cass Canfield suggested organizing his collection by subject, Gannett received from Thomas a list of Thomas's "favorites" from *Through Magic Casements*, which he had read as a child with his mother.[8]

Holt's and Thomas's correspondence with Stevenson and Gannett reveals as well the active mediations of publishing house personnel in determining the anthologies' shape. In the case of *The Home Book of Verse,* the title itself was partly the result of a wrangle between Holt and Stevenson, the editor. The publisher had insisted that the collection contain Latin hymns and certain other foreign-language texts that had fascinated him as a boy. Moreover, Holt and Harcourt privately disparaged Stevenson's judgment and ambition, and Holt had no qualms about exercising what he called "my little influence in determining what anthologies people shall have," and their contents. "I should like 'Carcassonne'—original *and* translation," he wrote Stevenson. "Mrs. Holt asks me why. I tell her I don't care to analyze that: I want it." When Holt prevailed, Stevenson's proposed title—"Favorite Poems in English"— became inaccurate, and the two settled on the alternative under which the book appeared.[9]

Such interventions were bound up with the understanding that, in part because of anthologies themselves, readers possessed a set of expectations about the contents of a household poetry book. Acknowledging that fact, Howells had urged compilers to bind poetry collections with blank leaves on which readers could paste in poems the editor had not included. Stevenson hoped to avoid that necessity by anticipating his audience's desires. Thus while he wrote that he aimed to make readily available the "poems which everyone ought to know," a 1937 article about his anthology made clear that it was devised not so much to teach as to serve its audience; it reprinted "familiar verse which everyone remembers and can never find," whether recognized masterpieces or well-known jingles. Along the same lines, the staff at the Harper firm instructed Gannett about the commercial value of including certain texts, whether or not they suited his taste. "Evan can't bear it if we don't have the Noyes' Highwayman," one editor told Gannett. "He's sure it's the one poem everyone will hope to find in the book." In another memo, she apprised Gannett: "[A] few poems like The Wreck of the Hesperus and The Highwayman—familiar to librarians, teachers and parents from their own childhoods—seem to us really essential: as sugar to catch flies." In remarks like these, anthology-making is clearly visible as a process of collaboration among publisher, compiler, and reader—each with a share of authority to determine the final product.[10]

Verse Reading as Affirmation of Domestic Order

As their marketers seem to have sensed, the cultural power of titles linking poetry and the home derived from, capitalized on, and further entrenched a vision of domestic order with a moral and a psychological dimension. Strong feelings attended both aspects of this drive for order, but, as one might expect, the use of poetry to attain psychological security within the family was the more emotionally charged.

In moral terms, reading in domestic surroundings was entangled with concepts of Christian nurture and self-improvement.[11] At least prescriptively, good parents read verse (and prose) to their children as they strove to make their households centers of virtue. Here, too, titles are revealing: well before the twentieth century, denominational periodicals adopted phrases like "Hours at Home" to identify sections containing poems and fiction. In practice, women in both modest and affluent economic circumstances took special responsibility for imparting cultivation through print. Remembering his mother, a single parent who made ends meet by running a boardinghouse and taking in sewing, George Creel, the leader of the American propaganda campaign in World War I, wrote in 1947: "Night after night, when she must have been ready to drop, she told us stories that made dead heroes live again, and actually had us believing that it was a privilege to learn the poems of Scott and Longfellow." Mary Ann Stewart, a Baptist minister's wife in Rochester who admonished herself to "Realise the Home idea—as fully as possible," repeatedly used her diary to take stock of her domestic obligations and shortcomings. These duties included overseeing her sons' and daughter's reading. "Get Arthur writing out, what he has read. Josephine also. Josephine read to me," she vowed in 1891. Shortly thereafter, Stewart promised to ensure that "Evg. after tea, Hugh & Norman read, learn poetry, games." As her goals proved elusive, she reiterated her intentions: "I would like to make for each child an individual record. I would like to direct Josephine's reading. Very important!" Such objectives stemmed from the same sense of duty that impelled Stewart to teach her children Bible verses on Sundays.[12]

During the interwar period, in the face of competition from new media and technology, the supposition that domestic reading bolstered Christian tenets was not only still current but also freighted with urgency. One writer in the *Christian Advocate* explained early in the 1920s that in homes where the church succeeds in encouraging reading, "the young people are not seeking excuses to be away." Instead, in the evening "the family is grouped around the big table, each with his own book or magazine. John Fox, Jr. or Gene Stratton-Porter is more interesting and far more helpful than the cheap moving picture or the village 'show.'" Stratton-Porter herself wrote a plea in 1925 entitled "Let Us Go Back to Poetry." As the daughter of an Indiana minister and farmer, she urged families to emulate her father's practice of reading aloud "the world's greatest poetry" in order to instill in his children an awareness of God in nature, a depth of sympathy, an aversion to "machine-made jazz music," and an animus against "moral laxity." Similarly, Ruth M. Carr, a twentieth-century Baptist missionary who stuffed a typed version of Edgar Guest's poem "Friendship" into the pocket of an undated notebook, copied lines from Whittier to construct the home as a bastion against changing mores: "And, weary seekers for the best, / We come back laden from our quest, / To find that all the sages said / Is in the books our mothers read."[13]

There was nothing exclusively middle-class in these visions; the proponents of domestic reading positioned their ideal as an alternative to popular culture, rather than to working-class identity. Yet there was certainly a consonance between verse recitation at home and middle-class affiliation. A Boston newspaper visually demonstrated that fact in its coverage of a 1925 "consecration" ceremony for a new house in the city's affluent suburbs. The homeowner, a professor of religious education, devised the ritual himself. Alongside a photograph depicting the professor's wife, son, and daughter reading next to the fireplace, the newspaper article explained that the dedication used poetry (as well as prayer, song, and "symbolic fire") to express the hope that the dwelling would epitomize "sacred" values, and thus offset a declining standard of home life.[14]

Among the moral tenets frequently in play at the site of domestic reading was the assumption that the proper nurture of children included laying the foundation for their gradual appreciation of the "higher" forms of literature. While the progression from newspapers and magazines to recognized classics was one type of print hierarchy, another was the putative climb from reading for excitement to edification as one's taste matured. With respect to poetry, the literary scholar Oscar Kuhns conceived of a movement from verse that illuminated "our everyday consciousness" upward to the works of "world-poets" who exhibited "high-seriousness." Not every commentator on the cultivation of reading habits embraced the necessity for continual improvement, nor did they all insist that the process should begin in childhood. But the ranks of those who believed that parents should guard against letting children read merely for entertainment included more than Victorian moralists alarmed by "dime novels." Self-consciously modern experts such as the organizers of the American Library Association's "Reading with a Purpose" book series in the 1920s and '30s revealed a similar outlook.[15]

The emotions underlying such moral uses of poetry in the home included both fervor and fear. But verse reading within the family derived even more of its affective presence from the psychological functions it served. In memoirs, diaries, and other reminiscences, individuals who came of age between 1890 and 1950 repeatedly connected the cadences they heard in the parlor and the bedroom to feelings of safety, well-being, and love.

The evidence from retrospective first-person sources is so plentiful, in fact, that a few cautions are in order before analyzing it. Prior to 1950, an account of reading was a convention of autobiography. Typically, life stories began with "I was born," moved on to a description of ancestors and family members, and continued with one or more chapters about childhood events and schooling—including "What I Read." Such virtually obligatory discussions re-

Ella Lyman Cabot reading to a young girl and boy, c. 1920. Domestic reading often signified order, innocence, and love. The Schlesinger Library, Radcliffe Institute, Harvard University.

flect the strength of the belief, in the early twentieth century, that literary culture shaped an individual's mentality, and that education was crucial to identity. But the formula also suggests that autobiographers might have unwittingly magnified their youthful reading experiences to ensure that their histories conformed to normative conceptions of the well-wrought narrative—to say nothing of the well-wrought life. Furthermore, even the historian disinclined to accept Freudian assumptions unquestioningly will recognize that memoir writers who chronicled only unalloyed pleasures in connection with domestic reading were probably exercising selective recall: ambivalence recedes as children mourn their parents' passing; the hardships of later life make youth appear in soft focus. Literary models of sentimentalism and, in certain cases, the pull of nostalgia alter the picture as well. These autobiographical records, to borrow from T. S. Eliot, mix memory and desire.

Despite some inevitable distortion and overstatement, it is nonetheless clear that one of the primary functions that sharing verse aloud acquired for American readers was to signify the shelter and stability of the family. A striking example comes from *Gramercy Park* (1958), a memoir by Gladys Brooks, the second wife of the literary critic Van Wyck Brooks. Brooks connected the practice of poetry reading with the repulsion of threats to both physical safety and sexual innocence. As a child, Brooks satisfied her "need" for "inner order" by memorizing poems indoors as her less controlled siblings played hopscotch on the pavement outside. On a weekend visit to a friend in the country, however, she discovered the disorderly—and frightening—consequences of her developing sexuality. While picking flowers in the woods, Brooks noticed a man watching her from behind a tree. As he moved toward her, she fled. Afterwards, she implored her friend to do "something safe and cosy [sic]," confiding that she had possibly seen a monster. "'Very well,' the girl answered. 'You can read to me out of the *Home Book of Verse*, while I go on with the red rose on my needlework. The Vision of Sir Launfal, maybe.'" Together with her invocation of Lowell's lines about a knight reasserting moral truth and her allusion to wholesome handicraft, Brooks's reference to Burton

Stevenson's anthology counterposed poetry reading to the unwelcome knowledge of human depravity and her own vulnerability. While aware (especially in retrospect) that she could not stave off the future, Brooks concluded the anecdote by reiterating her desire to get back to the safety—however temporary—of her family home, where poetry, allied with the past, produced a "quiet, dreamy feeling" and connoted her mother's antipathy to worldly concerns.[16]

Yet more often than signifying physical safety, listening to spoken verse within the home symbolized the stability of familiar arrangements (in both senses of "familiar"). When parents read poetry and prose aloud to children after the evening meal or at bedtime, they endowed home life with the features of predictable behavior and protective authority. Because of the influences of immigrant culture and religious belief, the practice cut across classes and locales. The novelist Jack Conroy, raised in a Missouri mining camp, listened almost nightly to his father and half-sister quoting "long ballads and sentimental poems . . . as entertainment, a custom imported, along with certain working-class radical attitudes, from Ireland." In the setting of rural Indiana, Stratton-Porter's father convened the family each evening for a study hour followed by Bible reading; seated at the head of the table, he heard each child recite poems memorized from McGuffey readers. "There was not a day of our lives," Stratton-Porter declared, "when some one was not learning a poem; often half a dozen of us were committing something to memory at once."[17]

More plentiful examples of reading as a source and sign of family cohesion, however, come from descriptions of middle-class families. The liberal Protestant minister Harry Emerson Fosdick, who was born in 1878, identified "a kind of fierce tribal loyalty" in his boyhood home. Although he lacked a college degree, Fosdick's father forged that bond in part through reading: Bible stories, Dickens, Scott, and poetry. The young Fosdick indelibly associated poetry reading with his father's role as "companion and chum": "I can hear [him] yet," he observed, "quoting the then popular" J. G. Holland's dreamy verses about sunsets.[18] Likewise, Elizabeth Borton de Trevino, a lawyer's daughter who had a varied career in publishing, journalism, and children's literature, implicitly emphasized the affinity between reading and comforting routine in describing her California childhood around 1910. "It was our happy family custom—after dinner at six o'clock, and when the table had been cleared and my sister and I had washed and dried the dishes—for Papa to read to us for half an hour," de Trevino explained. "This was a winter ritual. We sat around the fire in the fireplace, and we peeled and ate oranges as Papa read, occasionally handing him a juicy segment to keep his throat lubricated." De Trevino's classification of these performances, which included "Bobbie Burns," as rituals suggests their symbolic function: participation in them as listener or speaker affirmed the family's identity and stability. As de Trevino asserted after noting that reading was always "the chief joy . . . and often a lifesaver" throughout her childhood, "We were that kind of a family." The trope that de Trevino adopted to convey the warmth and pleasure her family supplied underscores the centrality of the fireside scene in her affective life: taking the image from Longfellow, she called her memoir *The Hearthstone of My Heart*.[19]

One of the richest revelations of poetry's use in creating feelings of domestic order comes from a fictional source: Dorothy Canfield Fisher's *Understood Betsy* (1917), a novel for young people that became one of Fisher's most enduring works. Betsy, a dependent, overprotected girl summarily removed from her city home to the care of her rural Vermont relatives, discovers on her second day in her new surroundings that her substitute father, Uncle Henry, "is just daft about being read aloud to" following the evening meal. When her uncle, aunt, and cousin gather around the table-lamp and take up various household repairs, Betsy, newly confident from performing her first chores, consents to satisfy her uncle's wish. From a "battered, blue-covered book," her aunt selects Scott's lines from "The Lady of the Lake" beginning "The Stag at eve." In the ensuing scene, two things happen. Betsy and her uncle, who "knew some of the places by heart," chant parts of the poem together, carried away by the sound and drama of the text. Their shared excitement is a consequence of the particular mode of reading that her adopted family (as opposed to the school) sanctions: "She did not know what all the words meant, and she could not pronounce a good many of the names, but nobody interrupted to correct her, and she read on and on, steadied by the strongly-marked rhythm, drawn forward swiftly from one clanging, sonorous rhyme to another." When she stops to ask about the definition of "copse," her uncle replies "indifferently" rather than pedantically that she can gather the meaning of the word from the "sense of the whole thing."

Thus the act of speaking the poem and joining with her uncle in visualizing its subject draws Betsy into the family fold. At the same time, it bolsters her sense of autonomy; like the character-building chores, reading poetry "for people to hear, not for a teacher to correct" is conducive to the self-reliance in which Fisher's beloved Vermonters specialize. Betsy, "very proud to think she could please a grown-up so much," acquires the "notion" that "the fact that she had never done a thing was no proof that she couldn't." Fisher's choice of a verse in which the quarry escapes capture—remaining proud and free—underscores the message of the reading tableau. Even more, her decision to locate the scene in a chapter she titled "If You Don't Like Conversation In A Book Skip This Chapter!" echoes the function of the poem within the fictional family by nurturing both affection toward the wise, motherly author and autonomy in the reader.[20]

Annis Duff, a former librarian and bookseller who, in the 1930s and 1940s, embarked with her husband on a concerted effort to share books with their young daughter and son, offered an explicitly didactic account of how the domestic reading of verse could function as a source of emotional security. When her daughter was an infant, Duff began speaking lines for the baby's (and her own) amusement and pleasure—not merely Mother Goose but also quotations from Blake, Housman, and other more sophisticated writers. Rhetorically, her explanation of the deeper impulse that prompted her to recite poems placed the genre within the family's Protestant framework: she and her husband were "two people who take poetry, along with books and music and all beautiful things, as major blessings; and who believe in sharing these things with children as freely and casually as daily bread." As her children became toddlers, Duff had them memorize verse in the service of the orderly household. To routines that included a daily morning walk and a baked potato at lunch, Duff added "all sorts of jolly verse" to "help with the endless training in habits of cleanliness and good manners" or to transform a "cross" young girl into one "beguiled into tranquillity." Millay's "Grown-up" deflected bedtime rebellion; a rhyme of Robert Herrick provided grace at table; Edward Lear's nonsense verse created a proper place for fun.

Later, Duff and her husband combined the organizational benefits they obtained from saying poems with their commitment to providing the "security and permanence" that children required to help preserve the "human family." In contrast to Stratton-Porter's girlhood home, where the *pater familias* exacted unquestioned homage, the Duff ménage of the 1930s took shape in the wake of progressive educational theory; consequently, along with her Protestant vocabulary, Duff's language reconfigured the family as an "ensemble" of junior and senior "members." Her self-consciously "modern" stance accommodated the teenager's need for "considerable privacy for the enjoyment of poetry" and the right of her adolescent daughter "to associate herself in feeling and interest with her contemporaries." In Duff's egalitarian view, books created domestic solidarity by bringing "reciprocal enjoyment into our companionship." Yet Duff's model of the companionate family strategically enabled her to act on convictions not so different from Stratton-Porter's—that "successful family living" resulted in passing on to the younger generation the "character," empathy, and self-confidence that would, she thought, ensure a "decent future" for themselves and society. Reading made children "secure within themselves" and hence competent as adults; "great" poetry, which "speaks to the feelings rather than to the intellect," was especially efficacious in achieving those ends. Thus the Duffs used verse in a way that "some might call indiscriminate"—drawing on anthologies that ranged by canonical standards "all the way from Edgar Guest to Robert Browning"—because, for Duff, the moral concern to instill respect for cultural hierarchy was less important than the psychological imperative to foster the "stability and encouragement" of the individual and the family unit.[21]

In the foregoing examples, the threats to domestic order that poetry reading promised to repel varied from the relatively timeless (the intrusion of sexual awareness in adolescent lives) to the urgently specific (the allusion, in Duff's second volume, to the specter of World War II and postwar juvenile delinquency).[22] Yet verse reading at home also acquired its affective functions against the backdrop of the history of the American (and in Duff's case, Canadian) family in the late nineteenth and early twentieth centuries. By 1890, families had lost their prior roles as centers of economic production and education; ideally, they had become sites for the nurture of individual development instead. The similarities among the reminiscences of Brooks, de Trevino, and Duff reflect that evolution. Although separated by decades, these memoirs confirm a model of the self-contained, nurturing family that remained unchanged in its broad outline up to at least 1950. One might speculate as well, however, that certain factors impinging on that ideal as the twentieth century wore on—the increase in divorce, the rise in married women's work outside the home, and the growth of an autonomous youth culture—intensified the attractiveness of the verse recitation for such observers in the face of those disturbing trends.[23]

As in the case of those who stressed the moral benefits of domestic reading, the danger of commercialized mass culture, with its attendant anti-intellectualism, lurks just offstage in Duff's and perhaps de Trevino's accounts of family stability. The accessibility of the "cheap and ugly," Duff implied, threatened more than Christian values and ideals of self-improvement. It also challenged parental control, potentially rearranging the tableau of deference that de Trevino and her siblings staged in feeding orange slices to their father. Aware that it was neither feasible nor entirely desirable to reverse what seemed to her the receding of her authority, Duff placed her hopes in a "reasonable policy of supervision" over children's reading, rather than in censorship. Nevertheless, she expressed relief that her daughter had developed an "appreciation of quality" that made her reject "best-sellers" and "fashions in reading" in favor of works upholding Duff's own taste.[24]

Duff's picture of home reading also occasionally implies the existence of pressure against the family from the school. In this instance, the conflict between parents and educators was not nearly as marked as in the nineteenth-century British situation which David Vincent explores in *Literacy and Popular Culture;* there schooling devalued and displaced knowledge gained outside of books. By contrast, the Duffs' access to an educational system that, for the most part, mirrored their approach to child training meant that the family did not ordinarily see its compromised autonomy as a loss. (The school's encouragement of parental involvement even allowed Duff to oversee the library containing the poetry anthologies her daughter's seventh-grade class read.) When an errant teacher "spoiled" "The Rime of the Ancient Mariner" by forcing analysis and memorization, however, Duff characterized the episode as an encroachment on her daughter's "right"—and the right of her classmates—to choose what they would "like" to read, and to do so in ways instilled at home.[25]

Poetry and Parental Approval

As it inscribed moral order and promoted psychological security in the family entity, poetry reading at the site of the home also operated to strengthen and certify particular bonds within the household—notably the approval of a parent toward a child. Participants in both father-son and mother-daughter relationships, as well as opposite-gender ones, found in literature and especially in verse a kind of code for affirming an emotional connection. For example, the Chautauqua publicist Edward Teall advised distant or estranged fathers and sons to improve their communication by using books (of any sort) to break the silence. A man "could not find a better way to set about improving the relation," Teall insisted, "than by talking to the boy about his reading." Similarly, one recalls Gray and Munroe's hypothesis that Mr. M's lifelong propensity for rereading Longfellow and Burns "once or twice a week" was linked to his vibrant memory of his "early home and his mother."[26]

Between fathers and daughters, reciting poems could take on a more complex psychological function, perhaps because of poetry's power to convey intimacy and yet to hold it at bay by spiritualizing it. One example comes from the 1910s, when Katherine Butler Hathaway, an adolescent invalid from New England, each night drew her father to her bed with "awful thoughts" of death that ended in her screams for "Papa." He "sat down close beside me," Hathaway recalled, "and put his healing and comforting hand upon me. Wonderful hand!" To this erotically charged gesture, her father always added "the same two poems": "I Wandered Lonely as a Cloud" and "Lochinvar."[27] Yet the possibility for such reassurance remained constant even when both the father-daughter pair and the texts they shared displayed the hallmarks of the modern. That fact is strikingly clear in the autobiography of the newspaper reporter Margaret Parton. The daughter of a couple who were both writers and political radicals, Parton was born in San Francisco in 1915. As a child, she met Carl Sandburg; in the late 1920s, while a student at the Lincoln School, she started writing verse seriously herself. Around the same time, her beloved aunt Sara, a poet and former missionary in Burma, married another poet, Charles Erskine Scott Wood. On visits to their home (which contained Wood's collection of erotic books), Margaret acquired an education of the senses. All of these early experiences combined to instill in her an admiration for individuals who possessed artistic natures—and a certain contempt for anyone who did not. After an encounter with a group of young people who made her feel socially awkward, she retaliated by writing in her journal, "I don't think they know any poetry at *all*."[28]

But evaluating others by their standards of aesthetic taste, a characteristic of Parton family style, could cut both ways. In the throes of the adolescent "pain" that drove her "deep into books," Parton kept her "'poetic thoughts'" from both of her parents, worried that, because they were "giant intellects," they would find her ideas "silly." As she grew older, she retained her conviction that her mother disdained her for her "poor little crippled mind" and her "small heart."[29]

Her relationship with her father was a very different matter. By the time she turned eighteen, Parton had come to recognize, and rejoice in, their shared outlook. On her birthday, she later wrote, he advised her to "lave your mind in poetry and it will sustain you all your life. I did, it has." Parton's father was as judgmental as her mother, but his tests came in the form of meter and metaphor. The crucial one occurred after Parton, who attended Swarthmore College, grew anxious that she was only a "pseudoscholar" who "might let down" her parents "by failure." She wrote home to "prepare them for this possibility." For the rest of her life, Parton explained, "I have treasured the letter my father wrote in answer to my fears." It read: "If, when I handed you that little Edna St. Vincent Millay poem, you had tossed off some flip crack, or had been insensitive to its quaint Elizabethan charm . . . I would have flunked you in Practical and Applied Aesthetics and I would not have felt the serenity and assurance which now, I give you my word, I feel about you." In that instance, poetry became the currency in a transaction that secured both approbation and relief. Moreover, the associations with cultural rebellion which the "new poetry" acquired at other sites did not diminish the "cash value" of the Millay poem in purchasing those emotional benefits at home.[30]

Parton's description of her encounter with Stephen Spender's "I Think Continually of Those Who Were Truly Great" demonstrates the same point. Along with Eliot's "Four Quartets" and the poetry of Yeats and Burns, Spender's words became a facet of the language she spoke with her lover when, in her thirties, she had a passionate affair with a married British diplomat. (Parton, herself equating poetry and life, revealingly characterized the relationship as a "lyric.") Yet, after Parton read Spender's poems with her father, "I Think Continually . . ." evoked the parent-child bond as well. Returning in middle age (with both parents dead) to the empty house where she had grown up, Parton recalled how the text gained her the attention and interest of her father: she imagined him "turning eagerly from the typewriter to listen to me as I shared my discovery of Stephen Spender with him. He was almost palpable in that dusty room."³¹

Bound up with their judgment of her, poetry finally certified for Parton her parents' (conditional) love—and hers for them. From her mother, she never received the acceptance she craved. Still, when Parton helped her move her belongings, she paused to reread her mother's favorite poem (Matthew Arnold's "The Buried Life") and "kept the book" *(British Poets of the Nineteenth Century)*—as if reading the poem enabled her to put their conflict to rest. Sighting "scores of my old poetry books" on her parents' shelves the day she returned to her childhood home, she concluded: "My God . . . the whole damned house is a museum of love. And not only that of my parents for each other, for me, for books, for beauty, but also of me and my life and those people and places I have loved."³²

In addition to garnering parental approval, sharing poems aloud could, on occasion, work the other way—signifying to a mother or father their secure place in their child's affections. In the context of her diary as a whole, which poignantly records her sense of loss as her children grew up and left home, Mary Ann Stewart's account of fireside reading with her married son suggests its function as a way of reversing his drift away from her. "Sunday is sometimes a strange, unhappy day for me," Stewart had mused in 1907. "What is all this rebellion in my heart? Is it because my children are going away one by one and the house is no longer filled with their voices[?]" When, on another Sunday some years later, her son Hugh and his wife paid her visit, her mood grew decidedly (if temporarily) better: "Hugh and I have had a most delightful hour together by my fire. We read poems—chiefly Matthew Arnold's, including Rugby and talked a good deal. How I *enjoyed* it." Stewart's reference to "my" fire, her daughter-in-law's absence from the scene, and her emphasis on what was, for her, a rare pleasure imply that poetry, by refilling the house with her son's voice, made it a space in which she could retrieve his undivided loyalty and love. One is tempted to read her final remark symbolically: "My heart is behaving rather noisily today."³³

The currency of poetry in parent-child relationships could be even more valuable when children performed memorized recitations. Such occasions were not without tension: the reciters might overestimate their mastery of a text; parents, especially when conscious of witnesses, might discover that their need for control and respect could quickly supplant pride in the child's accomplishment. Furthermore, some children wielded poems to gain power over their parents. The daughter of a woman who had escaped from Russia but lived in fear of deportation dutifully complied with her mother's demands that she cultivate proper speech by reciting poetry. The exercise at first was "a way to feel more loved." Eventually the daughter, who ultimately became an actress, learned to "please or punish" her mother by agreeing or refusing to perform. The poet Langston Hughes recalled that in order to embarrass his mother, he "deliberately and with malice aforethought" forgot the poem he was supposed to recite at a church program. Nevertheless, the reverse—a youth reciting on command to appease or give pleasure to a mother or father—was probably more common. In an autobiographical novel published in 1971, Linda Grace Hoyer, the mother of the writer John Updike, depicted a young girl who recites "The Raven" and "memory gems" to convince her aunt that she would not become "a disgrace to our whole family."[34]

Finally, when parents and children gave each other volumes of verse as gifts, the value of poetic texts as testaments of approval and understanding assumed material form. Presents of books no doubt frequently represented parental efforts to instill high-mindedness in their offspring, as when Mary Stewart dutifully gave each of her children a book (often poetry) for Christmas. If gifts became entwined, for the recipient, with memories of reading aloud, however, they took on an emotional significance that could last a lifetime. The distinguished librarian Lawrence Clark Powell, who ascribed his interest in poetry to his mother's "love" of it, remembered "how I loved to hear her, in the twilight at bedtime, recite" excerpts from *A Child's Garden of Verses*. Powell, who called that work "a key book in my life," later established a collection of *Garden* editions in his mother's memory at UCLA. He noted as well that on his ninth birthday in 1915, his mother gave him a copy of *The Home Book of Verse*, which he kept as an adult.[35]

In sum, poetry spoken in the social settings of the fireside and

Wife of a Farm Security Administration client reading to her son in 1939. Library of Congress.

bedside was frequently a way of preserving or restoring innocence, broadly understood. In carrying out those practices, readers drew on and perpetuated the affiliation of poetry with ideals of girlhood and domesticity which the figures of Millay, Crane, and Guest represented publicly. Verse reading afforded protection from distressing knowledge, not only about sexuality but also about change and loss; it supplied comfort by demarcating the haven of the household. Such emotional benefits could also accrue to children and parents reading silently. For instance, immersion in print—that is, the act of reading itself—could combat the attenuation or absence of family ties. Thus Mary Stewart, bereft again after losing "the 'togetherness' . . . we all enjoy" during her grown family's annual Muskoka vacation, revealed: "I had an hour or two of loneliness sharp and deep. I was tired, but the summer breaking up and scattering is hard. I took a book into the hammock and read Rabbi Ben

Ezra ["the best is yet to be"] and felt better." Reading Browning's lines helped Stewart to accept her diminished role in her children's lives. The silent reading of a particular text, Whittier's "Snow-Bound," even permitted one woman reader to imagine belonging to an ideal "large loving caring family" that she had "missed" in reality.[36]

Verse Reading as Liberation from Domestic Constraints

Yet when, instead of listening or reciting to their parents, children read poetry silently and alone, the experience often functioned not to signify domestic bonds but rather, in some measure, to undo them. That is, solitary reading could also accommodate or foster impulses at odds with familial expectations and values. Particularly in the case of young people from working-class backgrounds, reading provided a counterpoint to the rhythms of everyday life. For others, to curl up alone with a book was to revel in a liberating sense of disorder with respect to the act and consequences of reading itself. These emotional cross-currents sometimes merely rippled through the imagery in autobiographies and reminiscences, but they could also take a confessional or defiant direction. Whether, as children, such readers felt with the same intensity the rebellious impulses they reported as adults is another hazard of these retrospective sources, but the pattern of responses remains instructive.

For working-class readers like Jock Wilson, the Indiana coal miner's son, memorized verse provided a palpable break with the demands (although not necessarily the aspirations) of the family by altering the nature of labor. Both of Wilson's parents connected him with the world of print at an early age; to the boy's delight, his father read aloud *The Bears of Blue River,* and his mother taught him to decipher the alphabet and to recite "jingles and nursery rhymes" by heart "long before [he] started to school." Wilson encountered poetry with greater regularity, however, once he began formal education. A teacher who followed the custom of having children answer roll call with a Bible verse announced to Wilson's class one day that the pupils were instead to use lines from other sources, including poems. Revealing a more than perfunctory approach to the material, Wilson later created a painting from the images he discerned in Whittier's "Snow-Bound." When he reached the eighth grade, he relished studying Longfellow's "Evangeline," a requirement for the high school entrance examination; "interested in the melody of its words and rhythm," he again translated the verbal into the visual, noting that he "could see its rustic images" as he read.[37]

Wilson's references to Whittier and Longfellow—staples of the emerging national common curriculum—underscore the importance, as Roger Chartier has insisted, of resisting the temptation to make particular texts or genres "exclusive to a social group." At the same time, however, Wilson's working-class circumstances gave such poems special meanings. Before the entrance examination, Wilson learned that his father needed him to join him in the mines in order to augment the family income. Wandering alone by moonlight through the fields as he contemplated the prospect of leaving school, he invoked lines from "Evangeline"—stars situated "in the infinite meadows of heaven"—as a symbol of the expansive possibilities that contrasted with his narrowing circumstances. Buoyed by a teacher's encouragement, he resolved to continue preparing for high school, with the result that verse recitation (and similar tasks) became part of his mental life on the job: "I thought about the examination we were going to have in *Evangeline* and what the questions might be on the poem. I was lost in thought when my father called to me to help make up the powder for the holes I had drilled." Referring to "Enoch Arden" and mathematics problems as well as the Longfellow poem, Wilson likewise reported, "I would think about the things I studied while I was inside working." Needless to say, his ability to recite poetry did not excuse or even much ameliorate the hardships of coal mining. What Wilson did accomplish by interpolating poetic texts—and thus the promise of the upward mobility that education facilitated—into the work process was to separate himself in his mind from his father's way of life. Later, inspired by reading Carl Sandburg, he turned work into art, writing poems in the miner's voice. Eventually he secured from

Harriet Monroe the publication of one of his efforts in *Poetry* and brought out two collections of his verse.[38]

Rollo Walter Brown employed the verse that he memorized from his mother's borrowed cookbook in a fashion similar to Wilson's. Brown's father, who purchased a pot-shop in order to escape the clay mines, displayed what his son called "a pronounced trace of the poet." When Brown was growing up, however, his father's engagement with print epitomized the persistence of "intensive" practices in the late nineteenth century: the older man's reading repertoire consisted of a small-town newspaper that Brown characterized as "two-thirds 'boiler plate'"; a religious weekly that "devoted space to affairs of the day"; the *Sunday School Journal;* and "a Bible that included a concordance and plenty of maps." As Brown observed, his father, who always read with a dictionary on his knee, did so "with great concentration—leaning forward toward the page—and weighed every word, every sentence, every paragraph. . . . When he came upon something that seemed profoundly true he reread it a half-dozen times." On Sunday afternoon, "a special time for reading," he "read as if his life were at stake."[39]

Brown absorbed some of his father's approach to texts. As a youth, he owned "a library of three books" (*Aesop's Fables,* a simplified *Robinson Crusoe,* and a history of the Civil War), but he built a bookcase of a size that reflected his ambition to acquire at least a dozen volumes. What he did not own in material form he possessed through rereading and memorization: after his initial discovery of Byron, he, too, read favorite lines over and over. Thus Brown, like Wilson, transmuted through reading his experience of work. "I could drop back over my heels against a pile of clay and recite to myself with unvoiced eloquence these or any other poems I knew, and then sit up and rake the shovel across the gritty floor with pandemonium of approval." Poetry was one means he adopted to "sort out the choice parts of a world that ran off everywhere from the face of the clay," and to do so "uninterruptedly until a splash of roof somewhere" reminded him that he "was still in a clay mine." Brown left Ohio, went to Wabash College, acquired there a love of Whitman, Edwin Markham, and James Whitcomb Riley, and subsequently made his way to Harvard. Eventually he himself became a professor of literature and a writer. Yet the freedom from the mundane and the clarity of purpose that poetry reading had afforded him in the clay mine colored his engagement with the genre in those less "gritty" settings as well.[40]

A different kind of worker, Stuart Brent (originally Brodsky), the son of a Jewish tool and die maker in Chicago, transformed a summer-long house painting chore during the 1930s into an opportunity for escaping into "a glory of memorizing poetry and delivering noble dissertations." But Brent, who later changed the bookstore industry by combining book and record sales, approached reading as a means of escaping not only the tedium of labor but also the more abstract constraints imposed by adult prescriptions for purposive leisure. In contrast to the systematic pursuit of self-improvement, Brent happily reported that in his family "we read everything that took our fancy, whether we understood it or not, from Nick Carter to Kant and *Penrod and Sam* to Joyce."[41] While Duff's reference to indiscriminateness demonstrates that even the stabilizing rituals of the recitation could subvert aesthetic hierarchy, that impulse to ignore the counsel of parents and others especially flourished in circumstances that allowed solitary—and potentially secret—reading.

The result was an exhilarating sense of disarray, one which writers frequently captured in the language of unrestrained or immoderate appetite. In these instances reading (of both prose and poetry) became the antithesis of innocence, carrying instead the emotional valence of sophistication. Describing his attitudes as a book reviewer, the newspaperman Ben Hecht extended the appetite motif to include sex. "My chief drawback," Hecht explained, was "an inability to read any book through the assaying scale of my culture." Hecht "infuriated" an erudite friend by saying, "I liked all books in the manner that I liked all girls who were presentable. . . . And what did one gain by making oneself constantly toe the mark of preference—except fewer delights? In loving, or reading, a man was a fool to sit in judgment when he might lie in pleasure."

Hecht's reference to "my culture" (rather than merely to culture in general) suggests his awareness that his disregard for literary distinctions dissolved class as well as aesthetic boundaries. His summary of his outlook equated reading with a blurring of social conventions and categories: his approach, he declared, "was [the] lineal descendant of my young self in the attic room where I had found no difference in the charms of Nick Carter and Hamlet, nor outside the room, between hired girls and high-school princesses."[42]

The muckraker and reformer Ray Stannard Baker, who wrote more reflective essays under the pseudonym David Grayson, applied images of suspended self-control specifically to poetry reading. Alone and bedridden after surgery, he first recurred, however, to the well-worn metaphors of treasures and possessions in describing how "recaptur[ing] old poetry" alleviated his misery. Recalling "The Lady of the Lake," "The Prisoner of Chillon," "Thanatopsis," and Blake's "Jerusalem," among others, Grayson reported "a kind of satisfaction entirely apart from the content of the lines remembered, for it was a delight in itself to recover out of the mustiness of things forgotten, thoughts, impressions, beauties that had once thrilled me. I found that I could have my triumphs even as I lay in bed, silent, . . . and I had a sense that I was somehow getting the better of doctors and nurses who . . . never once probed the real secret of my life, what I had going on deep down with me—the struggles there, the voyages of discovery, the rich treasures I was now finding in forgotten caverns."[43]

Thereafter Grayson set himself the task of retracing the plots of novels. That exercise, although less interesting to him than reciting verse, also served as "anodyne" to his suffering. Summarizing that phase of his convalescence, Grayson switched metaphors; he compared the recollection of reading to "meeting friends once well known but half forgotten."[44] His greatest "adventures," however, still arose from remembered texts—and especially from poetry. Picturing his father's bookcase as it had been during Grayson's boyhood, he "revisited" not only the lines of a favorite poem (from John Gibson Lockhart's "Spanish Ballads") but the emotions accompanying his initial encounter, at age fourteen, with the text: "It was in the evening, I remembered, that I first came upon it, and it went straight to my head, like some divine intoxicant. After finishing the entire poem in one delicious draught I shut the book with a snap, seized my cap, and dashed out of the house. A young moon hung in the clear autumn sky; the silence of evening lay deep upon the world; cool airs had followed the heat of the day." One line—"My bed is cold upon the wold"—was especially evocative. Grayson doubted that, at the time, he knew what "wold" (an upland plain) meant. Nevertheless, its "charm," Grayson wrote, "set me thinking one night of the strange love affairs one may have with beautiful or desirable words." About one encounter, he said: "I had been hopelessly enslaved by a kind of modern flapper word"; in another, he found himself overcome by "infatuation." Recalling himself thrilled, drunk, passionate (albeit about the "beauty and mystery" of life), Grayson concluded that these "love affairs" with "one darling word after another" (most drawn from poems) together constituted "a new kind of autobiography of the heart."[45]

Grayson's elucidation of an alternative to domestic reading rituals that promoted order was almost as celebratory in tone as Hecht's description of his promiscuous choice of books. Yet Grayson's exuberant conceit, by casting the poetry reader as a victim of intoxication, nonetheless revealed a slight defensiveness about the genre's destabilizing effects. For other American readers, such disordering consequences of solitary reading were sufficient to produce conscious feelings of guilt along with liberation. "I'm a beast and deserve to be licked as much as any common drunkard does," the Maine minister's daughter Frances Wentworth Cutler wrote in 1903. Well acquainted with Tennyson, Browning, and Longfellow, Cutler noted that rereading the latter allowed her to enter a "Golden Age" and a "dream world" separate from her "dull round of lessons and trivial nonsense." She found herself especially susceptible, however, to the "intoxications" of fiction. "Can I never learn to control my craving for reading (of any kind, but especially romantic)," Cutler queried, "which corresponds to the craving for liquors? It isn't wrong, oh it can't be wrong, to like reading." In

Cutler's case, these emotional tensions were accompanied by physical distress: absorbing the warning that physicians and parents routinely gave children until the mid-twentieth century, she believed her excessive behavior was responsible for ruining her eyes.[46]

One might regard Cutler's observations as merely a continuation of the fears critics had attached to women's reading—especially of the novel—throughout the nineteenth century. Along the same lines, it is interesting to consider whether gender role expectations explain why, among the memoirs cited in this chapter, innocence and domestic order are a more prominent feature of those written by women than the ones by men, while the readers who speak with equanimity or boastfulness about poetry reading as rebellion are by and large male. One possibility is that, for Grayson and especially for a tough-minded journalist like Hecht, admitting to the enjoyment of a genre conventionally associated with femininity required masculinizing the reading experience by thinking of it as a boyish exploit. Yet just as not every man could tolerate the male domesticity typified by Edgar Guest, so some male readers could not remark on their pleasure in poetry without depicting it merely as illicit rather than freeing. Walter Locke, who in 1927 became the editor of the Dayton *Daily News*, suffered debilitating eye problems as a boy in the 1890s after he had "delighted intemperately in books." The solution thereafter to his "greed" and hunger for print was poetry, which he memorized and then repeated to himself as he walked. Even though Longfellow, Whitman and, later, Sandburg and Millay offered him a way to "carry on" a "life," however, Locke continued to associate reading with addiction, "intoxicant effects," and "indulgence."[47]

For Locke, as well as for certain practitioners of "omnivorous" reading, that sense of guilty pleasure derived not only from self-recrimination but also from a perception that his activities were socially unacceptable and, by implication, feminine. Locke saw his supposed deficiencies as in part the result of the modern American emphasis on efficiency and technological progress. "The age of speed was just then getting under way," he wrote of his turn-of-the-century young manhood. "The age was choosing between poetry and speed and it was not choosing poetry." Of special interest in Locke's account is his assimilation of early modernists to the "simple life" tradition he counterposed to mechanization and practicality; elsewhere in his autobiography, he referred to Sandburg in the same terms he used for Longfellow, as if the celebrant of Chicago's smoke and steel had belonged to a pre-industrial age.[48]

In any event, Locke's understanding that he had forged an "alliance with the poets the world was passing by" (because it was marginalizing poetry altogether) produced the same outcome that ignoring literary standards did: a clandestine reading life. As Teall put it, along with exhibiting an intelligent "social self" by talking about the books that others deemed worthwhile, "omnivorous" readers possessed a "Secret-Shelf collection"—including Longfellow's most sentimental poems and a "battered old volume of Tennyson"—to which they regularly turned but could not acknowledge in public. With poetry reading specifically in mind, Locke phrased that revelation even more forcefully: although his anti-technological mentality drew him back toward innocence, paradoxically his affinity for verse was his "secret joy and shame."[49]

Locke's language is especially jarring because of the dissonance it creates for twenty-first-century readers accustomed to regarding the schoolroom poets as bland and safe. Along with Teall and Grayson, Locke looked upon nineteenth-century poets not with the contempt one would expect from the "rebels against Victorianism" that historians have depicted but, rather, with a desire to reclaim the heady pleasures, the freedom from restraint, which they associated with their private reading. Those readers located the opportunity for unhampered emotional expression in the Victorian domiciles of their youth, rather than in an era of "terrible honesty" after World War I. The recognition that the vocabulary of intoxication and emotional surrender is itself conventional, belonging to the stock-in-trade of romanticism, only strengthens the point, because the survival of the romantic sensibility at the same time when Americans were bent on replacing illusions with hard truths and scientific facts has not appeared in most histories of the interwar period. It might be claimed that the individuals who emphasized the liberating effects of reading did so precisely because they were chafing against the repressive, decorous public behavior required by the American middle-class home at the turn of the century. Yet it seems equally possible that the order and safety these households enshrined were necessary preconditions for readers to let go emotionally in the encounter with print. In any case, Locke's furtive stance—like Brown's fantasy of audience approval, Hecht's willful indiscriminateness, or Grayson's imagined dalliance—is a reminder that the apparently solitary peruser of verse often was not entirely alone. Whether present in readers' thoughts or in their unconscious reactions, family members and other arbiters of youthful behavior hovered over armchairs and bedsides like ghosts.[50]

Poetry, Romance, and Friendship

It bears remarking that for a given individual, certain texts or genres might become affiliated with transgression while others satisfied a coexisting need for security. Harry Emerson Fosdick, for example, recalled of his rejection of fundamentalism: "What finally smashed the whole idea of Biblical inerrancy for me was a book by Andrew D. White . . . entitled History of the Warfare of Science with Theology in Christendom. It was a ponderous two-volume work, but I devoured it." Yet he acknowledged that "underneath my rebellions my appreciations were warm and lively—the love of nature, of music, of great books, and especially of poetry. . . . And most stabilizing and heart warming of all there was always my home."[51] Furthermore, the practices of reading verse silently and aloud, or individually and with others, were never entirely separable. When Duff's daughter eagerly drew her mother's attention to a poem she had just discovered, or when Parton brought her father into her mental world by speaking Spender's lines, they highlighted the ease with which one way of reading could shade into the other. Moreover, as the earlier discussion of poetry in the school has indicated, the home did not exist in isolation, however much reading verse may have contributed to defining its boundaries. When the progressive educator Howard Francis Seely described what he consid-

ered a typical middle-class encounter with a poetic text, he implic-
itly underscored how reading could slip from one modality and
milieu to another: the lone reader, moved by "the need to share the
melody of these lines with someone else," interrupts "whoever is in
the room or house" to "read passages to him," or, if no one is
home, runs down the street to show the poem to a neighbor.⁵²

As children grew to adulthood and faced the prospect of forging
new relationships outside the households of their youth, many of
the compensations that poetry reading supplied in the domestic
setting were mirrored in new social contexts. As in the home, read-
ing verse aloud played a role in forging or strengthening emotional
bonds; it established romantic ties and certified friendships. The
most familiar example of these functions is the phenomenon of
verse recitation in courtship. As an exchange concerning Jack
Conroy's proletarian novel *The Disinherited* (1933) reveals, the
practice carried messages over and above the profession of love. In
Conroy's story, the working-class protagonist garners the attention
of a young woman in a rubber heel plant by reciting lines from Ar-
thur Davison Ficke. (Actually, Conroy gives "Davidson" as the
poet's middle name.) Reviewing the book in the *Daily Worker,* the
Communist writer Mike Gold disparaged Conroy for overvaluing
bourgeois "literariness" and striking a "false note." The affronted
Conroy replied: "I have known many factory boys who quoted
fancy verses to appreciative girls without any perceptible damage
to the characters of either." He might have added that the poem in
question, beginning "I am in love with high, far-seeing places," was
widely anthologized despite Ficke's relative obscurity. Defending
the novel's verisimilitude, Josephine Herbst implicitly confirmed
the accessibility of such texts across social classes. Yet she neverthe-
less astutely noted that the Ficke poem signified the connection be-
tween reading and "'better[ing]'" oneself. From Herbst's perspec-
tive, the act of recitation thus contributed to "'a familiar and tragic
American dream'" of upward mobility without political struggle.
Whether or not one shares Herbst's anti-capitalist sense of futility,
her comment captures the importance, again, of not restricting par-
ticular texts and genres to a given class while exploring the distinc-

tive meaning a text might acquire in practice for working-class readers. In addition, the Conroy example illustrates the gender dimension of the courtship performance. The idea, as one reader put it, that men learned poetry "to impress girls" suggests that, again regardless of class, men who read poems to secure women's affection invoked the genre to express not only their aspirations to respectability, but also their willingness to meet feminine standards of cultivation and romance.[53]

At the same time, men as well as women used poetry reading in courtship to gauge whether or not an attraction would prove lasting. For example, Lee De Forest brought his lifelong appreciation for Victorian poets to the bond he forged with his future wife, Nora. De Forest had initially associated Tennyson, Longfellow, and Scott with parental nurturance—with his father's library and his mother's habit, when he was ill, of reading to him "by the hour" from *Ivanhoe* and "The Lady of the Lake." Love and verse coalesced around 1907 in his response to Nora, who "devoutly shared" his poetic inclinations. De Forest observed: "Together we memorized favorite passages. Down the long narrow passageway of my apartment, as we walked to her door in parting, we voiced in unison, from 'Ulalume': 'Here once, through an alley Titanic, / Of cypress, I roamed with my Soul— . . .' And surely never was a long narrow alley of a typical 'gay nineties' . . . apartment used in service more sweet than that!" Although less obviously judgmental, De Forest's anecdote conveys something of the same idea of the poem as prerequisite for acceptance that Margaret Parton's father imposed on their relationship.[54]

Sharing verse aloud also served as currency among friends. Between young men, poetic texts created camaraderie and a sense of emotional freedom. As an undergraduate at Williams College, the literary scholar Bliss Perry and his classmate Fred Bard "used to wander over the hills spouting Swinburne and *The Earthly Paradise* and *Sigurd the Volsung* to each other, and when Fred reported that his barber in New York (or it may have been a barkeeper) could declaim more pages of *Sigurd the Volsung* than either of us, our cup of delight was full." Later, when Perry joined the faculty at Harvard, he reported a kindred pleasure in listening to a brakeman and a barber recite poetry, as if assuring himself that workers and professors could speak the common language of Western culture. In his college days, however, Perry's wanderings with the eponymous Bard seem purely expressions of male exuberance, with poetry taking the place that alcohol might occupy for other revelers. More than forty years later, in *The Reading Interests and Habits of Adults*, Ruth Munroe depicted a similar recitation scene in psychological terms: a New Jersey man in his early twenties, "isolated" from his peers and burdened with a "feeling of inferiority," met a friend at college with whom he "enjoyed Shelley, Keats, and Omar Khayyam because of their emotional quality. At night they roamed around together reciting their literary tidbits." Reading poetry aloud became an "outlet" for an "emotional spree." Although the friend subsequently died, the salutary effects of the relationship on the young man's weak "ego" persisted. In that instance, where the friend was of unspecified gender, the case report noted that poetry recitation replicated the subject's only previous contact with a "truly sympathetic soul"—his mother.[55]

Accounts of young women who recited together as friends tend to convey a quieter, more soulful atmosphere, in part the consequence of the more romantic texts involved. M. Carey Thomas's intense attachment to Mamie Gwinn in the 1880s was founded on the conviction that their appreciation for Gautier, Rosetti, and Swinburne cast the two friends as "nous autres" (we others). Starting with Shelley, Thomas employed poetry to defy religious convention and to style herself as a woman of uncommon passion. For Thomas and Gwinn, the very meaning of the love they shared was inseparable from its embodiment in the pre-Raphaelite poetry which they both positioned at the center of their affective lives. Nevertheless, the consciousness among women friends of an "otherness" based on mutual pleasure in reading poems was less dependent on the quotient of romance within the texts than on the understanding that their distinctive sensibility—and their own poetic ambitions—set them apart from their less sensitive peers. Thus the same sense of "nous autres" appears in May Sarton's recollection of her adolescence in Cambridge, Massachusetts, around 1927: "Did we really spend hours in the Harvard Co-op smelling the different leathers of the expensive noteboooks we felt necessary as binding for the anthologies of our favorite poems by Francis Thompson, Edna St. Vincent Millay, H. D. and Carl Sandburg? I seem to remember that we did. . . . I had two intimate friends at this time. . . . We met after school to go on long expeditions up the Charles River, still lined in willows then, still open country back of Mt. Auburn Cemetery. We walked, reciting Francis Thompson's 'Hound of Heaven.'" Such friendships, in Sarton's view, were not sexual, but "our emotional temperature was high."[56] The fever could return when friends who reunited after long separations recalled the poems they had spoken together.

Yet for readers negotiating relationships with lovers and friends, the social dimension of silent reading was perhaps more noteworthy than the genre's oral uses, especially when texts enabled them to cope with the painful or disappointing aspects of relationships. One rich example appears in the diary of Clara Holloway. As a teenager in Iowa during the 1880s, Holloway, who eventually became a Baptist missionary to China, repeatedly fended off bouts of depression and loneliness. The erratic attentions of Addie Groesbeck, the young man she later married, heightened her propensity for self-blame, leaving her to wonder repeatedly whether she had imagined or caused his ill humor. When he failed to appear at her eighteenth birthday party, she was devastated: "I am *reckless* tonight," she wrote in her diary, "and would like to do something dreadful." After three days, however, Addie made amends, giving her a book of Wordsworth's poems as a birthday present. Like the recitation of romantic lines, proffering the slim volume of verse as a gesture of affection or desire was timeworn, predictable, even trite. Yet those qualities did not detract from (and possibly enhanced) the significance of the practice for individuals engaging in it anew. In any case, of more interest than the gift was Clara's response to it: "I was very much surprised," she wrote confessionally, "and I know I made him mad. Such a time as I do have. But the book is lovely, and I shall 'prize it for the giver's sake,' more than for anything else." That remark subordinates the content of the volume to its effect in consolidating the relationship.

Furthermore, when Clara two weeks later turned to the poems themselves, her sense of her literary preferences was inseparable from her romantic hopes and anxieties: "I have been reading Wordsworth and like it better all the time. Addie must have known my taste pretty well, when he selected that." As her dark mood returned over the next few days—"In the afternoon I was nearly sick with loneliness"—she recorded that she "settled myself with Wordsworth to comfort me," as if the book as object were a substitute for Addie's physical presence. Although, over the next few months, their relationship reassuringly evolved toward commitment, Clara still measured Addie's seriousness not only by his stolen kisses but also by the number of books (including Whittier's *Poems*) that he lent her. In August, she acknowledged his twentieth birthday by giving him a collection of Bryant's poems, which she thereafter read herself for the first time—a fact that suggests, again, that she chose the volume for its symbolic value, rather than for any particular sentiment within its pages. Although Clara's mental fragility continued to plague her as an adult, she did achieve some peace when, on her nineteenth birthday, Addie "asked me if I would take him for life." The same journal entry reporting her engagement captured both the emotional burden books bore within their relationship and, in a sense, the uncertainty their symbolic value helped assuage: "He ordered me a book for a birthday present but hasn't got it yet."[57]

Using poetry as a symbol or sign of intimacy also occurred in situations where actual relationships were painful or distasteful. In those instances the function of reading was not so much to create a liberating disorder as to permit readers to reorder their social worlds within their imaginations. Thus Harriet Monroe, who, by her own account, "grew up afraid of love" and suffered from an inability to be "simple and natural with anyone," gained from her time spent reading "fine editions" of the poets and novelists in her father's library "friends of the spirit to ease" her "loneliness." In her twenties, as she concluded that marriage was not to be her lot, she found consolation in "rapturous reading" of "the poets who had lived and suffered, as well as written, their poems."[58]

An extended example of the same phenomenon comes from the journal of Bernice Skidelsky, who traveled in literary circles during the 1920s and briefly served as a book review editor. As a college student at Swarthmore and Cornell just after the turn of the century, Skidelsky was often despondent. Convinced that she was physically unattractive, she longed for a setting in which sincerity counted more than appearance. Instead, she felt "like an alien . . . separated and secluded from everyone." (Part of her self-image derived from anxiety about gender expectations; her intellectual interests, she observed, would make potential suitors see her as a "masculine girl." The fact that she was Jewish may also have contributed to her sense that she was an outsider.) Books provided Skidelsky a refuge from her despair: in her journal, where snippets from Tennyson and Thomas Bailey Aldrich framed chronicles of her fluctuating moods, she recorded that she had read not only the "wonderfully true" verse of Browning but also Eugene Sue's *The Wandering Jew*, Owen Wister's *The Virginian* (where an appreciation for poetry defines the heroine), and numerous works of Dickens, George Eliot, Thackeray, and other nineteenth-century novelists.[59]

Skidelsky's mode of reading was often highly personalized, both in terms of her capacity to identify with fictional characters and her receptivity to the voice of the author. In a journal entry recording a walk in the woods, she herself measured the difference between the interpretive strategies her literature professors favored and her own stance as a reader: "It made me think," she wrote with some chagrin, "(not impersonally, I'm afraid, but applying directly to myself) of old Omar's lines" about wilderness as "Paradise enou." Yet she depended on that rejection of impersonality to construct, through print, an alternative social world. Her initial response to the heroine of *The Misdemeanors of Nancy*, for instance, a novel which she "attacked" and finished the day she obtained it, was to express her impatience with girls "so absolutely irresistible" to men. But her own fantasy—fueled by loneliness—soon overrode disapproval. "My day dreams, . . . aided by 'The Misdemeanors of Nancy,'" she observed several days later, "turn toward a soft warm room with an open fireplace and a red lamp, and other than my own thoughts for company." Her response to *The Flight of the Moth* was even more explicit: "Sometimes I read a book . . . in which the love part is very intense. I am half-ashamed to admit that under such circumstances I feel a longing that is by no means undefined but which is, on the other hand, extremely clear and acute. The love of a real man—a man in every sense—is a desirable thing, the most desirable thing in the world, and I do not think I am the least bit silly or sentimental in saying so."[60]

Such comments reveal that, in addition to enriching Skidelsky's knowledge of human experience, poetry and prose also enabled her to conceive of herself in relationships as a reconstructed, socially accepted individual. ("I should so like to be somebody else for a little while," she had written in the spring of 1905.) For that reason, as much as for the intellectual and aesthetic benefits that books conferred, Skidelsky exclaimed, "The greatest blessing of life is reading." Yet, as she well knew, immersion in print could not only mitigate but also intensify isolation by widening the gap between her mental life and that of her classmates. "The girls all wonder how I have time to do it [read extensively]," she reported during her first semester at Cornell, "but not half so much as I wonder how they manage to live without it." That sense of separateness might make more remote the possibility of deriving pleasure from relationships outside the social milieu that existed only on the page. As Skidelsky pointedly remarked after describing her impatience with "ordinary minds," the "world of books does us injury instead of good if it unfits us for life."[61]

Even if readers escaped that danger, their darker moods did not always yield to the compensations of the text. Mary Ann Stewart, whose self-deprecating remarks about her inability to maintain a household atmosphere of "unfailing brightness" make palpable her distress, observed that, at times when "life seems to have grown tasteless," she could not "sit to read." Nevertheless, those occasions when solitary reading alleviated solitude's discomforts argue that the figure of the poet as a companion or friend was not just an abstract metaphor; rather, the image attained a measure of reality in practice. As words and objects, poetry and books *were* friends— that is, they fulfilled the same needs friends served—especially for readers who found satisfactory human connections even more evanescent than those achievable with companions on paper.[62]

"I Like You, Carl Sandburg"

When readers imagined themselves emotionally linked to living poets who encouraged the sense of personal connection, those effects were magnified. One example comes from the voluminous correspondence of Carl Sandburg. Between his emergence as a "new poet" of the 1910s and his death in 1967, Sandburg's initial persona as political and literary radical gave way to a folksier, all-American image. The popularity of the biographies of Lincoln he published in the 1920s had something to do with this; so did the consonance between his affirmation of workers' lives in the poems of *The People, Yes* (1936) and the Popular Front ideals that informed so many aspects of American culture in the 1930s. After Sandburg, who brought out *An American Songbag* in 1927, began playing the guitar at his poetry readings (a combination he eventually exhibited on television in the 1950s), he became a less controversial (and arguably less authentic) version of Woody Guthrie. As with Edgar Guest and Edna St. Vincent Millay, the effect he created depended in part on his voice, which listeners characterized as unforgettable. Describing a Sandburg reading at the University of Chicago, the journalist Harry Hansen remarked on the "rapt attention" the poet commanded. Sandburg's auditors, Hansen added, "drift with the rich melody, the singing note, and the cadence with which he reads makes them forget that his verses will not scan by any rule of classic form." As the writer Oscar Cargill observed in 1950, "With a guitar to strum and a sympathetic audience, Carl Sandburg could make Harry S. Truman's budget message sound, if not like 'Lycidas,' at least like Allen Tate's 'Ode to the Confederate Dead.'"[63]

Sandburg's frequent public performances—he had no qualms about regularly courting readers and listeners—earned him the status of celebrity. "We are an Average American Family," a California woman wrote Sandburg in 1953, "to whom you, Lincoln and the flag are almost one as a symbol of America." Together with the plain language and realistic bent of his writing, however, his folksy persona and inclusive message had another result: they made him a prime example of the figure of the poet as intimate. Consequently, when members of his audiences took the next step of contacting him, they often addressed him in the vocabulary of friendship, sympathy, and love. Even requests from readers who wanted something tangible—material for a school report, the poet's own explanation of one of his lines, comments on their own verse—were emotional transactions as well as solicitations.[64]

Such letters came from both men and women, and both confided to Sandburg details about their lives. A Virginia man wrote the poet in 1938, "I call you my dear friend, Mr. Sandburg, because for the past five years I have had the pleasure to read and enjoy many of your poems and books. I have been graduated from high school a year and a half now but have never ceased to read your many bits of verse and your books." A self-described "housefrau [*sic*] and mother of three" who first encountered Sandburg's work while a schoolgirl told him that she and he were "comrades." Her subsequent comments mimicked the poet's studied simplicity: "It is a relationship, however vaporous, that has meant a great deal to me these years since 'Chicago' popped into my world. In this inadequate way, I wish to thank you, just for being. I like you, Carl Sandburg."[65]

More specifically, some readers presumed intimacy with the poet on the basis of their belief that they personified his subject. "I am an uneducated man who discovered your works quite by accident," a Brooklyn reader wrote. "Your great heart is with us, since I am the people you so deeply respect. . . . You have given me a new dignity in myself and my work." A woman seeking autographs for her children declared that the recording of *The People, Yes* was a family passion because "we feel you *know* of us, an American minority group (Latin Americans) with much love for our two daughters and the will to help educate them." A Connecticut high school girl who watched Sandburg's appearance on Arlene Francis's television show in the late 1950s echoed comments the poet had received since the 1920s: "Whenever I read any of your poems I cry, cry because I love them. . . . I know I'm important to you because I'm a person. Not because I'm a Sandburg fan but because I'm part of the human race. I'll never make the history books for doing anything outstanding. . . . No I will marry and raise a family but thanks to you I feel important. I live through your poems." She concluded her letter with a surge of emotion that underlined her assuredness about the poet's accessibility: "I know you'll read this letter and maybe write to me. I'm not a silly schoolgirl, but a person who loves poetry and a man who writes it."[66]

Other correspondents assumed a connection to Sandburg out of a conviction that they and the poet shared the same sensibility. One woman, writing in the late 1950s, alluded to the popular photographic exhibition of the period: "Your life and mine are worlds apart. However, your poetry enriches my life and brings me closer to half-realized ideas. In this manner we are related—we are the Family of Man." Among the readers who implicitly referred to Sandburg as a kindred spirit, several thanked him for the "inspiration" he provided, a state of mind they described in romantic terms of self-transcendence. "In all my life," a California woman wrote after hearing Sandburg lecture, "I think nothing else so completely carried me out of myself as your sympathetic insight. . . . When the evening was over, it was perhaps like coming out of a so-called trance into the realm of my every-day world. . . . I found it very inspiring, and even yet, I find myself many times recalling certain phrases and thoughts of yours as I go about my daily work. It made me somewhat sad, too, but perhaps that is even as it should be."[67]

Of all the letters expressing an emotional affinity with Sandburg, the most touching were those from readers whose sense of self seemed most precarious. For such individuals, reading Sandburg and then writing to him as a friend was a way of alleviating feelings of depression, loneliness, and social discomfort similar to those that plagued Skidelsky and Stewart. "It's good many a times to find out that you are not alone with your thoughts," a refugee from Austria wrote the poet after reading an interview in which Sandburg blamed intellectuals for neglecting "the common man." In the late 1920s, a Texas woman who described herself as a "care worn mother" assured Sandburg that she did "not want anything except to tell you how much I love you . . . with a holy sort of love." She went on to identify the source of that relationship: "You have spoken to me individually in the loneliness of my heart and I have found in your sympathy, [the] understanding and encourage-ment to go on telling the story of my kind of people."[68]

These missives testify to the sense of accessibility that Sandburg's persona created. Yet as Sandburg grew in celebrity, he actively nour-ished readers' fantasies of friendship by answering fan mail with what were, despite their personalized messages, in reality variants on a form letter. As early as 1930, he set the tone for such responses in an exchange with a Montana woman who had thanked him "on behalf of all youngest America" for *Good Morning, America,* which she and "Kathryn" had read late at night in one sitting. "Your letter has come along," Sandburg wrote back, "and all I know is we are grand neighbors for all of the rivers and mountains between us and it is blessed to know you and your Kathryn." Later he offered the same illusion of personal involvement by telling cor-respondents that their letter would "go among keepsakes that are cherished"; in the late 1950s, he pulled out all the stops with a form letter that said, "You are a thoughtful person and it is good to have you for a friend. I like your tone of voice."[69]

Sandburg's construction of himself as the reader's friend may be seen as one more strategy—like Untermeyer's anthology-making—to smooth the adjustment between modern American poets and their audiences; it was a form of mediation, however, that elimi-nated the critic as middleman. The strategy worked. In retrospect, perhaps the most remarkable feature of Sandburg's correspondence is the lack of cynicism his readers evinced upon receipt of the poet's calculated replies: they interpreted as generous gifts what others might regard as grudging attention. A woman who characterized herself as "one more statistic wife of a serviceman" thanked him in the 1950s as follows: "Your note will always be a treasure and a reminder that there's still a lot of goodness left if you just look for it long enough. I shall always think of you in terms of a friend." Even more revealing was the acknowledgment received by an editor at Sandburg's publisher, Harcourt, Brace, in 1959 from a "happy, married" middle-aged Ohio woman for whom the poet had autographed his *Remembrance Rock*. Distinguishing Sandburg's response from the prevailing ethos of impersonality and routine, she asserted: "He could have merely signed his name. . . . But he has written my name too, and the date (the latter in a highly individualistic way, I must say), and this is almost too much joy for me. . . . I went around all day yesterday feeling as though a very great and important person in our world LIKED me. . . . If we had more of this sort of communication instead of 'mass communication' we might somehow get our world back on its feet." Ironically, her concluding allusion to her special relationship with the poet might have been written by any number of readers who, over the course of Sandburg's career, had invested his poetry with the power to validate their self-worth: "Tell him his books are my intimate friends, and that through them he is my friend and as real to me as any of my friends here in the flesh,—MORE real than most of them, at times!" The greater irony, however, was that the editor had forwarded the letter to Sandburg in order to convince him that autographing books was not a waste of time.[70]

The feelings that Sandburg's poems elicited from his audience bore a direct relationship to the populist sentiments his work expressed. The reinforcement his persona provided was also an essential element in evoking those feelings, but, in contrast to much of the recitation before the family hearth or to the omnivorous diversions of the sickroom, it cannot be said that the poet's words were incidental to the results the act of reading produced. Yet even when content mattered, that act carried an emotional weight greater than what the text itself conferred. Regardless of the variable needs and circumstances involved—whether readers imbued poems with their desire for stability or with their urge for freedom, whether they read with others or alone, whether the site of reading was their childhood home or the one they established as adults—the practice touched the heart because of the social relationships it symbolized, certified, or subverted.

chapter ten

God's in His Heaven

Religious Uses of Verse

❧ "THE LEADING means of grace, next to prayer," advised the poet and critic Frederic L. Knowles in 1905, "is religious reading." For American Protestants (whether fundamentalist or liberal) in the early 1900s, the central text for that purpose was indisputably the Bible. Those who wanted to read more than scripture and the commentaries upon it, however, could turn, as Christians had for centuries, to devotional literature: writings that, as the Methodist Bishop William A. Quayle phrased it, "put the heart in the mood of prayer." Throughout the period, such works as Bunyan's *Pilgrim's Progress,* Thomas à Kempis's *Imitation of Christ,* and St. Augustine's *Confessions* continued to enjoy unquestioned stature as sources of piety. "Read helpful books, [such] as Wesley's journal to help keep me to high level," the Baptist missionary Edith Grace Traver resolved in the fall of 1929. In 1930, under the headline "Books for the Devotional Life," the Baptist *Watchman-Examiner* reiterated the seventeenth-century titles the theologian James Mudge had suggested many years earlier. Published by mainstream firms as well as denominational houses, devotional classics were "steady sellers," readily accessible to followers of Knowles's counsel.[1]

But while Knowles counted only "saints and men of worship" as "strictly devotional writers," his contemporaries did not necessar-

ily maintain his distinction between such figures and those he desig-
nated merely "literary masters." Many were willing to commend
poetry for devotional reading—even if written by other than "holy
men." The genre had in its favor a well-established body of schol-
arship and literary criticism that postulated the cordial relation-
ships between poetry and religion. Matthew Arnold's declaration,
in 1880, that "the strongest part of our religion to-day is its uncon-
scious poetry" had counterposed the knowledge of the poet to that
of the scientist. Scholars such as Jane Ellen Harrison and Francis
Gummere had documented the evolution of rhythmic chants from
primitive ritual, just as worship arose from incantations designed
to praise or appease unseen powers. Thus one of Knowles's fellow
essayists in the *Methodist Review,* a publication that resembled a
Methodist version of the *Atlantic Monthly* more than a theological
journal or denominational bulletin, declared in 1906 that poets,
who were the "best interpreters of life," were also "often the truest
theologians." Another contributor insisted in a 1907 article on
"The Spiritual Mission of Poetry" that the "true end" of verse was
"to awaken men to the divine side of things."[2]

Similarly, in 1900 George Santayana allied both poetic and reli-
gious expression with "intuitions" of the "ideals of experience and
destiny," elaborating on the figure of the poet as seer. Extending
that view, Charles G. Osgood explained in *Poetry as a Means of
Grace* (1941) that, as "probably our most powerful agent for rous-
ing, sensitizing, and energizing our sense of beauty in all things,"
the poem supplied "an intrinsic element of the Faith." Amos N.
Wilder, the theologian who made the most concerted effort at mid-
century to interpret early literary modernism in relation to Chris-
tianity, likewise announced that poetry was "always and inevitably
religious in its ultimate nature." The recognition that much of the
Bible itself—not only the psalms and songs of the Old Testament
but also the words of Jesus—derived from or sustained poetic pat-
terns of language strengthened the connection.[3]

Nineteenth-century Americans had already endorsed those
premises in the guise of the Protestant hymn, as well as by confer-
ring their blessing, as readers, on the verse of Phillips Brooks, Fran-

ces Ridley Havergal, Adelaide Procter, and other mid-Victorians who used the genre to extol God and evoke prayerful affirmations of belief. Such poets carried forward Christian traditions of sentimentalism or sensibility that, at least since the days of Wesley, had linked verse, faith, morality, and emotion in print.[4] Even as older texts continued to circulate, newer ones flowed from the pens of figures who made Protestant teachings their explicit and virtually exclusive subject matter. Among the most popular poets who perpetuated that tradition after 1900 were the British author John Oxenham, along with the Americans Susan Coolidge, Annie Johnson Flint, Grace Noll Crowell, and Henry Van Dyke, the latter a Presbyterian minister. In addition, many less famous individuals— amateurs who were often members of the clergy—turned to poetry as a congenial, natural form in which to express their vocational and spiritual commitments. Some of their writing remained lodged in copybooks, but much found an audience through scribal, serial, or even book publication.

At the same time, mainstream or liberal Protestants routinely commended for devotional purposes poets whose reputations rested on a body of work that transcended religious themes and deliberately admitted multiple meanings—figures, in other words, who had entered the British or American literary canon on a broader basis. Thus Gaius Glenn Atkins, a Detroit Congregationalist pastor, included Tennyson's "In Memoriam" on a list of devotional selections he assembled for Religious Book Week in 1923. In the same year, the leader of First Parish (Unitarian) Church in West Roxbury, Massachusetts, wrote that Dante, Milton, Wordsworth, Browning, Whittier, and Whitman came "inevitably to mind" as authors who stimulated worship.[5]

Yet, as presumably even those who chafed against Knowles's narrow definition would have acknowledged, not all religious poetry was devotional. That is, instead of quickening spiritual communion directly, a poem might reinforce other aspects of Christianity: it could, for example, provide moral instruction, exhort readers to service, assure them of eternal life, celebrate beauty, or even foster meditation without sparking the "mood" of supplication to which Quayle referred. Moreover, the terms "religious reading" or "religious poetry" are themselves problematic, as Wilder and others were quick to acknowledge. Was the poet's intended message the quality that made a work religious? If so, could the term apply (as Wilder insisted it could) even when that message repudiated a "decadent or coercive religious tradition"? Was a text religious because literary critics—sometimes dismissively—designated it so? (As T. S. Eliot observed, in classifying poetry the critic of his generation tended to equate "religious" with "minor.")[6] Was it the reader's response to a poem—not exclusively the development of an outlook preparatory to prayer, but also, for instance, the acquisition of philosophical perspective, denominational allegiance, or ethical sensitivity—that demarcated religious verse?

Wilder himself addressed those questions by distinguishing devotional poetry, in which the poet "engaged in the actual exercise" of addressing God, from works that merely contained "Christian motifs." He reserved separate categories for "mystical" writings and "sacred" texts that had been "taken up into" the liturgy. But those rubrics have not enjoyed universal acceptance and in any case derived from a consideration merely of a poem's content. Nor are they particularly helpful in getting at the reader's viewpoint. Prescriptively, devotional literature existed in contradistinction to texts for public services; it presumed reading that was private, deliberate, reverential, and—if not shared within the family—silent. Writings that were incontrovertibly suitable for rituals of devotion might also be read, however, more casually and cursorily, in impromptu moments of leisure instead of at an hour formally set aside for turning one's thoughts to God. As a poem reprinted in the *Watchman-Examiner* in 1930 underscored, even the Bible permitted readers not only to formulate competing interpretations of its words but also to act on a variety of attitudes and impulses. "Some read it as their duty once a week," the author of "How Readest Thou?" declared, "But no instruction from the Bible seek; . . . Some read it for the wonders that are there— / How David killed a lion and a bear; . . . One reads with father's specs upon his head, / And sees the thing just as his father said." (Recognizing such multiplicity, the poet nevertheless deplored the failure to read the Bible "prayerfully" and "right," the latter stipulation ironically mirroring the position of New Critics such as I. A. Richards, who in the previous year had excoriated wrong reading in *Practical Criticism*.) Furthermore, like schoolroom recitations, devotional works could survive in memory, recurring to readers as they went about their mundane chores. By the same token, lines of verse written from a humanistic standpoint might stir Judeo-Christian convictions—might become religious—by dint of how and where readers rendered them meaningful to themselves. Incorporated into the order of worship in the liberal Protestant and Jewish denominations that permitted liturgical modifications, such poems might even become, in Wilder's terms, "sacred."[7]

Fortunately, the history of reading not only raises but also implies a way out of such definitional difficulties. With appropriation in view, the task for the student of poetry in its cultural context becomes not delimiting the categories of "devotional," "religious," or "secular" reading—a pedantic exercise in any case—but, rather, appreciating their fluidity: that is, recognizing the capacity of some texts to support solitude and sociability, avant-garde performance and Protestant worship, stylistic experiment and convention, in both private and public settings. Like the pragmatists' conception of truth, poetry acquired its religious character in practice.

The Circulation of Religious Verse: Devotional Aids, Anthologies, and Periodicals

In the late nineteenth and early twentieth centuries, several forms of print (each shaped by its compiler's understanding of "religious" verse) made poems readily available to American Protestants as aids to faith. One was the collection of inspirational thoughts assembled expressly for devotional use. A representative example is Mary W. Tileston's *Daily Strength for Daily Needs* (1891). Such works were often organized as calendars and made pocket-size for portability. Especially insofar as they could substitute for, as well as supplement, the reading of devotional classics in full, they were akin to treasuries of memory gems. Some consisted of writings by a single figure; others brought together scriptural quotations, prose passages, and an assortment of poems by different authors. These were "patchwork texts," as David D. Hall has put it. In a sense, they also represented "women's work," resulting as they did from a fragmented process of gathering and copying that could be carried out in between other domestic obligations.[8]

The diary of Tileston's daughter Margaret affords a glimpse of that process, albeit with regard to another of her mother's projects. On vacation at the New England shore in the summer of 1881, Margaret, who was then fourteen, recorded: "Mr. Ames, the son of Mr. Charles G. Ames, called in the afternoon. He wants mother to collect a book on love and marriage." To "collect" (rather than to write) meant to draw upon habits already ingrained in the Tileston household. One was the practice, common among the Tilestons' contemporaries, of cutting and pasting excerpts from periodicals. "I found a great many Christian Registers up in the attic, and cut a great many poems out of them," Margaret noted one wintry day in 1881; the next week she discovered a stack of the *New England Farmer* and did the same.[9] Scrapbook-making was not only a type of entertainment but also an elaboration of the treasure-chest motif, a way of storing print for future needs. As such, the activity was a tangible representation of the idea that reading a poem (literally excised from the context of its production) was instantly and infinitely capable of renewing pleasure, providing guidance, instilling hope, bolstering resolve, rekindling memory, or affirming the compiler's identity and taste.

"Collecting" also meant transcribing texts, sharing them aloud, and spending part of each day in disciplined reading. While Margaret Tileston read and recited at school from poets such as Longfellow, verse was omnipresent at home as well. In that setting, as in the devotional volumes Mary Tileston pieced together, the genre shaded almost imperceptibly into scripture. "I copied one sonnet by James Russell Lowell, for Mother, in the afternoon," Margaret wrote about one Sunday's activities. "I read in 'The Wide, Wide World.' Mother read to us in the Bible, and played on the piano." Over the next several weeks, Margaret copied more poems ("two sonnets by Alfred Tennyson, for Mother"), while also noting: "I copied six sonnets by Mrs. E. B. Browning in the afternoon, for Mother. I copied a good many verses from the Bible, for each day, that is, I select one verse (generally) for a day, and selected verses for a good many days."[10]

It is hard to say whether Margaret's transcriptions were merely intended for her mother's enjoyment or were a form of research assistance; whatever the case, her publisher also wielded influence over Mary Tileston's compilations by furnishing her "some books to look over for poems to put in her collection." What is clear is that Margaret's determination to master both the Bible and a large poetry repertoire made her a repository of the same kinds of materials her mother amassed. In 1883, she began to read "a course of religious reading" that she had "decided on, a few poems & chapters [of the Bible] each day." The "course," she made plain in a subsequent entry, was the logical extension of her scrapbook-keeping. "I read each day now," she stated, "five or six pages in the 'Little Pilgrim' [Mrs. Oliphant], a chapter in Fenelon, a poem in Sunshine, a poem by Susan Coolidge and one chapter or more in the Bible." The "course" was also a reflection of the assumption, shared with her mother, that a poetic and scriptural "patchwork" qualified as "religious reading," the daily contemplation of which was both a duty and a comfort.[11]

One might expect Mary and Margaret Tileston, who were Unitarians, to assent to the devotional use of Oliphant and Coolidge— hardly "saints" but, rather, prime examples of poets imbued with Victorian uplift. More surprising is the appearance of such figures in perhaps the most influential twentieth-century devotional manual for American Protestants, Mrs. Charles E. Cowman's *Streams in the Desert*—surprising because Cowman identified herself as a fundamentalist. As Cheryl Forbes has compellingly argued, however, Cowman, in creating the volume and publishing it herself in 1925, ignored theology and sectarian debate. Instead, drawing especially on Tileston's *Daily Strength*, she too amalgamated Bible verses and brief passages of poetry and prose. Cowman also culled excerpts from "quasi-religious, high-toned Victorian moralists" like Harriet Beecher Stowe; she took lines of verse from such recent poets as Flint and Van Dyke. "Readers can also find writers quoted," Forbes observes, "whom no one would put into a Christian camp, not even the broadest and most inclusive camp we might imagine." Nevertheless, the result was that all of Cowman's disparate selections became Christian/religious/devotional because Cowman regarded each text as adaptable to her readers' spiritual needs. Thus, Forbes concludes, the book has always been particularly suited to women readers isolated in the "desert" of domestic drudgery and powerlessness. Acquired by Zondervan in 1965, *Streams in the Desert* has never been out of print since its first appearance, and has sold millions of copies.[12]

While *Streams in the Desert* may be said to have dominated the market for devotional aids in the first half of the twentieth century, it was one of a large quantity of such collections in circulation during that supposedly secularized modern era. Leaving aside the number of older compilations on readers' shelves, the *Cumulative Book Index,* which tracked new publications, listed thirty-eight entries under the heading "devotional exercises and meditations" in the volume for 1921–1924 (just before *Streams in the Desert* came out). Although the majority of such titles carried the imprint of a denominational press, certain trade firms—notably Macmillan, which issued six of the thirty-eight—played an active role in publishing these materials for daily observance.[13]

Macmillan was also a leader in producing a second form of print that disseminated poetry to the faithful: the anthology of religious verse. The distinction between religious anthologies and books published with the intent to aid devotion is admittedly fuzzy, but one key difference is that (in marked contrast to the author of "How Readest Thou?") anthologizers did not encode in their volumes prescriptions about how frequently or in what mood readers should approach their contents. For example, in her preface to *The World's Great Religious Poetry,* which Macmillan published in 1923, Caroline Miles Hill flexibly assigned her book more than a single "purpose": "to furnish delightful reading, to give comfort and consolation, to 'restore the soul' as well as to supply material for the study of the history and psychology of religion—the last

subject to be approached by scientific methods." The instruction
to use the book devotionally came not from the compiler but in-
stead from an external voice—the *Methodist Review*—which an-
nounced, "All who can afford it should own a copy and use it daily
as part of their devotional life."[14]

Hill's anthology typified those published after the First World
War in employing a thematic structure that permitted the juxtapo-
sition of texts radically different in style. Hill herself explained that
the collection made "strange combinations and sequences," rang-
ing from "the Psalms of David and the Hymn of Cleanthes to the
latest free verse." Poetry that affirmed the human potential for
goodness in language that admitted little ambiguity appeared in
abundance. Yet Hill's anthology also made room for poets whose
modern outlook privileged the ironic and the metaphorical rather
than the sentimental and the literal. Furthermore, the categories
undergirding *The World's Great Religious Poetry* accommodated
both poems of manifest Christian content and those for which the
designation "religious" seems optional or even forced. The heading
"God in the Life of Man" for instance, introduced twenty-nine se-
lections explicitly concerning God as "revealed in the life of Jesus
Christ": Goethe's "Easter Chorus from Faust" and Milton's "On
the Morning of Christ's Nativity" among the older choices, Edwin
Arlington Robinson's "Calvary" among the recent ones. The rubric
"God in Nature," however, admitted the lines from Whitman's
"Song of Myself" beginning "I think I could turn and live with ani-
mals, they are so placid and self-contained"—a stanza that includes
frank contempt for discussions of "duty to God." Likewise, from
Hill's perspective, "The Search After God" permitted expressions
of doubt: hence her choice of Sara Teasdale's lines "Of my own
spirit let me be / In sole, though feeble, mastery."[15]

Although the focus of this discussion is on Protestantism, it is
worth noting the similarities between Hill's volume and *The World's
Great Catholic Poetry* (1927), which Macmillan also published. (A
revised edition appeared in 1940.) While its editor, Thomas Walsh,
proceeded chronologically rather than thematically, he, too, faced
definitional difficulties which he resolved by adopting a capacious

selection principle. Like Joyce Kilmer, whose earlier anthology of Catholic poets, *Dreams and Images* (1917), had reflected similar assumptions, Walsh decided to include verse by non-Catholics that nevertheless rested "definitely and unmistakably" on "Catholic foundations." For that purpose, he created a "special division" of the book called "Catholic Poems by Non-Catholics"; among those texts were Henry Adams's "Prayer to the Virgin of Chartres," Edwin Markham's "The Lord of All," and William Rose Benét's "The Falconer of God."[16]

Anthologies of religious verse reflected the political orientations of their compilers as well. James Dalton Morrison's *Masterpieces of Religious Verse,* published by the house of Harper in 1948, grew out of his experiences as pastor and professor of homiletics. The broad headings "God" and "Jesus," which opened his collection, encompassed scriptural passages and verse rich in Christian references. Morrison's Social Gospel sympathies, however, colored a later section entitled "The Kingdom of God," which included poems of "social protest" and "race relations" that, to a compiler lacking Morrison's liberal Protestant orientation, could appear wholly areligious ("Sadly through the factory doors / The little children pass, / They do not like to leave behind / The morning sky and grass"). So could "The Nation and Nations," a part of the anthology that originated in Morrison's heightened consciousness of nationalism and war in the post-1945 era. By contrast, in *Inspirational and Devotional Verse,* assembled by the fundamentalist Bob Jones, Jr. in 1946, the category of "service" contained no poems construing that ideal as social or international responsibility.

Whatever their organization, anthologies of religious poetry, like the hodgepodge of texts Annis Duff relied on to promote family stability, mingled poets whose eventual reputations made them radically different in terms of their relationship to high culture and literary modernism. Walsh's volume, for example, contained both Kilmer and Ezra Pound. Hill and Morrison appear to have been well aware of aesthetic categories and debates; they each manifested a desire to rescue modern or experimental poetry from dismissal as "secular." As Morrison explained, "The criticism is frequently heard that modern poetry is . . . lacking in spiritual emphasis. While much modern verse *is* secular and even pagan in outlook and spirit, there is much also that is deeply religious. . . . Many poets who are not generally regarded as religious are nevertheless profoundly religious in their implications." Yet by disseminating the sentimental and the popular even as they self-consciously featured examples of the "new poetry," these anthologists contributed to the ongoing vitality of older poetic traditions. Like the compilers of works for school and home, they did so by valuing theme over form, in effect negating a text's relationship to modernism as the test of its literary standing. Hill went so far as to concede that some of her selections were not even "great," but were nonetheless "significant."[17]

A third practice that facilitated multiple definitions and uses of religious verse was the circulation of poems in denominational periodicals. By the late nineteenth century, American Protestants were awash in a sea of print. To take only one denomination, in 1900 Baptist concerns issued 99 publications (in addition to centrally-produced Sunday School materials). Among those were the major regionally-based weeklies: the *Watchman* and the *Examiner* (which combined in 1913), as well as the *Standard* (which became the *Baptist* in 1920, merging with the *Christian Century* in 1933). Each regularly used a poem to introduce its "home department," while usually running one or more others among its articles and editorials. Another locus of verse was the group of monthly magazines that various missionaries produced to review their activities and drum up support. In such journals as the *Baptist Missionary Magazine,* the *Helping Hand* (the voice of the Women's Baptist Foreign Mission Society), and the Free Baptist women's *Missionary Helper,* poetry enshrining faith and sacrifice often added a literary touch. The weekly *Indiana Baptist Outlook* typified the denomination's several statewide organs by carrying a poem on the second page of every issue. In addition, local church bulletins occasionally interspersed lines of poetry along with schedules of forthcoming events. Subsequently, beginning in the late 1930s, both the Southern and Northern Baptist Conventions published *Open Windows* and *The Secret Place,* respectively—each a monthly collection of daily devotions that from time to time included poetry.[18]

As in their non-Protestant counterparts, Baptist journals used verse to consume odd bits of space. The credit lines that followed poems sometimes read merely "Selected" or "Reprinted by request"—phrases implying a supply of filler made plentiful by the absence of copyright barriers. Yet here, perhaps even more than in scrapbooks and anthologies, the appearance of poetry also signified not only Christian faith but faith in the act of reading: the idea that an encounter with fifteen or twenty rhythmic lines of text interpolated between lengthier messages was a salutary, efficient form of therapy or uplift. The common characteristic of virtually all the poems in Baptist periodicals was their didactic quality— their lessons about the attributes and requirements of the moral life. Especially as printed in magazines for families, most also possessed the straightforward content and accessible diction that characterized sentimental verse. Apologetically returning a sonnet to the Baptist minister P. W. Crannell, the managing editor of the *Christian Endeavor World* explained: "It is our desire to print a great deal of poetry, but as many of our readers, and probably the majority of them, are young people, we try to obtain poems that are perfectly clear and easy of comprehension, while at the same time they are thoughtful and beautiful in form."[19]

In the pages of the *Watchman-Examiner,* which, under the ownership of Curtis Lee Laws, declared itself in 1930 "frankly and avowedly devoted to the simple old fashioned Baptist interpretation of the New Testament," the prevalence of the didactic and the sentimental throughout the first half of the twentieth century is not surprising. Yet, interestingly, the same was true even in the *Baptist,* which saw itself as "progressive" and from time to time featured poems by figures more identifiably literary: Louis Untermeyer, John Masefield, Bliss Carman. It may well be that copyright considerations and fees prevented the abundant reprinting of early modernist poetry even when editors found such texts congenial to their theology. In any case, the result was an occasional disjunction between the advice the *Baptist* offered its readers and the works it actually printed. In an essay entitled "Modern Poetry and Religion," for example, Thomas Curtis Clark hailed Millay, Sara Teasdale, John Hall Wheelock, Robinson, and Lindsay—along with Oxenham, Angela Morgan, and Ella Wheeler Wilcox, among others—as "just a few of the names that have shone in religious poetry since the turn of the century," although only poems in the style of the latter group appeared with any regularity. Put another way, whether for practical or ideological reasons, in these pages openness to both literary and religious modernism coexisted with the endorsement of older modes of expression. Moreover, precisely because of both its abundance and its accessibility, the poetry in denominational publications, while restricted in interpretive possibilities, nevertheless lent itself to more than one reading practice or behavioral outcome: a given text might provide a transitory thought at the breakfast table for one person while prompting emotional or even worshipful responses in another.[20]

Like anthologies, Baptist periodicals also expanded the opportunities for understanding poems in religious terms by routinely reprinting texts first published outside the Protestant media. In some instances, these reprints indicate the hospitableness of ostensibly secular magazines toward Christian messages, as when Grace Noll Crowell's poem specifying the "roads" that "lead to God" appeared in *Good Housekeeping* before it was picked up by the *Nebraska Baptist Messenger* for January 1930. Often, however, poets whose preoccupation with sentimental ideals far outweighed any specifically Baptist or even Protestant message made their way into denominational journals. In the *Indiana Baptist Outlook*, for example, works by favorite sons James Whitcomb Riley and Eugene Field appeared frequently. The *Watchman-Examiner* published Edgar Guest. Over a nine-month period beginning in the fall of 1899, the *Standard* included lines from Field, Richard Watson Gilder, Edwin Markham, and Wordsworth. While such poems unfailingly expressed at least vaguely Christian tenets, they did not necessarily contain the words "God," "Christ," or other doctrinal references. Wordsworth's "I Wandered Lonely as a Cloud" and Field's "Old Times, Old Friends, Old Love" are cases in point.[21]

It is possible to view these reprinting practices as contributing to—or at least symptomatic of—the vapidity that, as Ann Douglas and Jackson Lears have argued, overtook theological rigor in late-nineteenth-century America.[22] From one standpoint, they suggest that denominational distinctions had ceased to matter very much for the Baptist journals' publishers and subscribers. One might further propose that the importation of material from general-audience magazines may reveal editors' unspoken aspirations to proclaim the equal standing of the Christian and the non-Christian press (while, again, reflecting the exigencies of layout). Likewise, the *Examiner's* monthly summaries of contents in *Harper's*, the *Century*, and other intellectually respectable magazines (which offered similar synopses) can be regarded as a form of imprimatur but also as a declaration of cosmopolitanism. On the other hand, a poem's proximity to the sermons and mission reports that filled the pages of denominational journals could intensify and narrow the religious meanings of a text imported from a non-denominational source. Thus a figure such as Gilder, whom scholars have customarily characterized as a member of the urbane New York wing of the genteel tradition, and whose Episcopal affiliation accorded with his metamorphosis from Methodist minister's son to socially prominent editor, might emerge from the pages of the *Standard* as a homey Baptist poet. Whether reprinting magnified or obliterated theological differences, however, the use of poetry in denominational periodicals makes one point clear: even in a publication dedicated to the advancement of the church, the boundaries between the devotional, the religious, and the secular were shifting and permeable.

Poetry and Piety: The Reading Habits of the Devout

In addition to the devotional aid, the Christian anthology, and the denominational periodical, persons in search of "religious reading" obviously had at their disposal the entire corpus of Anglo-American verse, old and new, whether it came into their hands through other types of anthologies and magazines or through singly-authored collections. The question thus arises about the extent to which such individuals, confronting that spectrum of poetry, behaved like the editors and compilers of religious publications in seeing disparate texts through the lens of faith. Shifting the focus from editorial mediators to ordinary readers also invites further inquiries: What place did poetry occupy in the reading repertoires of church leaders? To what degree did the identifiably devout—for instance, pastors and missionaries—inflect prose and verse alike with values deriving from their Christian outlook?

Even with respect to a single denomination, these questions are impossible to answer in the aggregate. Individual differences in background, personality, geographic location, educational level, and attitudes toward orthodoxy made for different reading choices, regardless of allegiance to common tenets. Nevertheless, a sample of twenty-five diaries, journals, and unpublished memoirs produced by Baptist ministers and missionaries yields some instructive patterns.[23]

The authors of these documents were hardly alone among their contemporaries in making annual book lists or jotting down titles in daily entries; they shared with other Americans the assumption that a tally of reading signified an achievement worth noting for posterity. Yet it is safe to say that people who dedicated their lives to the service of the church were more likely to construe self-cultivation through reading as a Christian duty, a means of enhancing one's ability to carry out God's commandments. The calendar used by the missionary Edith Grace Traver in China suggests as much; it included a preprinted section labeled "Books Read" along with "Donations," "Conversions," and so on. By the same token, for those whose concept of Christian virtue demanded renouncing frivolity, the failure to read seriously might provoke remorse about wasting time—an emotion to which women seem to have been especially susceptible. "I am afraid my reading has been sadly neglected of late," Clara Holloway Groesbeck lamented, offering as a rationale that she had finished piecing a crazy quilt instead.[24] Hence for ministers and missionaries, references to reading were arguably more than a convention of autobiographical writing; they took on the quality of spiritual accountings and confessions.

To be sure, in several cases frustratingly brief notations ("Read, ate supper, read") imply the belief that perusing any book regardless of its contents demonstrated the writer's wise use of time. With respect to those reticent diarists, one cannot be sure whether the titles engaging them included poetic works or not. It is striking, however, that even among those who made fuller remarks—four left author/title lists, six more provided numerous details within entries—references to collections of verse appear in only seven documents in the sample. (Traver took with her to China the Hill anthology, another by Burton Stevenson, and Sara Teasdale's *Rainbow Gold*; other diarists referred to volumes by poets ranging from Holmes and Whittier to Rabindranath Tagore.) Against that relatively low number stands the fact that twenty-two of the sources contained allusions to reading or hearing poems. Together, those figures argue that, for the most part, these individuals did not "read thru" poetry (the term is Traver's) the way they did other genres. Dipping into a book of poems, recalling a memorized text, or listening to a recitation were more typical practices than reading a volume of verse from cover to cover. Poetry, one may conclude, suffused the mental world of these ministers and missionaries, but its position in their literary universe was less measurable—more amorphous—than the status occupied by novels and nonfiction.[25]

Given the desirability of recovering Americans' reading habits whenever the sources permit, a few general remarks about that wider universe are in order. Although they stretched out in steamer chairs or, especially during their seminary training, sat rigidly at desks, the twenty-five diarists most frequently identified the sites of their reading as the bedroom and the parlor. Curling up in bed with a book occurred typically but not exclusively in the evening hours, when, as for other Americans, the practice assumed the character of a ritual prior to sleep. More distinctive was the use of reading among those on foreign mission fields. Along with attendance at church functions, reading aloud in a group was among the most frequently tapped wellsprings of sociability in these missionaries' lives. Edith Grace Traver, writing in the 1920s, not only chronicled reading aloud at her home during and after meals, but also recorded the sharing of books in other missionaries' residences.

"I read 'Chinese Poems' and Mrs. Browning's & a sermon of Fosdick's to Margaret," she explained in April 1923, adding, "To-night I went to Clara's [probably Holloway Groesbeck] a minute & she read 'Chinese Poetry.'" In the same year, Traver, who imported books in her luggage and by mail, belonged to a reading club that chose *A Yankee on the Yangtze* for its first meeting and seems to have planned to meet weekly in members' homes. The missionary Sara Boddie Downer, also a reading club member in Asia at various times during the early 1920s, was involved in creating a "poetry room" for an unspecified audience. Further, she supplemented those activities, and her voracious solitary reading, with more informal sessions that entailed reading prose aloud with women friends. "Beulah finished the 'Silver Horde' [a novel by Rex Beach]," she commented from her sickbed in 1923. "My poor handkerchiefs."[26]

Downer's reference to the emotional impact of listening to a tearjerker prompts some speculation about the social and psychological functions that reading aloud performed in the mission setting. Whether the audience listened to a novel in installments or to poetry recitation, such gatherings of readers replicated similar scenes back in the United States; they were as much tokens of American identity—and of "civilization"—as the picture of home placed on the bedside table. Thus reading routines may have provided structure and the assurance of stable domestic arrangements for individuals who saw themselves as laboring among the unpredictable heathen. ("This is a very pleasant summer for me," Clara Holloway Groesbeck wrote in 1900. "It is so delightful to be outside Chinese walls and among people of my own race.") Undoubtedly, sharing books orally mitigated loneliness along with furnishing entertainment—both needs heightened by the omnipresent awareness of (and disdain for) cultural difference.[27]

Yet with respect to book selection, these foreign missionaries were not unique. Their domestic counterparts in missions and pulpits exhibited roughly the same range of taste in fiction. Three case histories drawn from the Baptist sample provide a closer look at some of the experiences and assumptions that these religious indi-

Isabel Crawford. Courtesy of the American Baptist Historical Society, American Baptist Archives Center, Valley Forge, Pa.

viduals brought to their private reading regardless of where they followed their calling. The three cases also contain extensive references to poetry, and, as such, redirect attention to the interplay readers constructed between poetic form and Christian purpose.

"Poetry," Isabel Crawford observed in 1913, "is my hobby." Born in 1865 to a Baptist preacher and his wife in Cheltenham, Ontario, Crawford spent much of her life as a missionary to Native Americans. Her first posting, beginning in 1893, was among the Kiowa Indians in Oklahoma. Feisty and independent by nature, she resigned from her work there in 1906 after a dispute with the Baptist leadership about the limits of her authority as a lay preacher. Subsequently she served on a reservation near Buffalo. When not on the mission field, she often gave public lectures, dressing in costume and demonstrating the 23rd Psalm in Indian sign language for eager audiences of churchwomen. Crawford incorporated verse into her performances as well. In the 1910s and '20s, as a roving ambassador for the home mission cause, she was constantly at the mercy of railroad schedules and church social committees, yet she made time to read "all the poetry I could lay my eyes on."[28]

Throughout her career, Crawford kept annual bound journals in which she recorded day-to-day events. At the back of these volumes, she usually made space for a yearly list of books read; from time to time, she also alluded to her reading in daily entries. Moreover, like Tileston's scrapbooks, Crawford's journals are a prime instance of the reader as compiler. Among the accounts of her activities, Crawford randomly inserted poems, anecdotes, and prose meditations, many cut and pasted in from periodicals, the others hand-copied. In 1931, to take just one example, Crawford created a journal page consisting entirely of printed verse, placing Longfellow's "I Hear Christ Say, 'Peace'" opposite the concluding stanza of Edna St. Vincent Millay's "God's World." The poet from whom Crawford borrowed most frequently was Edgar Guest, while "Invictus" appeared in four separate places.

The absence of singly-authored volumes of verse from her book lists suggests that anthologies and magazines furnished Crawford the materials for her homemade compilation. In a different context, the "patchwork" result might seem an incongruous jumble of styles and sensibilities, to say nothing of artistic merit. Within the pages of Crawford's journal, however, all the poetry she saved became consecrated to her faith and mission. A somewhat whimsical entry from September 1917 reveals that process of appropriation at work. Hungry and weak after speaking to the Cattaraugus Association of the Baptist Churches, she gratefully accepted both a plate of unappetizing chicken parts and twenty-five dollars in support of her efforts. Thereafter, "during the silent hours of the night," Crawford penned, "memories were awakened that had long been silent—scraps of poetry came to me such as 'Awake my soul. Stretch every nerve and press with vigour on[']—and Poe's masterpiece [']Quoth the Raven.' As often as possible during the remaining hours I thanked the people over and over again for their interest and living sympathy expressed through their gizzards and their cash!"[29] Crawford was apparently drawing a playful analogy between the raven and the chicken. Her slightly self-mocking, wry sense of humor percolates throughout her journals, lending them an unexpected note of worldliness. Whatever her intentions may have been, the serious point is that in her reverie she conflated the poems that came to mind, giving them new meaning as sources for the renewal of her Christian commitments. Moreover, as she read magazines or remembered schoolroom verse, the texts that Crawford saved in both her tangible and mental scrapbooks supported her sense of religious mission whether or not they expressly alluded to deity, creed, and ritual.

Needless to say, all the poems Crawford took the trouble to keep were ones she regarded favorably. One cannot say the same for her book lists, which contain every title she picked up; they are inventories of expectations, not seals of approval. Those expectations rested on Crawford's wide-ranging intellectual interests and on the set of moral precepts she derived from her Baptist convictions. Both sources are evident in a comment she made when she was confined to a sickbed in the summer of 1931: "Brother Bill the chaplain brings the denominational literature, but I want other reading too. I read so many books not worth while in the New

York hospital that this time I'm not going to indulge." Elsewhere, Crawford complained that of the fifty-two books she had read during her New York stay, only twelve fit her definition of "worth while." A remark she voiced in 1926 after reading *Wild Geese*, a novel she had received for Christmas, sheds further light on her exacting standards. "Every character was *extreme* and *unusual* and the whole thing not worth reading," Crawford declared. "I'm glad I had a mother who so guided and guarded my reading that I have no taste for anything that isn't elevating." In her reading list she repeatedly noted forays into the writing of her day, coupled with disappointment in the departure of current literature from her moral ideals. In the 1930s, she pronounced three contemporary best-sellers—*Anthony Adverse, Gone with the Wind,* and *The Good Earth*—all "abominable." Over the course of her reading life, the novelist Crawford liked best was Dickens, many of whose books she reread in 1933. As she phrased it, "They can't be beaten (for just stories)."[30]

Those aesthetic judgments mark Crawford as a representative of the mentality often disparaged as the "genteel tradition"; she seems an embodiment of Victorian values living on incongruously into the twentieth century. She was so wedded to decorum and rectitude that even the bold, "gaudy" colors of the 1933 Chicago Century of Progress Exhibition were an affront. At the same time, Crawford's reading—especially when one includes her taste in poetry—escapes neat classification by "brow" level or sensibility. Clearly, modernist experimentation lay beyond the pale (although she did manifest an interest in Amy Lowell and Vachel Lindsay). Yet she combined an affinity for the poetry of simple emotion with a venturesome attitude toward fiction and a willingness to risk assaults on her values for the sake of enlarged experience. Crawford read as a Christian, but she also read for a "hobby"—which meant that she read for edification, diversion, "relaxation" (her own word), and pleasure—all compatible qualities within her moral framework.[31]

In contrast to Crawford, who had a comfortable childhood as a minister's daughter, the Baptist clergyman William Edwin Darrow, who was born in 1864, led a hand-to-mouth existence as a youth;

the jobs that helped him survive included shelving books at a Brooklyn library and leading "exercises" at a Staten Island literary society. Following his graduation from seminary in 1892, however, the printed word assumed a more formal, predictable place in Darrow's life: he acquired a bachelor's degree and, in 1909, removed to the Midwest, where he held a series of pastorates until his retirement in 1931. He also became an Odd Fellow, a Mason, a certified teacher, a doctrinal conservative, a master's degree recipient (by correspondence), a compulsive list-maker—and a man so little inclined to reveal his thoughts and feelings that he used more space in his diary to describe which trains he took to a given destination than to report what he experienced when he got there.[32]

Nevertheless, Darrow, a voracious reader until his death in 1939, was also resident in a world of imaginative writing. Literary texts, and poetry in particular, entered his life through denominational periodicals, church bulletins, declamation contests, and attendance at lectures. At least in the early 1930s, however, Darrow's most consistent, substantial encounters with poetry and prose derived from his access to public libraries. One legacy of the rather stodgy personality he developed as he aged was his decision, first in Alton and then in Chicago, to keep a meticulous record of the books he borrowed and returned approximately every other Saturday. With respect to fiction, a striking facet of that record is its testimony to the ongoing life of nineteenth-century American literature, as an object not only of veneration but also of readers' continuing engagement. For example, in July of 1934 Darrow immersed himself in James Fenimore Cooper, taking up in succession *The Bravo, Mercedes of Castile, The Heidenmauer, Homeward Bound,* and *Home as Found.* He also read contemporary novels by Joseph Hergesheimer and Sinclair Lewis.

Darrow's reading record gave a prominent place to poetry and poetic criticism. Although he does not say so, Darrow's activities as a reader of the genre seem at least in part a search for models to emulate in his own writing. By the 1930s, he was composing poems in order to convey condolences, reinforce scriptural messages, and transmit religious fervor; these included "The Scales of Justice

Tilted," "Freedom through Truth," and "From Mother." (He also wrote some short stories with the same content.) Simultaneously, one finds him reading Longfellow's "Evangeline," Blake, and Sandburg. As if assenting to the assumption that he needed to stay abreast of recent language experiments, he took home *The Forms of Poetry* by Louis Untermeyer. He also borrowed studies of verse by Carl and Mark Van Doren and William Lyon Phelps. Yet he regarded as equally valuable the lessons in rhymed verse composition contained in George Lansing Raymond's *Poetry as a Representative Art,* a book he copied in longhand over a period of months in 1933. (His act of transcription suggests the desire to absorb viscerally the sensibility and craft that would match his aspirations.) In August and September of that year, Darrow withdrew from the library Charles H. Crandall's anthology *Representative Sonnets by American Poets,* the poems of William Blake and Sidney Lanier, Reverend Robert Aris Willmott's *The Poets of the Nineteenth Century,* an edition of Oliver Wendell Holmes, and Untermeyer's *Modern American and British Poetry.* He also displayed his sense of his own literary authority by addressing the Baptist Young People's Union on "Getting More Out of Reading." [33]

Two ironies attended Darrow's poetry reading. Despite his assiduous open-mindedness toward experimentation in form and language, he himself produced verse that admitted only literal interpretation. Whatever success he had in gaining an audience, moreover, resulted from his ability to commandeer means of dissemination that lay outside the usual mechanisms of distribution for the books he read. In 1932, for example, after hearing the keynote addresses at the Northern Baptist Convention, Darrow reworked the speaker's theme, "Let's Pray It Through," into rhyming stanzas. Borrowing "Let's Pray It Through" for his title, he then circulated mimeographed copies of his poem to about 75 ministers and other friends, and later sent out a revised version. At the same time, he submitted the poem to several Baptist publications. It appeared successively in the *Northern California Baptist Bulletin,* the *Baptist* (Chicago), the *Watchman-Examiner* (by which time credit to the originator of the title had disappeared), the *Illinois Baptist*

Bulletin, and *Adult Leader.* Whenever Darrow attempted to move outside the denominational press, however—he tried *Harper's,* the *Atlantic Monthly, Household Magazine,* and the *Ladies' Home Journal*—he met with failure. (The same was true on occasion even of Baptist periodicals.) During a two-week interval in March 1934, he noted five "returns" from journals around the country.

Darrow was, in plain words, a terrible poet, if one shares with the editors who rejected him a premium on subtle, inventive language. Nevertheless, that fact should not obscure his adherence to a sense of the "poetic" that encompassed schoolroom favorites, devotional sentimentalists, and early modernists alike. Darrow's apparent understanding that even his modest ambition to write simple Christian messages in verse required an education in the "literary" demonstrates the artificiality of divorcing a high culture aesthetic from popular religious expression, just as his intellectual energy precludes classifying him only as a clerical version of Lewis's Babbitt or Mencken's provincial member of the "booboisie."

John Alasko Curtis, the third of the three cases from the Baptist sample, was similarly eclectic. Born in 1870, Curtis was a Baptist missionary to India who eventually retired to Vermont. Initially religious values permeated all of Curtis's reading, in the broad sense that, like Crawford, he measured the written word against his stern understanding of Christian morality. By the 1940s, however, following his period of missionary service, Curtis's conventionally genteel taste had evolved into a perspective less easy to categorize. He found enjoyment in reading: he relished his subscription to the Book-of-the-Month Club, made proximity to a library part of his decision to relocate his household, and regularly traded volumes with friends. Yet, for Curtis, the pleasures of print did not derive only from morally edifying texts. For one thing, he was something of a scholar, with an appreciation for intellectual exchange that enabled him to countenance heterodoxy. "The long preface has proved stimulating," he wrote in 1949 of Shaw's *Saint Joan,* "though one disagrees often."[34]

Furthermore (in contrast to Crawford), Curtis developed a critical stance as a reader that permitted a distinction between literary craft and moral message. "Two Masefield story books dipped into," Curtis wrote in February of 1942. "Maybe it is satiety—cared little for them. They seem full of 'crudeties' and heaviness; characters & story lack reality or verisimilitude. Must try some of his poetry." In that statement, "crudeties" referred to infelicities of style, a signal of Curtis's distance from the moralism governing his youthful judgments. His remark a few days later that Masefield's *Collected Poems* were "more beautiful than I had remembered" but "uneven"—a word that Curtis absorbed from Masefield's biographer—demonstrated Curtis's understanding that reading poetry required responding to the text in aesthetic terms. Comparing Theodore Dreiser's *An American Tragedy* with Pearl Buck's stories of China, Curtis declared Dreiser's "natural pagan[ism]" preferable to Buck's betrayal of the "missionary enterprise," while nevertheless conceding that Buck's writing was itself "fairly skillful."[35]

Yet, as his condemnation of Buck indicates, Curtis's openness, by the 1940s, to risking the dislocations of modern literature did not entirely negate his religiously-based animosity toward what he saw as moral laxity. More than that, Curtis's sensibility continued to accommodate the romantic and idealist poetry of the nineteenth century. "In P. M. read Tennyson for a long time," he wrote in February of 1943. "Enoch Arden and [other] pieces. He is powerfully idealistic in thought as well as constantly producing gems of beauty and clarity & insight." In the same period he began composing verse himself, turning for instruction to a spectrum of writers that included Whitman and Poe along with Tennyson and Masefield.[36] Less ambitious than Darrow, Curtis evidently did not publish the ballads, autobiographical pieces, tokens of friendship, and commemorations of loved ones' deaths that he wrote. Nevertheless, even as an amateur he brought to the endeavor a sense of himself as an apprentice to literary authority. Like Crawford, Curtis never extended his reading repertoire to the poetry of high modernism. Still, both the texts he juxtaposed—in one entry, he described temporarily setting aside Thomas Mann to pick up the latest *Reader's Digest*—and his critical assumptions reflect a mentality that, informed by his religious beliefs, was neither one-dimensional nor retrograde. Curtis read verse and prose alike for diversion, knowledge, delight, and writing instruction, ranging across genre, period, and canon.

The journals of Crawford, Darrow, and Curtis stop short of providing the sort of detailed reflection that would enable one to reconstruct fully the psychological and social imperatives their reading satisfied. Yet the examples of these three devout Protestants have in common signs that, over time, reading became a practice that involved blending fidelity to their interpretations of Christian tradition and responsiveness to the claims of modernity. Crawford's love for the poetry of sentiment and uplift functioned to anchor the values buffeted by her desire to keep up with contemporary fiction. Darrow used verse to propagate his faith by conventional means while exercising a degree of openness toward changing standards of taste. Curtis similarly balanced the residual moral strictures of his youth and the greater flexibility he developed in maturity. Verse reading was central to their conception of themselves as Baptists and as human beings.

In the Minister's Study

Pastoral responsibilities strengthened and supplemented the Protestant clergy's motives for the private reading of poetry. "A bookless minister," one essayist warned in the *Methodist Review* in 1907, "means a barren ministry."[37] The connections between print and the work of leading a congregation received their fullest expression not on the pages of a diary but instead in the images that coalesced around an actual physical space: the minister's study.

Early-twentieth-century contributors to the *Methodist Review* recurred with striking regularity to the figure of the preacher ensconced amid his beloved volumes. In a typical example, Lynn Harold Hough, writing in 1911, described a young man's visit to an elderly, devout reader in terms that implicitly likened the occasion to revelation and worship. As Hough (the eventual president of Northwestern University) set the scene, "The softly shaded lamp cast a quiet glow over the many shelves of books," while the inter-

mittent crackling of the library fire resembled the "flashing light"—
one might say the divine intuition—"of a sudden thought." As
in church, meaningful silences punctuated the encounter between
the humbled visitor and (as the capitalization suggests) the exalted
"Book-Lover," who was called to lead others to God through read-
ing. Leaving the house, the young man "gazed up at the stars and
was glad to be alive."[38]

The titles on the "Book-Lover's" study table, which included the
writing of the Anglican (and future Catholic) Gilbert Chesterton,
locate Hough as a religious (as opposed to a literary) modernist; in-
deed, one purpose of reading, Hough implied, was to acquire the
broad-mindedness that distinguished the liberal Protestant from
the ignorant backwater fundamentalist. The message of the entire
vignette was that being well-read in literature, history, and philoso-
phy (rather than simply in the Bible) was an essential attribute
of the effective pastor. Similarly, by assuming an audience that val-
ued the question, Charles Edward Locke's "What Does a Bishop
Read?," which the *Review* printed in 1926, both certified the liter-
ary authority of the clergy and argued that mastery of wide culture
was inextricably bound to the minister's sense of identity. The fre-
quency and forcefulness with which Hough, Locke, and their like-
minded colleagues asserted the value of non-biblical reading may
indicate some lingering reservations even on the part of liberal rank
and-file pastors about preoccupying themselves with such texts.[39]

In any event, the commentators who envisioned the minister in
his study invested his reading of poetry and other genres with sev-
eral purposes directly related to his obligations to his flock. The
first, and most personal, was respite. As the author of "Poetry
an Asset for the Preacher" (1913) melodramatically observed, the
poet's perspective offered "relief" for the "heavily burdened" clergy.
Beset by apathy and doubt, exhausted by the endless demand for
"words, words, words," the leader of a church risked becoming
"either sordid or insane." Yet, awakening on a "'blue Monday,'"
he might find renewal in Browning's reminder that "God's in his
heaven"; he might gain fortitude recalling Gilder's command to
"keep pure thy soul!" The *Methodist Review*'s use of the term

"lure" to designate the power of reading likewise alluded to the way books "take us out of ourselves." Moreover, respite in the setting of the study or library was allied with pleasure; for some preachers, the site offered both intellectual and decidedly sensual gratifications. "There is no reason," the author of "The Minister Among His Books" noted somewhat defensively, "why the minister should not put another log on his library fire, while the chill night wind rustles and whistles against the window shutters, and take down the poets. That Temple edition of Shakespeare, bound in red and printed in black, feels just right in the hand." As Bishop William A. Quayle (an eloquent book lover and collector) described his responses in similar surroundings, "I care to fondle the book as if the words could make my hands odorous as if wind from a clover field blew over them. . . . I dawdle over it and am refreshed." Elsewhere Quayle asserted that a beautiful book was a "luxury" to "possess, read, dream over, caress with the eyes."[40]

Yet, despite the temptation to retreat to the study for its therapeutic and hedonistic benefits, ministers' accounts of their solitary reading indicate that the social uses of books were never far from view. For one thing, like other busy professionals, the "telephoned-plagued, nerve-wracked metropolitan parson" could not readily evade the day-to-day responsibilities of his position. Hence more than one writer in denominational magazines augmented images of the minister's study with references to reading on the run: carrying a pocket-sized edition of Masefield's "Everlasting Mercy" on a trolley car, leaving books in every room of the house for use during spare moments. Given the demands of their schedules, harried ministers sometimes conducted private reading in the public eye.[41]

Even if the study was available as a cloister, however, liberal Protestant ideals precluded using it solely as such. For the clergy, reading had a second religious purpose: "general literature," as Hough put it in 1916, provided the inspiration and empathy that connected religious doctrine and human experience. Thus, creating a fictional conversation among five longtime friends, Hough had one of his characters, a professor of theology, voice the discovery (after reading Dickens) that "a book must be an introduction to the study of people and not a substitute for it." He insisted that reading was not an "escape" but, rather, a preparation for greater service through "contact with life." Likewise, Hough wrote elsewhere, "A man goes out from his library to serve the world as effectively as he may[,] . . . giving toil and the full measure of devotion to the tasks of his own time." He credited books with "the breaking of the barriers of our own lives so that we actually experience the meaning of other lives."[42]

Indeed, the metaphors upon which religious leaders relied to convey the effects of reading transformed the site of the study into a social milieu, sustaining the figure of the poet as companion or intimate. Echoing literary critics and educators in the same period, ministers depicted books as "portals" to other worlds, and reading as a form of transport. Yet whether they entered a realm of "magic," a "new world," or a "metropolis," the destinations to which literature conducted readers were populated with fascinating people: the "fairyland" held "a choice set of folk"; the city staged "the most wonderful kind of receptions" with "guests" who were "chosen from all ages." Again, the language of friendship suggests cultural as well as professional sources: for readers troubled by the impersonality of the urban environment—for those distressed more by a sense of isolation within the multitude than by the press of the crowd—Hough's idea that "when a man of books sits in his library he is not alone" might carry special force. So, too, the conceit that "when the logs have burned low on the hearth, the minister may go to his rest with the consciousness that he is heir to all the ages" not only buttressed the importance of the clergy but also intensified their social connections.[43]

The goals of respite, empathy, and sociability accommodated a wide spectrum of genres and titles. The practice of rereading older works especially promised "refreshment," resembling "cooling draughts from familiar fountains." According to one observer, revisiting devotional texts—for instance, an "occasional reading of good old Thomas à Kempis"—would rejuvenate the pastor's soul "like a breeze," taking the "fire of impatience out of his blood and brain." Contributors to the *Methodist Review* made frequent reference to rereading poetry. One writer explained that volumes of verse "really beat the 'best-sellers,'" for those who read them once read them over and over again." Oscar Kuhns, who taught at Wesleyan University, stated that he read Dante through "practically every year." Quayle, who praised works for their "haunting quality" and reread a book every time he acquired a new edition of it, observed of Longfellow that, despite the "jazz-like attack" on him, his poetry was "like the old clock on the stairs which beats out the life of men, living when they are all dead and dust." Other older poets who, in the eyes of the *Methodist Review*'s contributors, withstood repeated readings were Tennyson, Wordsworth, and Browning; articles about them pervaded the periodical's pages until it ceased publication in 1931. At the turn of the century, the same could not be said for Whitman; condemned in the *Review* for "crass materialism," he found much less favor among even liberal Protestant clergy than Gilder or Henry Van Dyke.[44]

Yet Hough urged open-mindedness toward recent or innovative literature, on the grounds that a knowledge of contemporary taste enabled the pastor to stay in touch with his congregation. Another of the characters in Hough's fictional conversation, a popular writer, praised the mixture of old and new that constituted the library of a preacher in the "foreign quarter" of town: it overflowed with Alfred Noyes, O. Henry, and Kipling; it "even had the Spoon River Anthology," several works on immigration, and three books by Walter Lippmann. "The poets who have stolen fire from heaven were there—copies which had been used, too," Hough's character marveled. "You ought to have seen the man's Browning." Conspicuously absent was "predigested theological brain food," the closest thing to sermon outlines being four volumes of *Yale Lectures on Preaching*.[45]

The best summary of liberal Protestant eclecticism came from the pen of William L. Stidger, a Methodist minister who, in *The Place of Books in the Life We Live* (1922), offered a paean to poetry that read in part: "My Goethe, Dante, Omar too; / One likes the old, one likes the new. / . . . Some Gibson, Lindsay, and Millay; / Where shadows laugh and run and play; / . . . Our ancient Keats and Shelley too; / Our Rupert Brookes; our old, our new; / Carl Sandburg and the Vers Libre— / 'Spoon River's['] Bleak 'Anthology' / Our Amy Lowell and her tribe / The Orthodox must scold and chide / A thousand poems and a song; / A hundred authors and a throng / Of characters to love / And hate!"[46] Stidger's tolerant, almost playful reference to the "Orthodox," as well as his disarming acceptance of both "new poets" and nineteenth-century verse, is a compelling refutation of the idea that the advent of literary modernism divided American culture into two warring camps.

Of course, not all inhabitants of the pastor's study accepted the "new poetry" to that degree. Ambivalence was common. One minister, writing in 1920, conceded the difficulty of becoming accustomed to free verse, but praised Edgar Lee Masters for his "striking contribution" to the genre. Carl Sandburg met with greater resistance: a 1923 review in the family-oriented *Presbyterian* condemned his inclusion in Hill's anthology. Granting that the Chicago poet was "spontaneous," the same writer who embraced Masters exclaimed with disdain: "It is easy to say that Sandburg's work, if poetry at all, is poetry of the sidewalk and the soap box. Certainly it is not the poetry of the study."[47]

As Hough implied, however, the boundary between sidewalk and study was fluid—and, by 1920, arguably growing more so. While ministers continued to retreat to their firesides to satisfy both individual needs and communal imperatives, poetry reading as a social act increasingly took religious forms that extended well beyond the metaphorical. The minister's private employment of verse coincided with and complemented numerous uses of the genre within the church itself.

Poetry in Worship Services

As already noted, psalms and lyrics to hymns transported poetry to the heart of liberal Protestant ritual. Henry Sloane Coffin remarked in 1946 that "any definition of poetry that excludes altogether the simple congregational hymn is surely a narrow definition." At the same time, another facet of Protestant worship—the sermon—

allowed not only the dissemination of poetic insight but also the display of the minister's erudition. As one observer commented in the *Methodist Review,* literature was "a homiletical treasure house for the preacher of the living Word." Thus in 1905 James Mudge reported that, of twelve prominent Methodist preachers whose sermons he investigated, all but two relied on "extracts from the poets."[48]

The degree of understanding that ministers conveyed about such quotations varied tremendously. As Andrew W. Blackwood of Princeton Theological Seminary complained in 1939, preachers "glibly refer to Milton and Dante, or Francis Thompson and Alfred Noyes, and perhaps repeat excerpts from Bartlett's *Familiar Quotations,* or Burton Stevenson's books" without grounding their remarks in genuine knowledge and love of art. Nevertheless, by the mid-1920s Protestant clergy in communities like Buffalo and Kenosha, Wisconsin, had begun delivering sermons in which they expounded at length on literary themes. *Publishers' Weekly* indicated that the practice was especially prevalent at vespers or mid-week services. One extant example of that development was William Forney Hovis's *Poetic Sermons* (1932), a series of talks based on poems such as Longfellow's "The Village Blacksmith" and Tennyson's "Enoch Arden." Hovis, a Methodist preacher from Milwaukee, earned some publicity for the sermons: the St. Louis *Post-Dispatch* featured one (written in rhyme) in its Sunday magazine. In 1941 a class in homiletics at the Colgate Rochester Divinity School specifically studied the use of poetry in the sermon. A Congregationalist minister who served for part of his career in Sandburg's home town of Galesburg, Illinois, spoke frequently about the poet, explaining at the beginning of one sermon that he liked "a liberal pulpit" because he was "free to preach about the inspiring qualities of certain non-Biblical lives."[49]

The book sermon found its most vocal proponent in the Methodist clergyman William L. Stidger. Pastor in the early 1920s of Linwood Methodist Church in Kansas City, Stidger was professor of homiletics at Boston University School of Theology from 1928 to 1949. A prominent author and lecturer with a gift for self-pro-

motion, he moved easily in the male world of love and ritual that
Edgar Guest inhabited. The two men were friends for over twenty-
five years, Stidger reporting to "Dear Eddie Boy" in 1944 that their
relationship made him "hilariously happy." Stidger also counted
Amherst College president Mark Hopkins, Luther Burbank, and
Henry Ford among his acquaintances,[50] but he especially liked hob-
nobbing with literati. He befriended Edwin Markham and, in 1932,
became his biographer; he cultivated Sinclair Lewis but then quar-
reled vituperatively with him over *Elmer Gantry*. This is not to
deny the substance behind the preoccupation with celebrity. Stidger's
essays from the 1910s, as well as his relationship with Markham,
reflect a sympathy for the Social Gospel. Later, his writings reso-
nated with a faith in American individualism, virtue, and manliness
that linked him to the circle of two of his other heroes, Theodore
Roosevelt and Edward Bok.

By his own admission, in 1917 Stidger fell for a ploy of Wil-
liam Allen White's publishers, who flattered him and other "lead-
ing" ministers by giving them autographed copies of White's latest
novel. Stidger used it as the basis for his first "Dramatic Book Ser-
mon," in which a contemporary or classic work furnished connec-
tions to biblical teachings. This innovation in homiletics, Stidger
explained, derived in part from "Jesus Christ Himself," who drew
his teachings from "the library of the Old Testament." Stidger even-
tually made the book discussion formula a fixture of the Sunday
evening service in his congregation. He also proselytized on behalf
of the device to his ministerial colleagues, who responded by repli-
cating "book sermons" throughout the United States.[51]

To that endeavor, Stidger brought a conception of reading that
enlisted it as a means of both grace and marketing. In *The Place of
Books in the Life We Live*, he echoed progressive teachers and
other moralists in viewing with alarm the emergence of a "Motion
Picture Mind" and the "poor empty shelves of the bookcases in the
average American home." Shaped as it was by new technologies
and commodities, the "life we live," Stidger implied, was an exis-
tence in which the role of reading required redefinition and defense.
Most important, books offered, as Stidger phrased it, the "regener-

ation of a human soul." Extending the promise of respite to ordinary readers as well as beleaguered clergy, he insisted that stories of "great men" enabled the reader to "leave behind him all of the petty things of the present Age to live in the spirit of the Ages." Such a voyage furnished a vision of the eternal that brought individuals closer to God. Second, in remarks derivative of Quayle's, he praised books as sources of "pleasure" and sensory "delight." Finally, the armchair travel permitted by reading—which Stidger characterized as "bulging back the world's horizons"—was instrumental to discovering "new ideas, new impulses, new ideals, new aspirations."[52]

At the same time, however, Stidger also invested reading with less lofty purposes. Interestingly, the metaphor he adopted to denote the power of print contained both material and mystical allusions: a book was a "magic stone that will turn the world to gold." Stidger was entirely comfortable with the language and techniques of business; if Bruce Barton was in a sense an adman turned preacher, Stidger may be seen as a preacher turned adman. Thus he described the assistance books could provide a floundering young person as "the big boost." To be sure, this "boost" was in part spiritual—"I needed Light[,] I needed an Epiphany," he wrote of his own struggles—but it was also an aid to professional advancement. This was especially true, Stidger claimed, for the clergy who followed his example by invigorating their messages with literary texts. The "book sermon," he observed, was the "finest drawing card" he knew. It resuscitated the midweek prayer meeting (which Stidger transformed into Family Night); it satisfied the demands of the college graduates who, by the end of the 1920s, dominated congregations like Linwood; and it enhanced the lives and stature of pastors who became "almost over night" more "effective" and "popular." In Stidger's view, there was "no more pragmatic preaching vehicle" at hand.[53]

Within Stidger's ideology of reading, poetry held a central place. An amateur poet himself, Stidger incorporated into his monographs numerous verses in praise of books ("And we thank Thee, God, / For the deep in them; / For the rhythmic swing / And sweep

Reverend William L. Stidger preaching. Reproduced by permission of John W. Hyland, Jr.

in them") Preaching through poetry, he maintained, was the most efficient way to strengthen faith and increase church attendance. As "the divinely ordained vehicle" of "spiritual truths," poems were "bright darts" that preachers could shoot into the "hearts" of their congregations. In another counterpoint to the view of mainstream publishers who bemoaned the paltry market for single volumes of verse, Stidger declared at the end of the 1920s that "the preacher who uses poetry is sure of a hearing today." The people, he contended, "not only need poetry in this age, but they are wistful for it. They love it. They respond to it. It works. It lures them. It fascinates an audience." Moreover, because poets had learned economy of expression, they furnished ministers with countless lines for exegesis and elaboration.[54]

In articulating his outlook toward poetry and reading generally,

Stidger adopted the stance of the expert: as he explained in the foreword to *There Are Sermons in Books* (1922), he publicized the book sermon as a response to "preachers all over America" who were seeking his recipe for success. Nevertheless, Stidger's position, although laced with the same rhetoric of "service" to the community that corporate leaders employed at the time, betrays a hint of uneasiness about the nature of religious authority in the "business civilization" of the post–World War I period. Stidger took it upon himself to advise the publishing industry about how to expand its sales, a role born of friendship with "book men" but expressive as well of his arguably wistful notion that "the word of a preacher in commendation of a book" carried greater weight than the judgment of a newspaper columnist. "I say that I believe that it would be a more direct way of getting to a new reading market," he explained, "if Book Publishers and Book Sellers would introduce their wares more and more through preachers. I believe actually that the Book World is missing a good guess by not more and more sending their books to Preachers for review." By dubbing the minister "the man of Books," Stidger may have evinced longings for an imagined earlier day when the public deferred to the clergy on aesthetic as well as ethical matters.[55]

Whether or not he felt himself on an insecure foundation, however, Stidger had his own angle of vision which determined his strategies of enticement. From his pulpit, as well as in his essay collections, he publicized poets both "old and new," in the bargain erasing dichotomies between serious and light or popular verse. Edwin Markham remained his chief enthusiasm, yet in *Planning Your Preaching*, issued in 1932, Stidger commended the poetry of Gilder, Van Dyke, Robinson, Frost, and Don Marquis (to indicate only the range of his American favorites). The sources he suggested as reference works encompassed Burton Stevenson's *Famous Single Poems* as well as the Untermeyer and Wilkinson collections. His volume *Flames of Faith* (1922), though divided by gender, brought together on equal footing Millay, Guest, and Strickland Gillilan, a humorist who, Stidger averred, "keeps faith alive in the hearts of a great group of men who never heard tell of Tennyson, or Browning, or Poe."[56]

Stidger constructed his blend of styles by implicitly casting all his subjects as "poet-preachers"—that is, he interpreted as confirmations or echoes of his own Protestant beliefs references in their work to faith, God, prayer, and the soul. While proponents of speaking choirs valued Vachel Lindsay, for example, primarily because of his manipulation of sound and rhythm, Stidger heard in "The Congo" and "General William Booth Enters Into Heaven" only the poet's affirmation of Christian tenets. Of course, Lindsay was possessed of a mystical and missionary temperament and thus provided a sizeable basis for regarding his efforts in such terms; although more Swedenborgian than Protestant, he saw himself as spreading a "gospel of beauty." A more striking appropriation is Stidger's reading of Millay—especially her poem "Renascence." The publisher Mitchell Kennerley had first printed "Renascence" in his anthology of 1912 entitled *The Lyric Year*. Kennerley, a maverick himself, had hoped to discover new, young poets and had arranged a contest to find them. While a good deal of its contents remained traditional in form and diction, the resulting volume had a Greenwich Village, bohemian cast. The *Methodist Review*, although mentioning Millay only in passing, judged the collection "peculiar" and sadly concluded there was "much" in it that Kipling (considered a model poet) would not "abide."

Stidger's interpretation of "Renascence" wrenched Millay from that context, transforming her into a conventionally religious poet. Specifically, while literary critics have construed the poem as a discovery of the goodness manifest in nature ("God, I can push the grass apart / And lay my finger on Thy heart!"), Stidger exclaimed: "Then came something into this soul . . . nothing less triumphant than a good old-fashioned experience of what we call conversion." In Stidger's hands, Millay's transcendentalist or romantic God turned into a Methodist one; the narrator's despair, self-doubt, and consciousness of evil became "a running narrative of a man who, buried in materialism, cynicism, hate and sin, was washed from his grave into a new life and a new birth."[57]

To be fair, Stidger discovered "Renascence" before 1920, the year when *A Few Figs from Thistles* and *Second April* spread Millay's reputation as a Greenwich Village radical. In fact, Stidger's account of encountering Millay's verse argues against a trickle-down model of diffusion: he reports that he first happened upon one of her poems not in an anthology but, rather, in the "literary magazine" where it was initially published; later he found an excerpt from "Renascence" in what he described as a "Book Column"; and finally he acquired the small edition entitled *Renascence and Other Poems* that Kennerley brought out in 1917. Yet Stidger still classified Millay as the greatest modern poet-preacher as late as 1932, when he praised all of her writings through *A Buck in the Snow*. To make that case, he had to ignore not only the verse in which Millay explicitly flouted Christian morality but also the sexual imagery in her other work. By reprinting much of "Renascence" that year in *Planning Your Preaching,* he completed his transformation of the text into an artifact of religious publishing.[58]

Stidger's "dramatic book sermons" thus both exemplify one form of reading "secular" poetry in the setting of the church and emphasize the importance of recovering, insofar as possible, the terms on which such reading occurred. Furthermore, by implying that the greatest poets buttressed entrenched theology, and by attaching business ideals to the rationale for reading them, Stidger's canon-making provides another corrective to the generalization that, in the twentieth century, anthologists have typically equated the "best" with reactions against dominant values.[59]

The sermon was not the only form in which worshippers encountered poetry in church. They listened to it as well at rites and observances marking the stages of life. At funerals, for example, the British texts from which schoolchildren absorbed Christian romanticism became bearers of empathy and talismans of recollection: "There is often a place," Blackwood counseled, "for the right sort of poem; it may be from Browning, Tennyson, or Wordsworth. At the close of the service, when one makes ready to leave, it is good to hand one of the friends a copy of this poem," with "anything else which will serve as a loving token that the minister shares their sorrow and their hope."[60]

Perhaps most worth remarking is the fact that in some services both leader and congregation recited non-biblical verse as prayer.

In general, the interpolation of poems into liberal Protestant ritual reflected the greater possibilities, by the early twentieth century, for augmenting a fixed liturgy. Although the freedom of the minister to use "words of his own choosing" was a matter of "old warfare" among denominations, as Blackwood had observed, the issue received renewed attention as non-fundamentalist twentieth-century Protestant clergy worried about waning piety. "Unless the free churches develop a more convincing, more compelling, and more satisfying worship," one writer declared in 1931, "Protestantism is doomed." Not only poetry but also music, drama, and the visual arts promised to achieve those results.[61]

Religious educators targeted for experimentation the less formal services conducted at a time other than Sunday morning, as well as assemblages of church youth, the latter on the grounds that adolescents were "peculiarly ready for . . . and responsive to" the "religious nurture" that "vital" language and image supplied. Thus Darrow's poem "Proving My Love," reprinted in the *Young People's Leader*, became part of a group of "Intermediate Worship Services." The evangelical theologian Kirby Page presented the poems he gathered in *Living Creatively* (1932) as useful not only for daily devotions but also for "church services, schools of religions, education, young peoples' meetings, boys' clubs, summer camps, student conferences, and similar gatherings." Page's political activism extended his range of choices: along with Oxenham and "God's World," he included works by Countee Cullen, Langston Hughes, and James Weldon Johnson, while poems cognizant of working-class life—Margaret Widdemer's "Factories," Sandburg's "Prayers of Steel," Reginald Wright Kaufman's "The March of the Hungry Man"—complemented Kilmer's "Trees."[62]

Perhaps the most suggestive work that appropriated poetry for public worship was *Services for the Open* (1923), arranged by Laura I. Mattoon, secretary of an association of girls' camps, and Helen D. Bragdon, general secretary of the Y.W.C.A. at Mt. Holyoke College. Designed primarily for young people at camps or schools meeting out-of-doors, Mattoon and Bragdon's interdenominational Christian services also provided material for adults wishing to commune with "the God of the open air." As the two women explained, "In such services, it has been felt that there is a rightful place—not only for passages from the greatest Book wrought out of human experience, but for the inspirations of seers and poets down to the present time." Crediting both biblical and poetic texts with equal standing as sources, Mattoon and Bragdon also sanctified Emerson, Thoreau, Whittier, Wordsworth, and six naturalists as "apostles of the out-of-doors" around whose lives leaders could devise services of their own.[63]

The result was a series of thematic scripts in which the order of worship moved seamlessly, for example, from the Doxology, a Bible quotation, "The Lord's Prayer," and a hymn in praise of summer to stanzas by Edward Rowland Sill and Wordsworth. In a service for the planting of a tree, worshippers sang both "Fairest Lord Jesus" and a musical version of Kilmer's lines. Some of the poetry in Bragdon and Mattoon's compilation, such as Carman's rhyme beginning "Lord of my heart's elation, / Spirit of things unseen," had already found its way into anthologies like Hill's. But other texts—for instance, Kreymborg's "Old Manuscript," a poem originally published by Knopf (rather than a denominational magazine) and strikingly lacking in references to the divine or supernatural—became "religious" by their transformation into prayer. Services for the Open's chronological and stylistic range included Shakespeare, Longfellow, Lowell, Van Dyke, Markham, Robinson, and Frost. Mattoon and Bragdon's decision to identify authors only in a list of references may have heightened the reader's experience of an unmediated spiritual encounter but diminished the possibility of discriminating among the selections in literary terms.[64]

As in the schoolroom, the eclecticism characterizing Services for the Open had its limits: obscurity and pessimism were out of bounds. Yet the volume overrode a number of the distinctions on which scholars have often relied in sorting literary production—between the sacred and the secular, Victorian piety and early modernist revolt, the "high" and the popular. It bears repeating that the self-definitions of poets who rejected the conventions of earlier generations were a casualty of this form of dissemination; their

Sunday worship at Camp Kehonka, where elements of *Services for the Open* survived into the 1980s. Courtesy of Roy Ballentine.

oppositional stance disappeared in the process. To go further, the performance of poetry as worship is a striking exception to the idea that, by the nineteenth century, the authority of a text was inextricably bound to the construction of authorship; in *Services for the Open,* dissemination occurred without reference to the author, and authority derived from the weight of Protestant ritual—in other words, from the site of worship itself.

That authority inhered, moreover, not merely in doctrine or in the impact of architecture but also in the modes of speech congregations habitually adopted. That is, worshippers were accustomed to delivering prayers at the slow pace and steady rhythm that reading as a body required; the unison form homogenized voices and inserted pauses in a way that discouraged flamboyance and idiosyncratic theatricality. By virtue of tone as well as content, the religious service thus bestowed solemnity and stature on any text read aloud; it made Edgar Guest's lines ("For who would strive for a distant goal / Must always have courage within his soul") and Shakespeare's sound alike—which is to say it made them both sound "good." Comparative judgments about a poet's use of form and language gave way to sacralization of the most literal sort.[65]

These varied uses of verse in actual worship offered the same consolations as their quasi-religious echo in the public school. Poetry as prayer, however, lent more precise meaning to the motive of reading for inspiration, while reframing other aims of the classroom recitation in Christian terms. Here, the goal of fostering community meant achieving the unity of shared beliefs and oneness before God; it also referred to the equal standing of leader and congregation. As one commentator observed, non-liturgical denominations (that is, Protestants apart from Episcopalians and Lutherans) minimized the "spiritual spectatorship and individualistic devotion" characteristic of Anglo-Catholicism.[66] Both unison and responsive reading served that end, but the latter device was particularly suited to the rendition of poetry antiphonally. There was irony as well as fellowship in this practice: like the participants in the verse speaking choirs of the same era, when congregations read as an affirmation of social bonds the words of poets resigned to the solitariness of human existence—one thinks of Robinson or Frost—they yoked them to a sensibility decidedly at odds with the poets' dominant message.

At the same time, church leaders joined progressive pedagogues in involving poetic texts in the promotion of "creativity." As one religious educator, Laura Armstrong Athearn, explained, "Worship is essentially a creative process. It makes possible the release of a spiritual dynamic which has hitherto been a potential rather than an actual fact." While some theologians insisted that "creative prayer" necessitated a loss of selfhood, Athearn stressed that it would help make "a man or a woman greater in power than he or she had ever dreamed." Although the appropriateness of direct moral instruction was not at issue, the double emphases on communal loyalty and self-expression thus imparted to the worship setting a share of the tensions that marked poetry reading at school.[67]

Poetry as Prayer in Reform Judaism

However popular poetry may have been in settings such as youth camps, its incorporation into Protestant services was—and continues to be—optional and unstandardized. That is, the uses of verse in the Protestant milieu have always depended entirely on the decisions of individual congregational leaders to include selected poems in the liturgy. The Protestant case thus differs markedly from Reform Judaism, where poetic texts are an integral part of the two books that, until recently, the denomination had relied on for communal worship: *Gates of Prayer* (1975; revised 1994), for weekday and Sabbath services, and *Gates of Repentance* (1978, revised 1997), for the High Holidays Rosh Hashanah and Yom Kippur. Although examining these documents involves jumping ahead to the 1970s, poetry in Reform Jewish ritual warrants investigation because the site has been particularly hospitable to the dissemination of modernist verse.

Historically, poems entered Jewish synagogue worship not only by means of scripture but also in a type of poetic writing known as the *piyut*. Beginning in the fifth century the authors of *piyutim* constructed complex "mosaics of words," to quote Lawrence A. Hoffmann's phrase, which they explicitly intended for liturgical purposes. Hoffman hypothesizes that the genre signified an impulse to infuse Jewish expressions of spirituality with the beauty of language, much as Christians were doing at the same time. In addition, these poems, which entailed intricate allusions and puns, made the worship service a locus of reading pleasure and even entertainment for the learned. One legacy of the *piyut* tradition was that it licensed flexibility and experimentation in Jewish religious ritual. While in general Jewish liturgy has balanced fixed and spontaneous prayer, these long-standing endorsements of creativity and change have been especially evident in the various versions of the order of worship, or *siddur*, produced by the Reform movement since its inception in Germany during the early nineteenth century.[68]

The most dramatic innovations obviously came in the first edition of the Reform prayerbook, which encapsulated the outlook that had impelled the break with orthodoxy: an emphasis on modernity, reason, and civility that distanced Jewish identity from medieval cultishness and separate nationhood. Those commitments dictated the substitution of unison prayers, a sermon, and a choir in place of the less decorous, more individualistic chanting, bowing, mumbling, and emotional display of orthodox ritual. For better or worse, these early Reform efforts brought the synagogue service into alignment with German Protestantism.

Leaving aside the social implications of that development, however, perhaps the most important corollary of modernization in terms of the *siddur* was the assumption that (like Protestants) Jewish congregations should understand and assent to the words they spoke in prayer. As Hoffman notes, even when worshippers could translate the Hebrew texts of the orthodox service, the power of those texts came from their symbolic value more than from their content; the act of recitation, one might say, constituted their meaning. The German reformers, insisting on the importance of literal comprehension, subordinated Hebrew to the vernacular, in the process demystifying the atmosphere of the service as a whole.

As a consequence of the fact that congregants could readily grasp the import of what they were reading, the introduction of the vernacular led to further changes in the *siddur* when Reform Jews migrated to the United States. The first *Union Prayer Book* (1895) largely rested on the *siddur* that Rabbi David Einhorn had devised in the 1850s. Revisions in 1918 and 1940 did not fundamentally alter the values it conveyed. In the mid-1970s, however, the Reform movement once again drew upon its heritage of liturgical adaptation by publishing a new *siddur, Gates of Prayer.* Subsequently it also issued *Gates of Repentance,* for the High Holidays. Both volumes built on the *piyut* tradition by presenting poems as prayers—not only the verse of psalmists and other ancients but also the work of nineteenth- and twentieth-century Europeans and Americans. The interpolation of those relatively contemporary texts into the order of worship is as clear an instance of appropriation as the history of the book affords. That is, while many of the poems allude to Jewish history (notably the Holocaust), for the most part the figures who produced them—unlike the composers of *piyutim*—did not set out to write Jewish liturgy. Strikingly, some of the poets selected were even non-Jews. Moreover, this was appropriation by committee—the Liturgy Committee of the Central Conference of American Rabbis, under the leadership of the volumes' editor, Rabbi Chaim Stern.[69]

Stern was, by his own reckoning, an "outsider" in the Reform rabbinate who came to write liturgy by accident. A poet himself, he counted his experience of reading Eliot's "Ash Wednesday" at age fourteen among the most formative of his life. Untermeyer's *Modern American Poetry* likewise shaped his affinity for the poetry of the early twentieth century. Stern's modernist preferences colored his first liturgical undertaking: the revision, beginning in 1962, of the British Reform movement's *Liberal Jewish Prayerbook,* which Stern carried out while temporarily serving in England. The resulting volume, entitled *Service of the Heart* (1967), eventually engendered a revised High Holiday prayerbook.[70]

At the same time when British congregations were growing accustomed to the new *siddur,* their American counterparts were becoming increasingly dissatisfied with the existing liturgy. In the climate of the late 1960s, the mimeographed alternative service (often incorporating poetry) seemed more inspiring to many than the nineteenth-century tone of the *Union Prayer Book.* What happened next reflects the impact of the market—albeit not the commercial realm of mainstream publishers. As use of the *Union Prayer Book* fell off, the Central Conference of American Rabbis, which derived almost all its revenues from sales of the *siddur,* found itself in need of a quick way to reverse its declining income. Rabbi Stern suggested a licensing agreement with the British synagogue organization that would enable the CCAR to acquire the rights to *Service of the Heart,* revise the text further, and publish the American version as its own book. It was under this arrangement that Stern assumed editorial responsibility for *Gates of Prayer,* thus bringing to the project a model (and a claim to authority) with which not everyone on the Liturgy Committee was entirely comfortable. *Gates of Repentance,* over which Stern exerted even more influence, was the logical extension of that role. Thus, as Hoffman observed, "the character of Reform worship" was "determined in large part by this one man."

Specifically, Stern selected, translated, or in some instances produced virtually all of the poetry in the two *Gates* volumes. He incorporated into Sabbath services numerous excerpts from both modern and ancient Hebrew poets, notably the twelfth-century writer Judah Halevi. In rendering the latter's work into English, Stern made repeated "free adaptations" of the text, including adding new lines of his own, on the grounds that writing always entails borrowing from and altering the received literary tradition. Because of Stern's view that the locutions of everyday speech offered the most appropriate language in which to cast the familiar rituals of Sabbath observance, however, *Gates of Prayer* performs a much more limited function as a point of dissemination for poetry than the High Holiday *siddur, Gates of Repentance.*[71] In the former, nineteenth- and twentieth-century examples of verse are concentrated outside the liturgy proper, in a section of meditations. Even so, offering Reform Jews meditations by Frost, for example, imposed on such texts the work of signifying the sophistication, high educational level, and Americanness of the congregants.

Because in their *Union Prayer Book* version the services for the Days of Awe already contained numerous poems, they seemed to Stern to present greater opportunity to enfold more recent examples of the genre into the liturgy itself—as prayers either spoken aloud to the assemblage, recited by the congregation en masse, or designated for silent reading. The evolution of the volume from its British predecessor, the preferences of Stern and his colleagues for certain contemporary American poets, and the determination not to bar quotations from non-Jewish writers all contributed to the contents of the High Holiday *siddur.*

As in *Gates of Prayer* (and *Services for the Open*), the decision of the editor to omit bylines subordinated the "author function" to the authority of the site itself. Stern quite consciously sought that outcome, partly in the belief that attribution would distract from the message of the poem and partly to minimize the reader's pro-

pensity to make invidious distinctions between the words of well-
known figures and the rest of the text. Yet the mix of individual po-
ets represented in *Gates of Repentance* bears comment, precisely
because their anonymous appearance endowed ancient and mod-
ernist verse with uniform weight. In terms of structure, Stern often
deliberately placed twentieth-century verse before older texts, in ef-
fect muting the reader's sense of a departure from tradition. Hence
a sonnet by the American Jewish poet Robert Nathan, published in
1935, precedes a psalm and a *piyut* by Halevi which Stern adapted.
It would be misleading to suggest that Nathan's or any other poem
was equal in importance to the prayers of praise and confession at
the core of the High Holiday services. On the contrary, several ex-
amples of twentieth-century verse in the volume fall into the pe-
ripheral section of "Additional Prayers." At the same time, how-
ever, the editor enlisted poetry to build intensity from the opening
Rosh Hashanah service through the memorial prayers and closing
rituals for the Day of Atonement. Hence another cluster, including
an excerpt from Karl Shapiro's "Travelogue for Exiles," appears in
the Martyrology portion of the Yom Kippur afternoon service. In
the penultimate service of the High Holidays, Stephen Spender's in-
timate revelation of vulnerability, "I Think Continually of Those
Who Were Truly Great" (the same poem that Margaret Parton
read with her lover and her father), resolves almost immediately
into the 23rd Psalm—a text that supplies comfort both in its mes-
sage and in its familiarity. Finally, the concluding service adopts
from *Gates of Repentance* Rainer Maria Rilke's "Autumn," one of
three Rilke poems in the *siddur*. As a German, Rilke was a contro-
versial choice in the aftermath of the Holocaust, but he was a fa-
vorite of an active member of the Liturgy Committee, Rabbi Her-
bert Bronstein.[72]

Another of Bronstein's contributions is worth special mention. In
a striking example of the operation of the politics of culture (in a
double sense), Bronstein was instrumental in securing a central
place in the Yom Kippur morning service for Anthony Hecht's
poem "Words for the Day of Atonement." Bronstein and Hecht
had come to know each other in Rochester, where both lived in

the mid-1960s before Hecht's term as American Poet Laureate; Hecht had already assisted Bronstein when the latter was editing the Reform movement's Passover Haggadah; and Hecht's indictment, within the poem, of the Vietnam War ("the child screams in the jellied fire") seemed to Stern and Bronstein alike a powerful form in which to reiterate Jewish opposition to unjust war.[73]

Because of its historical references and its level of diction, the Hecht poem especially prompts the question of how late twentieth and early twenty-first century congregations might experience reading more difficult modernist poetry as prayer. As the Vietnam context has faded (while the Holocaust has remained salient), the "jellied fire," one suspects, has become assimilated to general images of death. The poet's insistence that survival is not a sign of either goodness or wickedness, that "we" sin while dwelling in a "wilderness of comfort," urges Jews to avoid complacency. Yet the form and language of Hecht's poem—its Eliotic repetition of "thy name," its elliptical allusion to sinless creation—are sufficiently challenging that congregants silently following the recitation of the text in a service cannot readily grasp the literal meaning of Hecht's phrases. What they hear, instead, is the *sound* of modernism: obscure references, sentence fragments, variable rhyme schemes. Although its title makes it a natural choice for liturgical use, the formal worship setting precludes rereading and critical analysis, with the result that Hecht's poem here functions more to create a mood than to transmit its moral injunction; it furnishes the progressive educators' experience of "apprehension" rather than "comprehension." Coming full circle from the period prior to the infusion of the vernacular, certain modernist texts have thus come to play the same role in Reform Jewish worship that lengthy Hebrew passages occupied earlier: they create an aura of spirituality, even of sanctity, precisely because most in the congregation do not fully understand the words they are encountering.

The exchange of poetic opacity for Hebrew is ironic in the respect that those who saw early modernism as alien equated it with a repudiation of faith and certainty. For Stern, however, the boundary between sacred and secular was always porous, both in his self-definition as poet and rabbi and in his approach to liturgy. Whether the inclusion of contemporary verse will continue to do double duty as a signal of cosmopolitanism and a source of inspirational mystification is in question as the Reform movement moves right ward: in 1998, the Unitarian publisher Beacon Press issued Stern's anthology of readings for home use after the CCAR refused to sanction a volume containing so many poems by non-Jews. Rabbi Stern died in 2001. In 2005, the denomination scrapped *Gates of Prayer* for a new *siddur.* Yet *Gates of Repentance* survives intact, at least for the moment, with the result that some Reform Jews accustomed to praying in the words of Hecht or Spender now re-gard those poets' lines as elements of long-standing (if not immutable) tradition. Like many of the works appropriated for Protestant contemplation and prayer, their poems have become religious in practice.

chapter eleven

Lovely as a Tree

---

*Reading and Seeing
Out-of-Doors*

૭ THE FIRST issue of *Poetry*'s second volume, which appeared in the spring of 1913, carried twelve poems by Ezra Pound, collectively labeled "Contemporania." Pound's Imagist experiments were among the most controversial works Monroe ever printed; the debate surrounding them, as well as Monroe's subsequent break with Pound, remains the most famous chapter in the annals of the magazine. Yet for all of the attention that "Contemporania" generated, and for all of its importance to the history of the avant-garde, a contribution in the August issue of the same volume had direct impact on considerably more readers over time. The influential text was a series of six couplets, beginning: "I think that I shall never see . . ."

Joyce Kilmer's "Trees" has since become both an object of parody and, thanks to Brooks and Warren, an object lesson in the pitfalls of imprecision in poetic imagery. At the time of its first publication, however, the public, in Monroe's words, took "Trees" to heart. Kilmer's lines were a monument to the conventions that Pound and others in his camp had placed under siege. Part of the poem's appeal was no doubt its uncomplicated diction and easily felt—not to say singsong—rhythm, which helped readers to find it "beautiful." In any event, "Trees" made its way from Monroe's "little magazine" to newspapers and other periodicals in short order. In 1914, it appeared in William Stanley Braithwaite's anthology of magazine verse for the previous year. The work gained additional visibility when Kilmer called his second book *Trees and Other Poems* (1914). For his own part, Kilmer, a feature writer for the *New York Times,* cultivated a persona as urbane literatus—a guise he assumed with concealed self-mockery before lecture audiences of women's club and poetry society members. (That pose is evident in his use of the phrase "fools like me" at the end of "Trees.") As a result, Christopher Morley wrote, "A kind of Kilmer cult grew apace; he had his followers and his devotees."[1]

By the mid-1920s, after Kilmer had been glorified for dying on the battlefield in France, "Trees" had been reprinted in some thirty anthologies. The titles of those compilations indicate the adaptability of "Trees" to a range of audiences and uses: the poem was included not only in general collections such as *The Oxford Book of American Verse* and Stevenson's *The Home Book of Verse* but also in Marguerite Wilkinson's *Contemporary Poetry* and Harriet Monroe and Alice Corbin Henderson's *The New Poetry;* it appeared in schoolbooks such as *Through Magic Casements* and the junior high school poetry text that Elias Lieberman edited for Scribner's; it had a special life in publications for Arbor Day; it seemed suitable for *The Boy's Book of Verse* (1923); and it found a place among *The World's Great Religious Poetry,* which Caroline Miles Hill assembled for Macmillan. Kilmer's conversion from the Episcopal to the Roman Catholic church in 1913 and his own activities as an anthologizer also earned the poem a place among Catholic texts. Perhaps most commonly, "Trees" invited classification as a nature poem, as indicated by its inclusion in the "Outdoor" sections of textbooks. Thus "Trees" assumed its place alongside countless other famous representations of one of poetry's major subjects, joining Wordsworth's "I Wandered Lonely as a Cloud," Bryant's "To a Waterfowl," and Frost's "Birches"—all, needless to say, much better poems from a literary standpoint.

Even though almost no one takes "Trees" seriously any longer, its message turns out to be more instructive than one might think.

For "Trees" is not only a nature poem; it is also about nature and poems. Kilmer's opening couplet, when one actually stops to think about it, conveys a key aesthetic and cultural tension. That is, the beginning of "Trees"—"I think that I shall never see / A poem lovely as a tree"—counterposes human artifice to the natural world, suggesting that no assemblage of words can substitute for the direct experience of life. The poet's deprecation of himself as a "fool"—while he simultaneously demonstrates the power of the verbal to transmit sensory perception—thus becomes ironic. Only God can make a tree, to be sure, but only poets can help readers to understand that fact.

To the extent that Kilmer's "Trees" explored the relationship between poetry and nature, or between words and spontaneous sensation, it took up a central problem of romanticism. One line of thought characterized poets as "the favorite children of Mother Nature" because their special "gifts" enabled them to realize "sympathy with the Creator." Yet a contrasting view was that, as Thoreau discerned in *Walden,* people "spending their lives in the fields and woods" were often better observers of nature than poets, "who approach her with expectation." That insight notwithstanding, Thoreau, like Kilmer, had relied on the intervention of the printed word to valorize the transcendence of mundane reality. In the late nineteenth and early twentieth centuries this paradox intensified as middle-class Americans increasingly turned to nature to counteract their fears of "overcivilization." Enthralled with the beauty of the sunrise, a writer in 1902 queried: "Why does man civilize himself, anyway? Why does he write his vapid books, paint his ludicrous pictures, build his dark hideous streets, and fret his mind and strangle his soul all for nothing?" The vogue of interest in the "simple life," spurred by the appearance, in 1901, of the French priest Charles Wagner's volume of that title, contributed to this turn-of-the-century nature revival. From Theodore Roosevelt's advocacy of the "strenuous life" to the Country Life movement, Americans sought immersion in the "open"—a term laden with the sense of claustrophobia that "closing" land to settlement entailed.

There they hoped to escape from the debilitating effects of runaway materialism.[2]

Those preoccupations raised questions about Omar Khayyam's placement of "a book of verses underneath the bough" along with food, wine, and love. Prescriptively, what role, if any, did reading play in the simple life? Did books combat or contribute to the phenomenon that observers of urban frenzy dubbed "American nervousness"? Was poetry's effect to deepen or inhibit contact with the natural environment? When readers slipped a volume of poems into their knapsacks, what values were they also taking along? Whether they read about nature by winter hearth or summer campfire, how did they conceive of the connection between print and experience in the "open"?

"Pack Plenty of Poetry": Promoting Verse Reading in the Open

In considering these questions, it is helpful to remember what college students routinely demonstrate by cramming for exams while sunning themselves on the quad—that outdoor spaces can support all sorts of reading, for work and for pleasure alike. In some instances, the words on the page and the reader's physical surroundings may replicate and reinforce each other. As Charles Keeler sailed from San Francisco to Sandy Hook, for example, he wrote in his diary, "During a squall this noon I read an account of a storm at sea by Shelley in one of his poems, and it made it quite realistic." Yet reading *in* nature does not necessarily involve choosing texts *about* nature. Historically, some readers have preferred the opposite. Edward Thomas, a contributor to the *Atlantic Monthly* in 1903, acknowledged as "one taste" the preferences of an "authoress" who "always took a volume of Spenser or Wordsworth or Thoreau under the trees." Still, "the poets who are most happily read out of doors," Thomas demurred, "are the courtly writers, the men of wit and fashion," whose critically deprecated works profited from the broad-minded reader's repose. Likewise, in "Books in the Wilderness" (1921), Frederick Niven explained his selection of volumes for a canoe trip by noting that "one inevitably longs for a voice to describe the visible world" from which one is absent.[3]

Furthermore, even when the texts they selected described natural beauty, open-air readers might preoccupy themselves with other thoughts, using the book, and the scene, as a backdrop for self-examination, philosophical reflection, or romance. Harry Emerson Fosdick recalled the Saturday afternoons of his youth in Buffalo when, "with a book of poetry," he "slipped away to the lakeside in Delaware Park and had a high time in solitude. The content of these hours was vague, but Wordsworth's phrases concerning similar experiences in his boyhood—'Aeolian visitations,' 'Trances of thought and mountings of the mind'—describe them. They suggested no special vocation . . ., but their influence unwittingly was reorienting my life." With evidently no greater focus on the natural setting itself, Fosdick and his future wife later followed Khayyam's advice by taking "books, especially poetry, and driving a horse and buggy into the countryside" to "read together in some comfortable nook."[4]

In the post–Civil War era, publishers in search of a way to boost sales in the slow summer months intervened to shape such practices by promulgating their own conception of the suitable outdoor book. Beginning in 1877, *Publishers' Weekly* put out a "summer catalogue" (later a "summer reading" issue or "announcement") to stimulate purchases from buyers headed for resorts and cottages. As the trade journal explained to its audience, "Booksellers should remember that, while summer is usually a dull time, the sales of light literature, etc., can be pushed to make a successful business even in this season. The classes who travel are of course those who have money to spend." Among middle-class Americans, the institutionalization of the paid holiday and greater acceptance of the doctrine of healthful relaxation added impetus to such advertising campaigns. When *PW*'s "Summer Reading" issues included illustrated covers in the early 1920s, they depicted books or readers in bucolic locales; the covers featured such slogans as "Book Companions for Outdoor Days" or "Take Along a Book." The presumption that Americans who took seaside or country holidays were seeking respite from routine colored the marketing strategies adopted within those covers.[5]

Although fiction's promise of escape gave it the largest share of the "beach reading" market, both publishers and consumers recognized that poetry "made its special appeal" to vacationers. In the 1922 "Summer Reading" issue of *PW*, Marguerite Wilkinson prescribed "much poetry" (as well as "the world's dearest old romances") to "clerks, stenographers, salesmen, and others who work in figures"; she urged the "nervous stockbroker" to "fill his pockets full to bulging with the poetry of Walter de la Mare." Dorothy Scarborough, the author of the lead article in the previous year's "Summer Reading" issue, recommended the genre on the basis of its capacity to mirror the surrounding atmosphere—to be "delicate and airy" as the birds, as Hawthorne put it, or "solemn and magnificent" as the river. Scarborough's formulation postulated a reciprocal relationship between text and natural setting: "How much more there is in poetry . . . when it is read in the presence of the things that poets write about—trees and stars and birds. . . . And we get more out of nature if we read the books that rightly reveal its secrets to us. . . . We see more in summer and see the more as we read more. . . . The eyes corroborate what poets tell us, and poetry read in the open imparts to us eternally the magic of such moments." More frivolously, *PW* also advised: "No vacation being complete unless you quote poetry in the moonlight, it is always advisable to take along a volume of poetry, on the chance of finding the moon—and the girl."[6]

At the same time, publishers touting particular titles made more practical pitches. Under the headline "Pack Plenty of Poetry: Poems and Plays Make Ideal Out-Door Reading," an advertisement for *The Le Gallienne Book of English Verse* (1922) noted that "its convenient size and light weight contribute toward making this anthology by a real poet [that is, not a "lightweight"] an ideal 'take away' book to be read under the pines or from the depths of the canoe." Readers concurred. In 1921 Mary Frank, the driver of the Book Caravan which the Women's Educational and Industrial Union had sponsored the previous summer in New England, reported that to her clientele "anthologies were second only to the popular novel"; without specifying the reasons behind it, she noted a particular demand among hikers and beach-goers for Jessie Rittenhouse's and Louis Untermeyer's collections. The popularity of "camping and tramping" itself stimulated anthology production specifically designed to capitalize on, and renew, readers' sense of themselves as attuned to nature. Some of those volumes, such as *The Nature Lovers' Treasury* (1906), were packaged as hefty gift books. Other titles carried overtones of immediacy and utility, appearing to invite perusal on the trail; one example was *The Nature Lover's Knapsack: An Anthology of Poems for Lovers of the Open Road* (1927). Both types implicitly acknowledged the market created by the impulse to achieve the "simple life."[7]

For those in the business of selling books, a challenge of the sort that Kilmer's "Trees" posed to the assumption that print enhanced nature was simply inadmissible; so was the conviction that the best books for outdoor use might not include those of the current season. Nevertheless, alongside publishers' campaigns there were more disinterested commentators who declared otherwise. In *Great Possessions* (1917) Ray Stannard Baker, writing as David Grayson, opined that the ideal book for walking in the woods was one that furnished "conversation"—the "thoughtful remark" of a "book friend"—without intrusion. The author of such a book, Grayson explained, "never interrupts at inconvenient moments" to compete with "the great and simple things of nature." Although "submitted to such a test as this few writers, old or new, give continued profit or delight," Grayson singled out poetry collections as passing muster; asserting that he did "not want long books and least of all story books in the woods—these are for the library," he recommended instead *Traveller's Joy, Songs of Nature, The Spirit of Man* (by the English laureate Robert Bridges), and an anthology of Elizabethan verse. Such works, Grayson announced, spoke in measured ways that made each "a true companion of the spirit."

Yet, in contrast to some of the genre's more commercially-minded advocates, Grayson commended poetry as outdoor reading without assigning the text a crucial part in forging the reader's comprehension of the natural milieu. While delighting in a wood

With both flowers and a book at hand, a young reader experiences the lure of the "open." Courtesy of the Boston Public Library, Print Department.

"full of voices," he did not demand of the poems he carried that they help him interpret what he heard outside. On the contrary, Grayson valued poetry out-of-doors because he felt free to ignore it: "I like to take a book with me in my pocket," he asserted, "although I find the world so full of interesting things—sights, sounds, odours—that often I never read a word in it." With that remark, Grayson implicitly acknowledged the problematic relationship between print and experience. His impulse to subordinate the former to the latter—to silence the text—reflects the tension that "Trees" conveyed between the poet's tutelage and the reader's perceptions. Poetic insights might enhance an individual's consciousness, but they could also impede sensory liberation.[8]

Flora Neil Davidson, the librarian from Madison, Wisconsin, clipped and pasted into her voluminous notebooks two poems that, taken together, made the same point. One, "My Wish," by an unidentified author, expressed longing for a refuge on a wooded hilltop "far away from the road where the world goes by"; among its simple but essential furnishings was a shelf large enough "to hold the books I love." The other, Ethel Romig Fuller's "God's Poem," made texts superfluous: "God made a poem (or was it a wood?) / Out of sunshine and rain and solitude. / In it were words as lovely as these— / Columbines, ferns, anemones. / . . . And a tree erect in its armored bark / Was God's own exclamation mark."[9] Thus the outdoor site lent itself to responses ranging from romantic veneration of the poet's gifts to an equally romantic quest for pure sensation. Those possibilities, and the various meanings they held for the act of reading, come into full view in the career of another "simple life" proponent who was himself both poet and nature writer: John Burroughs.

The Poet-Naturalist and His Readers

Burroughs was a friend and champion of Walt Whitman, a camping buddy of Theodore Roosevelt, and the celebrated author of some twenty-seven books, produced over four decades, about literature and the out-of-doors. Born in 1837 on a farm near Poughkeepsie, he began his writing career by composing essays in an Emersonian mode—so much so that, in 1860, when he asked James Russell Lowell to consider printing "Expression" in the *Atlantic Monthly*, Lowell felt compelled to verify that the piece was not Emerson's before accepting it. In 1862, the year before he met

Whitman, Burroughs wrote a famous poem of his own entitled "Waiting." First published in *Knickerbocker's Magazine,* it acquired a wide following when it reappeared in Whittier's *Songs of Three Centuries* (1875). As Burroughs remarked, "It began to be copied by newspapers and religious journals, and it has been traveling on the wings of public print ever since." The poem was so widely disseminated that almost thirty years later Houghton Mifflin, Burroughs's publisher, had to make a point of insisting that the author's permission was still required to reprint it.[10]

In the 1870s, Burroughs also established himself as a writer on both nature and literature. His accomplishments in the former category included *Wake Robin* (1871), *Winter Sunshine* (1875), and *Locusts and Wild Honey* (1879); the latter category contained not only an enlarged edition of the *Notes on Walt Whitman as Poet and Person* he had first issued in 1867 but also *Birds and Poets* (1877). Subsequently, Burroughs augmented those ongoing interests with ventures into theology and philosophy, among them *The Light of Day* (1900) and *The Summit of the Years* (1913). In 1906 he published a book of verse, *Bird and Bough.* His last completed work was *Accepting the Universe* (1920), although two more volumes (edited by his lover and literary executor, Clara Barrus) appeared after his death in 1921.

Even though, strictly speaking, that body of work contained more prose than poetry, during his lifetime Burroughs became known as America's "poet-naturalist." His claim to the first half of that label derived in part from Burroughs's well-publicized friendship with Whitman. More important, revealing the porous boundary between the genres, readers routinely likened Burroughs's prose style to verse. As William Dean Howells remarked in a review of *Wake-Robin,* "Mr. Burroughs adds a strain of genuine poetry which makes his papers unusually delightful. . . . His nerves have a poetical sensitiveness, his eye a poetical quickness." Yet, for all that, the impact of "Waiting" would have been enough to define Burroughs as a poet in his own right. As Jessie Rittenhouse declared after hearing Burroughs trace the poem to a period of his life when he "saw no opening" to improve his circumstances, "Well, you have helped thousands to meet the same situation, and I am one of them." Decidedly un-Whitmanesque in its conventional form, the text asserted the inevitability of achieving one's desires in a benign universe: "Nor time, nor space, nor deep, nor high / Can keep my own away from me." The power of that message shines through in the surviving letters that Burroughs received from the poem's readers—or, more accurately, its rereaders. These documents reveal individuals making meaning from Burroughs's lines by finding in the poet's message either prophecy about or confirmation of their particular circumstances.[11]

A poignant letter that Burroughs received from his friend Willis Boyd Allen in 1906 provides a close look at that process, which in this case had dramatic consequences: "A few weeks ago," Allen related, "a man and a woman were together in a little village on the Maine coast. The man had loved the woman patiently, without any apparent return, but never hopelessly, for years. One day, as they were beside the sea, he handed her your little poem 'Waiting' to read. She glanced over it, met his eye, and gave back the paper with an impatient gesture. 'Do you believe that?' he asked. 'O,' she said, 'You make everything so *personal!* All the poet meant was a general statement that whatever of good a man is destined to receive, shall be his, sooner or later.'" The man (was it Allen himself?) realized that the woman grasped his "application" of the poem, and drew her attention to the third stanza, containing the line "The friends I seek are seeking me." The woman parried by switching tactics from the general to the literal: "'Yes,' she retorted, 'but in the second he says "*What* is mine shall know my face." That does not refer to—to—a person.'" At an impasse, the man nevertheless tried once more to endow the poem with predictive force, much as a listener might react to the pronouncements of a fortune teller (or a minister): "'I think the poet meant,' he said, after a bitter silence, 'that not simply the abstract Good, but . . . the one who is dearest in the world, shall somewhere, sometime—come—to him who has loved him—or her!—steadfastly. If not in this life, then in some other.'" He stood and repeated Burroughs's line with the phrase "my own," but the woman, Allen commented, "only shook her head, and was silent."[12]

In that episode, both figures attached significance to the import of the poem, not merely to the act of reading it. Yet even imputing such didactic weight to the text left room for readers to ponder the question of how justified they were in positioning themselves at the center of the poet's concerns—or, put another way, how much authority to grant the poet as sage and seer. Allen concluded his account by asking Burroughs whether it was the man or the woman who had voiced "the right interpretation of your words"; a subsequent letter from him to Burroughs suggests that the poet had, perhaps charitably, endorsed the man's "personal" way of reading. Other readers manifested a similar attachment to the belief that the text pertained specifically (although not exclusively) to them. Writing to Burroughs in 1905 for the third time, a woman explained that she had started out poor and alone in a New York City room but currently lived with her husband and daughter in a house in Colorado. "In all truth," she observed, 'my own has come to me.' . . . I wonder how many have been turned to the light by that tiny little poem." Another correspondent went further, defending himself against plagiarism charges after "Waiting" (retitled "The Tide of Destiny") appeared over his name in the Farmington, New Mexico, *Enterprise*. "Inasmuch as I have never read any of Mr. Burroughs' poems, nor seen any of them in print," a man named Will H. Hedley averred, "to my knowledge, I cannot vouch as to the alleged first authorship. I do know, however, and that very forcibly, that the poem is a vivid portrayal of my own PERSONAL experience."[13]

Several of Burroughs's other correspondents who wrote him about "Waiting" indicated that the poem, in performing prophetic or explanatory functions, had elicited reading practices that were essentially religious: the repetition of words to ingrain belief and supply comfort; reproduction of the text in a form that resembled the printing of devotions for easy reference. Burroughs's espousal of faith in nature while at the same time acknowledging the existence of an "omnipotent intelligence" rested on a Christian foundation; he observed about "Waiting" that "these verses show what form the old Calvinistic doctrine took in me." Yet the poem also accommodated an impulse to replace Christianity with a more amorphous spirituality. As Burroughs himself recognized, "It puts in simple and happy form some common religious aspirations, without using the religious jargon. . . . My little poem is vague enough to escape the reason, sincere enough to go to the heart, and poetic enough to stir the imagination."[14]

Thus Mary C. McDonaugh, a Brooklyn woman who had earlier visited Burroughs's cabin "Slabsides" with a "party of Manual Training boys," wrote him in 1907 to tell him how "Waiting" had changed her life. In language that echoes the rhetoric of conversion, she reported that she had undergone a period of gloom after her mother's death: "So heavy a cross did I seem to bear, that, at the close of each day, I thanked God that life for me was one day nearer its end." Then "Fate placed in my hands one day a copy of ["Waiting"]. I read it over and over," McDonaugh declared, "and unconsciously lived in its atmosphere. Need I say to you that it gave me hope, in fact it was, is and ever will be an inspiration." McDonaugh's comment is notable for the way it moves from Christian imagery to an invocation of Fate to a reference to modern psychology ("unconsciously"), as if to acknowledge the versatility of Burroughs's poem in helping the reader to shed outdated beliefs.[15]

Nothing in "Waiting" pertained directly to the out-of-doors (although the poem might be read "beside the sea"). Burroughs's belief that human happiness was inexorably increasing, however, indirectly reflected his faith in Darwinian evolution, modified to exclude its bloodier aspects. As a naturalist, Burroughs (in contrast to his friend John Muir) was likewise drawn to the less disturbing manifestations of the struggle for survival. Burroughs was especially interested in distinguishing the sounds of birds and documenting the habits of woodland creatures, both at home and in England. His correspondents routinely consulted him about the identification of botanical specimens or the probability that they had heard some particularly elusive birdsong. Beginning with *Wake-Robin,* Burroughs's first-person accounts of nature (and human beings participating in it) reflected his commitment to the scientific methodologies of careful observation and accurate description. In 1903, when the *Atlantic Monthly* published Burroughs's article "Real and Sham Natural History," he made his stance as a naturalist even plainer. The article inaugurated the episode known as the "nature-fakers" controversy—attacks on such popular writers as Ernest Thompson Seton for falsifying animal behavior by ascribing human emotions and faculties to them.[16]

Burroughs's persona as "poet-naturalist," however, was more than the sum of his efforts to write verse and defend scientific standards of truth. Rather, the phrase reflected Burroughs's ability to reconcile, or at least to balance, not only artifice and nature but also competing ways of seeing. His autobiographical writings and literary criticism repeatedly explored the relationship between poetic vision and empirical knowledge. Likewise, Burroughs's audience revealed that reading his "poetical" works both colored and certified their perceptions of the out-of-doors.

Burroughs's assumptions about the role of the poet fell into two broad patterns. On the one hand, he positioned architects of language on one side of a divide separating culture from untamed nature. In that scheme, poets and others who relied on printed words joined company with scientists given to classification and analysis: the efforts of both might interfere with direct experience by crowding out an individual's original responses to natural phenomena. To carry a book of poetry into the woods, or to carry a poem in one's head, could diminish the benefits of transporting oneself beyond civilization. Thus Burroughs reported the story of "an enthusiastic American who went about English fields hunting a lark with Shelley's poem in his hand, thinking no doubt to use it as a kind of guide-book to the intricacies and harmonies of the song. He reported not having heard any larks, though I have little doubt they were soaring and singing about him all the time, though of course they did not sing to his ear the song that Shelley heard." Likewise, Burroughs argued that regarding nature "in the spirit of technical science, our minds already preoccupied with certain conclusions and systems," produced less joy than encountering it as children or "gleesome" lovers did. From this vantage point, the library and its contents came to stand for second-hand, and hence incomplete, understanding. In *Birds and Poets,* Burroughs asserted that "there is something higher and deeper than the influence or perusal of any or all books . . . a quality of information which the masters can never impart, and which the libraries do not hold. This is the absorption by an author, previous to becoming so, of the spirit of nature, through the visible objects of the universe." Burroughs deemed "artificial" those of his own writings that he attributed solely to what, quoting Whitman, he called "'the push of reading.'"[17]

On the other hand, although he insisted that encountering nature "without any intermediate agency or modification" was a prerequisite for an author to achieve greatness, Burroughs's account of his own development made plain not his wholesale subordination of the library to the out-of-doors but instead his integration of the two milieus. Recalling the influences that had shaped his sensibility, for example, Burroughs cited his maternal grandfather, whom he remembered for "a love of angling, and a love for the Bible." As Burroughs remarked, "He went from the Book to the stream, and from the stream to the Book, with great regularity." Although Burroughs rejected his family's Baptist and Methodist background, he too went back and forth from books to nature, both literally and metaphorically. The life of Washington he read as a boy created in him a "cloud of feeling"—the same entrance into "exalted emotional states" that nature also induced in him. Likewise, he mused: "What sent me to nature? . . . My reading, no doubt, had much to do with it." The out-of-doors furnished Burroughs with tropes to make sense of print ("where can you find a better symbol of good style in literature than a mountain brook after it is well launched towards the lowlands?"); print likewise made sense of the woods and fields ("Nature's infinite book of secrecy"). Writing to a group of schoolchildren in 1887, Burroughs advised them to take along essays on literature while fishing and to "dip into" them while waiting for a bite on the line. On a visit to Yosemite in 1909, sitting before a fire of juniper brush, Burroughs, Barrus, Muir, and their camping party themselves matched nature and poetry to the same aesthetic standard. Barrus recalled, "We listened to Mr. Muir reciting some lines from Milton—almost the only poet one would think of quoting in the presence of such solemn, awful beauty."[18]

Furthermore, instead of consistently arraying both the poet and the naturalist on the side of culture, Burroughs often assigned poets a place closer to nature than scientists occupied. Contrasting the former with the false "sentimentalist" as well, Burroughs explained: "The true poet knows more about Nature than the naturalist because he carries her open secrets in his heart." Poets were the "best natural historians, only you must know how to read them. They translate the facts largely and freely." In Burroughs's formulation, two qualities distinguished the poetic stance from the scientific outlook: one was the poet's concern to express the "spirit of Nature," as he "walks the ideal world"; the other was the capacity of a great poem to reveal the personality of its author. As Burroughs put it in an essay on literary criticism, "It is not truth alone that makes literature; it is truth plus a man. Readers fancy they are interested in the birds and flowers they find in the pages of the poets; but no, it is the poets themselves that they are interested in." That conception of poetry entailed the paradox that only by enlarging the self—injecting it into their observations—could poets see things as they were and transmit their impressions to others.[19]

At the same time, Burroughs's tendency to subordinate the naturalist to the poet coexisted with his impulse to switch the pecking order. Differentiating his own approach from that of Emerson and Thoreau, Burroughs depicted himself as a scientist committed to eradicating the self from the data: "My books do not bring readers to me, but send them to Nature. . . . I always seek to hold the mirror of my mind up to Nature, that the reader may find her lineaments alone reflected there." In the preface to *Birds and Poets,* he emphasized his intention "to bring my outdoor spirit and method within, and still to look upon my subject with the best naturalist's eye I could command"; in the 1895 edition's concluding essay, he linked the future of poetry to "thorough assimilation of the modern sciences," which "in its present bold and receptive mood, may be said to be eminently creative."[20]

The contradictions and ambiguities that attended the figure of Burroughs as poet-naturalist are reminiscent of the similarly maddening reversals in the writings of his Transcendentalist mentors. Yet the salient question is what animated Burroughs's impulse to counterpose science and poetry in the first place. As the notoriety of the nature-fakers episode demonstrated, Burroughs was not the only late-Victorian figure to test nature writing for scientific accuracy. *Nature Knowledge in Modern Poetry* (1906), by Alexander Mackie, a Scot, systematically evaluated the botanical and ornithological skills of Tennyson, Wordsworth, Arnold, and James Russell Lowell. Likewise, on the American side, Charles Dudley Warner, in *The Relation of Literature to Life* (1897), argued for poetry as "the one thing" that could ameliorate "all the woe of which nature is so heedless." The defensive quality of these documents suggests that what one might call Burroughs's strategic inconsistencies were a response to the rising prestige of science in American culture, and particularly in American universities. Charles W. Eliot's "The New Definition of the Cultivated Man," which made scientific training an essential component of education, appeared the same year as the nature-fakers controversy. Science, in the form of Francis Gummere's specialty, philology, was even dictating literary study. By making space for both poet and naturalist, Burroughs kept alive a threatened humanistic perspective while at the same time paying homage to the modern specialization of knowledge that had lent him some of his authority.[21]

Burroughs's role as "poet-naturalist" yoked together two additional dichotomies: one related to gender, the other to genre. Several historians have demonstrated the link between the late-nineteenth-century American's turn to outdoor pursuits and the desire to reassert toughness and self-reliance as attributes of masculinity. Burroughs's affiliation with Theodore Roosevelt—not only in the nature-fakers controversy but as the President's companion on expeditions recorded in his *Camping and Tramping with Roosevelt* (1907)—lent Burroughs's stance as naturalist some of the same characteristics that Roosevelt the rancher and big-game hunter came to symbolize: in Gail Bederman's phrase, a "virile, hard-driving manhood." Roosevelt's advocacy of the "strenuous life" (in addition to the "simple life") explicitly involved the expectation that men should display aggressive mastery to ensure personal and national well-being. The ideal of strenuosity could not only license

imperialism, as historians have noted, but also contribute to an-
other American tradition: the anti-intellectualism that identified
contemplation with weakness. Burroughs did not go that far. One
of his complaints, in fact, was that Roosevelt turned everything,
including quoting poetry, into a contest. (In *A Book-Lover's Holi-
days in the Open* [1916], Roosevelt referred to periods when he
"voraciously devour[ed] poets of widely different kinds. Now it
will be Horace and Pope; now Schiller, Scott, Longfellow . . . and
again Emerson or Browning or Whitman.") Nevertheless, Bur-
roughs's well-publicized rustic residence at Slabsides defined him as
a figure committed to combating the decadent—and feminizing—
effects of "overcivilization." Similarly, the Roosevelt connection
and Burroughs's 1899 participation in the Harriman Expedition
to Alaska worked to offset the image of nature lovers as effemi-
nate butterfly chasers. Burroughs's embodiment of a version of the
"strenuous life" likewise argued for the virility of the poet as well
as the naturalist. Implicitly alluding to his own efforts (and pre-
sumably to Whitman), he called for "a race of writers who affiliate
with their subjects, and enter into them through the blood, their
sexuality and manliness, instead of standing apart . . . and writ-
ing *about* them through mere intellectual cleverness." The nature-
fakers episode itself can be read as a contest between "masculine"
tough-mindedness and "feminine" embroidery of the facts.[22]

Yet in the case of both Burroughs and his presidential camping
partner, the gender issue is complicated. Roosevelt personified both
progress and primitivism; as Brander Matthews noted, he was as
much "a denizen of the library as he was an explorer of the forest."
The former pursuit, associated with femininity, offset his "rough
rider" persona. As for Burroughs, he observed that from his grand-
father he had acquired "that almost feminine sensibility and tinge
of melancholy that, I think, shows in all my books." As several
commentators have noted, the poem "Waiting" was a prescription
for passivity; so was Burroughs's affirmation of Transcendentalist
surrender to the flow of impressions (as in Emerson's "transpar-
ent eyeball"). Burroughs equated his passive propensities with the
"want of a certain manly or masculine quality," which nevertheless

enabled him to become "pure spirit, pure feeling, and get very close to bird and beast." Finally, one might argue that Burroughs's trademark essays themselves struck a kind of gender balance. Without suggesting that Burroughs consciously chose a literary genre to blend masculine and feminine ideals, it is notable that he specialized in a form hospitable to direct assertion—one might say to "straight shooting"—while inflecting it with the "poetical" language that marked him as sensitive and spiritual.[23]

The antithetical positions that Burroughs combined as poet-naturalist extended to his relationships with his readers. Those relationships entailed the partial dismantling of another set of oppositions: between poet and audience. A man from Crawfordsville, Indiana, wrote to Burroughs in 1919 that his books "always give me the feeling of a breath of clean, fresh air blowing across the space that divides the author from the reader. . . . I suppose most of your readers bear the same testimony." In the view that Clara Barrus promulgated, Burroughs was "our friend." Barrus's explanation for the large volume of fan mail which Burroughs routinely received was that he had "so written himself into his books that we know him before meeting him." Moreover, she insisted that his "simplicity," "directness," and "genuineness" enabled "us" to appreciate the natural world through his eyes. By means of his personality, he offered his audience clear sight. That construct echoed Burroughs's conception of the poet's mediating function as translator of nature.[24]

The well-worn metaphor of "awakening"—the same imagery on which Burroughs relied in *Wake-Robin* to depict springtime renewal—pervaded accounts from readers who supported Barrus's view. A doctor from Indiana noted in 1907, "I call you friend because I have been reading after you so long that you are indeed my friend, and even now, for you have taught me to read and love nature. . . . Above all, reading your works has taught me, or given me the power, to observe and now I see goodness and beauty where all was darkness before." Similarly, a woman who worked at a school for girls in Massachusetts told Burroughs in 1914: "Sometimes when things indoors look wrong, we go through the pines, the big, bold bluffs, thinking of you and Walt Whitman and Col. Roosevelt, and then before we know it, we are seeing things as they really are. It must be good to know that thinking about you puts people on their feet and shines up their eyes for them and sets the world right as God made it." In that statement, the phrase "seeing things as they really are" is of special interest, because the reality the reader perceives is a case of life imitating art.[25]

Filtering outdoor excursions through Burroughs's writings in turn brought pleasure. The response of a 16 year old boy in 1896 was typical: "You choose such interesting subjects and see so much where an unobservant person would see nothing. I did more or less walking before reading your books, but I never took any real pleasure in it till I read your essays on your pedestrian trips and your trips through the woods." Another woman explained, "We are reaching the shady side of life and hope, always, to have your books in our home and your companionship through them. More deeply do we feel and see the artistic and beautiful in the world under your teaching." To be awake was also to be admitted to an exclusive circle of enlightened individuals. Thus a reader in 1912 sent Burroughs "a loving greeting, from the heart, for I am numbered among the 'privileged ones'—I have your delightful 'Riverby Edition'—and I have seen and heard the winter wren, when he did *not* know it."[26]

The sample of respondents to the *New York Times* query about the memorization of poetry in school corroborated the effects of heightened sensitivity to which Burroughs's readers testified. Several mentioned that three works—"I Wandered Lonely as a Cloud," Helen Hunt Jackson's "October's Bright Blue Weather," and James Russell Lowell's lines beginning "What is so rare as a day in June?"—indelibly colored their perceptions as, year after year, they noticed signs of seasonal change. Similarly, Flora Neil Davidson was one of countless diarists to copy the Lowell quotation as a June entry. On a trip to Quebec and New England in 1929, Davidson repeatedly assimilated the scenery she encountered to the prior knowledge she had gained from poets' observations. "Whittier might have been describing Wilmington Notch," she recorded in one instance, "when he wrote: 'We held our sideling way above / The river's whitening shallows.'" Elsewhere she alluded to poetry reading as preparation for (and as a standard against which to measure) experience: "Of course I read some of Whittier's local poetry before we started East and some of it seemed to describe things very accurately but I wasn't in a position then to realize how very exact his description of Haverhill was." Although her pilgrimage to Whittier country is further testimony to his enduring reputation in the interwar period, Davidson declared that "no one claims that Whittier is a great poet"; she conceded that his verse was "often imperfect and always simple and uncomplicated." Nevertheless, the aesthetic value Davidson placed on complexity did not interfere with the enjoyment she derived from her practice of seeing through the lens that Whittier (and other poets) held before her.[27]

Some of Burroughs's readers revealed a different basis for their bond with him. Instead of filtering experience, the poet's words in these cases affirmed prior experience; readers used poetical writings to corroborate their own natural impulses when out-of-doors. "Once in a while," a young woman who was a teacher wrote Burroughs in 1912, "I get so full of things I feel as though I'd burst if I couldn't speak to somebody that can hear grass singing on a hill top just as clearly as I can." Another woman declared in 1918, "Ever since my early girlhood, I have read and re-read your books with the keenest delight. . . . A library of your works stands in a shelf beside my writing table, and if they were not there, I would feel indeed as though I had lost a friend. . . . I have always been a lover of the country, and so often I find in your books the very echoings of my own feelings." Similar responses ranged from crediting Burroughs with articulating emotions that readers could not quite convey to claiming perceptual powers superior to the poet's. "Some people I have seen," explained a man from Ohio, "read [your works] and say they are striking examples of pure language and poetry in prose, etc., but with me it is different. I don't think so much of what you are saying as the way it meets and expresses my

John Burroughs at "Slabsides" around 1901. Library of Congress.

own feelings. It may seem rather impudent for me to say so but I really believe that in a *small* way I see things and understand them the same as you do."[28]

Both groups of readers included men as well as women, and the commingled gender ideals that Burroughs represented remained muted in most of those readers' responses to his work. Two readers, however, explicitly corroborated the idea that Burroughs's ability to balance strenuousity and sensitivity was an element in the friendship he proffered. In 1918, an Indiana man wrote to describe the death of a soldier and physician who had read the poet-naturalist "again and again," treating his books as "companions": "There was nothing maudlin in his admiration," the man reported. "It was real and virile." Likewise the poet Lloyd Mifflin, complaining to Burroughs in 1902 that women had "fallen" from patronage of poetry to the "worship of clothes," placed his hopes in their shared audience of "a few men who love nature and nature books." For them, Mifflin (allying himself with Burroughs) had "tried to treat Nature *poetically* and yet with strict regard to the actual facts as they exist here, at my door."[29]

The multiple perspectives that Burroughs both expressed and elicited as poet-naturalist thus effected a series of negotiations over the meanings of reading verse in conjunction with excursions to the "open": his work bridged literature and science, female and male, prose and verse, words and action, author and audience. The desire Burroughs accommodated was not merely that of flight from urban civilization. Importing the special sight of a poet to the natural environment could signify the preservation of culture—and even reiterate the value of reading itself—while compensating for the loss of simplicity and intensity that seemed ruinous to modern society. Put another way, poets' intensified perceptions made reading their works integral to leading the simple life. In addition, combining poetic texts—in print or in memory—with the naturalist's close observation was both a hedge against the threat that science would destroy spirituality and an embrace of modernity. As the responses to "Waiting" suggest, this conjunction of science and poetry was particularly important to readers who rejected belief in a supernatural God but who clung to a conviction that "spiritual laws" favored human happiness. Burroughs's simple, personal manner—what one admirer called his failure to be a "book-maker"—also allowed for the denial altogether that civilization had eliminated opportunities for unmediated experience; that posture implied rejection of the proliferation of print by which a civilized society measured itself. Yet words in the company of faith, nature, and candlelight exerted a powerful appeal for Americans grappling with change. Appropriately, a reader in charge of a lodge for men "who have lost the joy of living" summarized that point best in a poem he wrote to Burroughs: "The forest hush is o'er him / He bows his reverend head / Beside a lighted taper, / A book before him spread."[30]

Cowboy Poets at the Turn of the Century

Similar tensions surrounding the poetry of nature and the nature of print marked other cultural locations outside the circle to which Burroughs (and Roosevelt) belonged. One revealing phenomenon, spurred in part by the publication of Roosevelt's *The Winning of the West* (1889–1896), was a turn-of-the-century vogue of cowboy poets. Like Buffalo Bill's Wild West show, the most popular manifestation of the American fascination with the western hero, cowboy poetry corralled anxieties about the consequences of industrialization and urbanization into a celebration of the disappearing frontier. Yet in both print and performance, the character of Buffalo Bill differed in spirit from his literary counterpart. William Cody, who played Buffalo Bill, projected brawn and self-reliance, not the poet's sensitive temperament; Cody never appended a list of his publications to his metaphorical string of scalps. Even so, as Joy S. Kasson has observed, part of Buffalo Bill's success, especially on his European tours in the late 1880s, resulted from the effort to market him as "respectable" as well as heroic. "Cody's marriage, his educated daughters, and the middle-class respectability of his home . . . were all important parts of his public image," Kasson has noted, "guarantors of propriety that gave spectators a sense of safety." For all of his rough-and-ready attributes, the figure of Buffalo Bill was a tamer of wilderness as well as a representative of unspoiled nature. Symbolizing that fact, the program booklet for the Wild West show at the Columbian Exposition (and earlier) imposed literary convention—poetic form—on the Buffalo Bill legend by including verse about Cody's exploits. The dime-novel publications that had contributed to Cody's persona in the first place were a source of such poems.[31]

Cowboys, ranchers, or scouts who, unlike Cody, proclaimed themselves authors went even further than Buffalo Bill in epitomizing the conjunction of civilization and wildness, study fire and campfire. Eugene Manlove Rhodes, whom the critic Bernard DeVoto called "the novelist of the cattle kingdom," once slid off a pony that reared to protest Rhodes's incessant reading; the story goes that Rhodes sat on the pony's head while finishing the long Browning poem that had riveted him to the page. In contrast to Burroughs's figure of the poet-naturalist, who promised liberation through literature as well as through its absence, the cowboys who wrote verse tended to make the poet the emissary of order, as against the freedom of an uncultivated West. That balance was inherent in the biographies of many of the cowboy poets. William Lawrence Chittenden, a dry-goods salesman and newspaper correspondent who wrote "The Cowboys' Christmas Ball," suggested as much by referring to himself as the "poet-rancher." In 1893 Putnam's published Chittenden's *Ranch Verses,* the first poetry collection organized around the cowboy theme to issue from a mainstream house. In the same period, James Barton Adams, another newspaperman, brought out a volume of poems "based on a bare two years of ranch employment in New Mexico." Charles Badger Clark, who had even less ranch experience, also gained a reputation as a cowboy poet through the appearance in western periodicals of works like "A Cowboy's Prayer." In 1915 he self-published a collection called *Sun and Saddle Leather,* a steady seller which the Boston firm of Richard G. Badger, and then the house of Chapman and Grimes, eventually took over. Chittenden, Adams, and Clark were all educated migrants to the West with tenuous connections to the cowboy's occupation. As one expert has observed, Chittenden may have been a rancher, "but he was an opportunist as well," who "treaded the dilettante's path between the real cowboy's world and polite society." Bruce Kiskaddon, a slightly later figure, had more actual experience with livestock and thus a voice that some scholars have considered more "authentic," although he, too, was an easterner and wrote about his cowhand days retrospectively.[32]

In addition to the contradictions such circumstances imparted to the form, nineteenth- and early-twentieth-century cowboy poetry was highly social in practice, even as it lauded the opportunities for individualism which the frontier ostensibly preserved from the encroachments of industrialization. (The social element remains important in the ongoing tradition of cowboy verse, which today is institutionalized in centers, conferences, literary journals, and websites.) These texts circulated widely in newspapers, making them accessible and portable. Kiskaddon's poetry appeared monthly in the *Western Livestock Journal,* from which it was "often clipped, carried in purses and wallets and pocket notebooks, pasted into scrapbooks, and memorized." Print in turn facilitated a strong tradition of recitation. Although cowboy poets might praise the freedom of the open range, the price of not being fenced in was loneliness. Reciters (along with singers) in "chuck wagons and campfires, bunkhouses and line camps, and barrooms and hotel rooms" mitigated isolation through oral performance, strengthening communal bonds among listeners while providing entertainment. For eastern audiences, recitations of cowboy verse combined amusement with a glimpse of a wild environment that Americans regarded, in Kasson's terms, as the source of both nature and progress.[33]

Perhaps the best exemplar of the complexities that cowboy poetry encompassed around 1900 was John Wallace Crawford. Like Burroughs's moniker "poet-naturalist," the name by which Crawford came to be known is a sign of his multiple appeals: he was "Captain Jack, the poet-scout." Crawford was born in Ireland in 1847 and arrived in the United States in 1861, settling in Pennsylvania. Wounded in the Civil War, he felt entitled (like William Cody) to bestow a military title on himself. In 1876, during a period as a miner and newspaper correspondent in the Black Hills, Crawford was "chief of scouts" tracking Sioux warriors. Cody, who also laid claim to the "chief of scouts" title, subsequently offered Crawford a role in the Buffalo Bill Combination, the forerunner of the Wild West show. Like Cody, Crawford sported shoulder-length hair, fringed buckskin trousers, a large sombrero, and a gun. The two reenacted Cody's ostensible killing of a Cheyenne chief to avenge the death of General George Armstrong Custer. The literary side of Crawford, who had already published numerous newspaper poems, was also in evidence: the program included a paean he had written to Custer. Blood, however, was the play's dominant motif, and real blood flowed during one performance when Crawford received a stab wound that he blamed on Buffalo Bill. Thereafter, Crawford went out on his own with the Captain Jack Combination, which performed a series of melodramas. In the process, Crawford consolidated his identity as what the *Los Angeles Herald* called "the very beau ideal of a frontier hero." Over the next several years, Captain Jack was himself a "combination": he prospected in British Columbia, continued to perform with various troupes, and wrote plays and poems. In 1879 he paid H. Keller and Company of San Francisco five hundred dollars to publish the first edition of *The Poet Scout: Verses and Songs.*[34]

The full development of the "poet-scout's" double-edged persona, however, occurred in the 1880s, when Crawford moved with his family to New Mexico. After an initial effort to compete directly with Cody in an outdoor Wild West spectacle, Crawford hit on a different formula for celebrity. First, he secured a patron for an enlarged version of *The Poet Scout,* which Funk and Wagnalls issued in 1886. At the same time, he brought out an additional volume of verse that, his biographer surmises, was probably designed to advertise his main collection. Second, he shifted his usual mode of performance from drama to recitation, delivering a "frontier monologue and medley" he called "The Campfire and the Trail." Still dressed in buckskin and sombrero, with his long curls flowing, Captain Jack remained the natural man—an icon, as one reporter put it in 1889, of "the wild and wooly west." The introduction he often requested to precede his walk to the podium portrayed him as a veteran of "savage border warfare" who was "accustomed to scenes of bloodshed and violence." He frequently closed performances by re-enacting his technique for killing two outlaws at once with his six-shooter. Yet Crawford found his niche in the entertainment market by using poetry to moderate that image. Reading his poems along with telling jokes and stories, he traded some of the thrill of spectacle for a touch of refinement. His denunciation of dime novels (even though he figured as a character in three of them) and his endorsement of temperance added to the aura his recitations created.[35]

The Broncho Book (1908) typified the verse that Crawford offered his audience. Its contents sanctified cowboy culture, lamenting the passing of the "days of old" when the Captain roamed "in the borderland out yonder, / Whar' the hand o' God is seen." Some of his lines provided a vicarious experience of the excitement and intensity of life in the West, with references to "hostile Indians." They also transmitted his intimacy with and respect for nature: the "scout's retreat," for example, was "a mountain lair, above an eagle's nest." In Crawford's rendition, "Mother Nature" was the source of physical challenge and, more important, of psychic comfort; his poetry repeatedly emphasized the "bright sunbeams" and "cheer" that he had found on the "trail." In terms of gender, the "scout" aspect of the Captain Jack persona strengthened the association between love of nature and masculine toughness. In the early twentieth century, after Crawford had gained Theodore Roosevelt's attention and approval, he wrote a Thanksgiving poem praising both "bounteous harvests" and the "strong heroic" followers of "our Teddy." Just as Captain Jack addressed his Winchester rifle as a "sweetheart," he advised in "Hymn of Nature's Creed": "Mother Nature's hand is reaching— / You can hear her voice beseeching . . . If you're man enough to face her, / Don't abuse her but embrace her." Finally, echoing Burroughs, Crawford's natural hero possessed access to greater "truth" than "ever was contained in richest store / Of literature, of poetry, or art, / Where mechanism forms the greater part."[36]

As the sentimentalism of his rhymes makes obvious, however, the "poet" half of "Captain Jack, The Poet-Scout" worked to filter and soften the encounter with the frontier. Arguably, not merely the content—the optimism and faith in a benign God—but also the very familiarity of sentimental verse conventions enhanced the civilized dimension of Crawford's public identity. Captain Jack's insistence that manliness required submission to nature's "laws" likewise coexisted with a defensive awareness that the tearful worship of nature could seem "weak" as well as "crude"; in one poem, "God's Ante Room," he defended such ostensible femininity by assailing the "dude" who worships fashion instead. (Subsequently, Crawford formulated his endorsement of sensitive masculinity in a poem he called "The Womanhood of Man.") Moreover, Crawford's acknowledgment of the benefits of print, the acquisition of formal learning, and, in particular, the mastery of poetic language offset his homage to nature's higher "truth."

This balance is especially apparent on the title page of Crawford's *The Broncho Book* (1908), which the Arts and Crafts devotee Elbert Hubbard issued with two-color ink, decorative capital letters, and other allusions to fine printing. The page, which includes a "brand" mark, playfully describes the text in cowboy imagery while conveying its status as an artifact of eastern culture: these "buck-jumps in verse" were "corralled into a volume by The Roycrofters at their Book Ranch, which is in East Aurora, on Buffalo Creek." Even more explicitly, Crawford referred to his admired Roosevelt as "strenuous, cultured, read" and voiced his conviction that his "broncho" verse made an "excellent book" by exemplifying the "strenuous life." Although elsewhere he made into a virtue his paucity of knowledge apart from nature, one of Captain Jack's most telling stanzas announced that insights gleaned from nature required the poet's—and easterner's—intervention to realize their full meaning: "If I could clothe each jeweled thought / That comes to me from Nature's bowers / In classic language, such as taught / Away from western woods and flowers, / . . . From many a heart I'd strike the chains, / And give the star of hope new lustre."[37]

Such concessions and accommodations made the civilized/wild, feminine/masculine, refined/unlettered Poet-Scout a "natural" on the wholesome entertainment circuit that served as the turn-of-the-century equivalent to the G-rated movie. Crawford's first venue for his one-man show was a Methodist church in Brooklyn. His biographer notes that in 1897 and 1898, he "crisscrossed the northeastern states, speaking to chautauquas, veterans organizations, schoolboys, prison inmates, private clubs, YMCA boys, and middle-class Americans in general," on some occasions addressing more than a thousand listeners at a time. In New York City in 1902, Crawford performed at Delmonico's and the Waldorf-Astoria; entertained at the home of Mrs. Russell Sage, the philanthropist; became acquainted with the popular poet Ella Wheeler Wilcox; and garnered publicity that generated scores of invitations nationwide. Newspaper accounts depicted him as "a prince of entertainers," in "constant demand" as a "reciter for all sorts of religious and social organizations."[38]

During the 1907 season, Crawford met a fan who shared his surname: the missionary Isabel Crawford. Although the two were not actually related, they became friends and began calling each other "cousin." In her journal the next year, Isabel Crawford recorded meeting Cousin Jack for sightseeing in Washington. (Later she pasted his poetry alongside that of Longfellow and Millay.) Both Crawfords decided to take advantage of their shared appeal by giving occasional joint performances for church groups and similar audiences. One such event, held in Onekama, Michigan, on Sunday, July 11, 1909, furnishes an especially good illustration of the equilibrium that cowboy poets embodied because its outdoor setting made its double meanings palpable. Isabel Crawford, well-established in her career as a reciter in Indian costume, had been camping immediately prior to the appearance with Cousin Jack. Her comment about a bonfire entertainment she witnessed on July 7 suggests the standards she brought to her own performances: "Few platforms in any city," she remarked of a program featuring not only recitation but also a dog named Bronte who barked answers to arithmetic problems, "could have given a better programme." That observation bespeaks her awareness of the conflict between nature and civilization—although labeling the dog act "culture" is admittedly a stretch. In any case, when she and Captain Jack took to the stage four days later they personified that conflict themselves. Standing before two hundred people assembled in the woods, they each wore buckskin to dramatize their connection to nature and the West. (As a missionary, Isabel Crawford also dramatized her implicit belief in the exotic but inferior caliber of Native American culture.) Yet Captain Jack simultaneously submitted to the limitations the occasion imposed: he restricted his repertory to poems that were sufficiently uplifting for reading on Sunday. The participation of a minister, who led the Doxology and pronounced a benediction, was an additional taming influence. At the same time, the presence of a professional photographer and of "Kodak fiends" accentuated the myth-making functions of the

Crawfords' tributes to nature while symbolizing the technological incursions against the simple life.[39]

Following Poetry's Trail: Girl Scouting
and the Adventure of Verse Reading

About ten years before his death in 1917, Crawford had also begun to envision a tangible expression of his ideas in plans for a boys' camp. On property in Michigan, he started building a place where he could accompany young men on hikes, show them the benefits of sleeping under the stars, and "elevate their character" by entertaining them with his poems. In addition, after speaking on temperance at a reform school in 1911, Crawford had announced the establishment of Boy Heroes of the World, over which he planned to preside as "provisional chief of scouts." Because of financial constraints, neither of those efforts got very far. Crawford's interest in them, however, points to the early-twentieth-century cultural phenomena which exhibited the uneasy relationship between nature, print, and poetry in its most institutionalized form: the beginnings of the scouting movement and the summer camp. Scouting and camping likewise entangled ideals of reading as a means to simplicity with the uses that progressive educators and participants in religious ritual assigned to verse and prose.[40]

In the United States, the ideology of scouting, while in part a British import, drew heavily on images of the pioneer as the self-reliant, virtuous practitioner of the strenuous life. The Boy Scouts of America, launched in 1910, had roots in Ernest Thompson Seton's Woodcraft Indians program, Daniel Beard's Sons of Daniel Boone, and the Camp Fire Girls, all of which stressed the moral value of outdoor activity in a rugged environment. The creation of the Girl Scouts a few years later accentuated the gendered elements of the scouting movement: while the boys adhered to a Rooseveltian association of strenuous challenges with manliness, Girl Scout leaders stressed wholesomeness, innocent pleasure, and a feminized version of strenuosity that came to be known as "spunk."[41]

The symbol of Girl Scouting's physical and spiritual ideals was the pioneer grandmother, a woman who personified wisdom, hardiness, adaptability, and a perspective on life that derived from the quest to meet basic human needs. By the 1930s, "creativity" also figured prominently in the movement's lexicon: each troop, a 1935 national "Program Study" maintained, should furnish opportunities for members to develop their creative potential. As scouting evolved, however, that emphasis on self-development became linked to a promise that the movement could bring about wider social change. As one leader phrased it, the Girl Scouts hoped to equip modern American girls with the ability not only to perpetuate the pioneer spirit in the nation's remaining outdoor spaces but also to transfer that spirit to community service, the home, the school, and the arts.[42]

The assumption that all Girl Scouts either possessed a lineage traceable to old American stock or should be remade so as to resemble those who did reflects the class and racial prejudices of the movement's leadership. By the time of the "Program Study," in fact, the agency's national officers had embarked on a concerted effort to reach poor or uncultured girls, who they thought most needed to experience scouting's beneficial effects. The report of the "Program Study" further explained that Girl Scouting, together with the family and the school, was entering a period of greater democracy; thus, echoing the rhetoric of the New Deal, every goal delineated in the report committed the organization not only to personal enrichment but also to the creation of an intelligent citizenry.[43]

Poetry reading had a place within the Girl Scouts' framework as part of a larger belief that books could be instruments for the attainment of the movement's personal and political objectives. In *The Way of Understanding* (1934), Sarah Louise Arnold, an influential scouting official and a poet herself, insisted that "we must guide our Girl Scouts to an appreciation of the best in poetry." Familiarity with beauty in that form, Arnold explained, would enable a girl both to remember that "life itself is worth living" and to carry out her "Task" to "do something the world needs done and to take pride in doing it well." Thus Arnold's book interspersed among her own verse and essays excerpts from the poems of Longfellow, Whittier, Whitman, Henry Van Dyke, Markham, and Walter Rauschenbusch, among others.[44]

The same message appeared in the publications on which girls in the movement relied directly, the *Girl Scout Handbook* and *American Girl* magazine. The handbook, a compendium of Girl Scouting's credo and craft, served as a prized token of membership along with troop insignia and a sash displaying "proficiency badges." In its early editions, the compilers did not hesitate to prescribe "reference reading" for troop members and leaders. The 1920 version contained a reading list recommending "some of the best books of the world, with which all persons should be familiar"—endorsements which remained essentially the same until the revision of the *Handbook* in the mid-1930s. The poetry in the 1920 list included Andrew Lang's *Blue Book* and Burton Stevenson's *The Home Book of Verse*. The 1932 edition dropped Lang in favor of Louis Untermeyer's *This Singing World,* a recommendation that, if followed, would have brought examples of Millay, Frost, Sandburg, Robinson, and other "new poets" to girls' and leaders' attention.[45]

In addition to consulting the *Handbook*'s reading lists, throughout the 1920s Girl Scouts who sought to align their reading with the movement's priorities could also rely on the agency's official magazine, *American Girl*. The periodical featured a monthly column that reviewed books of special interest to Girl Scouts. From 1925 to 1927, its author was May Lamberton Becker, the "book advice" columnist for the *Saturday Review of Literature* and, later, the *New York Herald Tribune*. In an informal style that radiated empathy and good cheer, Becker conveyed her "especial pleasure" in alerting her readers to new works; typically, she couched her suggestions in reminiscences about her own experiences as both girl and mother. Her columns established and assumed an ongoing emotional bond with her fictive troop of Scouts: "Do you remember how I shouted in favor of a lovely book of verses last year . . .?" she asked in one column. Similarly, writing about the poems in a collection of stories and verse published for Girl Scouts by Doubleday, Page, she commented: "These were not written for the book, but selected for it with great care, from the writings of famous poets of today. . . . I was rejoiced to find *Velvet Shoes*, by Elinor Wylie, loveliest of poems about snow. I do not know why this poem should make me so happy, but it does; the kind of happy that makes you wonder if you are going to cry. Beautiful poetry can do that, you know." Becker's skill in combining friendly "girl talk" and didactic commentary is especially evident in her long endorsement of Simon and Schuster's "Pamphlet Poets" venture; in praising the series, she etherealized a purchase that Macmillan, as a rival publisher, had regarded merely as lost revenue: "I hope I may find some of you putting down your own pocket-money in exchange for so much loveliness."[46]

The appreciation of "loveliness" may have been a mark of the personal and social development which scouting advocates hoped books would foster in young women, but Arnold, Becker, and their colleagues among the Girl Scout leaders nevertheless betrayed their awareness of the discrepancy between the sedentary posture of the reader and that of the spunky pioneer. In a section entitled "Book Learning and Experience," Arnold argued that "books follow experience and can be rightly used and understood only by those whose experience has given them a key to their contents." Her maxim was "Life first; then words and letters." Similarly, although the 1947 *Handbook* advised that "the more you read and handle books, the greater will be your respect for the book itself," a pervasive subtext of the various explanations of badges was that the "book itself"—as an object of contemplation—was worth relatively little.[47]

More specifically, Becker upheld in her columns a model of poetry reading that emphasized the genre's centrality to the active life. "This enterprise," she declared approvingly in reference to the Pamphlet Poets, "gets poetry off the center table and into the pocket. The best place to carry poetry is in the head, and the next best is in the pocket, ready to pull out in a spare moment and read over and again until it has become a part of you. You never can tell when you are going to need it. When I broke my arm last Spring, I used to lie there in the hospital reciting poetry to myself, and the nurses, looking in at the door and seeing me so comfortable and happy, thought I had a heavenly disposition, but it was nothing of the kind. I was just bringing back out of my memory poems that I had not so much as thought about since I learned them in my teens." That mixture of advice and anecdote, while it implicitly re-iterated the storehouse image, in this context turned poetry into a piece of equipment—like rain gear or tin cans for emergency cooking—which enabled scouts to "be prepared." The conceit of roaming, by means of print, through uncharted worlds made ac-ceptable the image of a girl reading that accompanied several of Becker's columns: slouched in an armchair and dressed in fashion-able clothes and jewelry, the girl is sophisticated, comfortable—and decidedly remote from the hardscrabble existence of a pioneer grandmother.[48]

In *American Girl* for August 1930 (the same issue that reprinted a poem by the Imagist H. D.), and again in September, subscribers debated whether or not the periodical contained enough poetry—with inconclusive results. Subsequently, *American Girl* came more and more to resemble a generic magazine for teenagers, and corre-spondingly looked less like the organ of Girl Scouting. Moreover, in the spirit of cultural relativism that dominated much of the pe-riod's thought, the revisions of the *Handbook* that appeared in the late 1930s and 1940s declined to render judgments about "the best," omitting reading lists altogether. Within that altered context, however, Girl Scout publications did continue to present reading as a component of active girlhood. "The land of books," the 1933 *Handbook* implied, offered as much terrain for adventure as the "by-paths of the woods." In addition, the language of books as friends here served to underscore the scouting movement's empha-sis on democracy and community: through reading a girl might "share in the life and customs of her sisters across the sea" and would "seldom be lonely."[49]

Beginning with the 1938 guide for Girl Scout leaders, the pub-lished rationales and requirements for the revamped program's "Literature and Dramatics Field" were even more explicit about reading as a chance for exploration, in which books were like markers along a hiking trail. In the 1947 *Handbook*'s revision of the "Reader" badge, poetry loomed especially large. Girls could choose among the following options: learning how to use *Granger's Index to Poetry and Recitation*, making a poetry anthology about a favorite subject, reading "a number of poems by different poets in a good anthology or elsewhere," or reciting a text aloud "several times before deciding" whether they "liked it." The last provision also included instructions that reiterated the importance of the sociability the genre facilitated. The purpose of choosing favorite poems, the *Handbook* stipulated, was to use them "at a troop meeting or campfire."[50]

The insistence on configuring reading as a physical as much as a mental pursuit presumably indicates the commitment on the part of Girl Scout officials to make books as appealing as possible to the movement's clientele. Even so, the perceived necessity of promoting the image of the reader as a hiker seems a defensive move, a concession to an underlying distaste for weakling intellectuals of either gender. The image, in other words, tacitly recognized the tendency to dispense with print altogether that Kilmer, Burroughs, and others had evinced. That possibility remained submerged during the winter months, when in many areas there were few opportunities for campfires and Girl Scouts worked on their badges indoors. Yet the consonances and contradictions between the *Handbooks'* assumptions about the value of reading (especially poems) and the movement's reverence for the "simple life" came into sharp focus in warmer weather, when girls went outside to a site designed to revivify the pioneer experience directly and intensively: the summer camp. Whether in the Berkshires, on the shores of Lake Michigan, or at any of the similar locations throughout the country that provided a remaining space of "wilderness," Girl Scouts—like many other youth groups under non-profit or private auspices—sought, for a time, the purported virtues of life spent entirely in the elemental conditions of the "open."

By the Firelight's Glow

The sources of organized camping in the United States overlapped with those that gave rise to scouting, but additional factors were also at work. Among these were the encampments of the Civil War and the physical culture movement of the late nineteenth century. Religion was an even greater cultural influence on the summer camp phenomenon. In the early 1800s, evangelical camp meetings had begun drawing hundreds of families to set up tents and cook over wood fires. That expression of Christian fervor eventually stimulated Protestant church involvement in outdoor activities for youth. The Chautauqua Institution, founded in western New York in 1874 to promulgate self-culture and Protestant morality, also popularized the mental and spiritual value of outdoor life. In 1880, two boys' camp programs—one church-sponsored, one private but laced with "spiritual instruction"—began in New England. Five years later the YMCA founded its first camp.[51]

As the movement for summer camps grew, it coincided with the reaction against "overcivilization" and the drive for strenuosity, as well as the presumption of reformers like Charles Loring Brace that fresh air could combat the ill effects the city exerted on immigrant children. In the 1920s, the offspring of the expanding middle class joined the wealthy and the poor at both sectarian and non-denominational camps. By that time, camping had also absorbed the philosophy of progressive education, taking on the coloration of pedagogues' interest not only in child development but also in healthful play. Church leaders designed youth group activities to counteract the "cheap and vulgar" with high-minded "fun."[52]

Poetry reading at summer camps derived from that matrix of precedents and ideologies. Counselors incorporated recitations into Sunday and evening programs where groups gathered to sing, hear stories, and meditate before blazing logs. As H. W. Gibson, a camp director and former president of the American Camping Association, explained, the campfire was "the soul of the camp." Its fixed rituals, often concocted from "Indian" lore, exposed youths to a heady dose of romanticism; its traditions were made to seem mysterious in origin, its "signs and ceremonies" (such as the Council Ring) vaguely occult or primitive. The campfire was not all seriousness—"stunts" such as a cracker-eating contest, can and glove boxing, and a human "dog fight" might be part of the proceedings—

but words and music predominated. "You cannot have a complete fire," said Gibson, quoting from the psychologist G. Stanley Hall, "unless you have a good story teller along." Although leaders might read a tale aloud from a book, they tended (when not making up their own yarns) to paraphrase the plot of a classic from memory: *The Three Musketeers, Lorna Doone, Treasure Island.* Signaling the popularity of the "steady seller," the director of Sebago-Bear Mountain camp commented, "The good story is wanted again and again. Interest grows with repetition. Summer after summer boys will listen to *The Count of Monte Cristo.*"[53]

From story telling, campers might be led to the "realm" of poetry. At Camp Ahmek in Ontario, a dramatization of "Hiawatha's Departure" was the "crowning feature" of the Council Ring. Many of the selections in Helen Bragdon and Laura Mattoon's compendium, the author of a guide for leaders explained, "attract such attention that they are memorized by the boys and girls and are recited about the camp fire." Likewise, in *By the Firelight's Glow,* a volume in his self-published *Monthly Library on Camping* (1927), Gibson presented poems he thought suitable for the occasion: Robert W. Service's "Song of the Camp Fire," Kipling's verse beginning "Who hath smelt wood-smoke at twilight?" and two poems about fire reprinted from the magazine *Field and Stream.* Those choices reveal that, as a reader himself, Gibson approached texts by determining what they were "about" in literal terms. The same framework dictated his selection of several works dealing with the relationships ideally forged at camp—for example, Emerson's "The Mountain and the Squirrel" (about differing talents); Longfellow's "The Arrow and the Song" (about friendship). The schoolroom favorite "Invictus" also appeared. Such poems might help the campfire leader "direct the thought of the campers" to the "more serious things" appropriate at the close of the program, when quiet tunes and pauses for reflection replaced the rousing choruses sung earlier. Taps customarily followed. Then, at Gibson's camps, the director announced to the campers standing in silence: "And, now, may the blessing and the Spirit of the Great Camp Director be with us until we meet again."[54]

The richest source concerning poetry by firelight conveys an even sharper picture of memory and rereading as sources of shared experience. That document is *Magic Ring*. The book, published in 1926 and issued in a revised edition in 1937, began as a game played at the camp of the Seattle Camp Fire Girls. One evening a camper spontaneously recited some lines of verse about autumn, "and poem [on that subject] followed poem. To the ring of girls around the drift-wood fire, the evening had slipped away like magic." As the volume's editor, Ruth A. Brown, related, "There was such a glow of happy interest on the ring of faces round the fire that the game went on until some one noticed it was time for the goodnight song." Over the next five years, the game became the campers' "best loved" campfire activity, as "girl after girl of her own accord repeated her favorite poems." The campers also decided to trade recitations on the trail, while sailing, or wherever their circumstances called to mind a poetic theme. "One day," Brown wrote (perpetuating the usual misquotation of Masefield's "Sea Fever"), "we came upon some girls drying dishes, billowing their towels to the swing of 'I must go [sic] down to the seas again!' They explained they were having a nautical adventure by repeating all the water poems they knew." The campers also collected their favorite poetry in "fat notebooks." When Brown decided to publish *Magic Ring,* she drew on the contributions of more than three thousand girls; by the time of the second edition, the game was popular at camps nationwide.[55]

To the twenty-first-century historian, the fact that these young readers, for their own pleasure, unselfconsciously shared poems from memory is remarkable in itself. So is the language of transport and fantasy with which they described their mode of reading together: for them, poetry transformed time and place. (One is tempted to speculate as well about the refuge the game afforded homesick, bookish girls who were better in English than gym class.) Moreover, as with school curricula (which presumably furnished many of the poems the girls had learned), comparing the two editions of *Magic Ring* allows a particularly clear view of the assimilation of changing poetic styles, and of the continuities attending that process.

The 1926 version of the book contained 286 selections, most describing some aspect of nature. In the 1937 revision there were 355 poems, despite the deletion of 70 entries (including all of the psalms and Christmas carols in the earlier edition). Both volumes contained a preponderance of nineteenth-century British and American poets, with the old standby "Abou Ben Adhem" heading the table of contents. In both, Robert Louis Stevenson (with fourteen poems in 1937) and Shakespeare (with nine) accounted for the greatest number of selections. Tennyson, Bliss Carman, Emily Dickinson, Markham, and Van Dyke remained heavily represented in the later edition as well. Of the figures with five or more poems in 1926, only a poet unknown today, Helen Gray, had entirely disappeared eleven years later, although Harriet Monroe, who had three poems in 1926, is strangely missing from the revision. Her absence was offset, perhaps, by the inclusion in 1937 of Ezra Pound's "An Immorality"—the most striking evidence of the campfire's function in popularizing the "new poets" of the early twentieth century. Similarly, the later volume contained four poems by Frost (an increase of three over 1927), four by Sandburg (up one), and two each by Millay, Louis Ginsberg, and Louis Untermeyer (all of which had been in the earlier collection.) That tally bears out the comment of *Publishers' Weekly* in 1927 that Camp Fire girls were avid readers of contemporary verse and wrote poems themselves; they possessed copies of *Creative Youth* as well as *Magic Ring*. It also corroborates the remarks in 1937 of a bookseller who peddled his wares at girls' camps in Vermont. For older girls and counselors, he observed, the "primary requisite" was "plenty of poetry," with Millay, Teasdale, and "any of the less abstruse moderns" among the favorites, and a taste for Spender, Auden, and Eliot among the "notable exceptions."[56]

Even more worth remarking on, however, are the older poets who received more space in the second *Magic Ring* compilation than they had in the first. One of these was Emerson, whose allotment doubled from four poems to eight, making him the third most represented poet in the second edition. Longfellow's total went from one to three; Lowell's from three to four; Whittier's from zero to two; Wordsworth's from two to four. Although practical considerations may have affected those choices (for example, the waiver of permissions fees for reprinting texts out of copyright), the fact remains that, at least among Brown's Camp Fire girls, the venerated figures of the past had not grown obsolete by the late 1930s but instead retained currency and force.

Operating as a site for dissemination, the campfire also endowed poetry with additional ideological weight. Even (or perhaps especially) for camps without denominational missions, the quasi-religious functions of such gatherings are obvious: they entailed rites, hymns, silences, a benediction. Hence, like the worship service, the site elevated works that literary critics dismissed as "magazine verse" to the status of sacred texts. Adding to that effect was a rhetoric that endowed the campfire with memorability (just as poems became treasures in the mind). After describing one fireside program featuring poems about pirates, Richard James Hurley, a librarian affiliated with the Boy Scouts, mused, "There is a long sigh at the end—the kind of a sigh that comes from being filled with something very satisfying. We can hear the wind gently pattering sand upon our tents, the roll of the surf, the voices of night insects. Yes, it is another perfect campfire to tuck away in our memories."[57]

To be sure, some leaders acknowledged that not every poem deserved an aura of sanctity and timelessness. For example, the editors of *Camp-Fire Verse* (1917), intended for adult as well as young readers, made theme the organizing principle of their anthology but "discarded as doggerel" poems "devoid of literary merit." In fact, Hurley envisioned a purification of taste by fire: while initially some campers would "consider that the boy who stood on the burning deck was 'swell' poetry and a camp yell [was] superior to Vachel Lindsay's *The Congo*," the campfire ring could "smooth the sharpest edge and polish the roughest diamond." To the degree that leaders believed in developing aesthetic judgment, the campfire was to be as educational as it was religious. Yet Hurley's standards did not depend on adherence to modernism or high culture: he juxtaposed Frost and Guest, Mark Van Doren and Henry Van Dyke, and complained that Service was "evidently beneath [the] dignity" of anthologizers.[58]

By the 1920s, moreover, the education proffered in the "open" increasingly matched that of the progressive classroom. Here, too, creativity appeared as a prime value, associated with an "emotional release" more "satisfying" than "alcohol, jazz, petting, and lavish spending." The author of the Girl Scout position paper "Program Building for the Permanent Camp" (1930), Louise Price, described how reading and writing poetry were central to that psychic liberation. A camp with which she was acquainted, Price approvingly noted, set aside an afternoon hour every other day when a counselor read and analyzed poems for interested campers. The rapport between the counselor and the girls encouraged the campers to explore their feelings in poems of their own, efforts that Price judged quite successful in literary as well as emotional terms.[59]

While Price emphasized the impetus to (and reinforcement of) personal relationships that reading poetry provided, others stressed the wider social consequences of attention to creative self-expression. Like the Girl Scouts, the upstate New York camp of the Pioneer Youth of America (not to be confused with the Communist Young Pioneers) was especially committed to the goal of democratic citizenship as well as self-development. With support from such reformers as Sidonie Gruenberg and Caroline Pratt, the Pioneer Youth sought to produce self-reliant, socially adjusted young people who "lived" their educational ideals. Similarly, a 1929 report by the New York Section of the Camp Directors Association declared, "The concept of education which we accept . . . is of a continuing process whereby the individual is led on by interest from one experience to another in such a way that he acquires the knowledge, skill, habits and appreciations which will mean the greatest enrichment of his life." In such manifestos, the concern about well-spent leisure surfaced once again. In an essay entitled "The Educational Value of the Summer Camp," Bragdon outlined the philosophy at Camp Kehonka for girls (where Mattoon served as director): it would develop in campers the awareness that "worthy use" of free time depended on "being a productive member of society," not on "membership in a favored class." Alluding again to the power of memory, Gibson explained, "We are builders of a kind of community idealism which will effectively combat the materialism of the present day . . . [with] the beauty of life. . . . The camp fires, the rising sun, the sunsets, the stars, the moon, the storms, the darkness of the night, contribute the stimulation of all this creative imagination. Memory is photographing scenes and experiences that will never be forgotten. We are truly 'shaping a new human race.'" Poetry reading (and writing) was one of those scenes—at campfires, on rainy days in well-equipped camp libraries, in small groups of Pioneer Youth when they pursued activities growing out of their own interests, in the booklet *Echoes from Camp Winnepe* which published campers' "creative work."[60]

As in the schoolroom, however, reading verse also played a part in moderating the challenge which the progressive vision of release posed to the status quo. At the Pioneer Youth camp, where the staff strove to correct problems of "maladjustment," reading her own poetry aloud helped Selma, a "highly artistic and creative" 12-year-old, to win the approval of her tent mates. In such a case, the "comfort" and "sympathy" that poetry reading spurred were doubtless immediate and beneficial. So was the practice, at one camp, of leaving at a "Meditation Rock" a book of poetry (as well as a Bible and pencil and paper) for troubled campers wishing a response from the chaplain. Yet these therapeutic functions might simultaneously serve somewhat coercive ends. The broadest objective of Camp Ahmek, for example, as Hedley S. Dimock and Charles E. Hendry noted in *Camping and Character,* was to transmit "a way of living—the Ahmek Way." Quoting Dewey, they drew an admiring analogy between that task and the "great Soviet experiment." But what of campers who resisted the Ahmek Way? The answer, the authors suggested, lay in "collective activities" such as ceremonies and dramatic performances that could supply "control."[61]

Furthermore, the progressive camping movement placed limits on the use of reading to effect adjustment. The Pioneer Youth camp staff saw too much attachment to books as pathological; their stance recapitulated the theme that reading precluded authentic experience. For example, Jenny, a 13-year-old girl, read "continuously" during her first few days at a Pioneer Youth camp. She made "no effort whatever to become friends with the other girls or enter activities. Conversation with her disclosed a conviction on her part that she couldn't do anything well. Reading was obviously a compensation for her supposed inabilities." The counselors successfully drew her out with praise for her other skills. They failed, however, in the case of a male camper whose friends consisted of "over-intellectual boys."[62]

Like the figure of Theodore Roosevelt, that last phrase is another reminder of the constraints that definitions of masculinity imposed on boys who displayed an interest in reading verse. The introspective, inactive girl, while in need of correction, was not as distant from prescribed gender roles as the boy who preferred poems to sports. Fortunately for such boys, the summer camp setting could sometimes function to legitimate or "masculinize" bookishness. When Gibson recommended marking a hiking trail with signs quoting Tennyson, or when Hurley's Boy Scouts recited verses about the sea while gazing at a lake, or when poetry around the fire worked its "magic," reading became as natural as woods and water. The predominance of story telling without the intrusion of the printed book as object also naturalized the text. Furthermore, if boys experiencing the freedom of the wild gravitated toward poetry without coercion, one might plausibly conclude that an affinity for the genre was an inherent trait rather than a sign of feminization. Thus, noting that she had been called upon to defend children's books against charges of "femininity," the librarian Effie Powers commended Hurley's *Campfire Tonight!* as an instance of a work that was appropriately masculine.[63]

Still, as Powers's defensiveness reveals, the concern about bookish boys—and girls—in the camp setting signals the presence, once again, of the dissonance between text and site with which Kilmer and Burroughs had grappled. It was possible, around the campfire, to strike a balance, as the poet-scout Crawford had, but the anti-intellectual dimension of the commitment to "strenuous" action was always in the air. Moreover, for campers, as for Burroughs's readers, the poet might be at the same time a guide and an obstacle to contact with the "simple" and "elemental." Both *Services for the Open* and Gibson's *Recreational Programs for Summer Camp* (1938) alluded to the problem. In Bragdon and Mattoon's plan of worship for the opening day of camp, immediately following the Lord's Prayer, leader and spokesman were to read responsively the lines: "Up! Up! my friend, and quit your books; / Or surely you'll grow double; . . . Come forth into the light of things / Let Nature be your Teacher." Writing in his preface, Gibson spoke in his own voice: "A wise man said several thousand years ago that of the 'making of many books there is no end and much reading is a weariness of the flesh.' . . . Conscious of the warning of this old sage, the author dares to launch another book upon the sea of the printed word."[64] The anxieties to which those lines testified were as enduring in American culture as the emberglow was in campers' summertime recollections.

"Favorite" Poems and Contemporary Readers

It would be easy to see the history of poetry reading in America as a story of decline and fall. Memorization practices have virtually disappeared from our schools, a casualty of both disdain for rote learning and, ironically, the pressure for more quantifiable achievements. Girl Scout cookie boxes depict young women engaged in high-tech adventures such as aviation, not trading stanzas around campfires. The family dinner hour, let alone after-dinner reading, is under siege. The National Endowment for the Arts warns that Americans are reading less literature, poetry included. It appears we have lost our ear for language, along with the sense of shared traditions and common culture that the public uses of poetry supplied.

Yet the picture is actually more mixed. In 2005 the NEA embarked on an ambitious national recitation contest, "Poetry Out Loud," to reacquaint high school students with the pleasures of verse. Thanks to a generous bequest from Ruth Lilly, the Poetry Foundation (the NEA's partner in "Poetry Out Loud") oversees an endowment to publish *Poetry* magazine in perpetuity. More than that, since the 1990s a poetry "renaissance" has produced new sites and new vehicles for the genre's dissemination.[1] In 2004, the audience for the biennial Dodge poetry festival in New Jersey was estimated at 25,000 attendees. The number of young people at "poetry slams"—raucous oral performances at which individuals or teams compete before judges, Olympic-style, for points—has grown exponentially since the invention of the form in 1984 at a Chicago bar. The tenth annual National Poetry Slam in 1999 drew almost 3,000 spectators from a broad range of ethnic and racial backgrounds, who cheered, screamed, and hooted at the 200 poets on stage. Among the teams was one from the Nuyorican Poets Cafe in Manhattan's East Village, the source in the 1990s not only of slams (parts of which appeared on MTV) but also of a touring company of spoken-word artists that aimed to "bring an in-your-face poetry" with multicultural inflections to a national audience. A close relative of the poetry slam, the hip-hop performance, began offering audiences a similarly passionate experience, its combination of rhyme and music presenting what one reviewer called "raw, unfiltered life."[2]

Furthermore, the designation of April as National Poetry Month has generated an annual barrage of publicity since the Academy of American Poets established the observance in 1996. During the first National Poetry Month, the shoppers at the Mall of America in suburban Minneapolis celebrated the event by composing poems using magnetic letters on refrigerators in front of Sears. As a writer for the Boston *Globe* put it, poetry "may have long flourished in the cloistered halls of academe, but lately it's evolved into a kind of popular form that's hot even at the mall." Subsequently, National Poetry Month has fueled not only the magnetic poetry ("Mag Po") craze (with encouragement from the product's manufacturer) but also an increase throughout April in radio coverage, book promotions, readings, "open-mike nights," classroom poetry kits, and other activities related to verse. During the rest of the year, Americans also encounter poetry in the subway: the Poetry Society of America's "Poetry in Motion" program, begun in 1992 and funded by Barnes & Noble in New York, was by 1998 placing poems on subways and buses in six other cities. In the late 1990s, poems appeared as well in the Yellow Pages of telephone books in localities ranging from Tacoma, Washington, to Long Island. Behind that method of distribution was the American Poetry and Literacy Project, which has given away anthologies of verse on Amtrak trains and in hotels, airports, schools, and similar public sites. In 1999, Volkswagen cooperated with the project by putting 40,000 copies of *Songs for the Open Road: Poems of Travel and Adventure* into the glove compartments of its new cars. The contents of the 66-page volume included Frost's "The Road Not Taken," Whitman's "Song of the Open Road," and Dickinson's "There is No Frigate Like a Book."[3]

In addition, especially after September 11, 2001, when grieving Americans posted "huge numbers" of poems online, the Internet has functioned as a powerful stimulus to poetry's popularity. In 1997, one commentator reported over 8,000 poetry sites on the World Wide Web; by 2000, the search engine Lycos was listing more than 228,400 such sites. One website, Poetry Daily, offers a new poem each day. Another, Poetry 180, the creation of the recent Poet Laureate Billy Collins, aims to bring a daily poem to high school students. Lycos also ranked poetry eighth among the fifty most popular search terms its users employed in 1999. The Internet facilitates both conversation about poems and self-publication, along with its own slams, workshops, and journals (many of which are selective and distinguished).

At the same time, poetry in print form proliferated in the late 1990s. The non-profit literary center Poets House reported that 53 per cent more poetry titles were published in 1997 than in 1993—875 versus 570. While the print run for the typical volume of verse remains what it was in the early twentieth century (around 1,000 copies), the advent of superstores like Barnes & Noble and Borders, with their facilities for authors' appearances, have made it possible for certain poets (notably Collins) to achieve best-seller status. In 1998, the Book-of-the-Month Club offered *World Poetry: An Anthology of Verse from Antiquity to Our Time* as one of its selections—only the second time it has chosen a book of verse since it sent out *John Brown's Body* in 1928.[4]

All these new manifestations of interest in poetry have sustained and enlarged the capacity of the genre to furnish opportunities for

sociability. Yet there is a key difference between the audience spur-
ring the recent poetry boom and their late-nineteenth- and early-
twentieth-century predecessors: present-day poetry devotees are more
likely to be writers as well as—and in some cases, instead of—read-
ers. Much of the explanation for the poetry boom—apart from
the Starbucks phenomenon that revived the coffeehouse setting—
has focused on the latter-day American's quest for authentic com-
munication. As the founder of Mag Po put it in 1998, "We've
tapped into a pent-up desire for inner expression." All over the
country, people have turned to groups such as Long Island's Sa-
chem Poets Society to "share small epiphanies and personal con-
fidences" through lines and stanzas of their own creation. "With all
the automization and depersonalization in society," a Boston-area
poetry slam participant remarked, "people feel disconnected, and
this is a way to connect. People want to tell their story, they want
to say what is important to them." The considerable overlap be-
tween readers and writers is reflected in the membership statistics
for the Academy of American Poets, which increased from 2,000 to
10,000 between 1995 and 2001. It is also evident in the burgeoning
programs of the National Association for Poetry Therapy, an orga-
nization of mental health professionals who assist their clients by
having them write and publish poems (as well as responses to the
work of others) based on their own "experiences and emotions."[5]

Not everyone views such developments positively. Some poets
and readers decry the proliferation of slams and websites as "de-
basing" to the genre, on the grounds that such activities are
commodifying an art form. Others note that despite poetry's surge
in popularity, the sales figures for volumes of verse are still small
and the market fragmented, and that no poet today "has the cross-
over recognition in mainstream America" of a Robert Frost. None-
theless, while the merits of the poetry "renaissance" may remain
open to question, "this enormous reawakening," in the words of
Dana Gioia (currently head of the National Endowment for the
Arts), "is now an undeniable fact of contemporary American cul-
tural life."[6]

Although many of them are also writers, readers have become

very visible in one compelling artifact of the poetry "renaissance": the torrent of response to Robert Pinsky's Favorite Poem Project. In 1997, during his first term as the nation's poet laureate, Pinsky decided to document and celebrate the vital place of poetry in American culture. He invited readers to submit to him the title of their favorite poem, together with a brief statement of the reasons for their choice; his goal, he explained, was to assemble a video and audio archive of ordinary citizens reading beloved verse. Over the next year, Pinsky and his associates at Boston University (the project's administrative home and main supporter) received over 17,000 letters and e-mails taking him up on his invitation. The project also facilitated almost 1,000 readings at locales around the country, in which community leaders joined other residents to share favorite poems aloud. The results of this effort include a collection of fifty documentaries featuring an individual reciting and speaking about a poem. These videos were broadcast nationwide on the Jim Lehrer "NewsHour" and now reside permanently in the Library of Congress. In addition, the Favorite Poem Project issued three anthologies that reprinted some of the submissions. The first volume in the series reproduced readers' comments alongside each chosen poem; the second—designed to highlight the "pleasure" of reading verse—included remarks by Pinsky and his co-editor, Maggie Dietz, about certain selections; and the third, which resembled the first anthology in format, was packaged with a DVD drawn from the video archive. The Favorite Poem Project still receives online additions to its mammoth database.[7]

Pinsky's undertaking rested on two assumptions that dictated its activities and set its tone. The first, evident in the recordings and nationwide readings, was that poetry was inherently a vocal art. Its "medium," Pinsky observed in The Sounds of Poetry (1998), "is a human body: the column of air inside the chest, shaped into signifying sounds in the larynx or mouth." That circumstance made the genre not only "physical" but also "intimate" and "individual."[8] Yet, at the same time, Pinsky argued that poetry's "very voice evokes the attentive presence of some other, or its lack: an auditor, significantly absent or present." This second assumption, that a

Robert Pinsky at a Favorite Poem Project event celebrating the 150th anniversary of the Boston Public Library in 1998. Boston University Photo Services.

poem "always includes the social realm"—that language itself bespeaks "communal life"—shaped the Favorite Poem Project to the extent that its central purpose was to "reflect some of the social presence of poetry in the lives of Americans." Thus, by extending the social dimension backward to the very production of a poetic text, Pinsky's animating principles complement and amplify the argument of the foregoing chapters that the dissemination and reception of verse are the products of social mediations.[9]

Pinsky would be the first to acknowledge that the intent of his project was not to conduct a scientific investigation. For one thing, the database includes a disproportionate number of teachers, who frequently required their entire class to submit responses as an assignment, most of which were too cursory to be meaningful. For another, it does not consist of spontaneous comments only, but, rather, contains some of the remarks of the local celebrities whom the organizers of the community events approached. Even many of the unsolicited replies, moreover, reflect readers' self-conscious attempts to impress Pinsky with their sensitivity and their own poetic turn of mind. Because respondents could omit their age, ethnicity, and occupation if they so chose, the data available to characterize participants are not uniform. Some people submitted their own poems despite the instruction not to. Others omitted explanations for their selections. Perhaps half of the respondents wrote one-line comments that were too general to cast much light on their thinking. The nature of the database obviously also mirrors the composition of the audiences exposed to the project's publicity campaign.

Even though some respondents referred to the project as a contest, the anthologies do not consist of the poems mentioned most often by readers, nor are they a record of representative replies. Rather, they were deliberately "edited" (Pinsky and Dietz's own term) in keeping with three priorities. First, "an explicit criterion for selection," Pinsky has explained, "was the intensity and interest of what the reader had to say about the poem."[10] Second, the editors sought to convey the wide range of backgrounds among the poetry-reading public. Examples of readers from various ethnic groups, racial minorities, and social classes attest to that diversity, but their inclusion in the volumes is unrelated to their statistical presence in the database. Finally, while the first and third anthologies are designed to display the spectrum of texts that appeal to contemporary Americans, Pinsky's and Dietz's predilection for modernism and, as they freely admit, their own standards of taste dictated the degree to which they were willing to accommodate popular verse in the project's archive and publications. Hence Ernest Lawrence Thayer's "Casey at the Bat," the choice of 66 readers, appears in the first and third anthologies, but Robert Service is absent from all three. Kilmer's "Trees," a favorite of 78 respondents, was presumably too bad a poem for the editors to set aside their aesthetic standards; Edgar Guest and Eugene Field suffered the same fate; and Shel Silverstein, the frequent nominee of schoolchildren, was deliberately excluded. Kipling, Noyes, Bryant,

Whittier, Holmes, Masefield, Riley, Markham, and Teasdale are also absent. "I Wandered Lonely as a Cloud" is a notable omission, given that the number of readers who chose it equaled those who nominated Thayer's baseball narrative. In the first and third volumes, however, the editors were constrained by their desire to reprint those poems that had generated engaging comments.[11]

Despite these features, the Favorite Poem Project offers the basis for some meaningful observations about Americans' verse-reading practices of the last several years. It also permits some comparisons between present-day readers and their counterparts between 1880 and 1950. Any such comparisons are bounded not only by the aforementioned quirks of the sample but also by the particular question that Pinsky posed to potential respondents: the project explicitly asked readers to specify the "personal meaning" their favorite poem held for them, and judged responses by the "intensity" of that personal dimension. As a result, the comments in the database and the anthologies reveal relatively little about the ideologies and values governing various sites for reading. Furthermore, Pinsky's question directed readers' attention to the links between the content of the text and their own lives; its implicit demand that they justify their selection on the basis of the poem's sound, imagery, or theme tended to obscure the extraneous uses—those deriving from the act of reading itself—that the wider lens of autobiographies and diaries reveals. In spite of these limitations, however, certain similarities and differences between past and present are clear.

Like earlier readers, a large number of respondents in the Favorite Poem Project were either oblivious to or unintimidated by the restricted definition of poetry that has shaped the academic literary canon. Pinsky's announcement of the project asked merely for the submission of a well-loved poem—not a "serious," modernist, or even a good poem—and readers behaved accordingly. Along with the works of Field, Kilmer, Service, Guest, and Silverstein, the call simply for a poem produced Bible passages, song lyrics, excerpts from Robert Louis Stevenson, and passages from Kahlil Gibran. "I know that Kipling is less than highly regarded by many in today's literary community," a 68-year-old Oregon man conceded, "but I think that is basically 'snobbery' and that Kipling should be considered one of the great poets of the English language."[12] Sixty-five mainly teenage readers (perhaps from the same school) selected the popular Christian missive entitled "Footprints," a poem only because some of its promoters call it one. Ninety-four readers mentioned "Jabberwocky" and other poems by Lewis Carroll, mainly on the grounds that "nonsense" was enjoyable. The inattention to cultural hierarchy which the project elicited was consistent with Pinsky's declared unwillingness (despite his editorial decisions) to separate poetry and popular culture.[13] Moreover, in cases where respondents happened to indicate more than one choice of a "favorite," an individual's reading across canon boundaries is occasionally visible: one reader proposed poems by both Robert Frost and Ella Wheeler Wilcox; another declared, "Robert Frost notwithstanding, Guest is America's greatest poet."[14] In any event, the database demonstrates the independence in matters of taste that a reading public in a democracy takes for granted: of the 17,457 entries received, the largest number for any one poet—Frost—was 970, less than 6 percent of the total.

Moreover, certain steady sellers of the school curriculum continue to hold some appeal. One might expect that older readers would be more likely to single out nineteenth-century staples, having been taught them more frequently as children. That supposition is correct: of the 66 readers who named Henley's "Invictus" as their top choice, about three-quarters of the 46 who specified their age were over forty years old. Surprisingly, however, the presence of 13 Henley readers in their teens and twenties suggests that younger people are replenishing (albeit in smaller numbers) the ranks of the poem's devotees as the older generation dies out. (One astute reader in her sixties both certified the ongoing resonance of "Invictus" and suggested a reason for its diminished prominence: "The ideas in the poem," she wrote, "have become so ingrained in our culture that they are assumed, and are considered clichés.")[15] Similarly, 7 of the 39 respondents who wrote about Longfellow's "A Psalm of Life" were under the age of eighteen; most of those younger readers indicated that the poem has a continuing, if modest, place in school curricula. The majority of the 218 readers of all ages who mentioned any of Longfellow's work associated it with memories of first learning the poem at school or at home. Nevertheless, Longfellow's showing in the database fell significantly below that of the living African-American poet Maya Angelou, whose 299 fans included only 5 above the age of fifty, and whose "Phenomenal Woman" and "Still I Rise" have become relatively new staples of the curriculum.

The participants in the Favorite Poem Project both dethroned and upheld figures of the poet on which their counterparts in the past also drew. Inviting members of the reading public to comment on the meaning of best-loved verse for themselves as individuals crowded out whatever references readers might have been inclined to make about the poet's role in society as a whole; except for a few remarks pertaining to "The Building of the Ship" or "Barbara Frietchie," and those mentioning the Kennedy and Clinton inaugurations, neither the poet as civic sage nor the recitation of verse on civic occasions were much in evidence. Yet the project itself, with its Library of Congress connection, entailed a civic mission: to demonstrate the richness of American culture, to display (in the words of the book jacket for the first anthology) the nation's "collective history," and to furnish a "portrait of the United States through the lens of poetry." Furthermore, the idea of the poet as source of wisdom and insight continues to operate on the personal, if not the national, level. A preponderance of the 343 readers who named Frost's "The Road Not Taken" as their favorite read the poem for its perceived message about how to live. Specifically, many credited Frost with providing instruction or advice about choosing unpopular alternatives (concluding that the poem endorses nonconformity). As one 42-year-old woman put it, "The poem represents so well the choices we have to make as we travel down the road of life. . . . It invites the reader not to follow the crowd, but to follow your heart, even if that means going down a less traveled path." The figure of the poet as personal sage and seer likewise informed the outlook of the numerous participants who equated inspiration with guidance, valuing "The Road Not Taken" for the way its words assisted them "when making important decisions." Robert Frost, one wrote, "reminds me to lead my wavering choices toward a direction, a path, that no one may ever tread; without regret." The poem, another insisted, "holds the key to the future of our planet."[16]

A second venerable figure, the trope of the poet as companion or friend, was a surprising rarity in the database. Although the rhetoric of friendship turned up in connection with Walt Whitman ("a companion who echoes the passion and joy I find in every day life"), "A Psalm of Life," and the contemporary writer Jane Kenyon, the infrequency of the friend motif is striking here given its widespread appearance in the testimonies of the elderly population that responded to the *New York Times* query. It may well be that the diminution of the trope reflects the fading of the poet as innocent, or at least that the friend motif has become associated with a lack of sophistication which younger, well-educated readers addressing the poet laureate were at pains to avoid exhibiting. If the poet as friend seemed an outmoded conceit to most of Pinsky's respondents, however, the feelings the trope represented remained highly visible in readers' comments, which substituted the language of shared perception for the rhetoric of companionship. For example, one participant wrote of Millay, "She and I share the same whimsical outlook. We value life for the sheer beauty and enjoyment of it. We walk to the beat of a 'different drummer.'" Describing his reaction to "Second Fig," another Millay devotee declared, "Somehow, I felt as if there were somebody somewhere who understood." A 16-year-old woman, sounding like one of John Burroughs's awakened readers, summarized the "joy" she felt upon remembering Wordsworth's "I Wandered Lonely as a Cloud" by asserting: "Wordsworth and I for a moment were in the same place." These remarks reflect the social dimension of poetry in the sense that they concern a human relationship—the one between poet and audience. Readers were unhampered by canonical judgments in entering into that relationship; their identification with their chosen poet took the same form regardless of the poem's standing among literary critics. "Service is my favorite poet," a respondent wrote. "His outlook on life matches my own. His rhyme and rhythm speak to my soul. . . . This poem cuts right to the heart of the highest value of my life."[17]

A common variant on the construction of the poet as intimate was the statement that particular lines of verse conveyed the reader's ideas and emotions with greater clarity than did that reader's own words. In a response that incidentally provides a beautiful example of reading as a process of literally remaking a text, a 30-year-old New Mexico woman described her reaction to Millay: "The first time I read her poems I was shocked to find that it was as if she had gotten inside my head, collected all my thoughts and feelings, and sung them back to me in words more beautiful and pointed than I could ever have mustered. (Although sometimes I get mad at her using 'thee' and 'thy' too often. Secretly I'll change them to 'you' and 'yours' in my head to better match her modern sensibility.)" Likewise, another woman wrote about Elizabeth Barrett Browning's "My Heart and I" that it was as if Browning "read my soul and wrote everything I was feeling." Poets, several contributors implied, were especially adept at giving "a voice, a quiet articulation" to readers' unexpressed sentiments of love and grief; they spoke what one bereaved woman called "words heard only within my own head and soul."[18]

Among participants in the project whose favorite poets were recently deceased or still living, a sense of the poet as friend or intimate often arose as well from an opportunity for access to the writer in person, much as Edward Bok or William Dean Howells had experienced the schoolroom poets as within their reach. A New Jersey reader who submitted lines by a member of her book group represented an extreme example of that phenomenon: "Poetry and poets," she wrote, "continue to exist and they sit next to you at book discussion." Hearing poets read their own work aloud made some people imagine stronger connections between themselves and the figures to whom they had listened, a response that Pinsky's insistence on the importance of the sound of verse privileged. "I have heard [David] Whyte recite this poem ["Sweet

Dreams"]," a 48-year-old Pennsylvania woman noted, "and each time I read it I can hear him speaking to me." Yet the frequent references that respondents made to meeting admired writers, obtaining autographs, or hearing well-known individuals read poets' works also testify to the ongoing power of the culture of celebrity and the role of literary luminaries within that culture. Along with the book superstores that sponsor staged readings that perpetuate sociability in the tradition of Lindsay and Millay, the expansion of English Departments and the growth of academic creative writing programs in the years since World War II have made the university a common site for encounters with famous poets or their promoters. (As the poet Donald Hall observed, Carl Sandburg's travels with his guitar, Robert Frost's exhibitions of "studied charm," and Dylan Thomas's three American tours in the 1950s also greatly stimulated the institutionalization of the readings phenomenon; so did the concerted activity of lecture agents.) With its reference to the poet by his first name, the comment of a longtime high school English teacher from New Hampshire registered the effects the brush with celebrity could have on readers' enthusiasms: "I heard Dylan read the poem at Amherst College in the spring of 1953. After the . . . program, I introduced myself to him and he signed my copy of 'Complete Poems.' He died later that year. I have shared his poems with students throughout my career." Another example of that phenomenon was the report of a woman who stated only that Angelou's "Phenomenal Woman" was her favorite poem because she had heard Oprah Winfrey deliver it at the 1997 Wellesley College commencement.[19]

Along with revealing readers' perspectives on the poet, Pinsky's database also makes visible the emotional purposes with which participants in the project invested verse. Like other veterans of the classroom and hearthside recitation, these respondents noted the function of memorizing and recalling poetry in supplying a sense of continuity over a lifetime. In some instances the imagery or setting the poet employed stirred remembrances of related episodes in readers' lives. "The poem," one man observed of W. S. Merwin's "Strawberries," prompted reminiscences about "my younger days when I was lucky enough to experience the sound of strawberry vendors in our neighborhood. . . . Merwin's poem parallels my dreams and my memories." Other contributors focused on a different set of recollections: those involving their repeated turns to the poem itself. Offering to read Stephen Vincent Benét's "The Mountain Whippoorwill" for the project archive, a Georgia man explained, "I would like to do something in the later years of my life that I did at the first and still enjoy." An older woman who wrote to recommend Frost's "The Tuft of Flowers" declared, "I can identify stages in my life by the poems I was reciting from memory first as a young child, then as a student, English teacher, young woman betrothed, homemaker, mother, and now grandmother. . . . [The poem] spoke to me first in my adolescence and . . . still comforts me today in my golden years." A Maine woman stated that she had been using Dylan Thomas's "Poem in October" as a "morning wake-up ritual" on her birthday for more than twenty-five years, changing the text's opening phrase "It was my thirtieth year to heaven" to reflect her actual age. While many of the individuals who recurred to the same lines year after year traced their acquaintance with the poem to their childhood (and often to school), the practice of endowing a poem with the capacity to evoke earlier stages of one's life is not just the habit of the nostalgic senior citizens in the sample; younger readers also highlighted their first encounter with their favorite work and used the poem as a touchstone in looking back through their own histories. A 39-year-old woman, for example, wanted to recite Frost's "Acquainted with the Night," which she had found as a teenager: "I would like to read it for the fourteen-year-old girl I once was," she wrote, [as well as] for the woman I have become." Even children engaged in the same retrospection, charting their growth from grade school to high school.[20]

More important, the overwhelming majority of respondents in the Favorite Poem Project echoed earlier readers in calibrating the emotional weight of a particular text in terms of their relationship to parents, spouses, siblings, or acquaintances. Often participants owed their knowledge of a poem to a family member, and thus the text was inseparably intertwined with the milieu of the household. (The incidence of parents reading to children seems greater among readers over forty, although the failure of around a third of Pinsky's respondents to report their age makes this generalization problematic.) In numerous cases, rereading a work that was a relative's favorite called forth readers' conscious or unexpressed longings to resurrect memories of unalloyed love and attention—to recover a lost innocence—within a relationship that the vicissitudes of life and death had complicated or attenuated. (The only example of reading to reinforce anger toward family appeared in connection with the poem "Daddy" by Sylvia Plath.) "My New-England father loved poetry," a fan of Kipling asserted. "I was his shadow, growing up, and we split wood, took winter walks, built houses, . . . fixed cars together. As he worked, he recited long poems from memory. The one that became part of my own life, through wintery times, is Kipling's 'When Earth's Last Picture [Is Painted].' My father's deep, velvet voice is still part of the words." An upstate New York woman reported that her mother read Longfellow's "The Children's Hour" to the family whenever her father was working out-of-town: "I feel it was her way of keeping our father present in our memory as he was so loving, caring, and giving when he was home. He enjoyed coming home to us running to the end of the driveway to meet him." In that account, the rationale for the recitation of "The Children's Hour"—the mother's reliance on the poem to fill her husband's absence—operated to affirm family bonds. In contrast to the Kipling example, however, that use was integrally related to the content of the text: its evocative power depended partly on the picture Longfellow drew of a father joyfully engaged with his affectionate daughters, and the driveway scene replicated the reunion described in the poem. An Ohio man whose own father had bought him a book of Eugene Field's verse years earlier rediscovered the poet's famously sentimental "Little Boy Blue" while his son was suffering with cancer. "I read the poem again and again and cried each time," he said. "Fortunately my son recovered . . ., but this poem means everything to me, including fond memories of my father, who taught me about truth and beauty." There, too, meaning arose both from a mimetic reading of the text and from the extrinsic circumstance that the reader had received the Field volume from a parent.[21]

The intrinsic characteristics of a poem also elicited emotions about familial relationships in a different way: by conjuring up the presence of family members even when those individuals had played no part in transmitting the work to the reader. Seven of the twenty-five individuals who chose "Little Boy Blue" as their favorite poem, which Field wrote after his young son died, reported that they themselves had cared for a severely ill child or had lost to death a boy or girl whom the poem seemed to memorialize. Similarly, a Massachusetts woman, interpreting Frost's "Mending Wall" as an affirmation of "boundaries," wrote, "This poem touches me emotionally because it brings me back to my childhood, watching my gentle father with his 'rough hewn' hands, mending fences with his neighbor. His love for his 'neighbors,' shown by his actions, taught me a lesson." A stark example of the practice came from a student whose father, a man who appeared happy, had killed himself like Richard Cory when the reader was a young child.[22]

Like the anecdotes revealing the sense of intimacy between poet and audience, all the comments displaying the familial associations readers attached to their favorite poems demonstrated that the "personal meaning" they derived from the text was inextricably bound to social experience. Focusing on the spoken aspect of poetry, a 27-year-old Boston man offered an elegant summary of that point in nominating Robert Creeley's "The Flower": "It's not the literal event the poet writes about that makes the strongest connection, it's the emotion, the communication between poet and reader that neither can see before it happens. And, the fact that the effect this poem had on me is directly related to hearing it read by a familiar and loved voice goes to show that a good deal of the power of poetry rests in its sounds and the communication of those sounds from one person to another."[23]

As readers expressed sadness at the loss of family, they also documented the ongoing appropriation of poetry for religious purposes. Some respondents—notably the 134 readers who nominated

"God's Grandeur" and other poems by Gerard Manley Hopkins—credited verse with buttressing an explicitly Christian view of God and of nature as God's handiwork. ("It's all that keeps me Catholic, some days," one Hopkins reader admitted.) Many more, however, reported using poetry to achieve a heightened sense of spirituality that supplemented or substituted for formal theology. "Each time I read (or recite) this poem," an older woman from Massachusetts wrote of "The City Limits" by A. R. Ammons, "my dormant spirituality is awakened and I am stirred by an intense hopefulness. . . . It reaches into my inner life and I feel for the time 'religious' (which I am not)." More than eighty people accorded their favorite lines the status of a prayer or Bible verse, which some reported reciting daily; the poems so designated ranged from Kilmer's "Trees" to Wendell Berry's "Manifesto: The Mad Farmer Liberation Front." Referring to William Butler Yeats's "The Second Coming," a 33-year-old Connecticut woman characterized the similarity between Bible reading and verse reading in terms of the mental processes each stimulated: "The language in this poem," she noted, "has, for me, gained the power of Biblical language—the phrases and the words that are always swirling in the mind, coming unbidden, weighty and strong."[24]

Even more numerous were readers who sustained the practice of employing poetry to obtain the consolations that faith supplied in other contexts: the ability to accept death and suffering, the assurance of a power beyond the self, the promise of a better world to come. One manifestation of that impulse consisted of the two hundred or so responses that located the appeal of a poem in its universality or its commentary on the "human condition"; the readers who derived from poetic texts the view that their place in the procession of life transcended their own finitude and mortality formed what one might call (with apologies to Benedict Anderson) an "imagined congregation." As an 18-year-old college student observed, "I don't subscribe to any religion, but I have a deep spiritual curiosity. This poem [E. E. Cummings's "since feeling is first"] expresses nearly everything I could say about Platonic love—love progressing from the mundane to contemplation of the universal and ideal. By grounding oneself in love (for one person, for many people, or for humanity as a whole), one achieves a sort of immortality of feeling." We are "not separate but in communion . . . with one another," a disciple of Hopkins declared. "Everything is sacred." Referring to Whitman's "O Me! O Life!," a Brooklyn man who described the poet as "speaking directly to me" remarked that the universality of Whitman's verse derived from its acuity about human fears, yet Whitman "offers us great hope because he understands the beautiful and the God-like quality inside each individual."[25]

Those essentially religious perceptions are related to one of the more noteworthy facets of the Favorite Poem Project: its occasional documentation of reading across class and racial categories (where readers were willing to divulge the relevant data; only a smattering of participants are identified by "ethnicity" in the database). Most visibly, the concept of a transcendent connection to others enabled white readers to appropriate poems growing out of African-American life and African-Americans to acknowledge commonalities with whites. Along with the countervailing sentiment of race pride, the poetry of Langston Hughes, selected by 356 respondents, often prompted that reaction, in part as a result of Hughes's own preoccupation with themes of inclusiveness and his repeated invocation of "dreams." Because Hughes's work is widely assigned in inner-city schools (the majority of Hughes readers who supplied their age were under eighteen), many of the references to interracial understanding no doubt reflect the intervention of teachers. Nevertheless, some older readers joined younger ones in asserting that Hughes spoke for all people—or all Americans—regardless of their (and the poet's) race. A white high school American history teacher wrote that she was "continually amazed and thrilled at the simple beauty and important message" of "I, Too." A 19-year-old African woman living in Virginia noted that the "similarities between the speaker and addressee" in "Theme For English B" were "so universal that his words are no longer words from a young black man, but words that could be from any young man." An African-American student commented that "the feeling of despair" that Hughes conveyed in "Harlem" was something that "all people can understand." The most memorable instance of a reader who subordinated class identification to universalism was the construction worker for Boston Gas depicted in one of the nationally televised videotapes. The appeal of Whitman's "Song of Myself," he explained, was not that the poet wrote about "ordinary laborers," although that was a "nice touch." Rather, the poem mattered to him for its "upliftingness," its inspiring qualities that supplied a positive perspective on human existence.[16]

A more salient use of poetry to secure the consolations of religion concerns a different kind of self-transcendence: the achievement of serenity and hope in the face of pain and loss. No feeling person can read the contributions to the Favorite Poem Project without being moved by the record of despair and resilience they offer. Divorce, terminal illness, depression, suicide, and accidental death riddle readers' explanations of poetry's appeal. As the examples of reciting "Little Boy Blue" and "Richard Cory" have already indicated, a poem's personal meaning could be grounded in the tragic disruption of the reader's social milieu as well as in the continuity the act of reading furnished. "When I first heard of the Favorite Poem Project, I was already searching for an elegy which would help me cope with the slow, sad dying of my eleven-month-old grandson," a Connecticut woman wrote of Maxine Kumin's "The Height of the Season." Now, she continued, "I'm reeling from two more deaths, both sudden." The poem, she explained, furnished "solace" through images that "balanc[ed] the harshness of loss, private and public, with the priceless treasures of love and life." While a middle-aged Colorado woman joined Reverend Stidger in reading "Renascence" as a description of Christian conversion, another reader extracted a less doctrinally grounded but equally sustaining faith from Millay's lines: "At a time of despair in my life when all I could see was darkness, this poem gave me inspiration and the will to live." A Virginia man who had first read the poem at age seventeen reread it at forty-five while near Millay's home in Maine to memorialize his wife, who had died when their son was ten. "Again," he wrote, "it spoke to me of cruel sadness, and of ultimate renewal." A young woman from Texas who had learned "Renascence" in high school summarized the religious function of poetry reading in general for numerous readers: the text, she noted, "spoke directly to my battered spirit, [and] gave me a vision of the sacred to hold onto as I wandered in search of a path." Despite the impact, in the post–World War II period, of modernism and existentialism on American thought, most of the project participants who linked poems to "darkness," as Pinksy and Dietz headed one chapter in the second anthology, did so by way of endorsing the genre's uplifting impact. The poetry of Mary Oliver, whose work was the favorite of 129 readers, stood out as a means, especially for women, of affirming life in the face of illness and death.[27]

The vocabulary of spirituality, and of the quest for renewal, is a hallmark not just of denomination-based faith but also of the therapeutic ethos which Americans have increasingly espoused since the mid-twentieth century; in consequence, the religious uses of verse documented by the database shade readily into those that draw on pop psychology, twelve-step recovery programs, and other New Age regimens. Responses reflecting those influences came from readers of all ages and pertained to both recent and older verse. For example, the vaguely Judeo-Christian/Buddhist/New Age trope of life as a "journey" appeared in about a hundred responses; readers applied it, for example, to "The Road Not Taken" ("life is a journey of choices"), "Renascence" ("a little spiritual journey"), and Tennyson's "Ulysses" ("it's the journey, not the destination"). The response to Oliver's "The Journey," where the trope is explicit, epitomized the way in which readers often relied on such language to authorize a focus on self-realization; the poem, one woman explained, was "deeply supportive of self care and self love."[28]

Like the practitioners of poetry therapy, roughly one hundred readers also invoked the metaphor of "healing" in describing the effects of verse. "Grief overwhelms," a 39-year-old Montana woman observed of Millay's "Childhood is the Kingdom Where Nobody Dies," but "in this poem Millay's honesty about regret somehow is healing." Longfellow offered the same balm. "The

Rainy Day," declared a 73-year-old Missouri man, "serves to heal the sadness that comes to every human's life." One of the "gifts" of poetry, a nominator of Denise Levertov's "The Fountain" generalized, is its "great healing potential." Some readers were even more specific in relating the genre's curative effects to their own psychic travails. Jane Kenyon's exploration of depression in "Having It Out With Melancholy" prompted a 49-year-old woman to observe: "For me this poem had healing power. . . . [Kenyon's] words alleviate the very pain, isolation and hopelessness she so eloquently describes." A woman in her late thirties, writing of E. E. Cummings's "somewhere I have never travelled gladly beyond," described the transformative power of the text in terms that amalgamated the rhetoric of religious conversion and recovery from illness: "It reminds me of the end of long years of agony, when I who was clenched and fearful, angry and depressed, was miraculously saved, opened by the magic of tenderness . . . to me it is a poem about salvation and healing and transformation."[29]

Respondents also explicitly compared reading a favorite poem to undergoing psychotherapy. "I guess I just want to say," a 20-year-old woman wrote, "that poetry (in general) really got me through a lot of tough times. I feel like I had hundreds of therapists, Dr. T. S. Eliot, Dr. E. S. V. Millay, Dr. Donne." Selecting Frost's "The Pasture," a California man explained, "I regard the poem as having a therapeutic quality. When I feel the world is closing in on me I pick up the copy I have sitting on my desk in my bedroom and read it slowly." For several readers, poems were more effective than the "talking cure." A 45-year-old woman from Virginia who regarded certain poems as "mental life rafts" judged reading Robinson's "Richard Cory" as "better than a cocktail or psychotherapy or any other modern remedy" in rooting her in "the reality of the basic pleasures" of her life.[30]

A quasi-religious interest in mind-cure is hardly new in American culture. Neither (as the earlier discussion of poetry's emotional valence has demonstrated) is the employment of reading to feel better. Yet the large volume and revelatory nature of the responses centering on the reader's loss and pain arguably reflect the specific cultural context that produced them: they bear the mark of the premium on self-disclosure, on telling one's story, that is at the heart of many current therapeutic regimens. Moreover, the question the Favorite Poem Project posed—what is the personal meaning of the poem?—might be regarded as a product of the same cultural climate that has encouraged public confession (often in the form of television talk shows) as a necessary step toward repairing the self. Along those lines, the philosopher Troy Jollimore, criticizing the first Favorite Poem Project anthology in the *Boston Book Review,* disparaged it as a reflection of Americans' characteristic narcissism. "When they try to explain why they chose the particular poems they did, why they mean so much to them," Jollimore remarked about the readers whose comments Pinsky and Dietz printed, "you find that they're not talking about the poems at all; they're talking about themselves." These readers, Jollimore continued, held "the unspoken assumption that a poem can only matter to me if it is in some way about me. . . . One searches in vain through Americans' Favorite Poems for the person who would write, I love this poem because it describes a reality I knew nothing of." Jollimore's point is well taken, although Pinsky himself has eloquently refuted it in *Democracy, Culture, and the Voice of Poetry* by arguing that the comments in the anthology contain a "powerful familial and social component" that serves as a counterweight to the narcissistic—Pinsky would say "personal"—tendencies the project elicited.[31]

Yet, in addition to displaying the social dimensions of reading, the greatest contribution of the Favorite Poem Project may be to document the artificiality of Jollimore's implied distinction between the meaning of a poem and the reader's self-referential account of it. While the entire database echoes the historical record in testifying to the instability that reading confers on texts, this contribution is especially clear in responses that note the shifting meanings readers impute to poems over time. The comments of a Wisconsin woman about Edgar Allan Poe's "Dream within a Dream" allow a closer confirmation of that variability than a focus on the mediations at particular sites for reading usually permits: "At the age of 14, I spent my summer memorizing this poem because I liked Poe. I recited the poem for the flow, the lyrics, the mere ability to recite. At the age of 28, I entered a four-year college to begin my quest for a degree in English literature. . . . The depth of the poetry opened before me, the lyrical aspects were accented by the 'Romanticism' of the lines. . . . And now, at the age of 39, I will . . . obtain my license to become a registered nurse. The depth of the pain of my clients is echoed in the lines of this poem. . . . What began as a childhood task to pass the boredom of summer has now become a reminder to me of the physical, mental, and emotional pains of mental illness. I can't wait to learn what this poem will teach me in the future."[32]

The Favorite Poem Project likewise measures the degree to which the idea that readers remake texts has attained popular acceptance. Several project participants implied that poets had no stronger claims to establishing the meaning of their work than readers did. For all the respondents who kept alive the figure of the poet as sage and seer, others were unwilling to grant poets either superior moral or aesthetic authority. A 19-year-old Wisconsin woman declared, "If it means something to the reader, even if it is not necessarily the writer's meaning, then it is a good poem." Somewhat more diffidently, the daughter of a Cambodian refugee family remarked in an entry chosen for the first anthology, "My interpretation of this poem written by Langston Hughes ["Minstrel Man"] may not be the same as his but a poem is what I choose to make of it and how it is a description of me." Pinsky has observed, in countering Jollimore, that in the context of the young woman's entire comment, even such a "personal" declaration sustains the spirit of Hughes's poem. But one might also say that, while late nineteenth and early-twentieth century Americans generally assumed that a poet's intentions mattered, the insistence of some of Pinsky's correspondents on their interpretive prerogatives is only a more extreme, less constrained version of how earlier individuals appropriated verse in schoolrooms, civic celebrations, parlors, religious settings, and campfire recitations. In practice, the cultural values and social uses that mediated poetry at those sites placed historical readers in a relationship to the text not so different from the one a 78-year-old member of a study group in a retirement center described to Pinsky: "We no longer try to figure out what the poem means," she wrote, "as much as what the poem means to us in our lives now."[33]

NOTES ❧ INDEX

Notes

Introduction

1. George S. Carhart and Paul A. McGhee, *Through Magic Casements* (New York: Macmillan, 1927).
2. See, for example, Robert Darnton, *The Business of Enlightenment: A Publishing History of the Encyclopédie, 1775–1800* (Cambridge, Mass.: Harvard University Press, 1979); Roger Chartier, *The Order of Books: Readers, Authors, and Libraries in Europe between the Fourteenth and Eighteenth Centuries* (Stanford: Stanford University Press, 1994); Carlo Ginzberg, *The Cheese and the Worms: The Cosmos of a Sixteenth-Century Miller* (Baltimore: Johns Hopkins University Press, 1980); Natalie Zemon Davis, *The Return of Martin Guerre* (Cambridge, Mass.: Harvard University Press, 1983); David D. Hall, *Worlds of Wonder, Days of Judgment: Popular Religious Belief in Early New England* (New York: Knopf, 1989); and Hugh Amory and David D. Hall, eds., *A History of the Book in America*, vol. I: *The Colonial Book in the Atlantic World* (Cambridge: Cambridge University Press, 2000). The phrase "social history of culture" is in David D. Hall, *Cultures of Print: Essays in the History of the Book* (Amherst: University of Massachusetts Press, 1996), 171.
3. Robert Darnton, "First Steps Toward a History of Reading," in *The Kiss of Lamourette: Reflections in Cultural History* (New York: Norton, 1990), 170–171, 187; David D. Hall, "Readers and Reading in America: Historical and Critical Perspectives," in *Cultures of Print*, 180.
4. Joan Shelley Rubin, *The Making of Middlebrow Culture* (Chapel Hill: University of North Carolina Press, 1992).

5. Sacvan Bercovitch, ed., *The Cambridge History of American Literature*, vol. 5, *Poetry and Criticism 1900–50* (Cambridge: Cambridge University Press, 2003), 2; Robert Spiller et al., *Literary History of the United States: History*, 4th ed. rev. (New York: Macmillan, 1974); Paul Lauter, gen. ed., *The Heath Anthology of American Literature*, vol. 2, 3rd ed. (Boston: Houghton Mifflin, 1998), 207–246; Nina Baym et al., eds., *The Norton Anthology of American Literature*, vol. 2, 2nd ed. (New York: Norton, 1985), 866–872; Jay Parini, ed., *The Columbia History of American Poetry* (New York: Columbia University Press, 1993); David Perkins, *Is Literary History Possible?* (Baltimore: Johns Hopkins University Press, 1992), 3.

6. Parini, *Columbia History*, xii.

7. Chartier, *The Order of Books*, ix; Hall, *Cultures of Print*, 184; Guglielmo Cavallo and Roger Chartier, eds., *A History of Reading in the West* (Amherst: University of Massachusetts Press, 1999), 34. On appropriation, see especially the work of Barbara Sicherman, e.g., "Sense and Sensibility," in Cathy N. Davidson, ed., *Reading in America: Literature and Social History* (Baltimore: Johns Hopkins University Press, 1989), 201–225.

8. Chartier, *The Order of Books*, vii–xi; Robert Darnton, "What Is the History of Books?" (1982), rpt. in *The Kiss of Lamourette*, 112.

9. Cavallo and Chartier, *History of Reading*, 2–3.

10. Elizabeth Long, *Book Clubs: Women and the Uses of Reading in Everyday Life* (Chicago: University of Chicago Press, 2003), 28. See also Janice A. Radway, *Reading the Romance: Women, Patriarchy, and Popular Literature* (Chapel Hill: University of North Carolina Press, 1984).

11. Cavallo and Chartier, *History of Reading*, 4; Hall, "Readers and Reading," 178; Lawrence W. Levine, *Highbrow/Lowbrow: The Emergence of Cultural Hierarchy in America* (Cambridge, Mass.: Harvard University Press, 1988); Michael Denning, *Mechanic Accents: Dime Novels and Working-Class Culture in America* (London: Routledge, 1998); Amory and Hall, *Colonial Book*, 11. Chartier is quoted in Hall, "Readers and Reading," 178.

12. Raymond Williams, *Marxism and Literature* (Oxford: Oxford University Press, 1977), 122.

13. William S. Gray and Ruth Munroe, *The Reading Interests and Habits of Adults: A Preliminary Report* (New York: Macmillan, 1929), 232–234.

1. Seer and Sage

1. R. A. Yoder, *Emerson and the Orphic Poet in America* (Berkeley: University of California Press, 1978), 192.

2. Ralph Waldo Emerson, *Essays, First Series* (Philadelphia: David McKay, 1890), 37; F. O. Matthiessen, *American Renaissance: Art and Expression in the Age of Emerson and Whitman* (New York: Oxford University Press,

1941), 51; Robert E. Spiller et al., *Literary History of the United States: History*, 4th ed. rev. (New York: Macmillan, 1974), 303, 378, 380; Denys Thompson, *The Uses of Poetry* (Cambridge: Cambridge University Press, 1978), 55–63; Mary Kupiec Cayton, *Emerson's Emergence: Self and Society in the Transformation of New England, 1800–1846* (Chapel Hill: University of North Carolina Press, 1989), 74, 137–160.

3. Emerson, *Essays*, 9, 47; Cayton, *Emerson's Emergence*, 118–119.

4. Donald Pease, "Walt Whitman's Revisionary Democracy," in *The Columbia History of American Poetry*, ed. Jay Parini (New York: Columbia University Press, 1995), 162–163; Yoder, *Emerson and the Orphic Poet*, 169; Gay Wilson Allen, *The Solitary Singer: A Critical Biography of Walt Whitman* (New York: Grove Press, 1995), 166–168, 411.

5. Noah Porter, *Books and Reading, or What Books Shall I Read and How Shall I Read Them?* (New York: Scribner's, 1871), 246; David Pryde, *The Highways of Literature, or What to Read and How to Read* (New York: Hurst, 1883), 69; Charles F. Thwing, *The Reading of Books: Its Pleasures, Profits, and Perils* (Boston: Lea and Shepard, 1883), 70. On sacralization, see Lawrence W. Levine, *Highbrow/Lowbrow: The Emergence of Cultural Hierarchy in America* (Cambridge, Mass.: Harvard University Press, 1988).

6. Lawrence Buell, *New England Literary Culture: From Revolution Through Renaissance* (Cambridge: Cambridge University Press, 1989), 111; Emerson, *Essays*, 14, 38; Matthiessen, *American Renaissance*, 38; Pease, "Walt Whitman's Revisionary Democracy," 153, 166.

7. Buell, *New England Literary Culture*, 138; Thompson, *Uses of Poetry*, 113–115; David S. Shields, "Eighteenth-Century Literary Culture," in *A History of the Book in America*, vol. I, *The Colonial Book in the Atlantic World*, ed. Hugh Amory and David D. Hall (Cambridge: Cambridge University Press, 2000), 438, 442; James Spear Loring, *The Hundred Boston Orators Appointed by the Municipal Authorities and Other Public Bodies from 1770 to 1852* (Boston: J. P. Jewett, 1853), 405, 412–413, 417, 532.

8. Merle Montgomery Hoover, *Park Benjamin: Poet and Editor* (New York: Columbia University Press, 1948), 167; Cayton, *Emerson's Emergence*, 153–159; Buell, *New England Literary Culture*, 154.

9. Spiller et al., *Literary History*, 358; Bernard I. Duffey, *Poetry in America: Expression and Its Values in the Times of Bryant, Whitman, and Pound* (Durham: Duke University Press, 1978), 44; Loring, *Hundred Boston Orators*, 418.

2. Amateur and Professional

1. Ellery Sedgwick, *The Atlantic Monthly, 1857–1909: Yankee Humanism at High Tide and Ebb* (Amherst: University of Massachusetts Press, 1994), 141.

2. Dana Gioia, "Longfellow in the Aftermath of Modernism," in Jay Parini, ed., *The Columbia History of American Poetry* (New York: Columbia University Press, 1993), 64. The best recent study of the schoolroom poets as a group is Angela Sorby, *Schoolroom Poets: Childhood, Performance, and the Place of American Poetry, 1865–1917* (Lebanon, N.H.: University of New Hampshire Press, 2005).

3. Mark Twain, *Speeches* (New York: Oxford University Press, 1996), 2, 3, 6–7; Sedgwick, *Atlantic Monthly*, 141; Ellen B. Ballou, *The Building of the House: Houghton Mifflin's Formative Years* (Boston: Houghton Mifflin, 1970), 218.

4. Twain, *Speeches*, 3, 5.

5. William Charvat, *The Profession of Authorship in America, 1800–1870* (New York: Columbia University Press, 1992), 290. An exception is Parini, *The Columbia History of American Poetry*.

6. Charvat, *Profession of Authorship*, 290; William Dean Howells, *Years of My Youth* (New York: Harper, 1916), 205.

7. Charvat, *Profession of Authorship*, 30; William Charvat, *Literary Publishing in America, 1790–1850* (Amherst: University of Massachusetts Press, 1959), 62.

8. Charvat, *Profession of Authorship*, 121, 157, 178–179; Charvat, *Literary Publishing*, 66–67, 136; Ballou, *Building of the House*, 242–243; Sorby, *Schoolroom Poets*, 27–28..

9. Lawrence Buell, *New England Literary Culture: From Revolution Through Renaissance* (Cambridge: Cambridge University Press, 1989), 31, 39, 58, 386; Cheryl Walker, *The Nightingale's Burden: Women Poets and American Culture Before 1900* (Bloomington: Indiana University Press, 1982), 55–57, 76–79.

10. James T. Fields to Whittier, Sept. 27, 1866, in *The Letters of John Greenleaf Whittier*, vol. III, 1851–1892, ed. John B. Pickard (Cambridge, Mass.: Harvard University Press, 1975), 136; Whittier to E. L. Godkin, March 9, 1867, *Letters*, III, 149; Whittier to Harriet Minot Pitman, Jan. 20, 1869, *Letters*, III, 191; Whittier to Edward L. Pierce, Apr. 12, 1882, *Letters*, III, 447–448.

11. Edward Bok, *The Americanization of Edward Bok* (New York: Scribner's, 1921), 19, 33.

12. Ibid., 33, 41.

13. Frederick L. Luqueer, "In a Volume of Lowell's Letters," *Dial*, Sept. 16, 1897, 138.

3. *Absence and Presence*

1. Harriet Monroe, *A Poet's Life: Seventy Years in a Changing World* (New York: Macmillan, 1938), 117, 125, 131, 242.

2. Ellen Williams, *Harriet Monroe and the Poetry Renaissance: The First Ten Years of Poetry, 1912–1922* (Urbana: University of Illinois Press, 1977), 6, 20–21; Robert E. Spiller et al., *Literary History of the United States: History,* 4th ed. rev. (New York: Macmillan, 1974), 809–826.

3. "Tennyson's Last Hours," *New York Times,* Oct. 6, 1892, 1; Henry Van Dyke, "The View of Tennyson," *Century,* Feb. 1893, 539; "The Late Poet Laureate," *Review of Reviews,* Dec. 1892, 576; Hamilton Wright Mabie, "The Influence of Tennyson in America: Its Sources and Extent," *Review of Reviews,* Dec. 1892, 553–554; William T. Stead, "Tennyson The Man: A Character Sketch," *Review of Reviews,* Dec. 1892, 557–570.

4. Mabie, "The Influence of Tennyson," 553; "The Books of 1892," *Publishers' Weekly,* Jan. 28, 1893, 170; William Dean Howells, "The Editor's Easy Chair," *Harper's,* March 1902, 673.

5. Daniel H. Borus, *Writing Realism: Howells, James, and Norris in the Mass Market* (Chapel Hill: University of North Carolina Press, 1989), 40, 183–189; William Dean Howells, "Novel-Writing and Novel-Reading: An Impersonal Explanation," in William M. Gibson, ed., *Howells and James: A Double Billing* (New York: New York Public Library, 1958), 7, 10; Lawrence W. Levine, *Highbrow/Lowbrow: The Emergence of Cultural Hierarchy in America* (Cambridge, Mass.: Harvard University Press, 1988), 177; Alan Trachtenberg, *The Incorporation of America: Culture and Society in the Gilded Age* (New York: Hill and Wang, 1982), 182–207; Oscar L. Triggs, "A Century of American Poetry," *Forum* 30 (Jan. 1901), 640.

6. "The Books of 1896," *Publishers' Weekly,* Jan. 30, 1897, 219–221; "American Book Production in 1904," *Publishers' Weekly,* Jan. 28, 1905, 103; "Poetry and the Drama," *Publishers' Weekly,* Jan. 26, 1907, 140.

7. Williams, *Harriet Monroe,* 4–8, 14; Hermann Hagedorn, *Edwin Arlington Robinson: A Biography* (New York: Macmillan, 1938), 218.

8. "The Slump in Poetry," *Critic,* Mar.-Apr. 1905, 264, 268, 272, 274, 348–349. France was implicated in the discussion as well; as early as 1889, a French observer had anticipated Monroe by lamenting the absence of any homage to poetry in the Paris exposition that year. See Francis B. Gummere, *Democracy and Poetry* (New York: Macmillan, 1901), 302–303.

9. Spiller et al., *Literary History,* 809; Monroe, *A Poet's Life,* 109.

10. "The Books of 1892," *Publishers' Weekly,* Jan. 28, 1893, 170; "Record of American Book Production," *Publishers' Weekly,* Jan. 27, 1912, 278; "The Slump in Poetry," 270; *Bookman Year-Book,* 1898, 153; "The Books of 1900," *Publishers' Weekly,* Jan. 26, 1901, 87; *The American Book Publishing Record, Cumulative, 1876–1949: An American National Bibliography* (New York: Bowker, 1980).

11. Volumes not clearly identifiable as poetry by author, title, subtitle, or publisher's indication were omitted from the total. Translations were in-

cluded. Small presses were distinguished from mainstream houses on the basis of their brief treatment in or absence altogether from John Tebbel, *A History of Book Publishing in the United States*, vol. II, *The Expansion of an Industry, 1865–1919* (New York: R. R. Bowker, 1975). *The American Book Publishing Record* contains seven additional Badger titles for 1905.

12. These data come from "The Weekly Record of New Publications," *Publishers' Weekly* 67 (Jan.-June 1905) and *Publishers' Weekly* 68 (July-Dec. 1905).

13. Charles A. Madison, *Book Publishing in America* (New York: McGraw-Hill, 1966), 263–267.

14. Ellen B. Ballou, *The Building of the House: Houghton Mifflin's Formative Years* (Boston: Houghton Mifflin, 1970), 141–142, 484, 486.

15. John Tebbel, *History of Book Publishing*, vol. II, 403.

16. Alfred Harcourt (editor at Holt) to Robert Frost, July 21, 1915, Box 39, Henry Holt Archives, Manuscripts Division, Department of Rare Books and Special Collections, Princeton University Library, Princeton, New Jersey, reprinted by permission of Henry Holt and Company, LLC; Charles A. Madison, *The Owl Among Colophons: Henry Holt as Publisher and Editor* (New York: Holt, Rinehart, Winston, 1966), 165.

17. Monroe, *A Poet's Life*, 88.

18. Hagedorn, *Robinson*, 112; Emery Neff, *Edwin Arlington Robinson* (New York: William Sloane, 1948), 65, 87.

19. Carlin T. Kindilien, *American Poetry in the Eighteen Nineties: A Study of American Verse, 1890–1899* (Providence: Brown University Press, 1956), 22; David Perkins, *A History of Modern Poetry: From the 1890s to the High Modernist Mode*, vol. I (Cambridge, Mass.: Harvard University Press, 1976), 101; Jessie Rittenhouse, *My House of Life* (Boston: Houghton Mifflin, 1934), 139–140; Paula Bennett, "A Sheaf of Poetry by Late Nineteenth-Century American Women," in Paul Lauter, ed., *The Heath Anthology of American Literature*, 3rd ed. (Boston: Houghton Mifflin, 1998), vol. II, 207–210; Paula Bennett, "Not Just Filler and Not Just Sentimental: Women's Poetry in American Victorian Periodicals, 1860–1900," in Kenneth M. Price and Susan Belasco Smith, eds., *Periodical Literature in Nineteenth-Century America* (Charlottesville: University of Virginia Press, 1995), 202–219; Paula Bernat Bennett, *Poets in the Public Sphere: The Emancipatory Project of American Women's Poetry, 1800–1900* (Princeton: Princeton University Press, 2003), 152–158.

20. Sandra Gilbert and Susan Gubar, *No Man's Land: The Place of the Woman Writer in the Twentieth Century*, vol. I: *The War of the Words* (New Haven: Yale University Press, 1988), 142–147; Cary Nelson, *Repression and Recovery: Modern American Poetry and the Politics of Cultural Recovery, 1910–1945* (Madison: University of Wisconsin Press, 1989); Bennett, *Poets in the Public Sphere;* Mary Loeffelholz, *From School to Salon: Reading Nineteenth-Century American Women's Poetry*

(Princeton: Princeton University Press, 2004); Robert H. Walker, *The Poet and the Gilded Age: Social Themes in Late Nineteenth-Century American Verse* (Philadelphia: University of Pennsylvania Press, 1963), 294.

21. "The Slump in Poetry," 270, 271.

22. Will Carleton, *Farm Legends* (New York: Harper, 1887), 9; Will Carleton, *City Festivals* (New York: Harper, 1893), viii.

23. George Steele Seymour, ed., *A Bookfellow Anthology* (Cedar Rapids, Iowa: Torch Press, 1925), n.p.

24. Meredith L. McGill, *American Literature and the Culture of Reprinting, 1834–1853* (Philadelphia: University of Pennsylvania Press, 2003); "The Books of 1896," *Publishers' Weekly,* Jan. 30, 1897, 210; "The Slump in Poetry," 265; Hall, *Cultures of Print,* 61; Ballou, *Building of the House,* 243, 309, 321; advertisement for "Houghton Mifflin Company's New Books," *Publishers' Weekly,* Jan. 26, 1901, 122. On the "Hiawatha" revival, see Alan Trachtenberg, *Shades of Hiawatha: Staging Indians, Making Americans, 1880–1930* (New York: Hill & Wang, 2004), 236–256.

25. "The Slump in Poetry," 267–268, 271.

26. Francis B. Gummere, *The Beginnings of Poetry* (New York: Macmillan, 1901), vii; Gummere, *Democracy and Poetry,* 304–305.

27. William Dean Howells, "The Editor's Easy Chair," *Harper's,* Mar. 1902, 674; William Dean Howells, "The Editor's Easy Chair," *Harper's,* Sept. 1901, 640–645.

4. Sophisticate and Innocent

1. R. L. Duffus, *The Waterbury Record: More Vermont Memories* (New York: Norton, 1959), 175, 176, 181, 185, 186, 187.

2. Henry Crew to Grace D. Hollowell, May 23, 1933, Folder 1-12281, Century of Progress International Exposition Records, Special Collections, Richard J. Daley Library, University of Illinois, Chicago; "Press Veterans of '93 Bridge a Gap of 40 Years," Chicago *Tribune,* Aug. 13, 1933, I, 5.

3. Perkins, *Modern Poetry,* vol. I, 296.

4. "Can You Name These Modern Poets?" *Ladies' Home Journal,* Mar. 1928, 22; Joseph Harrington, *Poetry and the Public: The Social Form of Modern U.S. Poetics* (Middletown, Conn.: Wesleyan University Press, 2002), 48; Robert E. Spiller et al., *Literary History of the United States: History,* 4th ed. rev. (New York: Macmillan, 1974), 1347.

5. Nancy Milford, *Savage Beauty: The Life of Edna St. Vincent Millay* (New York: Random House, 2001), 160, 385.

6. Edmund Wilson, *I Thought of Daisy* (New York: Farrar, Straus, and Young, 1953), 7–10.

7. Lewis A. Erenberg, *Steppin' Out: New York Nightlife and the Transformation of American Culture, 1890–1930* (Chicago: University of Chicago Press, 1984), 54.

8. Christine Stansell, *American Moderns: Bohemian New York and the Creation of a New Century* (New York: Metropolitan, 2000), 4; Wilson, *Daisy*, 128.

9. Milford, *Savage Beauty*, 94; Rittenhouse, *My House of Life*, 223.

10. Stansell, *American Moderns*, 164–165.

11. Max Eastman, *Enjoyment of Poetry* (New York: Scribner's, 1930), 15, 17, 90–92, 168–169, 188.

12. *Letters of Edna St. Vincent Millay*, ed. Allan Ross MacDougall (New York: Grosset & Dunlap, 1952), 76; Wilson, *Daisy*, 25; Milford, *Savage Beauty*, 47, 49, 329, 384.

13. Duffey, *Poetry in America*, 232; Elizabeth Atkins, *Edna St. Vincent Millay and Her Times* (Chicago: University of Chicago Press, 1936), 71; Erenberg, *Steppin' Out*, 219; Sandra Gilbert and Susan Gubar, *No Man's Land: The Place of the Woman Writer in the Twentieth Century* (New Haven: Yale University Press, 1988), 91.

14. "The Literary Spotlight XIV: Edna St. Vincent Millay," *Bookman*, Nov. 1922, 272; Milford, *Savage Beauty*, 288; Sarah Carlton, "Edna St. Vincent Millay," *American Girl*, Nov. 1930, 13.

15. An equally prominent "girl" poet was Hilda Conkling. On Crane, see Louis Untermeyer, *From Another World* (New York: Harcourt, Brace, 1939), 288–294; Nunnally Johnson, "Nathalia From Brooklyn," *American Mercury*, Sept. 1926, 52–59; Hughes Mearns, introduction to *Nathalia Crane* (New York: Simon and Schuster, 1926), 5; "The Muse in the Nursery," *Current Opinion*, July 1924, 51; "Nathalia Crane in Recital," *New York Times*, Dec. 21, 1925, 7.

16. "What Child Poet 'Loves,'" *New York Times*, May 4, 1924, IX, 2; "Child Poet Picks Big Words From Air," *New York Times*, Nov. 17, 1925, 11; James C. Young, "Child Poet Explains Her Lines 'Just Come,'" *New York Times*, Nov. 22, 1925, IX, 8.

17. Nathalia Crane, *The Janitor's Boy and Other Poems* (New York: Thomas Seltzer, 1924); "In Praise of Fairies, Elfins, and a Red-Haired Boy," *New York Times*, June 8, 1924, III, 6.

18. Harriet Monroe, "Edna St. Vincent Millay," *Poetry*, Aug. 1924, 266; Milford, *Savage Beauty*, 332, 384. On the "titaness," see Ann Douglas, *Terrible Honesty: Mongrel Manhattan in the 1920s* (New York: Farrar, Straus, and Giroux, 1995), 240–243.

19. Gilbert and Gubar, *No Man's Land*, 77; Milford, *Savage Beauty*, 80, 144, 321.

20. Robert L. Gale, "Guest, Edgar Albert," *American National Biography*, vol. 9 (New York: Oxford University Press, 1999), 698–699; Joe Grimm, "Edgar A. Guest: The People's Poet," *www.freep.com/jobspage/club/guest.htm;* "Guest, Edgar A(lbert), *Current Biography* 1941 (New York: H. W. Wilson, 1941), 354–356; Royce Howes, *Edgar A. Guest: A Biography* (Chicago: Reilly & Lee, 1953).

21. Advertisements for Reilly & Britton, *Publishers' Weekly,* Sept. 23, 1916, 943 and Sept. 30, 1916, 1099; John Bakeless, "Laureate of the Obvious," *Outlook and Independent,* Aug. 6, 1930, 528; "American Poet Tours America," *Publishers' Weekly,* May 14, 1921, 1418.

22. Edgar A. Guest, *Harbor Lights of Home* (Chicago: Reilly & Lee, 1928), 54, 75, 97; Edgar A. Guest, *The Light of Faith* (Chicago: Reilly & Lee, 1926), 73; Edgar A. Guest, *A Heap O' Livin'* (Chicago: Reilly & Lee, 1916), 28.

23. Mrs. W. E. Adams, Ringling, Mont., to Edgar A. Guest, Thanksgiving Day, 1924, folder 1924, Edgar A. Guest Papers, Burton Historical Collection, Detroit Public Library, Detroit, Michigan.

24. Bakeless, "Laureate," 527, 529; Eugenia Hughes Papers, 1926, Box 6, folder 1, Manuscripts and Archives Division, The New York Public Library, Astor, Lenox, and Tilden Foundations, New York City.

25. Howes, *Edgar Guest,* 80.

26. Charles Johanningsmeier, *Fiction and the American Literary Marketplace: The Role of Newspaper Syndicates, 1860–1900* (Cambridge: Cambridge University Press, 1977), 23–24; Elizabeth J. Van Allen, *James Whitcomb Riley: A Life* (Bloomington: Indiana Univ. Press, 1999), 168; Howes, *Edgar Guest,* 78, 127.

27. Harriet Monroe, "Newspaper Verse," *Poetry,* Mar. 1922, 325, 327; "Guest Day," *Time,* Feb. 24, 1936, 51.

28. Howes, *Edgar A. Guest,* 210, 222; Guest, Edgar A(lbert), *Current Biography,* 354; "Guest of Detroit is Guest of Philadelphia," *Publishers' Weekly,* Mar. 19, 1919, 898; "American Poet Tours America," *Publishers' Weekly,* May 14, 1921, 1418.

29. Guest, *Harbor Lights,* 151; Carroll Smith-Rosenberg, "The Female World of Love and Ritual: Relations between Women in Nineteenth Century America," *Signs* 1:1 (1975), 1–29; Albert Kennedy Rowswell to Edgar A. Guest, Nov. 27, 1940, folder 1940 J-R, Edgar A. Guest Papers; George Matthew Adams to Edgar A. Guest, folder 1929 A-C, Edgar A. Guest Papers, Dec. 27, 1929.

30. "News Notes," *Poetry,* May 1926, 117; E. V. Baugh to Edgar A. Guest, Dec. 31, 1928, folder 1928 A-L, Edgar A. Guest Papers.

31. Louis Untermeyer, "Poetry and the Common Man," *Rotarian,* Apr. 1935, 14.

32. Edwin Markham, ed., *The Book of Poetry* (New York: W. H. Wise, 1926).

33. Flora Neil Davidson Diary, 1921, Box 1, Flora Neil Davidson Papers, Wisconsin Historical Society, Madison, Wisconsin.

5. Celebrity and Cipher

1. On the *Tristram* event, see Edwin Arlington Robinson File, Macmillan Company Records, Manuscripts and Archives Division, The New York

Public Library, Astor, Lenox and Tilden Foundations, New York City; Carl Van Doren, *Three Worlds* (New York: Harper, 1936), 202–207, and Emery Neff, *Edwin Arlington Robinson* (New York: William Sloane, 1948), 226–228. The Scribner's figure is from the card files, Archives of Charles Scribner's Sons, Department of Rare Books and Special Collections, Princeton University Library, Princeton, New Jersey.

2. Fanny Butcher, "You Can Never Sell Poetry," *Publishers' Weekly,* Sept. 27, 1924, 1152–1153; William Stanley Braithwaite to Elizabeth Hollister Frost, Feb. 18, 1929, Box 1, Elizabeth Hollister Frost Papers, Rare Books and Special Collections, University of Rochester Libraries, Rochester, New York.

3. "Book Titles Published by Classes in the United States, 1880–1927," *Publishers' Weekly,* Jan. 19, 1929, 278–279; "American Book Production, 1940," *Publishers' Weekly,* Jan. 18, 1941, 225; John Hall Wheelock to Mrs. C. R. Murphy, Box 4, July 24, 1936, Perkins-Wheelock General Files, Scribner's Archive.

4. Louis Untermeyer, *Modern American Poetry,* 6th rev. ed. (New York: Harcourt, Brace, 1942), 13; David Perkins, *A History of Modern Poetry: From the 1890s to the High Modernist Mode,* vol. I (Cambridge, Mass.: Harvard University Press, 1976), 320; Mark W. Van Wienen, *Partisans and Poets: The Political Work of American Poetry in the Great War* (Cambridge: Cambridge University Press, 1997).

5. Joseph Harrington, *Poetry and the Public: The Social Form of Modern U.S. Poetics* (Middletown, Conn.: Wesleyan University Press, 2002), 190; Gladys Hasty Carroll, *To Remember Forever: The Journal of a College Girl, 1922–23* (Boston: Little, Brown, 1923), 5–7.

6. Marion E. Dodd, "The College World and Poetry," *Publishers' Weekly,* Mar. 7, 1931, 1146.

7. Edward N. Teall, *Books and Folks* (New York: G. P. Putnam's, 1921), 208; "The Selling of Poetry," *Publishers' Weekly,* May 17, 1924, 1584; Harrington, *Poetry and the Public,* 49.

8. Roger Burlingame, *Of Making Many Books: A Hundred Years of Reading, Writing, and Publishing* (New York: Scribner's, 1946), 248; "Who Publishes Poetry?" *Publishers' Weekly,* Nov. 26, 1932, 2034; John Hall Wheelock to Mrs. John D. Leitch, May 10, 1937, Box 4, Perkins-Wheelock General Files, Scribner's Archive; John Hall Wheelock to Mrs. C. R. Murphy, July 24, 1936, Box 4, Perkins-Wheelock General Files, Scribner's Archive.

9. Perkins, *Modern Poetry,* 321–322; "Personal Notes," *Publishers' Weekly,* May 12, 1914, 1886; Elizabeth McHenry, *Forgotten Readers: Recovering the Lost History of African American Literary Societies* (Durham, N.C.: Duke University Press, 2002), 251–269; Louis Untermeyer, *From Another World* (New York: Harcourt, Brace, 1939), 219; Burton Rascoe, *A Book-*

man's Daybook (New York: Liveright, 1929), 234; Constance Babington Smith, *John Masefield: A Life* (Oxford: Oxford University Press, 1978), 142, 208.

10. Harrington, *Poetry and the Public,* 28; Amy Schwartz Oppenheim diary, Feb. 5, 1936 and April 25, 1932, Amy Schwartz Oppenheim Papers, Box 9, Manuscripts and Archives Division, The New York Public Library, Astor, Lenox and Tilden Foundations, New York City; "Who Are America's Literary Stars?" *Publishers' Weekly,* July 29, 1922, 411.

11. Burlingame, *Many Books,* 270; Percy Boynton, *A History of American Literature* (Boston: Ginn, 1919), 453.

12. Butcher, "You Can Never Sell Poetry," 1155; Lulu S. Teeter, "Do You Sell Poetry?" *Publishers' Weekly,* Sept. 27, 1924, 1155–1156.

13. George Brett, Jr., to John G. Neihardt, Aug. 27, 1925, Box 101, Macmillan Co. Records.

14. M. Lincoln Schuster to Edwin Arlington Robinson, June 19, 1926, Box 108, Macmillan Co. Records.

15. Maxwell Perkins to Louise Bogan, Dec. 4, 1928, Box 16, Scribner's author files (Bogan), Scribner's Archive; John Hall Wheelock to Louise Bogan, Dec. 6, 1928, Box 16, Scribner's author files (Bogan), Scribner's Archive; John Hall Wheelock to Louise Bogan, Dec. 10, 1928, Box 16, Scribner's author files (Bogan), Scribner's Archive; John Hall Wheelock to Louise Bogan, Sept. 11, 1935, Box 16, Scribner's author files (Bogan), Scribner's Archive.

16. "Merchandising Poetry," *Publishers' Weekly,* July 4, 1936, 24.

17. George Brett, Jr., to John Neihardt, Aug. 27, 1925, Box 101, Macmillan Co. Records; Edgar Lee Masters to George Brett, Jr., Feb. 23, 1916, Box 93, Macmillan Co. Records; George Brett, Jr., to Edgar Lee Masters, Feb. 25, 1916, Box 93, Macmillan Co. Records; George Brett, Jr., memo, June 28, 1926, Box 108, Macmillan Co. Records.

18. Amy Lowell to George Brett, Jr., Dec. 11, 1916 and Jan. 20, 1917, Box 89, Macmillan Co. Papers; Richard Benvenuto, *Amy Lowell* (Boston: Twayne, 1985), 16; S. Foster Damon, *Amy Lowell: A Chronicle* (Boston: Houghton Mifflin, 1935), 547; Edgar Lee Masters to George Brett, Aug. 9, 1920, July 20, 1928, and May 1, 1931, Box 93, Macmillan Co. Records (quoted by permission of Hilary Masters); Ernest Filsinger to Harold Latham, June 26, 1928, Box 115, Macmillan Co. Records; Louise Bogan to John Hall Wheelock, May 1, 1944, Box 16, Scribner's author files (Bogan), Scribner's Archive; Edmund Wilson to John Hall Wheelock, Dec. 1, 1947, Box 13, Scribner's author files (Bishop), Scribner's Archive; John Peale Bishop to Maxwell Perkins, May 28, 1940, Box 13, Scribner's author files (Bishop), Scribner's Archive.

19. Harold Latham to John Neihardt, Aug. 31, 1942, Box 101, Macmillan Co. Records; John Neihardt to Harold Latham, Sept. 18, 1942, Box 101,

Macmillan Co. Records (quoted by permission of Coralie J. Hughes, Trustee, John G. Neihardt Trust).

20. Ransom is cited in Harrington, *Poetry and the Public,* 39; Thomas Strychacz, *Modernism, Mass Culture, and Professionalism* (Cambridge: Cambridge University Press, 1997), 28–29.

21. Catherine Turner, *Marketing Modernism Between the Two World Wars* (Amherst: University of Massachusetts Press, 2003), 141 and passim; John Hall Wheelock to Jean Starr Untermeyer, July 3, 1936, Box 2, Perkins-Wheelock General Files, Scribner's Archive; jacket copy, Box 4, Perkins-Wheelock General Files, Scribner's Archive; John Hall Wheelock to Mrs. Clinch Calkins, Nov. 16, 1937, Box 16, Scribner's author files (Bogan), Scribner's Archive.

6. *Alien and Intimate*

1. John Ciardi, "A Close Look at the Unicorn," in *Dialogue with an Audience* (Philadelphia: J. B. Lippincott, 1963), 74–79. I have written at length about the Ciardi-Lindbergh controversy in "The Genteel Tradition at Large," *Raritan,* Winter 2006, 70–91.

2. Norman Cousins, "John Ciardi and the Readers," in Ciardi, *Dialogue,* 84; "Letters to the Editor," in Ciardi, *Dialogue,* 79; John Ciardi, "The Reviewer's Duty to Damn," in Ciardi, *Dialogue,* 90–92; Lord Dunsany, "The Poets Fail in their Duty," in Ciardi, *Dialogue,* 130.

3. Stanton A. Coblentz, *My Life in Poetry* (New York: Bookman Associates, 1959) 48; Charles H. Compton, *Who Reads What? Essays on the Readers of Mark Twain, Hardy, Sandburg, Shaw, William James, the Greek Classics* (New York: H. W. Wilson, 1934), 61–62.

4. Babette Deutsch, *This Modern Poetry* (New York: W. W. Norton, 1935), 25–26.

5. William Aspinwall Bradley, "The New Poetry," *Bookman,* Oct. 1914, 202–203.

6. Louis MacNeice, "Eliot and the Adolescent," in *T. S. Eliot: A Symposium,* ed. Richard March (Chicago: H. Regnery, 1949), 147–150.

7. Harriet Monroe and Alice Corbin Henderson, eds., *The New Poetry: An Anthology of Twentieth-Century Verse in English* (New York: Macmillan, 1923), vi.

8. Marguerite Wilkinson, *New Voices: An Introduction to Contemporary Poetry* (New York: Macmillan, 1919), 7, 9, 122; rev. ed. (1928), 459.

9. On Untermeyer's life, see his memoirs *From Another World* (New York: Harcourt, Brace, 1939) and *Bygones: The Recollections of Louis Untermeyer* (New York: Harcourt, Brace, 1965); Untermeyer, *From Another World,* 26.

10. Untermeyer, *Bygones,* 60.

11. Craig S. Abbott, "Untermeyer on Eliot," *Journal of Modern Literature* 15:1 (Summer 1988), 105–106.

12. Louis Untermeyer, *Modern American Poetry,* 1st ed. (New York: Harcourt, Brace, 1919), 60–63; Louis Untermeyer, *Modern American Poetry: A Critical Anthology,* 6th rev. ed. (New York: Harcourt, Brace, 1942), vi, 31.

13. Louis Untermeyer, "Disillusion as Dogma," *Freeman* 17 (Jan. 1923), 453; Abbott, "Untermeyer on Eliot," 112; Edmund Wilson, "The Critic as Politician," *New Republic,* Dec. 2, 1925, 42–43; Louise Bogan to John Hall Wheelock, Nov. 8, 1935 and Mar. 21, 1936, Box 16, Scribner's author files (Bogan), Scribner's Archive.

14. Carl and Mark Van Doren, *American and British Literature Since 1890* (New York: Century, 1925), 19–20.

15. Dana Gioia, "Longfellow in the Aftermath of Modernism," in Jay Parini, ed., *The Columbia History of American Poetry* (New York: Columbia University Press, 1993), 79; T. S. Eliot, "The Metaphysical Poets" (1921) in *Selected Prose of T. S. Eliot* (New York: Harcourt, Brace, Jovanovich, 1975), 65; Harold Kastner to Carl Sandburg, Oct. 10, 1942, Box 348, Carl Sandburg Papers, University of Illinois Library, Urbana-Champaign, Illinois.

16. Deutsch, *This Modern Poetry,* 26.

17. Robert Hillyer, "Poetry's New Priesthood," *Saturday Review of Literature,* June 18, 1949, 8; Beth Bishop, "Letters to the Editor," *Saturday Review of Literature,* July 16, 1949, 22.

18. Randall Jarrell, "The Obscurity of the Poet" (1950), *Poetry and the Age* (New York: Knopf, 1953), 7–9.

19. Ibid., 12–13; Wyndham Lewis, "Early London Environment," in *T. S. Eliot: A Symposium,* 24; Harold Kastner to Carl Sandburg, Oct. 10, 1942, Box 348, Carl Sandburg Papers.

7. Listen, My Children

1. John T. Morse, Jr., *Life and Letters of Oliver Wendell Holmes,* vol. 2 (Boston: Houghton Mifflin, 1896), 130. I am grateful to Ellen Gruber Garvey for this reference.

2. Arthur H. R. Fairchild, *The Teaching of Poetry in the High School* (Boston: Houghton Mifflin, 1914), 84–85; Hughes Mearns, *Creative Youth* (Garden City, N.Y.: Doubleday, Doran, 1925), 118–119; Donald E. Stahl, *A History of the English Curriculum in American High Schools* (Chicago: The Lyceum Press, 1965), 14–15, 88–89; Howard Francis Seely, *Enjoying Poetry in School* (Richmond, Va.: Johnson, 1931), 208–209; Clarence Poe, *My First Eighty Years* (Chapel Hill: University of North Carolina Press, 1963), 17–18. For purposes of this discussion, I have separated Shakespearean drama—a standard feature of the high school curriculum—from the category of "poetry."

3. Ruth Miller Elson, *Guardians of Tradition: American Schoolbooks of the*

Nineteenth Century (Lincoln: University of Nebraska Press, 1964), 211–242; Stahl, *History of the English Curriculum,* 88.

4. W. H. Lambert, *Memory Gems: Graded Selections in Prose and Verse for the Use of Schools* (Boston: Ginn, Heath, 1883); Herbert M. Kliebard, *Forging the American Curriculum* (New York: Routledge, 1992), 8–9. On the commonplace book, see, for example, Mary Thomas Crane, *Framing Authority: Sayings, Self, and Society in Sixteenth-Century England* (Princeton: Princeton University Press, 1993).

5. Barbara Sicherman, "Reading and Middle-Class Identity in Victorian America: Cultural Consumption, Conspicuous and Otherwise," unpublished paper in my possession; Lawrence Levine, *Highbrow/Lowbrow: The Emergence of Cultural Hierarchy in the United States* (Cambridge, Mass.: Harvard University Press, 1989), 177; T. J. Jackson Lears, *Fables of Abundance: A Cultural History of Advertising in America* (New York: Basic Books, 1994).

6. W. H. Williams, *Memory Gems for School and Home* (New York: A. S. Barnes, 1907), v–vii; Raymond Williams, *Culture and Society, 1780–1950* (New York: Harper, 1958), 34–38.

7. Lawrence Buell, *New England Literary Culture: From Revolution Through Renaissance* (Cambridge: Cambridge University Press, 1989), 108.

8. Henry Wadsworth Longfellow, *Evangeline,* in *Favorite Poems of Henry Wadsworth Longfellow,* ed. Henry Seidel Canby (Garden City, N.Y.: Doubleday, 1947), 316, 333, 359; Dana Gioia, "Longfellow in the Aftermath of Modernism," in Jay Parini, ed., *The Columbia History of American Poetry* (New York: Columbia University Press, 1993), 87.

9. Henry Wadsworth Longfellow, "The Courtship of Miles Standish," in *Favorite Poems,* 17; Henry Wadsworth Longfellow, "A Psalm of Life," in *Favorite Poems,* 302–303; Buell, *New England Literary Culture,* 116.

10. Oliver Wendell Holmes, "The Chambered Nautilus," in *Through Magic Casements,* ed. George S. Carhart and Paul A. McGhee (New York: Macmillan, 1926), 182; James Russell Lowell, "The Vision of Sir Launfal," in *Through Magic Casements,* 378; John Greenleaf Whittier, "Snow-Bound," in *Through Magic Casements,* 267, 270.

11. Leigh Hunt, "Abou Ben Adhem," in *Through Magic Casements,* 235; William Ernest Henley, "Invictus," in *Through Magic Casements,* 461; Sir Walter Scott, "Lochinvar," in *Through Magic Casements,* 67.

12. Gioia, "Longfellow," 78; Lambert, *Memory Gems,* iii; F. T. Oldt, *Memory Gems Graded for Use in School* (Lanark, Ill.: Gazette Steam Printing House, 1891), 2; Nan Johnson, "The Popularization of Nineteenth-Century Rhetoric: Elocution and the Private Learner," in *Oratorical Culture in Nineteenth-Century America: Transformations in the Theory and Practice of Rhetoric,* ed. Gregory Clark and S. Michael Halloran (Carbondale: Southern Illinois University Press, 1993), 157.

13. Anne M. Boylan, *Sunday School* (New Haven: Yale University Press, 1988), 44; Hoxie Neale Fairchild, *Religious Trends in English Poetry* (New York: Columbia University Press, 1949, 1957), vol. III, 3–18, 504; vol. IV, 3–17, 61–167; Charles A. McMurray, *Special Method in the Reading of Complete English Classics in the Grades of the Common School* (Bloomington, Ill.: Public-School Publishing Company, 1899), 55–56.

14. Henry Wadsworth Longfellow, "The Day is Done," in *Through Magic Casements*, 227; Gioia, "Longfellow," 87; William Wordsworth, "I Wandered Lonely as a Cloud," in *Through Magic Casements*, 89; Ralph Waldo Emerson, "The Snow-Storm," in *Collected Poems and Translations*, ed. Harold Bloom and Paul Kane (New York: Library of America, 1994), 34.

15. Noah Porter, *Books and Reading, or What Books Shall I Read and How Shall I Read Them?* (New York: Scribner's, 1871), 247, 258; W. H. Williams, *Memory Gems for School and Home*, vi; Will P. Hart, *Memory Gems of Poetry and Prose* (Indianapolis: The Normal Publishing House, 1899), 5; Wilbur Cross, *Connecticut Yankee: An Autobiography* (New Haven: Yale University Press, 1943), 90.

16. Hart, *Memory Gems of Poetry and Prose*, 9; L. C. Foster and Sherman Williams, *Selections for Memorizing* (Boston: Ginn, 1892), iv; William E. Woodward, *The Gift of Life* (New York: Dutton, 1947), 91.

17. Harris is quoted in Herbert M. Kliebard, *The Struggle for the American Curriculum, 1893–1958* (Boston: Routledge & Kegan Paul, 1986), 37. Matthew Arnold, "The Study of Poetry," *Essays in Criticism*, 2nd ser. (New York: Macmillan, 1924), 7.

18. Elson, *Guardians*, 226–227.

19. In the Library of Congress the latest use of the phrase as a title is 1924, but it is the only example from that decade. Arthur H. R. Fairchild, *Teaching of Poetry*, 92. The courses of study cited are organized alphabetically by place in Special Collections, The Gottesman Libraries, Teachers College, Columbia University, New York City.

20. Mearns, *Creative Youth*, 124.

21. I have discussed those anxieties in *The Making of Middlebrow Culture* (Chapel Hill: University of North Carolina Press, 1992).

22. On copyright constraints, see "Course of Study in English for Rochester Senior High Schools," vol. II, Literature, Rochester, N.Y., 1929, 219.

23. Charles and Frank McMurray, *The Method of the Recitation* (New York: Macmillan, 1921), 329–332.

24. Edwin Greenlaw and Dudley Miles, *Literature and Life, Book Four* (Chicago: Scott Foresman, 1932), 743–776.

25. Claudia Goldin, "America's Graduation From High School: The Evolution and Spread of Secondary Schooling in the Twentieth Century," *Journal of Economic History* 58:2 (June 1998), 345–374; James Bryant Conant, *The American High School Today* (New York: McGraw-Hill,

1959), 6–8; Lawrence A. Cremin, *American Education: The Metropolitan Experience, 1876–1980* (New York: Harper & Row, 1988), 212–242; Henry Suzallo, introduction to Arthur H. R. Fairchild, *The Teaching of Poetry*, viii; Arthur H. R. Fairchild, *The Teaching of Poetry*, 163.

26. Kliebard, *Struggle*, 18–20, 34, 44–49, 67–68; Angela Sorby, *Schoolroom Poets: Childhood, Performance, and the Place of American Poetry, 1865–1917* (Lebanon, N.H.: University of New Hampshire Press, 2005), 5–8; Sam C. Stephenson, *Poems and Stories Required by the Elementary Schools of Nebraska* (Lincoln: Lincoln School Supply Co., 1925), 43.

27. Kliebard, *Struggle*, 67, 69–122, 162; Robert B. Westbrook, *John Dewey and American Democracy* (Ithaca: Cornell University Press, 1992).

28. Arthur H. R. Fairchild, *The Teaching of Poetry*, 12, 101, 127, 135–137, 164; Charles Swain Thomas, *The Teaching of English in the Secondary School* (Boston: Houghton Mifflin, 1927), 28–32, 224.

29. Lee Emerson Bassett, *Handbook of Oral Reading* (Boston: Houghton Mifflin, 1917), 4, 114. See also Wayland Maxfield Parrish, *Reading Aloud: A Technique in the Interpretation of Literature* (New York: Thomas Nelson and Sons, 1933), and H. H. Fuller and Andrew Thomas Weaver, *How to Read Aloud: A Guide to Interpretive Reading* (New York: Silver, Burdett, 1935).

30. James Fleming Hosic, comp., *Reorganization of English in Secondary Schools* (Washington: Government Printing Office, 1917), 32, 63–65, 97.

31. Seely, *Enjoying Poetry*, viii; "Course of Study in Literature for Junior High School," Minneapolis, 1931.

32. Sterling Andrus Leonard, *Essential Principles of Teaching Reading and Literature* (Philadelphia: J. B. Lippincott, 1922), 5, 49; Paul McKee, *Reading and Literature in the Elementary School* (Boston: Houghton Mifflin, 1934), 475. Abbott is quoted in Blanche E. Weekes, *The Influence of Meaning on Children's Choices of Poetry* (New York: Teachers College, 1929), 4. See also John Hooper, *Poetry in the New Curriculum* (Brattleboro, Vt.: Stephen Daye Press, 1932).

33. Leonard, *Essential Principles*, 56, 201–212, 226; Seely, *Enjoying Poetry*, 65, 91, 145; McKee, *Reading and Literature*, 548.

34. Leonard, *Essential Principles*, 201–202; Hooper, *New Curriculum*, 38, 79.

35. Mearns, *Creative Youth*, 19; Weekes, *Influence of Meaning*, 6; "Course of Study for Senior High Schools, English, Grades 10, 11, 12," 1927, 161.

36. May Sarton, *I Knew a Phoenix: Sketches for an Autobiography* (New York: Norton, 1959), 111–113.

37. Leonard, *Essential Principles*, 125, 248; Seely, *Enjoying Poetry*, 41, 214; Mearns, *Creative Youth*, 108. Mearns's title also alluded to Edward Yeomans, *Shackled Youth: Comments on Schools, School People, and Other People* (Boston: Atlantic Monthly Press, 1921).

38. National Council of Teachers of English, *An Experience Curriculum in English* (New York: D. Appleton-Century, 1935), 20, 22, 55–59; "Courses of Study for High Schools, Part II, English" (1921), State of Kansas, 1927, 14; "Course of Study in English for Junior High Schools," Berkeley, 1939, 66–67; "Course of Study in English for Grades I–VI," Kansas City, 1932, 36; "Course of Study," Rochester, 210; "Design Bulletin, Junior and Senior High School English," Montgomery County, Md., Sept. 1939, 1; "A Brief Guide to Teaching English in the Secondary School," Florida State Department of Education, 1946, 41.

39. John Erskine, *The Kinds of Poetry* (Indianapolis: Bobbs-Merrill, 1920), 64.

40. Seely, *Enjoying Poetry,* 113, 137; Mearns, *Creative Youth,* 28, 128; Cary Nelson, *Repression and Recovery: Modern American Poetry and the Politics of Cultural Recovery, 1910–1945* (Madison: University of Wisconsin Press, 1989).

41. Elizabeth E. Keppie, *The Teaching of Choric Speech* (Boston: Expression Co., 1939), 11.

42. Cecile de Banke, *The Art of Choral Speaking* (Boston: Baker's Plays, 1937), 11.

43. Marjorie Gullan, *Choral Reading* (New York: Harper, 1937), 211; Keppie, *Teaching of Choric Speech,* 28; de Banke, *Art of Choral Speaking,* 70. In its attention to immigrants' speech (as well as in its implied concern with professionalization), the speaking choir movement perpetuated some of the developments within the practice of elocution at the turn of the century that widened the space for the career of the African-American poet Frances E. W. Harper and her elocutionist daughter, Mary E. Harper. The speaking choir proponents placed less value, however, on the naturalness and spontaneity that, as Mary Loeffelholz has observed, their predecessors attributed to African-Americans. See Loeffelholz, *From School to Salon: Reading Nineteenth-Century American Women's Poetry* (Princeton: Princeton University Press, 2004), 124–127.

44. Keppie, *Teaching of Choric Speech,* 13, 92.

45. Bonaro Wilkinson, *The Poetic Way of Release* (New York: Knopf, 1931), 17, 51, 70–76, 112.

46. H. A. Overstreet, *A Guide to Civilized Leisure* (New York: Norton, 1934), 48–50.

47. Cecile de Banke, "Notes on the Verse-Speaking Choir," in *Practical Methods in Choral Speaking,* ed. Marguerite E. DeWitt (Boston: Expression Co., 1936), 71; Marguerite E. DeWitt, "Shall We Recite As Groups?" in DeWitt, *Practical Methods,* 62; de Banke, *Art of Choral Speaking,* 27.

48. de Banke, *Art of Choral Speaking,* 26; Virginia Sanderson, "Choirs That Speak," in DeWitt, *Practical Methods,* 119.

49. Keppie, *Teaching of Choric Speech,* 16, 37; de Banke, *Art of Choral*

Speaking, 128, 130; Marion Parsons Robinson and Rozetta Lura Thurston, *Poetry for Men to Speak Chorally* (Boston: Expression Co., 1939), 10, 31; Dorothy Kaucher, "The Verse-Speaking Choir," in DeWitt, *Practical Methods,* 147; Marjorie E. Burdsall, "Choral Speech in the English Class," in DeWitt, *Practical Methods,* 181; Helen Gertrude Hicks, *The Reading Chorus* (New York: Noble and Noble, 1939), 7; G. F. Reynolds, "Concerted Reading," in DeWitt, *Practical Methods,* 167.

50. Gullan, *Choral Reading,* 241–242; Hicks, *Reading Chorus,* 7; Kaucher, "The Verse-Speaking Choir," 150–151.

51. Kaucher, "The Verse-Speaking Choir," 147; Gullan, *Choral Reading,* 29; de Banke, "Notes on the Verse-Speaking Choir," 71.

52. Milton Allen Kaplan, *Radio and Poetry* (New York: Columbia University Press, 1949), 119, 240.

53. The sample resulted from my "Author's Query" that appeared in the *New York Times Book Review* on April 16, 1995. Eliot is quoted in Allys Dwyer Vergara, *A Critical Study of a Group of College Women's Responses to Poetry* (New York: Teachers College, Columbia University, 1946), 2.

54. Bettie L. Snyder, Sharon, Conn., Apr. 19, 1995. All of the responses to the query are in my possession. An earlier summary of this material appeared in my essay "'They Flash Upon That Inward Eye': Poetry Recitation and American Readers," *Proceedings of the American Antiquarian Society* 106: Part 2 (1997), 273–300, and was reprinted in Barbara Ryan and Amy M. Thomas, eds., *Reading Acts: U.S. Readers' Interactions with Literature, 1800–1950* (Knoxville: University of Tennessee Press, 2002), 259–80. I am grateful to the informants from whose letters I quote directly for their permission to do so.

55. Doris K. Goga, Mayfield Village, Ohio, Apr. 30, 1995; Edward J. Brennan, Copake, N.Y., May 14, 1995.

56. Richard Phelan, McGregor, Tex., May 30, 1995; Jane E. Lewin, Bethesda, Md., May 25, 1995; Arlynn Nellhaus, Jerusalem, Israel, June 22, 1995.

57. Victor Nell, *Lost in a Book: The Psychology of Reading for Pleasure* (New Haven: Yale University Press, 1988), 5.

58. L. Barry Barrington, Arlington Heights, Ill., Apr. 17, 1995; Robert Stark, Cranberry, N.Y., Apr. 20, 1995; Betty Hurwich Zoss, E. Falmouth, Mass., July 24, 1995.

59. Joan C. Browning, Ronceverte, W.Va., Apr. 19, 1995; Edith Spilka, Westport, Conn., Apr. 19, 1995; Gilda Sferra, Long Beach, N.Y., Apr. 17, 1995; John David Burton, Red Bank, N.J., June 6, 1995.

60. Isabel Bliss, Chelsea, Mich., Apr. 26, 1995; M. Maxine Garner, Liberty, N.C., Apr. 16, 1995; Helen H. Baker, West Milford, N.J., May 15, 1995; Henry Exall, Jr., Dallas, Tex., Apr. 18, 1995; Joan Flint, Tulsa, Okla., May 16, 1995; John J. Goodwin, Bedford, N.Y., Apr. 19, 1995.

61. Ruth Limmer, New York, N.Y., Apr. 18, 1995; Martin Goldstein, Teaneck, N.J., June 20, 1995; Dorothy Helfeld, San Francisco, Calif., May 13, 1995; Patricia M. Fort, DeLand, Fla., Apr. 17, 1995; Julius LaRosa, suburban New York City, Apr. 18, 1995.

62. Robert Finley, New York, N.Y., Apr. 18, 1995; Elizabeth Bosland, Glen Rock, N.Y., June 10, 1995.

63. Richard H. Freeman, Washington, D.C., Apr. 17, 1995; Edith D. Weber, Augusta, Maine, May 14, 1995.

64. Harold C. Cannon, Greenfield Center, N.Y., Apr. 22, 1995; John A. Nelson, Saratoga Springs, N.Y., Apr. 17, 1995.

65. Frederica Fox Winter, Rockville, Md., Apr. 16, 1995.

66. For example, Joan D. Ensor, West Redding, Conn., May 2, 1995.

67. Solita Sheehan, Brooklyn, N.Y., Apr. 20, 1995; Howell D. Boyd, San Antonio, Tex., June 15, 1995; Alice Nichols, Damariscotta, Maine, Apr. 25, 1995; Enid Pensack, Trenton, N.J., Apr. 21, 1995; Howard Goldberger, Katonah, N.Y., Apr. 16, 1995; Robert L. Bancroft, Amherst, Mass., Apr. 19, 1995; James C. Lee, Chattanooga, Tenn., Apr. 24, 1995.

68. Mary Ann Shubert, Selkirk, N.Y., Apr. 21, 1995; Joan Fillmore Hooker, Brooklyn, N.Y., Apr. 15, 1995; Helen Winters, Naples, Fla., Apr. 13, 1995; Margaret P. Gurler, Plymouth, Minn., June 14, 1995.

69. J. Lawrence Pool, West Cornwall, Conn., Apr. 21, 1995; A. G. Medlicott, Jr., Haverhill, N.H., Apr. 22, 1995; Frances D. Rothman, Philadelphia, Pa., Apr. 17, 1995.

70. Anna T. Lelbach, Maplewood, N.J., May 4, 1995; Marcy S. Powell, Oxford, Ohio, Apr. 18, 1995.

71. Alma R. Price, Shawnee Mission, Kans., Apr. 25, 1995.

72. Mrs. Sanford W. Weiss, New Orleans, La., Apr. 23, 1995.

73. Mary Louise Cuneo, Bridgeport, Conn., Apr. 18, 1995.

74. Nelda Brehm, South Hadley, Mass., May 5, 1995.

75. Jane E. Lewin, Bethesda, Md., May 25, 1995.

76. Roy R. Burns, Nashville, Tenn., July 13, 1995

77. Thomas E. Norton, Kennebunkport, Maine, Oct. 14, 1995.

78. Poe, *My First Eighty Years*, 16; Stephen J. Kudless, Staten Island, N.Y., Apr. 17, 1995; Mary Bingham, Los Alamos, N.Mex., May, 1995.

79. William R. Woods, Ben Avon, Pa., Apr. 25, 1995; Eugene W. McArdle, St. Charles, Ill., Apr. 14, 1995; Joan D. Ensor, West Redding, Conn., May 2, 1995.

80. Margery Meyer, Stamford, Conn., Apr. 20, 1995; Mary Margaret Sloan, San Francisco, Calif.; Apr. 16, 1995; Isabelle N. Woodrow, Jamesburg, N.J., Apr. 26, 1995; James J. McElroy, Farmington, Mich., Apr. 24, 1995.

81. Helen B. Neuhaus, Upper Montclair, N.J., Apr. 22, 1995; Hava Rogot, Bethesda, Md., Apr. 28, 1995; Nancy McNulty, Leeds, Mass., Apr. 23, 1995; Rita B. Kushner, Oakdale, N.Y., Apr. 28, 1995; Olivene S. Longino,

Kansas City, Mo., May 21, 1995; Earle A. Taylor, Portland, Ore., May 19, 1995; Allan Schindle, Macomb, Ill., June 27, 1995; Grace M. Wallace, Memphis, Tenn., Apr. 19, 1995; Beverly Marzuk, New York, N.Y., June 19, 1995.

82. Roger Chartier, *The Order of Books* (Palo Alto: Stanford University Press, 1992), 16; Florence Dober, Forest Hills, N.Y., Apr. 24, 1995; Nancy Jane B. Cheffey, Deckerville, Mich., Apr. 17, 1995; Jacob Korg, Seattle, Wash., Apr. 18, 1995.

83. Allyn Leidig, White Plains, N.Y., Apr. 27, 1995; Esther B. Sundel, San Diego, Calif., Apr. 17, 1995; Reva Brown, New York, N.Y., Apr. 27, 1995; Richard W. Hudgens, St. Louis, Mo., Apr. 16, 1995; Norma Marder, Champaign, Ill., Apr. 17, 1995.

84. Carolyn Daniels, Rochester, N.Y., May 10, 1995.

85. I. A. Richards, *Practical Criticism: A Study of Literary Judgment* (New York: Harcourt, Brace, 1929), 7–8, 11, 15, 191, 229, 231, 234, 258–261, 313.

86. Cleanth Brooks, Jr., and Robert Penn Warren, *Understanding Poetry: An Anthology for College Students* (New York: Holt, 1939), iv, xi, 23, 32.

87. Brooks and Warren, *Understanding Poetry*, 11–12, 14–18, 171, 200, 390–391.

88. Richards, *Practical Criticism*, 321, 339; Brooks and Warren, *Understanding Poetry*, iv, 4–6, 25.

89. "A Tentative Course of Study for Literature for the Senior High School, Fort Worth, 1939," 52–60, 93–116; "Tentative Manual—State of Oregon High Schools—Language Arts," 1945, 35; "Course of Study in High School English, Grades 9–12," St. Paul, 1945, 38.

90. Kliebard, *Struggle*, 242, 251; "A Suggested Course of Study in English for Selected Superior Pupils," St. Paul, 1946, 89.

91. Vergara, *College Women's Responses*, 5, 33, 54, 148–149; Kliebard, *Struggle*, 209–239.

92. Vergara, *College Women's Responses*, 90–91. Lionel Trilling made the same observation about his students that Lewis did in "On the Teaching of Modern Literature," reprinted in Trilling, *The Moral Obligation to be Intelligent: Selected Essays*, ed. Leon Wieseltier (New York: Farrar, Straus, and Giroux, 2000), 398.

93. Vergara, *College Women's Responses*, 60, 62, 96, 127.

8. I Am an American

1. Lawrence Thompson and R. H. Winnick, *Robert Frost: The Later Years* (New York: Holt, Rinehart, Winston, 1976), 282.

2. Jeffrey Meyers, *Robert Frost: A Biography* (Boston: Houghton Mifflin, 1996), 324.

3. Michael Ignatieff, *Blood and Belonging: Journeys into the New Nationalism* (New York: Farrar, Straus & Giroux, 1993); Gary Gerstle, *American Crucible: Race and Nation in the Twentieth Century* (Princeton: Princeton University Press, 2001). See also Rogers Smith, *Civic Ideals: Conflicting Visions of Citizenship in American History* (New Haven: Yale University Press, 1997).

4. Werner Sollors, *Beyond Ethnicity: Consent and Descent in American Culture* (New York: Oxford University Press, 1986).

5. On "civil religion," see, for example, Robert N. Bellah and Phillip E. Hammond, *Varieties of Civil Religion* (San Francisco: Harper & Row, 1980).

6. *The Official Records of the Centennial Celebration, Bath, Steuben County, New York, June 4, 6, and 7, 1893* (Bath, N.Y.: Press of the Courier Co., 1893), 75; *Geneseo's Centennial, September 11, 1890: Report of the Celebration, Literary and Other Exercises, and Poem and Addresses as Delivered* (Geneseo?, N.Y.: s.n., 1890); *1794–1894 Centennial Celebration, Mount Morris, New York, August 15, 1894*, comp. Rev. Levi Parsons, D. D., and Samuel L. Rockfellow (Mt. Morris, N.Y.: J. C. Dickey, 1894), 11, 49; *Centennial Day Celebration, Rochester, New York, 1912*, comp. and ed. Charles E. Ogden and Thomas T. Swinburne (Rochester, N.Y.: The Centennial Committee, 1912); Brooks McNamara, *Day of Jubilee: The Great Age of Public Celebrations in New York, 1788–1809* (New Brunswick, N.J.: Rutgers University Press, 1997), 152.

7. John Bodnar, *Remaking America: Public Memory, Commemoration, and Patriotism in the Twentieth Century* (Princeton: Princeton University Press, 1992), 32–34; *Proceedings of the Bi-Centennial Celebration of Richmond County, Staten Island, New York* (New York: s.n., 1883), 52.

8. *Proceedings of the Centennial Celebration of the Incorporation of the Town of Longmeadow, October 17, 1883, with numerous Historical Appendices and A Town Genealogy* (Longmeadow, Mass.: Town of Longmeadow, 1884), 135.

9. Leigh Eric Schmidt, "From Arbor Day to the Environmental Sabbath: Nature, Liturgy, and American Protestantism," *Harvard Theological Review* 84:3 (1991), 303, 306.

10. Robert Haven Schauffler, *Memorial Day* (New York: Moffatt, Yard, 1911), 184–186; W. Lloyd Warner, *American Life: Dream and Reality* (Chicago: University of Chicago Press, 1962), 31.

11. *To Commemorate the Foundation of the Village of Cooperstown and its Corporate Existence of One Hundred Years, This Memorial Celebration Was Held August 4th 10th, 1907* (Cooperstown, N.Y.: The Otsego Republican, 1907).

12. Boston Committee on Compilation of the Tercentenary Celebration, *Tercentenary of the Founding of Boston* (Boston: Printing Department,

1931), 212; "Harding Dedicates Lincoln Memorial; Blue and Gray Join," *New York Times*, May 31, 1922, 1, 3.

13. *Tercentenary of the Founding of Boston*, 63; *Centennial Celebration of Richmond County*, 16; David Glassberg, *American Historical Pageantry: The Uses of Tradition in the Early Twentieth Century* (Chapel Hill: University of North Carolina Press, 1990), 30.

14. David B. Little, *America's First Centennial Celebration: The Nineteenth of April 1875 at Lexington and Concord, Massachusetts* (Boston: The Club of Odd Volumes, 1961), 35.

15. *Life and Letters of Bayard Taylor*, vol. II, ed. Marie Hansen-Taylor and Horace E. Scudder (Boston: Houghton Mifflin, 1885), 689.

16. Glassberg, *American Historical Pageantry*, 43, 53–54, 57, 62, 149.

17. Ibid., 147–148, 184, 191.

18. Mary Master Needham, *Folk Festivals: Their Growth and How to Give Them* (New York: B. W. Huebsch, 1912), 1, 3.

19. Arvia MacKaye Ege, *The Power of the Impossible: The Life Story of Percy and Marion MacKaye* (Falmouth, Maine: Kennebec River Press, 1992), 16, 56, 107, 235, 369.

20. Percy MacKaye, *Poems and Plays*, vol. I (New York: Macmillan, 1916), xi; Percy MacKaye, *Saint Louis: A Civic Masque* (Garden City, N.Y.: Doubleday, Page, 1914), x, xiii–xiv.

21. Illinois Federation of Women's Clubs annual meeting program, October 18–21, 1898, folder biographical material I, Box I, Martha Foote Crow Papers, Special Collections, Syracuse University Library, Syracuse, New York.

22. Theodora Penny Martin, *The Sound of Our Own Voices: Women's Study Clubs, 1860–1910* (Boston: Beacon Press, 1987), 57, 61–62, 172; Anna Ruggles Gere, *Intimate Practices: Literacy and Cultural Work in U.S. Women's Clubs, 1880–1920* (Urbana: University of Illinois Press, 1997), 227; McHenry, *Forgotten Readers*, 191–217, 240. Sicherman is cited in Gere, *Intimate Practices*, 232.

23. Martha Foote Crow, "Notes About the Poetry Prize and Other Notes," *General Federation of Women's Clubs Magazine*, April 1917, 24; Gere, *Intimate Practices*, 231; WPA interview with Mrs. W. C. Patrickson, *www.loc.gov*.

24. Martha Foote Crow, "Literature—Poets of Today," *General Federation of Women's Clubs Magazine*, July 1915, 27; Andrew DuBois and Frank Lentricchia, "Modernist Lyric in the Culture of Capital," in *The Cambridge History of American Literature*, vol. 5, *Poetry and Criticism 1900–50*, ed. Sacvan Bercovitch (Cambridge: Cambridge University Press, 2003), 29; Martha Foote Crow, "The Mind of America as Represented in the Poets of Today," Box 1, folder biographical material, Crow Papers.

25. "Department of Literature and Library Extension," *General Federation of*

Women's Clubs Magazine, Nov. 1918, 26; Martha Foote Crow to Lillian A. Lilly, Sept. 2, 1920[?], Box 2, Crow Papers.

26. Anna Hempstead Branch to Martha Foote Crow, Jan. 14, 1920, Box 1, Crow Papers.

27. Anna Hempstead Branch, *The Shoes That Danced* (Boston: Houghton Mifflin, 1905), 156; Vachel Lindsay to Anna Hempstead Branch, Dec. 3, 1910, folder 63 (June-Dec. 1910), Anna Hempstead Branch Papers, Smith College Library, Smith College, Northampton, Mass. (quoted by permission of Nicholas C. Lindsay); Helen Lefkowitz Horowitz, *Alma Mater: Design and Experience in the Women's Colleges from Their Nineteenth-Century Beginnings to the 1930s* (Amherst: University of Massachusetts Press, 1993), 172–175.

28. Anna Hempstead Branch to Mary Bolles Branch, Apr. 16, 1899, folder 38, Branch Papers.

29. Anna Hempstead Branch, draft of letter to the Poetry Society of America, 1917, folder 256, Branch Papers.

30. Vachel Lindsay to Anna Hempstead Branch, Apr. 18, 1916, folder 77, Branch Papers; Margaret Widdemer to Anna Hempstead Branch, Nov. 21, 1919, folder 85, Branch Papers (quoted by permission of John D. Widdemer); Anna Hempstead Branch to Mary Bolles Branch, Jan. 14, 1919, folder 84, Branch Papers; "College Women Are Told About Poets in Slums," Feb. 21, 1935, scrapbook 17, Branch Papers; Julian T. Baird, Jr., "Branch, Anna Hempstead," in *Notable American Women, 1607–1950: A Biographical Dictionary,* vol. I, ed. Edward T. James (Cambridge, Mass.: Harvard University Press, 1971), 226–228.

31. "College Women Are Told About Poets in Slums"; Margaret Widdemer to Anna Hempstead Branch, Nov. 21, 1919; Edwin Markham to Anna Hempstead Branch, Nov. 22, 1919, folder 85, Branch Papers; Anna Hempstead Branch to John Masefield, Dec. 13, 1930, folder 256, Branch Papers; reprint from *Smith Alumnae Quarterly,* n.d., folder 257, Branch Papers; Edwin Arlington Robinson to Anna Hempstead Branch, Dec. 10, 1919, folder 86, Branch Papers; Marie V. de Nervaud, "The Poets [*sic*] Guild of Christodora House," c. 1922, scrapbook 17, Branch Papers.

32. DuBois and Lentricchia, "Modernist Lyric," 29; *Smith Alumnae Quarterly.*

33. de Nervaud, "The Poets Guild"; Katherine Lee Bates to Anna Hempstead Branch, Apr. 14, 1924, folder 102, Branch Papers.

34. Mary Louise Pardee, "The Unbound Anthology and the Daughters of the American Revolution," typescript, folder 258, Branch Papers.

35. Winifred M. Gillis to Anna Hempstead Branch, Nov. 28, 1924, folder 104, Branch Papers; DuBois and Lentricchia, "Modernist Lyric," 35, 46–48.

36. Anna Hempstead Branch, solicitation letter, n.d., folder 259, Branch Papers; DuBois and Lentricchia, "Modernist Lyric," 29.

37. "Report to the Executive Committee," May 1936, folder 182, Branch Papers; Anna Hempstead Branch, "Dear Fellow Board Member," June 3, 1936, folder 256, Branch Papers.
38. Edward G. Hartmann, *The Movement to Americanize the Immigrant* (New York: Columbia University Press, 1948), 38, 42, 125–126, 218.
39. Ibid., 259, 262–263.
40. Thomas J. Archdeacon, *Becoming American: An Ethnic History* (New York: The Free Press, 1983), 184; Herbert Adolphus Miller, *The School and the Immigrant* (Cleveland: The Survey Committee of the Cleveland Foundation, 1916), 93–94.
41. M. Catherine Mahy, "The Differentiation of English Classes in the High School," *Education* 36 (May 1916), 576, 578–579; Robert A. Carlson, *The Americanization Syndrome: A Quest for Conformity* (Croon, Helm, 1987), 116–117; Myra Kelly, *Little Citizens: The Humours of School Life* (rpt. New York: Peter Smith, 1931), 324–326.
42. Peter Roberts, "The Library and the Foreign Speaking Man," in *Americanization,* ed. Winthrop Talbot (New York: H. W. Wilson, 1920), 248; Peter Roberts, *The Problem of Americanization* (New York: Macmillan, 1920), 140–144.
43. Huldah Florence Cook and Edith May Walker, *Adult Elementary Education* (New York: Scribner's, 1927), 11–12, 73–77.
44. Sollors, *Beyond Ethnicity,* 172; Gerstle, *American Crucible,* 153; E. J. Irwin, "An Americanization Program," *Bureau of Education Bulletin* 1923, no. 30 (Washington, D.C.: Government Printing Office, 1923), 8; Frances A. Kellor, "What Is Americanization [sic]," in *Immigration and Americanization,* ed. Philip Davis (Boston: Ginn, 1920), 638; Henry Neumann, "Teaching American Ideals Through Literature," *Bureau of Education Bulletin* 1918, no. 32, 9–12. See also John J. Mahoney, "Training Teachers for Americanization," *Bureau of Education Bulletin* 1920, no. 12, 15.
45. Sollors, *Beyond Ethnicity,* 89; Roberts, *Problem of Americanization,* 31; Nellie B. Sergent, "High School Poets," *Progressive Education* VI:3 (Sept.-Oct.-Nov. 1929), 268–283.
46. Leonard Covello, *The Heart Is the Teacher* (New York: McGraw-Hill, 1958), 81, 109–110, 192, 242.
47. "Dr. Elias Lieberman Dies at 85," *New York Times,* July 14, 1969, 35; Gilman Hall to Elias Lieberman, Apr. 14, 1916, Box 1, Elias Lieberman Papers, Manuscripts and Archives Division, The New York Public Library, Astor, Lenox and Tilden Foundations, New York City; Sollors, *Beyond Ethnicity,* 103–105. Among studies of "whiteness," see Linda Gordon, *The Great Arizona Orphan Abduction* (Cambridge, Mass.: Harvard University Press, 1999), and Matthew Frye Jacobson, *Whiteness of a Different Color: European Immigrants and the Alchemy of Race* (Cambridge, Mass.: Harvard University Press, 1998).

48. Clipping of review of *Paved Streets, New York Sun,* n.d., Box 1, Lieberman Papers; Abraham Zivinitsky to Elias Lieberman, June 30, 1920, Box 1, Lieberman Papers; Warren T. Powell to Elias Lieberman, Dec. 18, 1928, Lieberman Papers; Clipping *re* oratory contest, *New York Journal-American,* May 3, 1949, Box 1, Lieberman Papers.

49. Louella D. Everett to Elias Lieberman, Dec. 12, 1939, Box 1, Lieberman Papers; "New Citizen Rally" program, Nov. 25, 1941, Box 1, Lieberman Papers; Sollors, *Beyond Ethnicity,* 222; Jean Barondess to Elias Lieberman, May 3, 1939, Box 1, Lieberman Papers.

50. Michael Schudson, *The Good Citizen: A History of American Civic Life* (New York: The Free Press, 1998); Arthur William Dunn and Hannah Margaret Harris, *Citizenship in School and Out: The First Six Years of School Life* (Boston: Heath, 1919), xix, 40, 58–59, 69; Roy Winthrop Hatch, *Training in Citizenship* (New York: Scribner's, 1926), 54, 160, 178, 280; Rachel Davis DuBois, *Build Together Americans* (New York: Hinds, Hayden & Eldredge, 1945), 22–23, 114–115.

51. DuBois, *Build Together Americans,* 71–72, 115–116; Covello, *Heart,* 217.

52. Nicholas V. Montalto, "The Intercultural Education Movement, 1924–41: The Growth of Tolerance as a Form of Intolerance," in *American Education and the European Immigrant: 1840–1940,* ed. Bernard J. Weiss (Urbana: University of Illinois Press, 1982), 142–160.

53. Sollors, *Beyond Ethnicity,* 75–79, 191, 222–223; Covello, *Heart,* 40–41. See also Constantine Panunzio, *The Soul of an Immigrant* (New York: Macmillan, 1921).

54. Alan Trachtenberg, *Shades of Hiawatha: Staging Indians, Making Americans, 1880–1930* (New York: Hill & Wang, 2004), 149, 162; M. E. Ravage, *An American in the Making: The Life Story of an Immigrant* (New York: Harper & Brothers, 1917), i–ii, 138, 150–155, 177–178, 191, 249, 260, 266; Sollors, *Beyond Ethnicity,* 89.

55. Mary Antin, *The Promised Land* (New York: Penguin, 1997), 1–2, 114, 124, 161, 166.

56. Ibid., 175–181.

57. Ibid., 184, 186, 230; Mary Antin, "How I Wrote The Promised Land" (1912), in Antin, *The Promised Land,* 296; Angela Sorby, *Schoolroom Poets: Childhood, Performance, and the Place of American Poetry, 1865–1917* (Lebanon, N.H.: University of New Hampshire Press, 2005), xxxiii–xxxvii.

58. Antin, *The Promised Land,* xvii, 169, 210, 267, 281.

59. Betty P. Fotis, Tucson, Ariz., June 4, 1995; Leonard Grumbach, Roslyn, N.Y., June 29, 1995; David Nasaw, *Going Out: The Rise and Fall of Public Amusements* (New York: Basic Books, 1993), 45–46.

60. Charles H. Gold, Evanston, Ill., Apr. 17, 1995.

61. Panunzio, *Immigrant,* 236; James Weldon Johnson, *The Book of American Negro Poetry* (New York: Harcourt, Brace, 1922), xxxiii, xl; James

Weldon Johnson, *Along This Way* (New York: Viking, 1933), 158–159; Sollors, *Beyond Ethnicity*, 245, 250; James Weldon Johnson, *God's Trombones: Seven Negro Sermons in Verse* (New York: Penguin, 1990), 7–9.

62. Johnson, *American Negro Poetry*, xli–xlii.

63. Johnson, *Along This Way*, 153–156.

64. Rose Cohen, *Out of the Shadow: A Russian Jewish Girlhood on the Lower East Side* (Ithaca: Cornell University Press, 1995), 242, 267.

65. Charles W. Chesnutt, *The Wife of His Youth: And Other Stories of the Color Line* (Ridgewood, N.J.: The Gregg Press, 1967), 1, 4, 7, 17.

66. Ibid., 133, 147, 152, 156, 163.

67. Mark W. Van Wienen, *Partisans and Poets: The Political Work of American Poetry in the Great War* (Cambridge: Cambridge University Press, 1997), 6, 175; Cary Nelson, *Repression and Recovery: Modern American Poetry and the Politics of Cultural Recovery, 1910–1945* (Madison: University of Wisconsin Press, 1989), 149.

68. Van Wienen, *Partisans and Poets*, 15, 144.

69. Harold G. Campbell to Elias Lieberman, June 6, 1916, Box 1, Lieberman Papers; Elizabeth Antermann(?) to Elias Lieberman, Feb. 1, 1944, Box 1, Lieberman Papers; Louise Girling to Elias Lieberman, May 30, 1952, Box 1, Lieberman Papers.

70. Edmund Chambers, "The Timelessness of Poetry," *The English Association*, Dec. 1940, n.p.; Babette Deutsch, "War Poetry Then and Now," *New Republic* 104 (Apr. 21, 1941), 565–567.

71. Max Hertzberg, "English Teachers' Wartime Role and the Victory Corps," *Education for Victory*, Feb. 1, 1943, 21; "Aims of Pre-Induction Training in English," *Education for Victory*, Dec. 1, 1943, 16; Allan M. Winkler, *The Politics of Propaganda: The Office of War Information, 1942–1945* (New Haven: Yale University Press, 1978).

72. Ralph W. Tyler, "Wartime Interests and Needs and Their Relation to Reading Programs," in *Adapting Reading Programs to Wartime Needs: Proceedings of the Conference on Reading Held at the University of Chicago*, vol. V, ed. William S. Gray (Chicago: University of Chicago Press, 1943), 15; Hertzberg, "English Teachers' Role," 21; Neal Cross, *Teaching English in Wartime: A Brief Guide to Classroom Practice* (Pamphlet Publication of the National Council of Teachers of English, No. 4, 1943), 1; Meyers, *Robert Frost*, 115. See also *Of the People*, ed. Harry R. Warfel and Elizabeth Manwaring (New York: Oxford University Press, 1942).

73. Earl H. Robinson and John LaTouche, "Ballad for Americans," *lyricsplayground.com/alpha/songs/b/balladforamericans.shtml*; Hal Borland, "Creed," *www.buchanan.org/h-114.html*; Cross, *Teaching English*, 7.

74. "Literature as a Resource in Pre-Induction Training," *Education for Victory*, Dec. 1, 1943, 23; Edith E. Shepherd, "Experience, the Key to Literature in Secondary Schools," in *Adapting Reading Programs to Wartime Needs*, 152.

75. Bernice E. Leary, "A Workshop Approach to Literature in the Middle Grades," in *Adapting Reading Programs to Wartime Needs*, 144; "Correlating English, Literature, and the Social Studies," *Education for Victory*, Apr. 3, 1944, 28–29.

76. Shepherd, "Experience," 151; John J. DeBoer, "Current Importance of the Literature of Power and Imagination," in *Adapting Reading Programs to Wartime Needs*, 136–137.

77. Paul Fussell, *Wartime: Understanding and Behavior in the Second World War* (New York: Oxford University Press, 1989), 245; Norman Cousins, *A Treasury of Democracy* (New York: Coward-McCann, 1942), xiv, 98, 116; William Rose Benét and Norman Cousins, *The Poetry of Freedom* (New York: Random House, 1945), xxix–xxxiv; John Kieran, *Poems I Remember* (Garden City, N.Y.: Doubleday, Doran, 1942), ix. See also *The Poems of Henry Wadsworth Longfellow*, ed. Louis Untermeyer (New York: The Heritage Press, 1943), xv.

78. Fussell, *Wartime*, 241.

79. Ibid., 249; *As You Were: A Portable Library of American Prose and Poetry Assembled for Members of the Armed Forces and the Merchant Marine*, ed. Alexander Woollcott (New York: Viking, 1943), xi.

80. Fussell, *Wartime*, 174.

81. Charles A. Fenton, *Stephen Vincent Benét: The Life and Times of an American Man of Letters, 1898–1943* (New Haven: Yale University Press, 1958), 58, 80, 86.

82. Ibid., 141, 213; "Epic on an American Theme: Stephen Vincent Benét and the Guggenheim Foundation," *The New Colophon*, vol. II, part V (1949), 1–12; Stephen Vincent Benét, *John Brown's Body* (New York: Rinehart, 1928), 48.

83. Fenton, *Stephen Vincent Benét*, 213, 219, 220; John Tebbel, *A History of Book Publishing in the United States, vol. III: The Golden Age Between Two Wars, 1920–1940* (New York: R. R. Bowker, 1978), 301.

84. Fenton, *Stephen Vincent Benét*, 209; M. M. Hart, Jr. to Stephen Vincent Benét, Nov. 21, 1928, Box 17, folder H, Stephen Vincent Benét Papers, Beinecke Rare Book and Manuscript Library, Yale University, New Haven, Conn.; William Minor Lile to Stephen Vincent Benét, Jan. 29, 1929, Box 20, folder L, Benét Papers; William Mann Fincke to Stephen Vincent Benét, June 14, 1935, Box 15, folder F, Benét Papers; Edith Rossiter Bevan to Stephen Vincent Benét, Oct. 14, 1940, Box 2, folder B, Benét Papers; Avedis Derounian to Stephen Vincent Benét, Jan. 31, 1938, Box 13, folder D, Benét Papers; Holmon Carson to Stephen Vincent Benét, n.d., Box 12, folder C, Benét Papers.

85. Stephen Vincent Benét, *A Summons to the Free* (New York: Farrar and Rinehart, 1941), 30; Elizabeth Woodward to Stephen Vincent Benét, Aug. 13, 1940, Box 26, folder W, Benét Papers.

86. Fenton, *Stephen Vincent Benét*, 363; Stephen Vincent Benét, *We Stand*

United and Other Radio Scripts (Farrar and Rinehart, 1945), 139, 147, 152; Stephen Vincent Benét, *America* (New York: Farrar and Rinehart, 1944), 60; Ron Robin, *The Barbed Wire College: Re-educating German POWs in the United States During World War II* (Princeton: Princeton University Press, 1995), 98.

87. Fussell, *Wartime,* 164–180.
88. Ibid., 178; *Selected Letters of Stephen Vincent Benét,* ed. Charles A. Fenton (New Haven: Yale University Press, 1960), 377, 378, 382, 383, 385, 392, 410.
89. Kathleen Sutton to Stephen Vincent Benét, July 7, 1941, Box 24, folder S, Benét Papers; Elizabeth Woodward to Stephen Vincent Benét; James Byrnie Shaw to Stephen Vincent Benét, July 6, 1941, Box 24, folder S, Benét Papers.
90. Marianne Oswald Lorraine, prospectus for a series of radio plays, n.d., Box 20, folder L, Benét Papers; James Byrnie Shaw to Stephen Vincent Benét.
91. *The American Citizens Handbook,* ed. Joy Elmer Morgan (Washington, D.C.: National Education Association of the United States, 1946), 6.
92. Ibid., 5, 11, 13, 598.
93. Ibid., 79.
94. Jay Nordlinger, "Hand It to Them: Rediscovering American Scripture," *National Review,* May 14, 2000, 42–43.
95. *The American Citizens Handbook,* 71.
96. Ibid., 71; Schudson, *The Good Citizen,* 173, 202–204, 250.
97. *The American Citizens Handbook,* 6, 365, 373, 398.
98. Ibid., 23; Nordlinger, "Hand It to Them," 42–43.

9. Grow Old Along with Me

1. George S. Carhart and Paul A. McGhee, *Through Magic Casements* (New York: Macmillan, 1927), xxxii.
2. Ormeida Curtis Keeler diary, Aug. 30, 1900, Carton 13, folder 5, series 3, Charles Augustus Keeler Papers, The Bancroft Library, University of California, Berkeley; Oscar Kuhns, *A One-Sided Autobiography: Containing the Story of My Intellectual Life* (New York: Eaton & Mains, 1913), 159–160.
3. Lee De Forest, *Father of Radio: The Autobiography of Lee De Forest* (Chicago: Willcox & Follett, 1950), 106.
4. Charles A. Keeler diary, March 8, 1893, Carton 8, folder 10, Keeler Papers. The unidentified story, clipped from a magazine, is pasted in a volume of the journal of the Baptist missionary Isabel Crawford. Crawford journal, 1915–1916, 110–111, Box 4, Isabel Crawford Papers, RG 1024, American Baptist Historical Society, American Baptist–Samuel Colgate Historical Library, Rochester, New York; cited hereafter as ABHS.

5. Margaret de Angeli, *Butter at the Old Price* (Garden City, N.Y.: Doubleday, 1971), 32; Rollo Walter Brown, *The Hills Are Strong* (Boston: Beacon Press, 1952), 74, 83; John Minnich Wilson, *The Dark and the Damp: An Autobiography of Jock Wilson* (New York: Dutton, 1951), 67–68; Ellen Gruber Garvey, "Scissorizing and Scrapbooks: Nineteenth Century Reading, Remaking, and Recirculating," in *New Media: 1740–1915*, ed. Lisa Gitelman and Geoff Pingree (Cambridge, Mass.: MIT Press, 2003), 207–227.

6. Alan C. Golding, *From Outlaw to Classic: Canons in American Poetry* (Madison: University of Wisconsin Press, 1995), 20–21.

7. Excerpts from Henry Holt letter to Burton L. Stevenson, Nov. 15, 1911, folder 2, Box 122, Henry Holt Archives, Manuscripts Division, Department of Rare Books and Special Collections, Princeton University Library, Princeton, N.J., reprinted by permission of Henry Holt and Company, LLC; quote from Henry Holt letter to Alfred Harcourt, Oct. 22, 1912, Box 122, Holt Archives, reprinted by permission of Henry Holt and Company, LLC; Burton L. Stevenson to Mrs. Bromley, Apr. 10, 1923, Box 122, Holt Archives; Burton Stevenson to Richard H. Thornton, May 2, 1935, Box 122, Holt Archives; Henry Holt to Burton L. Stevenson, Nov. 21, 1911, Box 122, Holt Archives.

8. Evan Thomas to Lewis Gannett, Jan. 15, 1959 and Feb. 5, 1959, folder 531, Lewis Gannett Correspondence and Compositions, MS Am 1888(531), Houghton Library, Harvard University, Cambridge, Mass. Quoted by permission of HarperCollins Publishers.

9. Henry Holt to Burton L. Stevenson, Nov. 21, 1911; Henry Holt to Alfred Harcourt, Sept. 29, 1911, Box 162, Holt Archives; Henry Holt to Burton L. Stevenson, Nov. 15, 1911.

10. Box 162, Holt Archives; William Dean Howells, "The Editor's Easy Chair," *Harper's*, June 1907, 149; Harold R. Walley, "Librarian to a Nation: The Story of Burton Stevenson '94, Editor of Stupendous Yet Lively Reference Books," *Princeton Alumni Weekly*, Sept. 24, 1937, 27–29; Frances Lindley to Lewis Gannett, c. Oct. 1960 and Oct. 17, 1960, folder 531, Gannett Correspondence. Quoted by permission of HarperCollins Publishers.

11. On domesticity and Christian nurture, see, for example, Colleen McDannell, *The Christian Home in Victorian America* (Bloomington: Indiana University Press, 1986), and Louise Stevenson, *The Victorian Homefront: American Thought and Culture, 1860–1880* (New York: Twayne, 1991).

12. George Creel, *Rebel at Large: Recollections of Fifty Crowded Years* (New York: G. P. Putnam's Sons, 1947), 19; Mary Ann Stewart diary, Apr. 1, May 10, and Nov. 23, 1891, RG 1173, ABHS; Alexis McCrossen, *Holy Day, Holiday: The American Sunday* (Ithaca: Cornell University Press, 2000).

13. Ralph A. Felton, "Speaking of Home," *Christian Advocate*, Oct. 7, 1920, 1146; Gene Stratton-Porter, "Let Us Go Back to Poetry," *Good House-keeping*, April 1925, 200; Ruth M. Carr, undated notebook, Box 16, Ruth M. Carr Papers, RG 1161, ABHS.

14. The account of the suburban Boston home dedication appears in an un-dated newspaper clipping in Isabel Crawford's diary, vol. 1924–25, 104, Box 6, Crawford Papers, ABHS.

15. Kuhns, *A One-Sided Autobiography*, 178; Maurice Francis Egan, *Confes-sions of a Book Lover* (Garden City, N.Y.: Doubleday, 1922), 2.

16. Gladys Brooks, *Gramercy Park: Memories of a New York Girlhood* (New York: Dutton, 1958), 38, 72, 211.

17. Douglas Wixson, introduction to Jack Conroy, *The Disinherited: A Novel of the 1930s*, ed. Douglas Wixson (Columbia: University of Missouri Press, 1991), 20; Stratton-Porter, "Let Us Go Back to Poetry," 35.

18. Harry Emerson Fosdick, *The Living of These Days: An Autobiography* (New York: Harper, 1956), 33–34, 37.

19. Elizabeth Borton de Trevino, *The Hearthstone of My Heart* (Garden City, N.Y.: Doubleday, 1977), 64, 113.

20. Dorothy Canfield Fisher, *Understood Betsy* (New York: Holt, 1917), 127, 129–132. The same text was a staple in the Hudson River Valley par-sonage where the prominent banker Thomas W. Lamont grew up. See Lamont, *My Boyhood in a Parsonage: Some Brief Sketches of American Life Toward the Close of the Last Century* (New York: Harper, 1946), 79.

21. Annis Duff, *"Bequest of Wings": A Family's Pleasures with Books* (New York: Viking, 1946), 16, 30, 58, 69, 72, 73, 76, 79; Annis Duff, *"Longer Flight": A Family Grows Up with Books* (New York: Viking, 1956), 11–14, 109, 112.

22. Duff, *"Longer Flight,"* 23.

23. On the history of the American family, see Stephanie Coontz, *The Social Origins of Private Life: A History of American Families, 1600–1900* (Lon-don: Verso, 1988); *Family and Society in American History*, ed. Joseph M. Hawes and Elizabeth I. Nybakken (Urbana: University of Illinois Press, 2001); and Steven Mintz and Susan Kellogg, *Domestic Revolutions: A So-cial History of American Family Life* (New York: Free Press, 1988).

24. Duff, *"Longer Flight,"* 31–32.

25. David Vincent, *Literacy and Popular Culture: England, 1750–1914* (Cam-bridge: Cambridge University Press, 1989); Duff, *"Longer Flight,"* 110–144.

26. Edward N. Teall, *Books and Folks* (New York: G. P. Putnam's, 1921), 188; William S. Gray and Ruth Munroe, *The Reading Interests and Habits of Adults* (New York: Macmillan, 1929), 232–234.

27. Katherine Butler Hathaway, *The Little Locksmith* (New York: Coward-McCann, 1942), 35–37.

28. Margaret Parton, *Journey Through a Lighted Room* (New York: Viking, 1973), 34.

29. Ibid., 27–28.

30. Ibid., 5, 48, 168.

31. Ibid., 180.

32. Ibid., 5.

33. Mary Ann Stewart diary, Mar. 10, 1907 and Feb. 8, 1914, ABHS.

34. Linda Polan, London, England, May 23, 1995 (in *New York Times* query sample); Langston Hughes, *The Big Sea* (New York: Hill and Wang, 1993), 25–26; Linda Grace Hoyer, *Enchantment* (London: Andre Deutsch, 1971), 14.

35. Mary Ann Stewart diary, Dec. 25, 1898 and Oct. 28–31, 1897, ABHS; Lawrence Clark Powell, *Fortune and Friendship* (New York: R. R. Bowker, 1968), 5.

36. Mary Ann Stewart diary, Aug. 22, 1907 and Sept. 2, 1907, ABHS; Anna D. Skinner, Ipswich, Mass., May 12, 1995 (in *New York Times* query sample). See also de Angeli, *Butter at the Old Price*, 22.

37. Wilson, *The Dark and the Damp*, 17–18, 68.

38. Guglielmo Cavallo and Roger Chartier, eds., *A History of Reading in the West* (Amherst: University of Massachusetts Press, 1999), 272; Wilson, *The Dark and the Damp*, 54. The first of his poetry volumes, *Man with a Pick*, was printed for his friends in an edition of 150; the second, *Black Diamonds*, was published in 1947 by Exposition Press.

39. Brown, *The Hills Are Strong*, 32–33.

40. Ibid., 74–75.

41. Stuart Brent, *The Seven Stairs* (Cambridge, Mass.: Riverside Press, 1962), 133.

42. Ben Hecht, *A Child of the Century* (New York: Simon and Schuster, 1954), 69.

43. David Grayson [Ray Stannard Baker], *More Adventures with David Grayson* (Garden City, N.Y.: Doubleday, 1946), 166–168. For other accounts of reading as liberation or indulgence, see Teall, *Books and Folks*, 10; Bliss Perry, *And Gladly Teach: Reminiscences by Bliss Perry* (Boston: Houghton Mifflin, 1935), 58–60; Clyde Brion Davis, *The Age of Indiscretion* (Philadelphia: J. B. Lippincott, 1950), 40–41, 49; Egan, *Confessions*, 1, 92; and Kuhns, *One-Sided Autobiography*, 118–121, 151–158.

44. Grayson, *More Adventures*, 168.

45. Ibid., 189, 190, 194.

46. Frances Wentworth Cutler, *The Minister's Daughter: A Time-exposure Photograph of the Years 1903–04* (Philadelphia: Dorrance, 1974), 61, 107.

47. Walter Locke, *This World, My Home* (Yellow Springs, Ohio: Antioch Press, 1957), 85, 92–93.

48. Ibid., 92–93, 148–150.
49. Teall, *Books and Folks,* 159–163; Locke, *This World,* 91.
50. On "rebels against Victorianism," see, for example, T. J. Jackson Lears, *No Place of Grace: Antimodernism and the Transformation of American Culture, 1880–1920* (New York: Pantheon, 1981), 5. Lears's book begins with a description of the "educated bourgeoisie" of the late nineteenth century who, feeling increasingly confined to "the airless parlor of material comfort and moral complacency," wished to "smash the glass and breathe freely." See also Stanley Coben, *Rebellion Against Victorianism: The Impetus for Cultural Change in 1920s America* (New York: Oxford University Press, 1991).
51. Fosdick, *Living of These Days,* 60–61.
52. Howard Francis Seely, *Enjoying Poetry in School* (Richmond, Va.: Johnson), 1931), 8–10.
53. Wixson, "Introduction," 11, 27; Cavallo and Chartier, eds., *Reading in the West,* 274; Richard W. Hudgens, St. Louis, Mo., Apr. 16, 1995 (part of *New York Times* query sample).
54. De Forest, *Father of Radio,* 46, 106, 224.
55. Perry, *And Gladly Teach,* 287, 558–560; Gray and Munroe, *Reading Interests,* 252–254.
56. Helen Lefkowitz Horowitz, "'Nous Autres': Reading, Passion, and the Creation of M. Carey Thomas," *Journal of American History,* June 1992, 68–95; Sarton, *I Knew a Phoenix,* 137–138.
57. Clara Holloway Groesbeck diary transcript, Dec. 1, 1885, Dec. 4, 1885, Feb. 19, 1886, Apr. 22, 1886, June 14, 1886, Aug. 13, 1886, Nov. 30, 1886, RG 1169, ABHS.
58. Harriet Monroe, *A Poet's Life: Seventy Years in a Changing World* (New York: Macmillan, 1938), 37, 56–58, 60–62.
59. Bernice C. Skidelsky journal, Oct. 20, 1904, Dec. 28, 1904, Oct. 13, 1905, Box 3, Bernice C. Skidelsky Papers, Manuscripts and Archives Division, The New York Public Library, Astor, Lenox and Tilden Foundations, New York City.
60. Skidelsky journal, May 17, 1905, Nov. 10, 1905.
61. Ibid., Dec. 8, 1904, May 11, 1905, Oct. 14, 1905, Apr. 9, 1906, Apr. 22, 1906.
62. Mary Ann Stewart diary, Aug. 29, 1897, Mar. 10, 1907, ABHS. A similar comment is in the Skidelsky journal, Oct. 13, 1904. In contrast to these examples, Barbara Hochman has argued for what she calls the "erosion of friendly reading" in the conventions of reader-author interchanges that dominated the rise of realistic fiction in the late nineteenth century. See Barbara Hochman, *Getting At the Author: Reimagining Books and Reading in the Age of American Realism* (Amherst: University of Massachusetts Press, 2001), 29–47.

63. Harry Hansen, *Midwest Portraits: A Book of Memories and Friendships* (New York: Harcourt, Brace, 1923), 22–23; Oscar Cargill, "Carl Sandburg: Crusader and Mystic," *College English* 11:7 (April 1950), 365.

64. Jean H. Morsch to Carl Sandburg, Feb. 18, 1953, Box 348, Carl Sandburg Papers, University of Illinois Library, Urbana-Champaign, Illinois.

65. Harry M. Saltzman to Carl Sandburg, Feb. 23, 1938, Box 357, Sandburg Papers; Norma L. Bagley to Carl Sandburg, June 23, 1962, Box 348, Sandburg Papers.

66. Robert Lemkowitz to Carl Sandburg, n.d., Box 348, Sandburg Papers; Mrs. J. L. Duran to Carl Sandburg, n.d., Box 357, Sandburg Papers; Peterann Rich to Carl Sandburg, Sept. 4, 1957, Box 348, Sandburg Papers.

67. Martha Ann Hartzog to Carl Sandburg, Oct. 1, 1959, Box 348, Sandburg Papers; Marguerite Angelo to Carl Sandburg, Oct. 16, 1937, Box 350, Sandburg Papers.

68. Hans Engel to Carl Sandburg, Jan. 24, 1942, Box 349, Sandburg Papers; Mrs. O. W. Groene to Carl Sandburg, Dec. 16, 1927, Box 350, Sandburg Papers.

69. Frances Manley to Carl Sandburg, May 28, 1930, Box 348, Sandburg Papers; Carl Sandburg to Frances Manley, c. May 28, 1930, Box 348, Sandburg Papers; and form letter, folder Indexed Form letters (no box no.), Sandburg Papers. Quoted by permission of Maurice C. Greenbaum on behalf of the Trustees of the Carl Sandburg Family Trust.

70. Mrs. George L. Hauger to Carl Sandburg, n.d., Box 348, Sandburg Papers; Jane Ridgeway Harsha to Catherine McCarthy, Apr. 15, 1959, folder Harcourt, Brace additional mss., 1938–1966 (no box no.), Sandburg Papers.

10. *God's in His Heaven*

1. Frederic L. Knowles, "The Relation of Reading to Christian Character," *Methodist Review,* Sept. 1905, 735; William A. Quayle, "The Literature of Devotion," *Methodist Review,* Jan.-Feb. 1904, 36; Edith Grace Traver diary, Oct. 16, 1929, 254, Box 10, Traver Papers, RG 1078, ABHS; "Books for the Devotional Life," *Watchman-Examiner,* Aug. 7, 1930, 1002.

2. Matthew Arnold, "The Study of Poetry" (1880), in *Essays in Criticism, Second Series* (London: Macmillan, 1888, 1903), 1–41; David G. Downey, "Some Present-Day Opportunities," *Methodist Review,* Sept. 1906, 780; Homer G. Curley, "The Spiritual Mission of Poetry," *Methodist Review,* Sept. 1907, 785.

3. George Santayana, "Interpretations of Poetry and Religion," *Works of George Santayana,* Triton Edition, vol. II (New York: Scribner's, 1936),

198–201; Charles G. Osgood, *Poetry as a Means of Grace* (Princeton: Princeton University Press, 1941), 18–19; Amos N. Wilder, *Modern Poetry and the Christian Tradition* (New York: Scribner's, 1952), 19, 6–8.

4. Fred Kaplan, *Sacred Tears: Sentimentality in Victorian Literature* (Princeton: Princeton University Press, 1987), 11–38; Janet Todd, *Sensibility: An Introduction* (London: Methuen, 1986), 1–31, 49–64.

5. "Religious Book Lists," *Publishers' Weekly*, Mar. 17, 1923, 942; Harold Greene Arnold, "A Wider Use of General Literature in Church," *Publishers' Weekly*, Mar. 3, 1923, 630.

6. Wilder, *Modern Poetry*, 19.

7. Ibid., 8–9; "How Readest Thou?," *Watchman-Examiner*, Feb. 6, 1930, 170.

8. David D. Hall, *Worlds of Wonder, Days of Judgment* (New York: Knopf, 1989), 28–29.

9. Margaret Harding (Tileston) Edsall diaries, July 14, 1881; Aug. 4, 1881; Jan. 8, 1881; Jan. 15, 1881, Box 1, Margaret Harding (Tileston) Edsall Papers, MC 354, Schlesinger Library, Radcliffe Institute for Advanced Study, Harvard University, Cambridge, Mass.

10. Edsall diaries, May 15, 1881; May 29, 1881, Box 1, Edsall Papers.

11. Edsall diaries, Aug. 4, 1881; Feb. 1, 1883; Feb. 5, 1883, Box 1, Edsall Papers.

12. Cheryl Forbes, "Coffee, Mrs. Cowman, and the Devotional Life of Women Reading in the Desert," in David D. Hall, ed., *Lived Religion in America* (Princeton: Princeton University Press, 1997), 117.

13. I discuss the role of trade firms in religious publishing in "The Boundaries of American Religious Publishing," *Book History* II (1999), 207–217.

14. Caroline Miles Hill, *The World's Great Religious Poetry* (New York: Macmillan, 1923), xii; "Book Notices," *Methodist Review*, July 1923, 656–657.

15. Hill, *World's Great Religious Poetry*, xi and passim.

16. Thomas Walsh, *The World's Great Catholic Poetry* (New York: Macmillan, 1927; rpt. 1940), vii; Joyce Kilmer, *Dreams and Images: An Anthology of Catholic Poets* (New York: Boni and Liveright, 1917; rpt. 1926).

17. James Dalton Morrison, *Masterpieces of Religious Verse* (New York: Harper, 1948), xiii, 481, and passim; Hill, *World's Great Religious Poetry*, xi.

18. The figure on Baptist publications comes from inventorying the holdings of the American Baptist Historical Association, Rochester, New York.

19. Amos R. Wells to P. W. Crannell, May 3, 1906, Box 1, Crannell Papers, RG1023, ABHS.

20. "The *Watchman-Examiner* and Its New Ownership," *Watchman-Examiner*, Oct. 2, 1930, 1255–1256; "The *Baptist* Merges with the *Christian Century*," *Christian Century*, Jan. 14, 1933, 3; Thomas Curtis Clark, "Modern Poetry and Religion," *Baptist*, Feb. 20, 1931, 237–238.

21. *Nebraska Baptist Messenger,* January 1930, clipping in William Edwin Darrow Papers, Oct.-Dec. 1933, Box 19, RG 1397, ABHS. Guest's "Daddies" appeared in the *Watchman-Examiner* for Jan. 8, 1925, 46.

22. Ann Douglas, *The Feminization of American Culture* (New York: Knopf, 1977); T J. Jackson Lears, *No Place of Grace: Antimodernism and the Transformation of American Culture, 1880–1920* (New York: Pantheon, 1981).

23. The entire sample was drawn from the collections of the American Baptist Historical Society, Rochester, New York.

24. Clara Holloway Groesbeck diary, Sept. 21, 1885, RG 1169, ABHS.

25. Edith Grace Traver diary, n.d. 1923, 273, Box 10, ABHS. Those who left author-title lists were Isabel Crawford, William Edwin Darrow, Elmer Davis, and Edith Grace Traver; those who provided detailed entries were Helen Hovey Parshley, John Alasko Curtis, Clara Holloway Groesbeck, Luella M. Dodge, Mary Ann Stewart, and Alvah Strong. Ella Marie Holmes Swanson, Groesbeck, Traver, Rittenhouse Neisser, Curtis, Darrow, and Parshley referred explicitly to reading volumes of poetry.

26. Traver diary, Apr. 22, 1923, Apr. 16, 1923, Box 10, ABHS; Sara Boddie Downer diary, Sept. 8, 1923, Oct. 7, 1923, Box 1, RG 1044, ABHS.

27. Groesbeck diary, July 23, 1900, ABHS.

28. Isabel Crawford journals, Sept. 10, 1913, 30, Box 3, and annual report, 1918, Box 4, RG 1024, ABHS; Isabel Crawford, *Joyful Journey: Highlights on the High Way* (Philadelphia: Judson, 1951).

29. Crawford journals, Sept. [n.d.], 1917, 5–6, Box 4, ABHS.

30. Ibid., Aug. 9, 1931, 62, Box 7; Jan. 8, 1926, Box 6, 4–5; 1937 reading list, journal 1937–38, n.p., Box 8; Nov. 17, 1932, 1, Box 7, ABHS.

31. Crawford journals, June 4, 1933, 79, Box 7; Sept. 10, 1913, 30, Box 3; annual report 1918, Box 4, ABHS.

32. William Edwin Darrow diary, Jan. 12, 1885; Jan. 18, 1885; Jan. 31, 1885; all in Box 1, RG 1397, ABHS.

33. Ibid., Mar. 9, 1934; Mar. 10, 1934; Mar. 13, 1934; Mar. 31, 1934, all in Box 20, ABHS; Sept. 10, 1932; Aug. 5, 1933, Aug. 19, 1933; Aug. 27, 1933; Sept. 2, 1933; Sept. 9, 1933, all in Box 19, ABHS.

34. John Alasko Curtis diary, Sept. 30, 1892; Sept. 13, 1893; June 17, 1893; Aug. 8, 1893, all in Box 3, ABHS; Apr. 4, 1949, Box 2, RG 1025, ABHS.

35. Ibid., Feb. 18, 1942; Mar. 2, 1942; June 7, 1944; Feb. 24, 1949; July 11, 1949, all in Box 2, ABHS.

36. Ibid., Feb. 21, 1943; July 26, 1942, Box 2, ABHS.

37. George W. Farmer, "The Minister Among His Books," *Methodist Review,* Nov. 1907, 948.

38. Lynn Harold Hough, "The Lure of Books," *Methodist Review,* May 1911, 383–392.

39. Charles Edward Locke, "What Does a Bishop Read?" *Methodist Review,* May 1926, 404–415. See also Thomas W. Lamont, *My Boyhood in a Parsonage* (New York: Harper, 1946), 39–41.

40. David Keppel, "Poetry an Asset for the Preacher," *Methodist Review*, July 1913, 556–565; e.g., Hough's title "The Lure of Books"; Farmer, "The Minister Among His Books," 954; William A. Quayle, "On Reading Beautiful Books," *Methodist Review*, May 1914, 365, 368–369.

41. Lynn Harold Hough, "The Preacher as a Reader of General Literature," *Methodist Review*, Sept. 1916, 702–703.

42. Hough, "The Preacher as a Reader," 703; Hough, "The Lure of Books," 392; Lynn Harold Hough, "The Magic of a Book," *Methodist Review*, Sept. 1914, 696.

43. Hough, "The Magic of a Book," 696; Hough, "The Lure of Books," 388; Farmer, "The Minister Among His Books," 947, 954; Hough, "The Lure of Books," 389.

44. Locke, "What Does a Bishop Read?," 405; Farmer, "The Minister Among His Books," 949; review of Oscar Kuhns, *A One-Sided Autobiography*, *Methodist Review*, Nov. 1913, 997; William A. Quayle, "The Haunting Quality," *Methodist Review*, Sept. 1924, 706; Downey, "Some Present-Day Opportunities," 982.

45. Hough, "The Preacher as a Reader," 701.

46. William L. Stidger, *The Place of Books in the Life We Live* (New York: Doran, 1922), 133.

47. Caleb T. Winchester, "The New Poetry," *Methodist Review*, Jan. 1920, 17, 21; "Book Notes," *Presbyterian Magazine*, March 1923, 181.

48. Henry Sloane Coffin, *The Public Worship of God* (Philadelphia: Westminster, 1946), 104; Lewis H. Chrisman, "The Arena: Literature and the Preacher," *Methodist Review*, Sept. 1918, 787; James Mudge, "Present-Day Methodist Preaching," *Methodist Review*, Jan. 1905, 72.

49. Andrew W. Blackwood, *The Fine Art of Public Worship* (Nashville: Cokesbury, 1939), 71; Jack R. Noffsinger to Carl Sandburg, Nov. 26, 1941, Box 357, Carl Sandburg Papers, University of Illinois Library, Urbana-Champaign, Illinois; Alan Jenkins to Carl Sandburg, Jan. 1, 1958, Box 416, Sandburg Papers.

50. William L. Stidger to Edgar A. Guest, c. March 27, 1944, Box 5, folder 1944, Guest Papers; William L. Stidger, *The Place of Books in the Life We Live* (New York: Doran, 1922), 70.

51. William L. Stidger, *There Are Sermons in Books* (New York: Doran, 1922), xv.

52. Stidger, *There Are Sermons*, xi, 24, 67, 146, 194–198; Stidger, *The Place of Books*, 125.

53. Stidger, *The Place of Books*, 83, 88, 41–42, 101, 109.

54. Stidger, *There Are Sermons*, xix; William L. Stidger, *Planning Your Preaching* (New York: Harper, 1932), 44–45; William L. Stidger, *Preaching Out of the Overflow* (Nashville: Cokesbury, 1929), 204.

55. Stidger, *There Are Sermons*, foreword; Stidger, *The Place of Books*, 102, 115.

56. Stidger, *Planning Your Preaching*, 46; William L. Stidger, *Flames of Faith* (New York: Abingdon, 1922), 171.

57. William L. Stidger, *Giant Hours with Poet Preachers* (New York: Abingdon, 1918), passim; review of *The Lyric Year, Methodist Review,* May 1913, 492–98; Stidger, *Planning Your Preaching*, 54; Matthew J. Bruccoli, *The Fortunes of Mitchell Kennerley, Bookman* (San Diego: Harcourt, 1986).

58. Stidger, *Planning Your Preaching*, 54.

59. Alan C. Golding, *From Outlaw to Classic: Canons in American Poetry* (Madison: University of Wisconsin Press, 1995), 20–21.

60. Blackwood, *Fine Art of Public Worship*, 191.

61. Ibid., 60; G. Walter Fiske, *The Recovery of Worship* (New York: Macmillan, 1931), 55.

62. Laura Armstrong Athearn, *Christian Worship for American Youth* (New York: Century, 1931), 29; Darrow Papers, folder Sept.-Dec. 1932, Box 19; Kirby Page, *Living Creatively* (New York: Farrar and Rinehart, 1932), 99 and passim. See also Margaret T. Applegarth, *Bound in the Bundle of Life: Worship Services for Adult Church Groups* (New York: Harper, 1941); Albert A. Susott, *A Practical Handbook of Worship* (New York: Fleming H. Revell, 1941), 134–135; Alice Anderson Bays, *Worship Services for Youth* (New York: Abingdon-Cokesbury, 1946).

63. Laura I. Mattoon and Helen D. Bragdon, *Services for the Open* (New York: Century, 1923), vii and passim.

64. Ibid., 3, 28–29, 70–71.

65. Roger Chartier, *The Order of Books* (Stanford: Stanford University Press, 1994), 5–59; Mattoon and Bragdon, *Services*, 83.

66. Edwin H. Byington, *The Quest for Experience in Worship* (Garden City, N.Y.: Doubleday, Doran, 1943), 33.

67. Athearn, *Christian Worship*, 72.

68. Lawrence A. Hoffman, ed., *Gates of Understanding 2* (New York: Central Conference of American Rabbis, 1984), 68, 76–77; Rabbi Herbert Bronstein to author, Dec. 18, 1998; Lawrence A. Hoffman, ed., *Gates of Understanding* (New York: Central Conference of American Rabbis, 1977), 15.

69. Hoffman, "The Liturgical Message," *Gates of Understanding*, 129–168.

70. My account of Stern's role relies on my interview with him on February 14, 1999, in Chappaqua, N.Y. See also Hoffman, *Gates of Understanding* 1, vii.

71. One instance of Stern's interpolation of his own poetry as prose occurs in a passage beginning "Let me hear you . . . ," in *Gates of Prayer* (New York: Central Conference of American Rabbis, 1975), 232.

72. *Gates of Repentance* (New York: Central Conference of American Rabbis, 1978), 295–297, 378, 389–390, 430, 487, 499.

73. Ibid., 331–332; Hoffman, *Gates of Understanding 2*, 128–129; Bronstein to author, Dec. 18, 1998.

11. Lovely as a Tree

1. Harriet Monroe, *A Poet's Life: Seventy Years in a Changing World* (New York: Macmillan, 1938), 352, 386; "Joyce Kilmer," *Literary Digest*, Sept. 7, 1918, 33.

2. David Pryde, *The Highways of Literature* (New York: Jurst & Co., 1890), 67–70; Henry D. Thoreau, *Walden and Resistance to Civil Government* (New York: Norton, 1992), 141; Lynn Tew Sprague, "At Dawn of Day," *Outing*, July 1901, 478. On "overcivilization" and the search for the "simple life," see T. J. Jackson Lears, *No Place of Grace: Antimodernism and the Transformation of American Culture, 1880–1920* (New York: Pantheon, 1981); David E. Shi, *The Simple Life: Plain Living and High Thinking in American Culture* (New York: Oxford University Press, 1985); Roderick Nash, *Wilderness and the American Mind*, 3rd ed. (New Haven: Yale University Press, 1982), 141–160.

3. Charles A. Keeler diary, Mar. 19, 1893, Charles Augustus Keeler Papers, The Bancroft Library, University of California, Berkeley; Edward Thomas, "Reading Out of Doors," *Atlantic Monthly*, Aug. 1903, 276; Frederick Niven, "Books in the Wilderness," *Bookman*, Jan. 1921, 351.

4. Harry Emerson Fosdick, *The Living of These Days* (New York: Harper, 1956), 50, 68.

5. Between 1923 and 1933, the catalogue was sold separately from the periodical. Advertisement for summer catalogue, *Publishers' Weekly*, May 22, 1880, 524; cover, *Publishers' Weekly*, May 15, 1920, May 28, 1921, May 27, 1922. *Publishers' Weekly*, May 27, 1922, 1537–1538.

6. Marguerite Wilkinson, "Take Along a Book," *Publishers' Weekly*, May 27, 1922, 1537–1538; Dorothy Scarborough, "Summers [*sic*] the Time For Books," *Publishers' Weekly*, May 15, 1920, 1530; "Some Chat of Books for Vacation Reading," *Publishers' Weekly*, May 24, 1913, 1865.

7. Advertisement, *Publishers' Weekly*, May 27, 1922, 1561; Mary Frank, "Caravaning With Books," *Bookman*, Feb. 1921, 533–534.

8. David Grayson [Ray Stannard Baker], *Great Possessions: A New Series of Adventures* (Garden City, N.Y.: Doubleday, Page, 1917), 64–65.

9. Flora Neil Davidson diary, Box 1, folder 4, 1921, Flora Neil Davidson Papers, Wisconsin Historical Society, Madison, Wisconsin; Flora Neil Davidson diary, Box 1, folder 5, Aug. 7, 1931, Davidson Papers.

10. Perry D. Westbrook, *John Burroughs* (New York: Twayne, 1974), 11; Clara Barrus, *Our Friend John Burroughs* (Boston: Houghton Mifflin, 1914), 177–178; Houghton Mifflin Company to Alfred Bartlett, Jan. 1, 1903, Box 68, folder 68.15, John Burroughs Papers, Vassar College Li-

brary, Poughkeepsie, N.Y. In 1918, "Waiting" headed the predictions in the *Old Farmer's Almanac.*

11. *The Heart of Burroughs's Journals,* ed. Clara Barrus (Boston: Houghton Mifflin, 1928), 77; Edward J. Renehan, Jr., *John Burroughs: An American Naturalist* (Post Mills, Vt.: Chelsea Green Publishing Company, 1992), 95; Jessie Rittenhouse, *My House of Life* (Boston: Houghton Mifflin, 1934), 170.

12. William Boyd Allen to John Burroughs, Dec. 15, 1906, Box 68, folder 68.15, Burroughs Papers.

13. John Burroughs to William Boyd Allen, Jan. 7, 1907, Box 68, folder 68.15, Burroughs Papers; Mrs. R. P. Belazzi to John Burroughs, Sept. 10, 1905, Burroughs Papers; Will H. Hedley to John Burroughs, Dec. 5, 1906 and Dec. 14, 1906, Box 68, folder 68.16, Burroughs Papers.

14. Barrus, *Our Friend,* 43, 178.

15. Mary C. McDonaugh to John Burroughs, April 1, 1907, Box 68, folder 68.17, Burroughs Papers.

16. John Burroughs, "Real and Sham Natural History," *Atlantic Monthly* 91 (March 1903), 298–309. See also Burroughs, "The Literary Treatment of Nature," *Atlantic Monthly* 94 (July 1904), 38–43.

17. John Burroughs, *The Writings of John Burroughs,* vol. III: *Birds and Poets with Other Papers* (Boston: Houghton Mifflin, 1904), 18; 216; *The Writings of John Burroughs,* vol. X: *Literary Values and Other Papers* (Boston: Houghton Mifflin, 1904), 141; Barrus, *Our Friend,* 130.

18. Burroughs, *Birds and Poets,* 215; Barrus, *Our Friend,* 14, 113, 121–122, 125, 144–145, 236.

19. Burroughs, *Birds and Poets,* 18, 58; Barrus, *The Heart of Burroughs's Journals,* 48, 70; Burroughs, *Literary Values,* 105.

20. Barrus, *The Heart of Burroughs's Journals,* 241; Burroughs, *Birds and Poets,* v, 241, 243, 246. See also John Burroughs, *Indoor Studies* (Boston: Houghton Mifflin, 1889), 43–78.

21. Charles Dudley Warner, *The Relation of Literature to Life* (New York: Harper, 1897), 29.

22. John Burroughs, *Camping and Tramping with Roosevelt* (Boston: Houghton Mifflin, 1907); Gail Bederman, *Manliness and Civilization: A Cultural History of Gender and Race in the United States, 1880–1917* (Chicago: University of Chicago Press, 1995), 184, Renehan, *John Burroughs,* 250; Burroughs, *Birds and Poets,* 62.

23. Brander Matthews, "Theodore Roosevelt as a Man of Letters," in *The Works of Theodore Roosevelt,* vol. XII (New York: Scribner's, 1926), xiii–xiv; Richard Slotkin, "Nostalgia and Progress: Theodore Roosevelt's Myth of the Frontier," *American Quarterly* 33:5 (1981), 613; Hermann Hagedorn, *The Boys' Life of Theodore Roosevelt* (New York: Harper & Bros., 1918), 60–62; Barrus, *The Heart of Burroughs's Journals,* 110–111.

24. Henry Scott Miller to John Burroughs, April 4, 1919, Box 66, folder 66.95, Burroughs Papers; Barrus, *Our Friend,* 114.
25. G. C. Mason, MD, to John Burroughs, Jan. 9, 1907, Box 66, folder 66.94, Burroughs Papers; Faith Bickford to John Burroughs, March 3, 1914, Box 69, folder 1, Burroughs Papers.
26. Herbert Sproull to John Burroughs, Feb. 29, 1896, Box 68, folder 68.1, Burroughs Papers; Mrs. John W. Holt to John Burroughs, Jan. 17, 1920, Box 66, folder 66.94, Burroughs Papers; Mary Cadwallader Benedict to John Burroughs, April 1, 1912, Box 68, folder 68.16, Burroughs Papers.
27. Robert Finley, New York, N.Y., April 18, 1995 (in *New York Times* sample); Flora Neil Davidson diary, June 27, 1905, Box 1, folder 3, Davidson Papers; Flora Neil Davidson diary, 1929, Box 2, folder 3, Davidson Papers.
28. Edna Albert to John Burroughs, April 21, 1912, Box 68, folder 68.9, Burroughs Papers; Paulina Brandreth to John Burroughs, Feb. 2, 1918, Box 66, folder 66.94, Burroughs Papers; J. B. Alger to John Burroughs, Dec. 2, 1892, Box 66, folder 66.94, Burroughs Papers.
29. Earl Williams to John Burroughs, Jan. 2, 1918, Box 67, folder 67.41, Burroughs Papers; Lloyd Mifflin to John Burroughs, Feb. 27, 1902, Box 67, folder 67.41, Burroughs Papers.
30. Mary Alderson Chandler to John Burroughs, Jan. 31, 1903, Box 68, folder 17, Burroughs Papers; Elizabeth Mason Lanier to John Burroughs, Dec. 12, 1905, Box 68, folder 68.11, Burroughs Papers (Lanier is quoting Hiram Corson, professor at Cornell University); Harry Lee to John Burroughs, Dec. 7, 1915, Box 66, folder 94, Burroughs Papers.
31. Edward Larocque Tinker, *The Horsemen of the Americas and the Literature They Inspired* (Austin: University of Texas Press, 1967), 110–111; Joy S. Kasson, *Buffalo Bill's Wild West: Celebrity, Memory, and Popular History* (New York: Hill and Wang, 2000), 107, 132, 227.
32. Tinker, *Horsemen,* 116; *Cowboy Poets and Cowboy Poetry,* ed. David Stanley and Elaine Thatcher (Urbana: University of Illinois Press, 2000), 7; Hal Cannon, "Cowboy Poetry: A Poetry of Exile," in Stanley and Thatcher, *Cowboy Poets,* 65.
33. David Stanley, "Cowboy Poetry Then and Now: An Overview," in Stanley and Thatcher, *Cowboy Poets,* 3, 9; Kasson, *Buffalo Bill's Wild West,* 235–236.
34. Darlis A. Miller, *Captain Jack Crawford: Buckskin Poet, Scout, and Showman* (Albuquerque: University of New Mexico Press, 1993), 68, 77; Kasson, *Buffalo Bill's Wild West,* 35–36.
35. Miller, *Captain Jack Crawford,* 122, 162, 203.
36. Jack Crawford, *The Broncho Book: Being Buck-Jumps in Verse* (East Aurora, N.Y.: The Roycrofters, 1908), 14, 16, 22, 25, 27, 29, 35, 49, 139.
37. Ibid., 16, 18, 36, 43, 48, 52, 143; Miller, *Captain Jack Crawford,* 262–263.
38. Miller, *Captain Jack Crawford,* 201, 251; Isabel Crawford journals, Nov. 11, 1916, [n.p.], Box 4, Crawford Papers, ABHS.

39. Isabel Crawford journals, 1930–31, 38, Box 7; Isabel Crawford journals, [n.d.] 1908–1910, 127–28, 129, Box 3, ABHS.

40. Miller, *Captain Jack Crawford,* 263–264.

41. Shi, *The Simple Life,* 206–212; Nash, *Wilderness,* 141–160.

42. Louise Price, "Program Building for the Permanent Camp" (1930), File Camp and Camp Activities—General, Girl Scouts of the United States of America Archives, New York, N.Y.; hereafter cited as GSA. "Report of the Girl Scout Program Study" (1935), 62, Publication Development Files—General, GSA.

43. "Report of the Girl Scout Program Study," 24–27.

44. Sarah Louise Arnold, *The Way of Understanding* (New York: Girl Scouts, Inc., 1934), 57, 133.

45. *Scouting for Girls: Official Handbook of the Girl Scouts,* 2nd ed. (New York: Girl Scouts, Inc., 1920), 540–547; *Girl Scout Handbook,* 8th ed. (New York: Girl Scouts, Inc., 1932), 455–460.

46. May Lamberton Becker, "Start the New Year with a Book," *American Girl,* Jan. 1926, 28; Becker, "Books for April's Rainy Days," *American Girl,* April 1926, 34; Becker, "New Plays to Give and Other Books," *American Girl,* Feb. 1927, 32.

47. Arnold, *The Way of Understanding,* 38; *Girl Scout Handbook* (New York: Girl Scouts, Inc., 1947), 210.

48. Becker, "New Plays to Give," 32–33.

49. *Girl Scout Handbook* (New York: Girl Scouts, Inc., 1933), 531.

50. *Girl Scout Program* (1938), 79, file Publications—G, GSA; *Girl Scout Handbook* (New York: Girl Scouts, Inc., 1947), 205, 450; *Girl Scout Handbook* (New York: Girl Scouts, Inc., 1944), 376.

51. Floyd Todd and Pauline Todd, *Camping for Christian Youth* (New York: Harper, 1953), 119.

52. Ibid., 13; E. O. Harbin, *Recreational Materials and Methods* (Nashville: Cokesbury Press, 1931), 37, 62.

53. H. W. Gibson, *The Monthly Library on Camping,* vol. V: *Making Rainy Days Attractive* (Watertown, Mass.: The Gibson Publications, 1927), 47; Gibson, *The Monthly Library on Camping,* vol II: *By the Firelight's Glow* (Watertown, Mass.: The Gibson Publications, 1927), 12.

54. H. W. Gibson, *Recreational Programs for Summer Camp* (New York: Greenberg, 1938), 9, 228; Hadley S. Dimock and Charles E. Hendry, *Camping and Character: A Camp Experiment in Character Education* (New York: Association Press, 1931), 75; J. W. Frederick Davies, *Out of Doors with Youth: For Leaders of Boys' and Girls' Camps* (Chicago: University of Chicago Press, 1927), 44; Gibson, *By the Firelight's Glow,* 22–31.

55. *Magic Ring: A Collection of Verse,* ed. Ruth A. Brown (Seattle: Newman-Burrows, 1926; rev. 1937), vii, ix.

56. Rowe Wright, "Red-Blooded Program for Girls and Boys Based Upon Books," *Publishers' Weekly* 112 (Oct. 15, 1927), 1465–1468; Sanford Cobb, "Girls Are Intelligent Customers," *Publishers' Weekly* 132 (August 28, 1937), 679.

57. Richard James Hurley, *Campfire Tonight!* (Ann Arbor, Mich.: The Peak Press, 1940), 5.

58. Williams Haynes and Joseph LeRoy Harrison, *Camp-Fire Verse* (New York: Duffield, 1917), xiii; Hurley, *Campfire Tonight!*, 33, 80.

59. H. W. Gibson, *The Monthly Library on Camping*, vol. XII: *Stimulating the Creative Imagination* (Watertown, Mass.: The Gibson Publications, 1927), 26; Price, "Program Building for the Permanent Camp," 3.

60. Joshua Lieberman, *Creative Camping: A Coeducational Experiment in Personality Development and Social Living* (New York: Association Press, 1931), vii; Gibson, *Stimulating the Creative Imagination*, 6, 25; Helen D. Bragdon, "The Educational Value of the Summer Camp," in H. W. Gibson, *The Monthly Library on Camping*, vol. VI: *Objectives, Ideals, and Standards* (Watertown, Mass.: The Gibson Publications, 1927), 57–60; Gibson, *Objectives, Ideals, and Standards*, 25.

61. Lieberman, *Creative Camping*, 179; Dimock and Hendry, *Camping and Character*, 320.

62. Lieberman, *Creative Camping*, 193, 202.

63. Hurley, *Campfire Tonight!*, vi.

64. Laura I. Matoon and Helen D. Bragdon, *Services for the Open* (New York: Century, 1923), 3; Gibson, *Recreational Programs for Summer Camp*, 2.

Coda

1. Sally Jacobs, "A Renaissance of Verse: There's a Reason for Rhyme's New Popularity: the Need to Feel Connected," *Boston Globe*, April 14, 1995, 75; Don O'Briant, "Poetry in Motion: Rhyme Renaissance Under Way with People Embracing Verse as Antidote to High-Stress Lives," *Atlanta Journal-Constitution*, April 15, 1999, F1; Gail Bush, "The Poetry Renaissance," *School Library Journal* 44:2 (Feb. 1998), 40–41.

2. Dodge poetry festival information at *www.dukefarms.org/page.asp?pageId=366*; Bruce Weber, "Slammers Shake Up an Interest," *New York Times*, Aug. 16, 1999, E1; Ed Morales, "Grand Slam," *Village Voice*, Oct. 14, 1997, 62–63; Roberta Smith, "Hip-Hop as a Raw Hybrid," *New York Times*, Sept. 22, 2000, E31.

3. Jacobs, "A Renaissance of Verse," 75; Bush, "The Poetry Renaissance," 40–41; Jane Henderson, "Watch on the Rhyme," *St. Louis Post-Dispatch*, April 16, 1998, G3; Karen Angel, "Poetry in Motion," *Publishers Weekly*,

April 4, 1998, 22–25; O'Briant, "Poetry in Motion," 1; Glenn Elsasser, "Poetry Project Has Simple Mission: Spread the Words," *Chicago Tribune*, June 12, 1997, 1.

4. Carol Muske Dukes, "What Matters Most," *Los Angeles Times*, April 20, 1997, 9; Karen S. Peterson, "For Better or Verse, Poets Embrace Net," *USA Today*, Feb. 10, 2000, 11D; Jon Spayde, "Who's Afraid of Poetry?" *Utne*, Sept.-Oct. 2004, 42–46; Angel, "Poetry in Motion," 22; Henderson, "Watch on the Rhyme," G3.

5. Mona Van Duyn, "Matters of Poetry" (Washington, D.C.: Library of Congress, 1993), 1; Angel, "Poetry in Motion," 22; Naomi Serviss, "Smitten with Words, Theirs and Others'," *New York Times*, Oct. 3, 1999, L129; Jacobs, "A Renaissance of Verse," 75; Academy of American Poets website, *www.poets.org*; National Association for Poetry Therapy, *www.poetrytherapy.org*.

6. Jacobs, "A Renaissance of Verse," 75; Troy Jollimore, "Songs of Ourselves," *Boston Book Review*, March 2000, 35; O'Briant, "Poetry in Motion," 1; Martin Arnold, "Finding a Place for Poets, Perhaps Not for the Giants," *New York Times*, Jan. 14, 1999, B3; Dinitia Smith, "Laureates Convene, Waxing Poetic," *New York Times*, April 28, 2003, E1. For a thoughtful reflection on the limitations of the quest for a democratic poetry (with particular reference to the poetry slam audience), see Paul Breslin, "The Sign of Democracy and the Terms of Poetry," in Andrew Michael Roberts and Jonathan Allison, eds., *Poetry and Contemporary Culture: The Question of Value* (Edinburgh: Edinburgh University Press, 2002), 165–183.

7. Favorite Poem Project website, *www.favoritepoem.org*.

8. Robert Pinsky, *The Sounds of Poetry* (New York: Farrar, Straus and Giroux, 1998), 8.

9. Robert Pinsky, *Democracy, Culture, and the Voice of Poetry* (Princeton: Princeton University Press, 2002), 22, 30, 50.

10. Ibid., 66–67.

11. The data on numbers of readers, and the testimony of respondents which forms the remainder of this chapter, come from the Favorite Poem Project database, a copy of which is in my possession. The database is searchable by the title of a poem and the name of a respondent, as well as by keyword.

12. Claude Brown, Grants Pass, Ore.

13. Pinsky, *Democracy*, 17.

14. Janice Whatcott, Layton, Utah; George McClellan, Marietta, Ga.; C. Cluver, Maroa, Ill.

15. Marilyn Sisson, Walton, Ind.

16. Catherine Smentkowski, St. Louis, Mo.; Jennifer Dahlke, LaCrosse, Wis.; Safiyyah Muhammed, East Orange, N.J.; Kathy Juline, Pasadena, Calif.

17. C. Papini, Wheeling, W.Va.; Peggy Sapphire, New Fairfield, Conn.; Meredith Butterworth, no address given; Stan Martin, Walhalla, S.C.; Erin Kinter, Chardon, Ohio; Kim Engle, Asheville, N.C.

18. Sally Rauber, Albequerque, N.Mex.; Mimi Slaughter, no address given; Kimberly Stammer, Los Angeles, Calif.

19. Denise Laude, Cresskill, N.J.; Dyan Tichnell, Jenkintown, Pa.; Donald Hall, "The Poetry Reading: Public Performance/Private Act," *American Scholar* 54:1 (Winter 1984–85), 63–77; Robert Fay, Hancock, N.H.; Nancy Kwach, Kalamazoo, Mich.

20. Allan McGuffey, Louisville, Ky.; William Barker, Summerville, Ga.; Marion Rowell, Waterville, Maine; Iris Selig, Damariscotta, Maine; Wendy Galgan, New York, N.Y.

21. Cynthia Torres, Jersey City, N.J.; Kajira Berry, Vashon Island, Wash.; Muriel Albright, Spencerport, N.Y.; Thomas Cahill, Cincinnati, Ohio.

22. Shirley Money, Centerville, Mass.; Amanda King, Barnhart, Md.

23. Andrew Clark, Boston, Mass.

24. Alisa Slaughter, Mentone, Calif.; Norma Johnson, Montague, Mass.; Florence Burnett, Glen Carbon, Ill.; Sarah Bartos, Canton, Ohio; Michelle Moon, Mystic, Conn.

25. Lindsay Jones, Bellingham, Wash.; Kay Holzmeister, La Grange Park, Ill.; Timothy Ryan, Brooklyn, N.Y.

26. Barbara Pafundi, Palm Harbor, Fla.; Paulina Haikola, Burke, Va.; Apphia Taylor, Toledo, Ohio; John Doherty, Braintree, Mass. (at *www.favoritepoem.org*).

27. Sheila Murphy, Portland, Conn.; Susan Cunningham, Colorado Springs, Colo.; Suzanne Lovelace, Marietta, Ga.; Stuart McCausland, Virginia Beach, Va.; Lisa Ammann, Austin, Tex.

28. Kathy Freeman, Floss Moor, Ill.; Christine Weber, Charlotte, N.C.; Cathy Moran, no address; Ann Todd Jealous, Pacific Grove, Calif.

29. Becky Cox, Bozeman, Mont.; Walter Parkinson, Rolla, Mo.; Mae Koppman, Forest Hills, N.Y.; Geraldine Madak, Bridgewater, N.J.; Leslie Britt, Winston-Salem, N.C.

30. Rachel Castignoli, Milford, Conn.; Ronald Burke, Capitola, Calif.; Linda Jemison, Alexandria, Va.

31. Jollimore, "Songs of Ourselves," 35; Pinsky, *Democracy*, 72–73.

32. Lisa Hendricks, Sheboygan, Wis.

33. Courtney Hoppus, West Allis, Wis.; Pov Chin, Stockton, Calif.; Pinsky, *Democracy*, 67–71; Madalene Barnett, Newville, Pa.

Index